Cherokee Power

New Directions in Native American Studies
Colin G. Calloway and K. Tsianina Lomawaima, General Editors

Cherokee Power

Imperial and Indigenous Geopolitics in the
Trans-Appalachian West, 1670–1774

Kristofer Ray

University of Oklahoma Press : Norman

This book is published with the generous assistance of the McCasland Foundation, Duncan, Oklahoma.

Library of Congress Cataloging-in-Publication Data

Names: Ray, Kristofer, author.
Title: Cherokee power : imperial and indigenous geopolitics in the Trans-Appalachian West, 1670–1774 / Kristofer Ray.
Other titles: Imperial and indigenous geopolitics in the trans-Appalachian west, 1670–1774 | New directions in Native American studies ; v. 22.
Description: Norman : University of Oklahoma Press [2023] | Series: New directions in Native American studies ; volume 22 | Includes bibliographical references and index. | Summary: "Considers the scope of Cherokee influence on British and French trans-Appalachian imperial power and policy along a 'corridor' stretching along the Tennessee River to the Illinois country and the Wabash River"—Provided by publisher.
Identifiers: LCCN 2023008282 | ISBN 978-0-8061-9296-3 (hardcover) | ISBN 978-0-8061-9297-0 (paperback)
Subjects: LCSH: Cherokee Indians—History—17th century. | Cherokee Indians—History—18th century. | Appalachian Region—History—17th century. | Appalachian Region—History—18th century. | United States—History—Colonial period, ca. 1600–1775.
Classification: LCC E99.C5 R28 2023 | DDC 975.004/97557—dc23/eng/20230313
LC record available at https://lccn.loc.gov/2023008282

Cherokee Power: Imperial and Indigenous Geopolitics in the Trans-Appalachian West, 1670–1774 is Volume 22 in the New Directions in Native American Studies series.

The paper in this book meets the guidelines for permanence and durability of the Committee on Production Guidelines for Book Longevity of the Council on Library Resources, Inc. ∞

Copyright © 2023 by the University of Oklahoma Press, Norman, Publishing Division of the University. Manufactured in the U.S.A.

All rights reserved. No part of this publication may be reproduced, stored in a retrieval system, or transmitted, in any form or by any means, electronic, mechanical, photocopying, recording, or otherwise—except as permitted under Section 107 or 108 of the United States Copyright Act—without the prior written permission of the University of Oklahoma Press. To request permission to reproduce selections from this book, write to Permissions, University of Oklahoma Press, 2800 Venture Drive, Norman OK 73069, or email rights.oupress@ou.edu.

For B, B, and V

Contents

List of Illustrations	ix
Acknowledgments	xi
Introduction	1
1. Cherokees, England, France, and Imagined Empires before 1715	17
2. (De-)Constructing an Anglo-Cherokee Chain of Friendship, 1700–1730	36
3. Cherokees, Europeans, and the Tennessee Corridor, 1730–1750	58
4. Of Fortifications and Chains of Friendship, 1750–1759	83
5. The Overhills and the Limits of the European Imperial Imagination after 1759	103
Epilogue. Cherokees, Trans-Appalachia, and the Era of the American Revolution, 1774–1800	128
Appendixes	135
A. Transcription of the 1730 Anglo-Cherokee Treaty and Cherokee Responses Thereto	135
B. Transcription and Translation of the 1756 Franco-Cherokee Treaty of Friendship	141

List of Abbreviations	157
Notes	159
Bibliography	223
Index	251

Illustrations

Fanni Mingo map ... 2
Map of Overhill towns ... 3
Tennessee corridor ... 5
Cherokee regions in the eighteenth century ... 6
Jacques Bellin map, 1755 ... 10
Oconostota's Commission from Gov. Louis Billouart,
    Chevalier de Kerlérec ... 112
Map of the Indian Nations in the Southern
    Department, 1766 ... 113

Acknowledgments

This book took a lot longer to get to the finish line than I ever expected (or intended). It began at a moment just prior to a stunning level of personal upheaval, and it was repeatedly put aside as other matters took precedence. That I *did* finish was almost entirely due to advice, critiques, and support from the following friends and colleagues.

Theda Perdue planted the seeds of this project in 2003 when she asked me some tough but eminently fair questions about my first book. Whether or not she agrees with my conclusions here, I sincerely appreciate the insight and advice she's offered me over the years. A 2007 short-term fellowship at the Robert H. Smith International Center for Jefferson Studies at Monticello further cultivated the seeds Theda planted, for which I thank Andrew O'Shaughnessy, Frank Cogliano, and Victor Enthoeven. As the project evolved, Austin Peay State University granted me a leave of absence and then a sabbatical to work on it, which I greatly appreciate. Thanks to the staff at both the William Clements Library and the Huntington Library for their help and for insight into their incredible collections. Thanks to SUNY-Binghamton's Upstate Early American Seminar, the Kentucky Early American Seminar, the D'Arcy McNickle Center for American Indian and Indigenous Study's seminar series, and to students and colleagues at Dartmouth College for patiently discussing draft material. Thanks to Ben Marsh, David Stirrup, and the virtual workshop at the University of Kent's Centre for Indigenous and Settler Colonial Studies, as well as to Bruce Baker and Shane

McCorristine at the University of Newcastle for inviting me to discuss the project in the United Kingdom. At the University of Hull, sincere thanks to Amanda Capern and Glenn Burgess for going out of their way to help an ignorant 'Murican as he attempted to make sense of (what to him was) an entirely new way of doing things. Thanks also to Martin Wilcox, Alison Price-Mohr, Matt Pooley, and David Bagchi for listening to my rambling over pints at Old Grey Mare, Pave, or the Lockdown Arms.

I am indebted to the following institutions and people for listening to my incoherent babbling over pints, lunches, and dinners; for letting me stay with them; for reading draft material; for helping me translate French documents; for giving me office space; or for granting access to databases so I could finish writing: the Eisenberg Institute for Historical Studies, University of Michigan; the William Wilberforce Institute for the study of Slavery and Emancipation, University of Hull; the Departments of Native American and Indigenous Studies and History at Dartmouth College; and the History Department at the University of North Carolina Wilmington; and Matt Adkins, Jonathan Schiff, Charles Hogan, Robert Engelbert, Joseph Gagne, Karen Sorenson, Lance Parker, Stephen Warren, Maureen Meyers, Rose Stremlau, James Rice, Paul Musselwhite, Rex Weeks, François Furstenberg, Greg Dowd, Tiya Myles, Greg Smithers, David Preston, Sarah Gardner, Stephen Berry, Emily Richmond, Peter Mancall, Alejandra Dubcovsky, Jacob Lee, Natalie Inman, Frances Kolb Turnbell, Noel Smyth, David La Vere, and Paul Townend.

The following people went well above and beyond the call of duty by reading multiple chapter drafts, honestly evaluating various theories, tolerating my ADD, paranoia, and endless tinkering, and for generally putting up with my lack of filter: Colin Calloway, Alessandra Tamulevich, Daniel Tortora, Paul Kelton, Bruce Duthu, Robert Bonner, Spencer Lone Fight, Kate Fullagar, Denise Bossy, Bernie Perley, Melanie Benson-Taylor, Dale Turner, Brad Austin, Michael McDonnell, Trevor Burnard, and Susan Gaunt Stearns.

I could not have formed several of the ideas in this book without the help of David Britton. He was the first person with whom I chatted about the Tennessee corridor, and he has served as a patient and steadfast sounding board ever since. I hope the end product meets his high standards.

To Angela Pulley Hudson, Daniel Usner, Greg Waselkov, Stef Ramsden, Duncan Jamieson, Josh Piker, Harry Watson, Raymond Orr, Kevin Barksdale, Ann Toplovich, and particularly Andrew Frank, Tyler Boulware, and Brady DeSanti: thank you for reading drafts, offering support when I desperately needed it, and for being my friend during a few dark moments. I hope I can somehow return the favor.

Andrew Frank and Greg Waselkov also deserve medals for taking time out of their busy schedules to critique swaths of the revised manuscript. All mistakes are mine, of course, but they have saved me from making a great many more. Thanks very much!!

Other than my immediate family, Robbie Ethridge is unquestionably the most positive influence in my life. Thanks for your help and support, much of which I don't deserve. Finally, thanks to B, B, and V for sticking by me through an incredible level of tumult, when others chose to peel away. Your patience and grace mean more than you'll ever know.

Introduction

In 1723 a Lower Chickasaw man known as Fanni Mingo (also Fanimingo, loosely translated as "Squirrel King") delivered a deerskin map to British officials in South Carolina. In addition to the major river systems crisscrossing trans-Appalachia, the map designated South Carolina's paths to and through the Native South as well as routes through the Illinois country (or, as the French called it, the *pays des Illinois*), with which Carolina had only minimal contact. The map also located dozens of Native settlements across the eastern and central portions of the continent.[1]

Whether or not they understood it, the map gave Carolinians a snapshot of the *Native* realities defining the eighteenth-century trans-Appalachian world. And while scholars long have understood the importance of the Mississippi and Ohio valleys to this world, Fanni Mingo suggested that the interconnected Tennessee, (lower) Ohio, and Wabash River valleys deserve equal scrutiny. European witnesses concurred, describing both how Native southerners traveled this "corridor" and how "westward" and "northward" people came southeast from American Bottom, Illinois, the Great Lakes, and the upper Ohio valley.[2] Native political, economic, and diplomatic endeavors in this Tennessee corridor blew apart European political labels and boundaries, upending newcomer claims of sovereignty and jurisdictional extension.[3]

Cherokee Power: Imperial and Indigenous Geopolitics in the Trans-Appalachian West, 1670–1774 offers insight into these complex realities. It focuses upon how Overhill Cherokee trade, negotiation, and

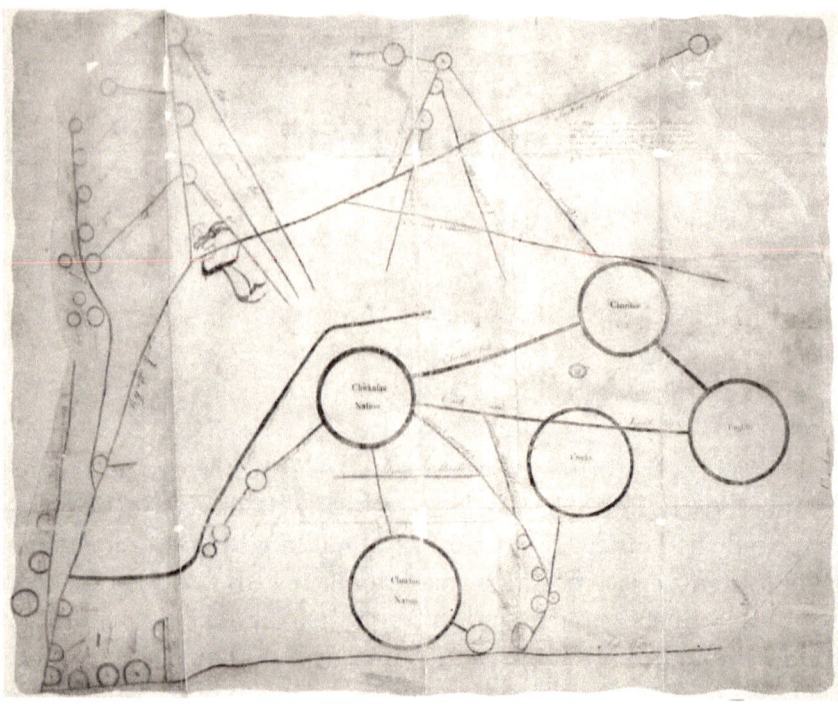

British replica (1725) of Fanni Mingo's map (1723), showing trans-Appalachia's major rivers systems, paths to and through the Native South, and routes to and through the *pays des Illinois*. Printed by permission of the British National Archives (CO_700_NORTHAMERICANCOLONIESGENERAL6_2_1725–1725).

confrontation with other Indigenous polities along the Tennessee-Ohio-Wabash system shaped the parameters of British and French western expansion—both real and imagined—between 1670 and 1774. It makes two interconnected arguments. First, it contends that scholars have oversimplified both Cherokee and British North American political coalescence by constructing narratives in which a monolithic, increasingly dependent—and, after 1760, declining—Cherokee people allied themselves to an expansive British North American empire. While in some contexts they maintained a certain cohesion, the inner workings of both of these polities were more complex than such narratives allow.[4] Second, it emphasizes that over the course of the eighteenth century the British and French struggled to overcome a dissonance between their visions of western

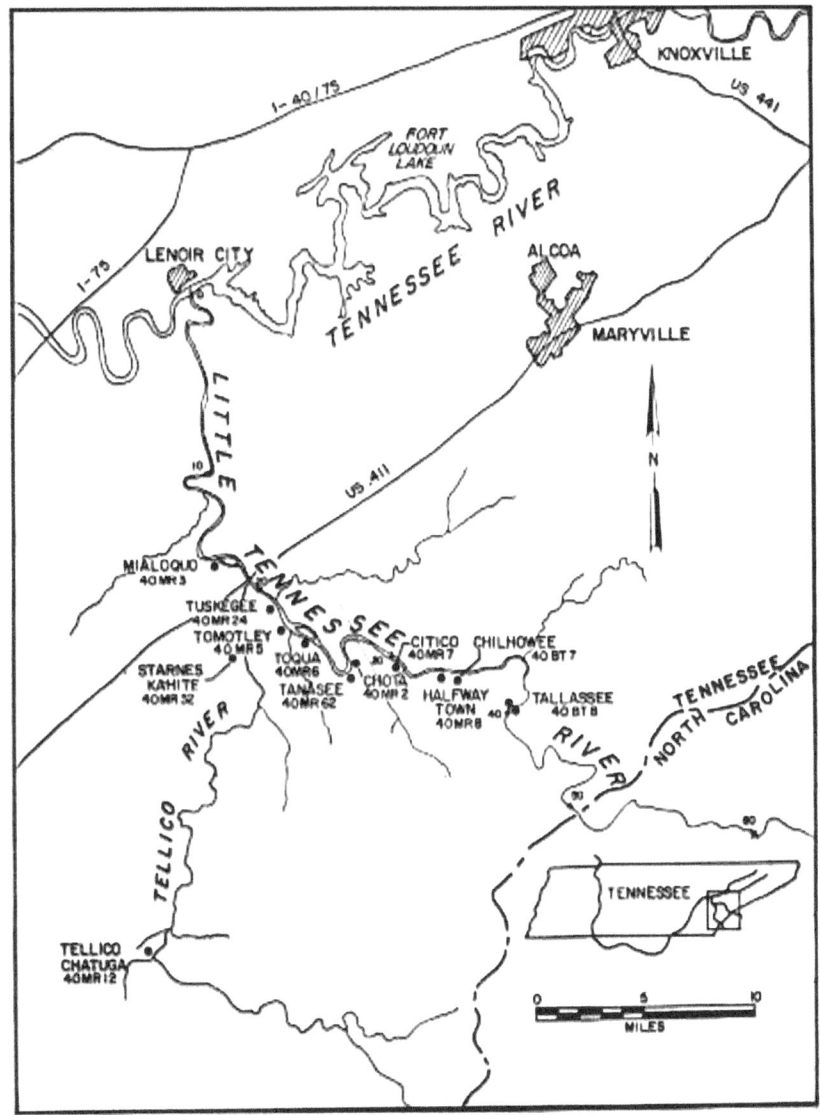

Map of Overhill Cherokee sites, eighteenth century. Frank H. McClung Museum, University of Tennessee Knoxville, preserved in the Digital Library of Georgia.

empire and Overhill mobility and agency. Along the way, *Cherokee Power* suggests that understanding the origins of the American Revolution requires closer inspection of British responses to the Native realities defining the Tennessee corridor specifically and trans-Appalachia more generally.

I focus on Overhill Cherokees because of their ubiquitous presence across trans-Appalachia. European witnesses placed this westernmost of five Cherokee settlement areas in the Tennessee corridor as early as the 1670s. (The other settlement areas were known by Europeans as the Lower towns, Middle towns, Out towns, and Valley towns.) Their presence came at a period of already intensive Indigenous mobility. Between the 1650s and 1680s, for example, people archaeologists call "Fort Ancients" departed the lower and mid-Ohio valley in five directions, traveling to the upper Ohio valley, Cumberland River valley, and even as far as the Savannah River on the edge of Southern Carolina. At roughly the same moment, Quawpaws left the Ohio valley to settle along the Arkansas River.[5] In response to increasing Haudenosaunee (Five and Six Nations of Iroquois) pressures, Illinois-based "Twightwees" (Miamis) and Mascoutens began in the late seventeenth century to resettle in western Ohio and the Wabash valley.[6] As those polities' presence diminished, Kickapoos and Piankeshaws moved into Illinois, while Anishnaabeg and Wendats (Wyandots, or Hurons) traveled south from the Great Lakes to reinforce links to the region. After the 1720s, meanwhile, Lenapes (Delawares) and Senecas began to move from Pennsylvania and New York (among other areas) into the Ohio valley, as did the Shawnees after a four-decade diaspora.[7]

The more visible were the Overhills in the Tennessee corridor, the more they encountered these other polities—with powerful consequences for the bewildered Europeans watching from the periphery.[8] They may have *claimed* ever greater swaths of the continent, but between 1670 and 1774 both the British and French grew convinced that a Cherokee alliance would be a crucial aspect of *actually* extending their empires across the Appalachian Mountains.

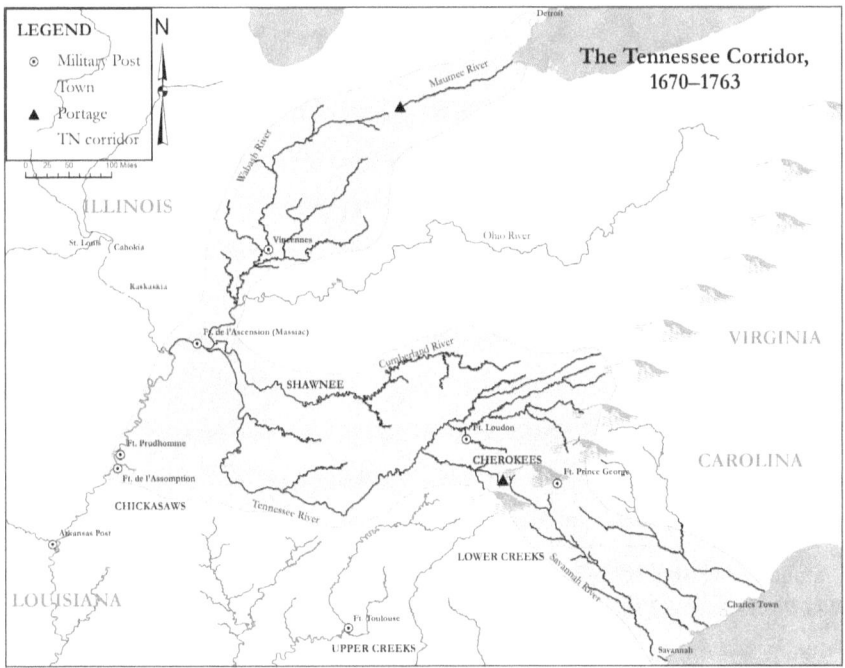

The Tennessee corridor. GIS mapping by David Britton on behalf of the author.

Cherokee Nationhood and Alliance in the European Imagination

The location of the Overhills' settlement region begins to explain their importance. In 1754 South Carolina governor James Glen observed that the Tennessee River "has its rise in the Cherokee Nation and runs a great way through it."[9] An author for the London *Gentleman's Magazine* went further: although they seemed only to inhabit approximately five hundred miles of territory in the mountains, Cherokees had "undoubted" ownership over land adjoining the Tennessee. Said territory was "of a prodigious extent; [it reaches] from our back settlements quite to the Mississippi, on both sides of the Tennessee River, that is, from east to west eight hundred miles." Its reach included "one of the finest countries in America, which is [Cherokee] hunting ground, and to part of which no other nation ever pretended any right or claim."[10]

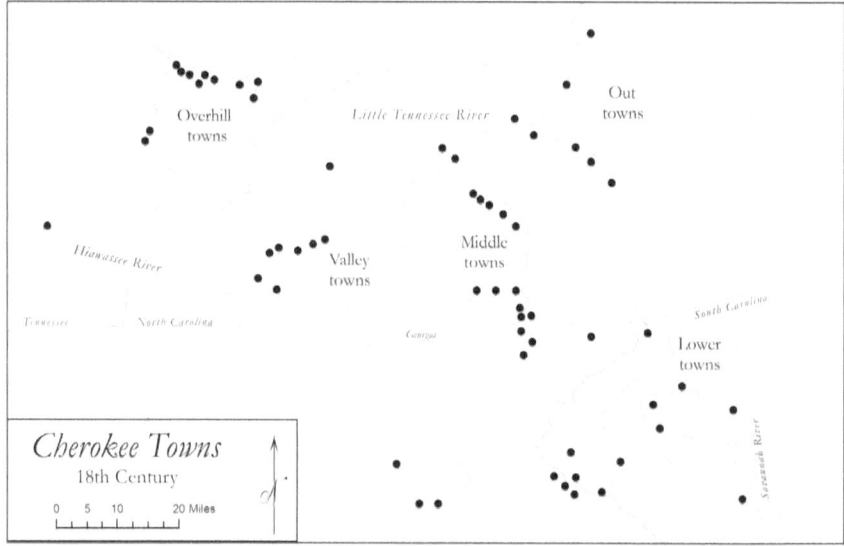

Location of Cherokee towns in trans-Appalachia and the Tennessee corridor. GIS mapping by David Britton on behalf of the author.

Carolinians, Virginians, Georgians, and the evolving British Empire all hoped to exploit this perceived geopolitical advantage at various points in the eighteenth century. One opportunity particularly sparked imaginations: the Cherokees could potentially serve as a southern counterpart to the powerful Haudenosaunee presence in the North.[11] In 1720 Virginia governor Alexander Spotswood wrote to the Board of Trade that the Cherokees "are the nearest to and most considerable Body of Indians on our Southern Frontier . . . so they have been generally very friendly & affectionate to the English and are the only Indians we ought to depend on to ballance the Northern Nations." Ten years later Martin Bladen and others were more explicit, explaining to the Duke of Newcastle and the Board of Trade how the Five Nations served as their northern "Frontier Guards, always ready to defend our outsettlements and to make war upon any other Nation whenever we require them to do so." It was in the power of the British Empire "to put the Cherikees upon the same footing," they insisted, which would be extremely advantageous given their ability to "bring three thousand fighting men upon Occasion into the Field."[12] To employ this "great advantage," however, the British would need to establish something akin to the Covenant Chain, which they believed subordinated the (then) Five Nations to British interests.[13] An agreement could have profound consequence: "Upon future Disputes with any European Nation," Newcastle was led to believe, it would "greatly strengthen our Title in those Parts, even to all the Lands which these People now Possess."[14] Combined authority over the Iroquois and the Cherokees, in other words, could provide a means by which to claim the entirety of trans-Appalachia.[15]

In 1730 the empire used a Cherokee visit to London to establish a "Chain of Friendship" that would frame Anglo-Cherokee interaction into the 1770s. As we shall see, four significant issues contaminated this so-called alliance. First and foremost, British decision makers misunderstood the complexities of Native diplomacy, agency, and lifeways. Second, British officials at both the colonial and imperial levels adhered to the idea of a fictive and singular Cherokee Nation that for most of the eighteenth century the Cherokees rejected. Third, and directly related, British visions of western empire depended on an Overhill acquiescence that seemed perpetually elusive. Finally, competition between Virginia and South Carolina (and eventually Georgia) undermined the Anglo-Cherokee relationship for decades on either side of the 1730 "agreement."

There is an irony in this latter problem: for all their insistence upon a singular Cherokee Nation, the British could offer no such unity in return. Because it was a new entity in 1730, there was no more cohesion in the British Empire's constituent parts than in the five Cherokee regions. Markers were becoming clear, to be sure. Scholars understand that early-eighteenth-century Anglo-Americans extolled the superiority of British maritime power. They committed themselves to the ideas of liberty embedded in the 1689 English Declaration of Right, and to the expansion of a Protestant interest.[16] And, given the alignment of French, Spanish, and Indigenous challenges around the periphery of their colonies, they insisted that defense form an essential part of the imperial American experience. The only catch was that the metropole would have to pay for it—not the colonies.[17] That insistence would form a major element of dispute as the eighteenth century progressed.

Linguistic, spiritual, and material similarities, however, are not the same as political and diplomatic unity.[18] If a sense of "Britishness" was emerging, the colonies did not naturally connect it to a singular geopolitical interest. It seriously complicated Indigenous affairs, energizing debates over such questions as: Were Native people truly subjects of the Empire? Did they represent independent polities? Something in between? Where should power concerning Indigenous affairs rest—at the colonial level or the imperial? If the latter, what level of centralization was acceptable? No answers were immediately apparent, and the result was a cacophony of diplomatic demands upon Native societies extending from metropolitan, continental, colonial, and local authorities.

If the British never fully understood either Cherokee nationhood or the Chain of Friendship, it nevertheless catalyzed spirals of paranoia amongst French North Americans. Louisianans had feared a Carolina-Cherokee alliance throughout the early eighteenth century, and after 1730 they grew convinced that the British were behind Overhill excursions into the *pays des Illinois* and Wabash valley. They believed that the British would manipulate Overhill towns to settle along La Belle Rivière ("the beautiful river"—the name the French applied to the Ohio), thereby putting a stop to potentially lucrative commerce between the lower Ohio and the Mississippi.[19] In 1731, for example, Louisiana governor Étienne Perier warned that Cherokees might abscond with significant amounts of the estimated "100,000 pounds of flour" he hoped would move from the *pays des Illinois* to New Orleans that year.[20] He insisted that such an attack would mark the beginning of a larger push against French trans-Appalachian interests. It could lead, he feared, to the erection of British "forts on the Cherokee [Tennessee] River" that would disrupt "the communication of Canada with Louisiana."[21] To protect against such a disaster France would need to fortify the Tennessee corridor.

At the same time, Louisiana officials came to believe that they could present the Cherokees with a meaningful diplomatic and commercial alternative to the British Chain of Friendship. Given that Overhill (and Valley) townsfolk were reasonably close to Fort Toulouse (at the forks of the Coosa and Tallapoosa Rivers, in Mvskoke country near modern Montgomery, Alabama) and seemed to reach posts in the *pays des Illinois* and Wabash valley with little difficulty, a program of trade and fortification could lure them into an exclusive relationship.[22] Franco-Overhill interaction accelerated as imperial tensions mounted in the 1740s and 1750s, culminating in a 1756 Treaty of Friendship.[23]

After 1763 the French presence gradually receded from trans-Appalachia, but the Overhill Cherokees continued to enter the Tennessee corridor to trade, negotiate, and fight with western polities such as Odawas, Piankeshaws, Peorias, Kaskaskias, Mascoutens, and Potawatamis. As a consequence, Britain would not simply take control of locations "ceded" by the French in the Seven Years' War. And that, combined with the staggering costs of stabilizing North America in the aftermath of the war, convinced British officials of the desirability of centralizing Native affairs. Their decision limited local autonomy at the same moment that the empire restructured colonial financial obligations, a combination that catalyzed significant debate over the nature, meaning, and future of British North America.[24]

Cherokee Nationhood and Alliance: The Indigenous Perspective

To Europeans, much of the above narrative indicated Cherokee schizophrenia, diplomatic simplicity, and, more nefariously, duplicity. The reality was far more complicated. Perhaps the biggest issue was that European trade and diplomacy were anchored by the false assumption that Cherokees comprised a singular nation.[25] It is certainly true to say that all postcontact Aniyunwiya, as the Cherokees call themselves, were matrilineal, spoke different dialects of the Iroquoian language, and were intimately connected by the sinews of seven clans.[26] (Although when focusing on political development, it is important for historians not to overlook the presence of *sodalities*—society members who share common interests crosscutting kinship ties.) They also maintained similar religious and cultural beliefs across the five settlement regions. Merely one example: the spiritual significance of rivers. Eighteenth-century Indian trader James Adair pointed out that Cherokees generally were "strongly

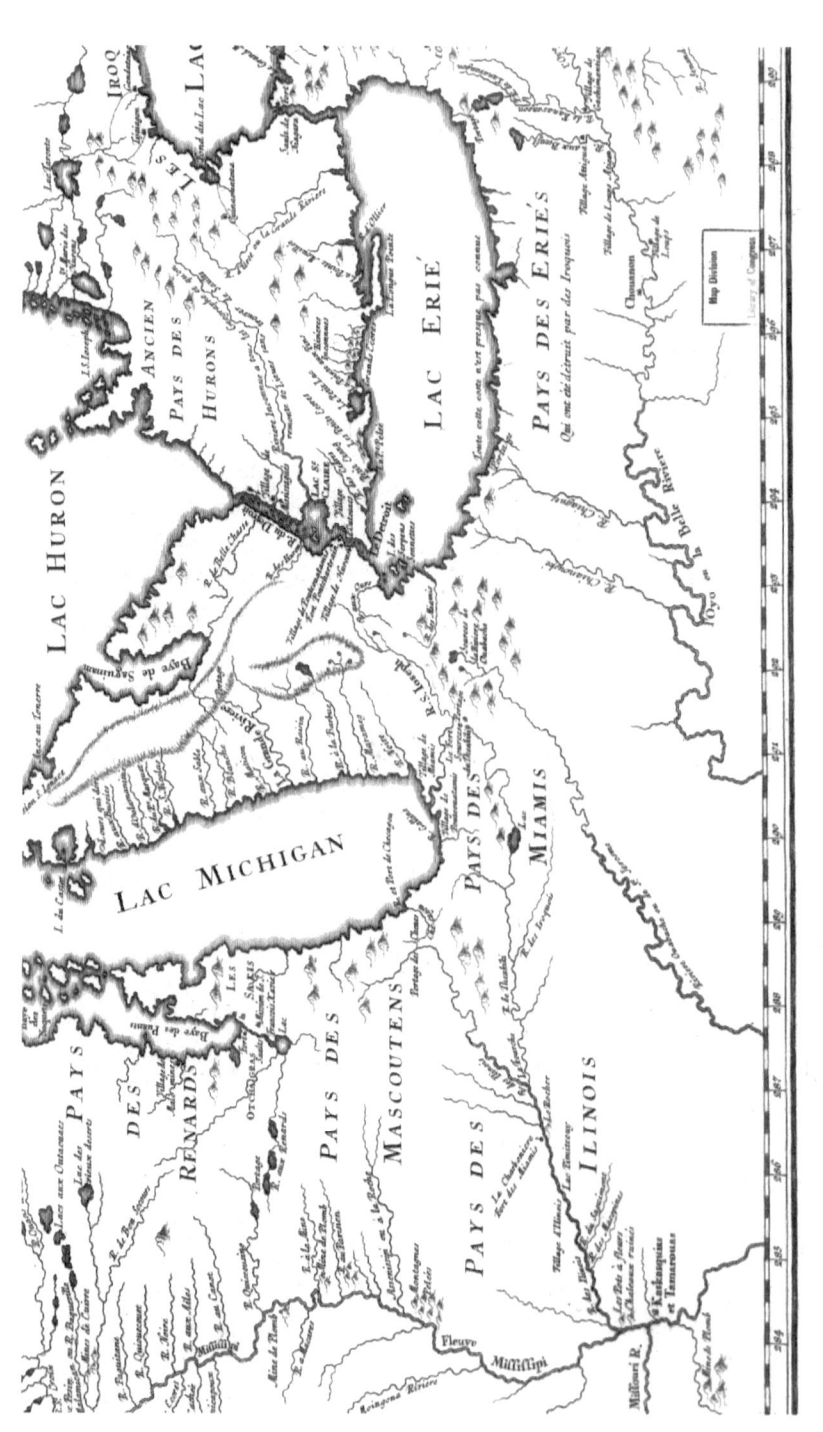

In this map, French cartographer Jacques Bellin identified major Indigenous polities of the Ohio valley and *pays des Illinois*. Jacques Nicolas Bellin and Homann Erben, *Partie occidentale de la Nouvelle France ou du Canada*. [Nürnberg, 1755]. Library of Congress, Geography and Map Division, https://www.loc.gov/item/73694802/.

attached to rivers—all retaining the opinion of the ancients, that rivers are necessary to constitute a paradise. Nor is it only ornamental, but likewise beneficial to them, on account of purifying themselves, and also for the services of common life—such as fishing, fowling, and killing of deer, which come in the warm season, to eat the saltish moss and grass, which grow on the rocks, and under the surface of the waters."

Because rivers originated in the Lower World, Cherokees believed, they provided both "fertility and healing" and could be used for myriad purposes, from cleansing rituals to tools by which to mitigate epidemics.[27] The Tennessee River was particularly important to them. The early twentieth-century anthropologist James Mooney once observed that the Cherokees thought of that river, called "Long Man," as "a giant with his head in the foothills of the mountains and his foot down in the lowland, pressing always, resistless and without stop."[28]

Spiritual, material, and cultural connections are not the same as political and diplomatic ties, however, even if contemporary Euro-Americans showed a maddening willingness to conflate them. Modern historians have fared little better, embracing a narrative constructed via ubiquitous—if biased—British sources that an emerging eighteenth-century Cherokee Nation uniformly came to support that empire. In this narrative, the Aniyunwiya became so reliant on Charles Town commodities that by midcentury they at best only occasionally played their Anglo allies off the French to secure their diminishing independence.

Archeologists Ted Gragson and Paul Bolstad offer a different approach. "The pre-1776 Cherokee literature," they note, "has often relied on interpretations that outrun evidence, which compounds the difficulties of making sense of a sparse and often ambiguous record. Grand narrative and evocative imagery have been used to present global generalities that apply neither any*where* nor any*time*."[29] Anthropologist Charles Hudson would have agreed, once noting that there was no linear relationship between sixteenth- and eighteenth-century Cherokees and that the latter comprised culturally and linguistically diverse peoples. The political and economic dynamics shaping one settlement region, he believed, could differ markedly from the forces shaping others.³⁰ Archeologist Christopher Rodning reinforces Hudson's point by noting that intra-Cherokee relations were in flux from the outset of the contact period. "Community dynamics within towns and social relations between towns," he observes, "were... different in 1540, when Spanish colonists first reached the Southern Appalachians, than they were in 1670, when Charlestown was founded, and in 1715."³¹ He spells out the political implications of this reality. "Leaders of [Cherokee] towns were spokespersons for their communities," he writes, "but their status did not grant them power over people in other towns. Different towns likely formed alliances with each other in different situations, but there were not paramount chiefs that ruled whole groups of towns."³² Historian Tyler Boulware puts these dynamics in broader terms: postcontact Cherokees (politically) thought of themselves in relation to town and region, with only gradual—and incomplete—development of "national" solidarity.³³ Despite Europeans' best efforts to create a singular Cherokee Nation, the five settlement areas developed distinct (albeit overlapping) geopolitical interests. The Overhill towns were easily the most mobile in terms of the Tennessee-Ohio-Wabash system. By consequence, then, they rooted their realities in trans-Appalachia in ways other Cherokees did not. It made "westward" polities and affairs—as well as the French in Louisiana, Illinois, and even Canada—meaningful parts of their calculations.

Inseparably intertwined with the issue of geopolitical unity is the problem of assuming exclusive commercial relationships. Unlike their British (and French) counterparts, Cherokees thought of trade in terms of what the Haudenosaunee described as the *kaswentha* concept. Historian Jon Parmenter reminds us that *kaswentha* signifies "a separate but equal relationship between... two entities based on mutual benefit and noninterference. The spatial metaphor bound up in *kaswentha* asserts the right of each entity to free movement in its own 'canoe' along the paths represented in white wampum. Neither side in a *kaswentha* relationship may attempt to 'steer' that of the other." Such a relationship, Parmenter suggests, meant "mutual recognition of the patterns of spatial mobility that brought the two entities into contact, and a subsequent mutual commitment to recognizing and preserving those patterns of mobility."³⁴ It also hinged on the idea that the relationship did not connote exclusive ties, a reality that European polities never seemed fully to accept.

Directly related for Overhill Cherokees was a commercial reality that few contemporary Europeans understood and that modern scholars tend to overlook: while they certainly could (and did) arrive via formal French, Spanish, or English (British) networks, informal inter-Indigenous markets for European commodities also developed.[35] One of the most striking examples in the long eighteenth century was in the *pays des Illinois*. Upon encountering Peorias for the first time in 1673 Jacques Marquette observed that they "use guns, which they buy from our savage allies who trade with our French."[36] Only a few decades later Antoine Denis Raudot observed that trans-Mississippi people were not as warlike as the Illinois, but that "having need of their trade to get axes, knives, awls, and other objects, the Illinois buy these things from us to resell to them."[37]

Pierre de Liette offers even more telling insight into the commercial allure of the region. In his 1721 journal he chronicles an abundant variety of game animals, edible and medicinal flora, lead mines, and other exploitable natural resources. He also describes a striking number of guns, horses, and European commodities—along with brief explanations for how they arrived in the *pays des Illinois* and Wabash valley. Like Marquette and Raudot before him, he observed that Illinois polities received horses and Spanish goods from the Panis, Osage, and others to the west.[38] Meanwhile, they received French commodities through the Jesuits, voyageurs, and Anishnaabeg traveling into the region, which, as per Raudot, they in turn traded in multiple directions. Scholars can add that over the course of the eighteenth century a stream of British supplies entered the region as well. And that does not include the curious emergence of horse theft and markets observed by Carolinians, Georgians, Virginians, the French, and the Spanish in the eighteenth-century Native South. Merely one example: in 1761 South Carolina rangers taking provisions to Fort Prince George in the Lower Cherokee town of Keowee reported losing "125 horses to the Indians."[39]

Because the heart of the continent represented such a confluence of interests, it is hardly surprising that the Overhills (and the Chickasaws, among other Native southerners) would become visible there.⁴⁰ Liette provided a fleeting reference to one other commodity drawing Overhill Cherokee interest: slaves.⁴¹ (More on that point in chapter 2.) For now, it is worth noting that the region's potential was more than enough to justify Overhill projection and for Illinois-Wabash polities to respond in kind along the Tennessee River.⁴² For most of the period under examination, the Aniyunwiya seemed able to acquire goods relatively smoothly via alternatives to officially sanctioned trade paths.⁴³ Despite hubristic claims to the contrary, Europeans were only indirectly necessary for the growth and sophistication of markets for European commodities. It is a fact that significantly complicates standard alliance narratives. At the very least, scholars should contextualize eighteenth-century British descriptions of Native southern "nakedness" and "starvation" more carefully than is typically the case.

To be clear, there is no question that the British colonies represented a crucial element of Cherokee trade and decision making.⁴⁴ Nevertheless, the concept of an eighteenth-century alliance is deceptive. Overhill towns used the Tennessee corridor to engage in acts of trade, war, and diplomacy to which Britons only indirectly mattered and to which they most often were not privy. They were on the margins, recording snapshots of situations first manipulated by Indigenous representatives and then filtered through idealized notions of empire and commercial opportunity. The standard narrative of Cherokee history—in which the British-allied Aniyunwiya used Louisiana to maximize their bargaining power with Charles Town—cedes too much influence to Western ideas of jurisdictional control and Indigenous nationhood. The reality more likely was that European polities misinterpreted regional Cherokee political and diplomatic cues to extend their imagined empires. From this perspective, the seemingly inconsistent and frustrating Indigenous behaviors described by British (and other European) sources make *much* more sense.⁴⁵

• • • •

The historian Donald Fixico has observed that studying American Indian history requires using what he calls the "Medicine Way." "In the Medicine Way," he explains, "different understandings of history prevail over Western linearity. In this genre Indians control the discourse, so interested non-Indians must lower their mainstream guard if they want to learn what Indians were really like and how and why their cultures and histories matter."[46] This book is inspired by this idea. While it is broadly linear, readers will find significant topical overlap between chapters.

At the broadest level, each chapter weaves European imaginations and actions with Native and trans-Appalachian realities. Chapter 1 introduces patterns of Cherokee mobility and coalescence before turning to seventeenth-century iterations of English and French interest in trans-Appalachia (generally) and the Tennessee corridor (specifically). It lays out the Indigenous realities lurking behind European imaginations, demonstrating how Indians established a "native ground" through which they framed European projection into the west. It concludes with the English realization that trans-Appalachian "empire" would require the careful cultivation of Cherokee alliances, with Overhill towns perhaps the most crucial of the settlement regions. Focusing primarily on the first three decades of the eighteenth century, chapter 2 explores the wider context for the construction of what became known as the Anglo-Cherokee Chain of Friendship. It frames British North American developments with Native realities; illuminates Cherokee regional variations and the rejection of diplomatic unity and exclusivity; and investigates the impact of British intercolonial squabbling on the Anglo-Cherokee relationship.

Chapter 3 concentrates on how Overhill agency and mobility (as well as Indigenous geopolitical complexity broadly) influenced British and French trans-Appalachian imaginations between 1730 and 1754. It manifested most clearly in fear and paranoia over inter-Indigenous interactions to which Europeans were only sporadically privy. It also emerged, however, in responses to the activities of individuals such as Christian Priber, Cornelius Docherty (spelled Doherty or Dougherty in several sources), James Maxwell, and the Overhill leader Attakullakulla. Chapter 4 explores how, as the Seven Years' War unfolded, British officials saw the Overhills as both an essential bulwark against French invasion from the west and a tool for trans-Appalachian expansion. For Overhill leadership, however, it remained clear that the British could not (and would not) fulfill long standing promises. The Anglo-Cherokee relationship grew strained as Overhill towns pursued their own diplomatic and economic agendas, including negotiating a 1756 Treaty of Friendship with French Louisiana. At the heart of their efforts was a crucial, generally unexplored issue. In a nutshell, the Overhills had a "westward" problem: they consistently dealt with Indigenous threats from the *pays des Illinois* and the Ohio valley that challenged access to trade goods at a moment when those seemed increasingly difficult to acquire from French and British sources. Such complexity framed their responses to European demands stemming from the Seven Years' War.

Starting with the Anglo-Cherokee War, chapter 5 explores the freneticism defining trans-Appalachia in the 1760s. It contextualizes that conflict with French diplomacy and Native complexities before showing how, after 1761, the Overhills continued to struggle with westward polities in the Tennessee corridor. Yet despite (or perhaps because of) these powerful pressures, the Aniyunwiya remained where they had been for a century: crucial players in an Indigenous trans-Appalachia that continued to set the parameters of Euro-American expansion. The chapter also dives into the fact that the Cherokees (along with other Native southerners) increasingly had to grapple with land encroachment on the part of British North American colonials. This combination of trans-Appalachian concerns and eastern infringement encouraged the Cherokees to reformulate their understanding of political identity just as the British North American empire was undergoing an identity crisis of its own. An epilogue briefly touches on trans-Appalachia and the Tennessee corridor in the extended era of the American Revolution (1774–1800). One final observation: readers will find that the Spanish sporadically appear in this book. I focus on the French and British because they were the most visible European polities in the Tennessee corridor, but I cheerfully concede that the Spanish presence is crucial for understanding the broader trans-Appalachian story. Alas, I must leave Overhill-Spanish encounters for other scholars to consider.

CHAPTER 1

Cherokees, England, France, and Imagined Empires before 1715

The Cherokees have always lived in the Appalachian Mountains. On this point there is no dispute. In their cosmology the Earth is a floating island in a sea of water, "suspended at each of the four cardinal points by a cord hanging down from the sky vault, which is of solid rock." Early on, the ground was flat, soft, and wet, facts that frustrated the animals then living in the upper world of Gălûñ′lătĭ. Anxious to "get down," they sent several birds to see if the Earth had dried, but with no success. Finally, they sent a Great Buzzard, who, like his predecessors, found the ground too soft for habitation. It was an exhausting journey. By the time the Great Buzzard made it to Cherokee country, "his wings began to flap and strike the ground, and wherever they struck the earth there was a valley, and where they turned up again there was a mountain. When the animals above saw this, they were afraid that the whole world would be mountains, so they called him back, but the Cherokee country remains full of mountains to this day."[1]

But if they always have been mountain people, Western notions of time and historical migration insist that they must have moved there from other locations.[2] And from this perspective it is impossible to know with certainty "where they originated, or even when they first arrived on their traditional lands in the Southeast."[3] The influential anthropologist Charles Hudson argued that the earliest migration of Cherokee-speakers had occurred by the twelfth century—early enough to embrace certain Mississippian traditions but recent enough that their "Mississippianization" began "two or three centuries after their northern and southern neighbors."[4] For evidence he pointed to Cherokee mound centers, which he interpreted as "smaller, more recent, and less elaborate" than older neighboring chiefdoms. For that matter, he observed, the "paraphernalia and symbolism of the Southeastern Ceremonial Complex is virtually absent from the mountains."[5]

Non-Cherokee traditions suggest a more recent range of dates for their arrival. Shawnees, for example, hold that Cherokees may first have lived around Lake Erie, arriving in the Southern Appalachians as recently as the postcontact era.[6] Mvskoke speakers agree that the "Tsalagis" were relative newcomers, insisting that some of them seized Mvskoke land when they settled west of the Appalachians.[7] Catawba oral tradition, meanwhile, argues that migrating Cherokees first settled in the upper Catawba River valley near where the Spanish stumbled into the town of Joara (in modern Burke County, North Carolina).[8] Protracted conflict between the two Native groups ultimately led Cherokee ancestors to move west, deeper into the mountains.[9] Many of their descendants remained there for centuries afterward, eventually forming the Middle and Valley towns.[10] It was not a uniform cultural population, however, as nineteenth-century Cherokees believed that the Middle towns also "received an influx of people from the French Broad [River]." Other oral traditions explain that some Middle town ancestors drew from the Chiscas territory in southwest Virginia.[11]

Murky migration experiences indicate a multiplicity of chronological and geographic settlement possibilities, which in turn enhanced the development of distinct (if overlapping) polities. Historian Paul Kelton speaks to the point when he notes relatively recent and stark "differences between peoples who lived in eastern Tennessee and Iroquoian speakers deeper in the mountains." In roughly only one hundred years, he observes, "settlement patterns, housing styles, and ceramic patterns changed considerably," suggesting an infusion of new ideas and customs.[12] Many of these newcomers came to inhabit the fertile lands surrounding the Little Tennessee River that, depending upon the tradition, had either been vacated by the Coosa Chiefdom or required the departure of Coosa's Mvskokian descendants. Over time they became known as the Overhill towns. Like the Middle and Valley towns, these settlements were not culturally uniform.[13] Still another group of Iroquoian speakers settled on or near the headwaters of what have become known as the Savannah and Chattahoochee Rivers. Eventually called Lower Cherokees, they, too, incorporated non-Iroquoian populations—in this case from what is now Georgia and South Carolina.[14]

At any rate, by the last third of the seventeenth century a core Cherokee area was coming into focus: from four to five highly mobile town clusters comprising "culturally and linguistically diverse peoples" amidst forty thousand square miles in southern Appalachia and the Piedmont plateau.[15] Altogether, the area incorporated part or all of the "New River system, the South Fork of the Holston River basin, the Watauga River basin, the Nolichucky River basin, the French Broad River basin, the Big Pigeon River basin, the Little Tennessee River basin, the Hiwassee River basin, the tributaries of the Upper Savannah River system, and the Coosa River and its affluents."[16] Archeologist Jon Marcoux adds Tuckaleechee Cove and the Little River to the list.[17] And from this broad area the Cherokees "followed gravity west, north, and south along the branched headwaters of the Tennessee, Kanawha, and Savannah rivers."[18] The nineteenth-century anthropologist James Mooney framed the territory by observing that "the Cherokees extended from the Ohio River southward to present-day central Georgia, and from what are now the states of Tennessee, Kentucky, and Alabama to the Wabash River."[19]

Power in these Cherokee regions was nearly entirely localized as of 1670. At that point they were also largely unaffected by the utilitarian lure of European goods (and the epidemiological carnage that came with them).[20] Shortly thereafter the Spanish seem to have provided a trigger moment, however. According to Chief Charles Hicks, a nineteenth-century Cherokee leader, Cherokees first acquired guns and other European commodities around 1671, and a 1673 report by Virginia traders James Needham and Gabriel Arthur indicated that these goods came from Spanish sources.[21] Within ten years English goods and guns would begin to affect whatever Spanish-Cherokee connection may have existed. According to archaeologist Gregory Waselkov, by 1681 "Chichumecoes, Uchizes [probably Yuchis], and Chiluques [possibly Cherokees]" had begun traveling south to attack the Guale missions in La Florida, "even though they had previously traded with the Spaniards 'in good friendship.'"[22] This movement speaks to a crucial point: by the 1680s Native southerners faced mounting pressure from Carolina's deerskin and Indian slave trades.[23]

Over the course of the seventeenth century, English and French Atlantic world pressures gradually extended to trans-Appalachia (generally) and the Tennessee corridor (specifically) as well. Rumors of exploitable resources to the west of their seaboard outposts had captured the English and French imaginations from the moment of their continental invasions, leading both groups to pursue expansionist schemes ranging from halting to unrealistic to outright absurd. Regardless of the category into which they fell, subsequent efforts to procure these resources developed in tandem with paranoia that each emerging "empire" represented an existential threat to the other. This combination of imagination and paranoia became particularly forceful by the time of Queen Anne's War (c. 1702–13) and would underpin both empires' western policies for most of the eighteenth century.

The process of Cherokee migration and settlement makes it abundantly clear, of course, that European expansionism never entailed simple forays into *vacuum domicilium*.[24] Understanding that point—and properly contextualizing Overhill power in the Tennessee corridor—requires a brief turn to the first iterations of English and French interest in trans-Appalachia. The chapter will then conclude with the English realization that western empire would require the careful cultivation of Cherokee alliances, with Overhill towns playing perhaps the most crucial role.

The Origins of the English Invasion of Trans-Appalachia

On some level, the "west" captured imaginations from the outset of the English invasion.[25] Inspired by eighty years of Spanish travel accounts, rumors, and legends, and committed to their own narrative of Edenic boosterism, members of the 1585–86 Roanoke expedition described an abundance of pearls, gold, silver, and copper they believed were tantalizingly nearby. As with other European invaders, men like Ralph Lane and Thomas Harriot also felt sure a western passage to the "South Sea" lay within their grasp, if only they knew where to look.[26] The Lane expedition was a disaster from start to finish, but twenty years later the Virginia Company picked up where the Roanoke invaders left off. The 1606 Virginia Charter specifically authorized settlers "to dig, mine, and search for all Manner of Mines of Gold, Silver, and Copper, as well within any Part of their said several Colonies, as of the said main Lands on the Backside of the same Colonies."[27] Even as disease and starvation decimated the earliest English settlers, a German called William Volday convinced London merchants to fund an expedition "to find silver in the mountains to the west and beyond." He landed in Jamestown with Lord De La Warr in 1610, allegedly carrying maps to the mines. As with nearly everyone else landing in Virginia, he died not long thereafter.[28]

The specter of death notwithstanding, English intruders remained intoxicated by the potential wealth both near their scattered settlements and further west. By the 1620s the commercial explosion of tobacco had focused most attention on cultivating that crop. The concomitant need for land and the persistence of Spanish rumors, however—combined with the conviction of "rich Mines of Copper and Yron" further west and the hope of "farre richer Minerals" soon to be discovered—continued to encourage blindly optimistic western boosterism.[29] The 1622 John Pory expedition provides an excellent example.[30] In January and February of 1621–22, Pory traveled to the vicinity of the Chowan River in modern-day North Carolina. He returned with descriptions of remarkable "discoveries." Not only was the ground itself fertile and available, Pory explained, he also had "past through great forests of Pynes 15. or 16. Myle broad and above 60. Myle long, which will serve well for masts for Shipping, and for pitch and [t]are, when we shall come to extend our plantations to those borders."[31] Drawing a direct connection to the Roanoke experiment, he further praised the large amount of "silke grasse which growes there monethly of which Maister Harriot, hath affirmed in print many yeeres ago." And although he did not cross the river, he nevertheless reported that "on the other side . . . there is a fruitfull Countrie blessed with aboundance of Corne, reaped twise a yeere: above which is the Copper Mines, by all of all places generally affirmed."[32] Notably, Pory did not see these mines himself.

Pory's expedition occurred just prior to a major Powhatan attack on the Jamestown settlements. When combined with the exploding value of tobacco, his description offered a rosy forecast to counteract the existential peril Virginians felt in that moment. That he returned not only with Edenic descriptions but also with a few bits of copper given him by the Chowans was enough to pique interest at the highest echelons of English power. In 1629 it helped convince Charles I to confer a patent for the colony of "Carolana" upon his attorney general Sir Robert Heath. The declared boundaries of this proposed colony were "between thirty one and thirty six degrees latitude," and, as with Virginia, would extend "to the west & soe fare as the Continent extends itself."[33]

Heath never exploited the patent and by 1637 had sold it to Henry Frederick Howard, Lord Maltravers, who likewise could not take advantage before civil war turned his attention to other matters. With Charles I's execution in 1649, however, Carolana reemerged as an object of interest.[34] Inspired by Pory and Harriot, a few influential boosters encouraged their audiences to support what they hoped was an imminent settlement. A 1649 entry in the (London) *Moderate Intelligencer* by a "well-willer," for example, assured potential Carolanians that they would "be plentifully fed and cloathed with the natural commodities of the Country, which fall into your hands without labour or toyle, for in obtaining of them you have a delightful recreation."[35] A year later, *Virgo Triumphant* author Edward Williams declared his intention to exploit not only "the beauties of a long neglected Virgin the incomparable Roanoke, [but also] the adjacent excellencies Carolana, a Country home God and Nature has indulged with blessings incommunicable to any other Region."[36] He explained that Carolana was "within ten dayes West toward the setting of the Sunne"—close enough to justify exploitation, he believed, even if it was far enough away to require forays into territory (and geopolitics) he did not know.[37] Dangerous, perhaps, but the abundance of copper and pearls would make it worthwhile.

There was so much of the latter, in fact, that "the Indians used to make and adorn Babies [dolls] with them."[38]

Both "well-willer" and Edward Williams cited Pory's 1622 narrative, various statements to Virginia governor Sir William Berkeley, and "Mr *Heriots* Report" to support their assertions.[39] It meant that their calls to exploit Carolana relied on sources that never physically accessed anything of value. On the contrary, Native communities and guides merely *told* the English about potential riches. And as Williams himself admitted, wealth always seemed just far enough away that the English would have to depart from the territories of the Indigenous polities with which they were interacting and move into what for them was terra incognita. A careful observer might have detected a pattern that stretched back a century. When in 1540 Hernando de Soto's expedition encountered the Cofitachequi Chiefdom, for example, his chroniclers reported that the paramount chief, "Lady of Cofitachequi," pointed them toward wealth further west, away from her borders.[40] Twenty years later Juan Pardo heard about mineral wealth near Joara, away from the settlement areas of those who told him about it. He never was able to cash in. Harriot and Ralph Lane heard similar reports at Roanoke in 1585–86, as did Pory in 1622.[41]

These experiences reveal how Native southerners manipulated European interests for Indigenous geopolitical purposes. Variously viewing the invaders as potential (but subordinate) allies, serious enemies, and destructive forces, people across the Mississippian and Powhatan worlds actively channeled this "other." Leaders adjusted combat tactics to neutralize European horses and technological advantages, as illuminated several times by Soto's chroniclers (most prominently in their descriptions of confrontation at Mabila in 1541); sent spies to gather intelligence, such as when Roanoke Weroan Wingina sent Manteo and Wanchese with Arthur Barlowe to London in 1584; incorporated English leaders into their chiefdoms (John Smith in 1608); steered European expeditions toward enemy or rival chiefdoms, in the process subordinating invader interests to geopolitics they could not understand (as described both by Soto's chroniclers and Ralph Lane); and informed Europeans that mineral wealth was just over the horizon, effectively moving them away before damage could become catastrophic.[42] Historian Kathleen DuVal has called this manipulation evidence of a "native ground": a theoretical location wherein Indigenous polities "were more often able to determine the form and content of inter-cultural relations than were their European 'colonizers.'"[43] A major consequence for dreamers like Thomas Harriot, John Pory, "well-willer," or Edward Williams was that they embraced rumors of wealth that obfuscated more than they revealed.[44]

A related point: as was the case with colonies across the eastern seaboard, the proclaimed boundaries of Carolana were meaningless. Everything west of the small, scattered coastal settlements was Native country, shaped by millennia of competition, commerce, diplomacy, war, and mobility by myriad Indigenous polities. The complexity was more than the first Europeans could negotiate. They chose to downplay their near-helplessness, instead emphasizing imperial expansion through Edenic imagery, imagined barriers, cultural and technological superiority, and claims of sovereignty that only made sense to them. The language had long-term consequences, of course, because it lulled subsequent generations into thinking that early European power was firm and thus that their land claims were clean. In this evolving narrative Indigenous people became static, apolitical, dangerous curiosities on the margins of the European colonial experience.

The legal and philosophical somersaults undertaken by men such as Edward Williams, however, illuminate that the first generation of invaders understood Indigenous realities quite well. That awareness formed the core of Williams's *Virgo Triumphant*: Native sovereignty and geopolitical strength, he believed, represented roadblocks to the English exploitation of Carolana. To get around such thorny issues, he recommended an insidious process by which to secure the colony's hypothetical riches.[45] "The fastest way" to secure dominion was "by degrees" to seize "places of advantage, very frequently found in that Contry, which we may progressionaly fortifie at every twenty or five and twenty miles distance." Once established, the English could then stabilize the posts by a constant stream of "supplies of victuals and ammunition, not only for the men there

Garrisond, but for our owne reception and maintenance in the Discovery."[46]

These improved if remote outposts would serve as the sharp point of the English spear. "By conference with the Indians" garrison officers would discover a route to the South Sea, along with "what distance, what accesse, what harbours, what frequentation, and by what people the neighbor Sea consists of." Simultaneously, Indigenous people would reveal to the English discoverers "all Mineralls, Drugges, Dies, Colours, Birds and Beasts, drawne to the life in colours." Such behavior would be safer and far more productive than sending "multitudes of people, whose number commonly (as in the example of *Fernando Soto* in Florida) hastens no other discovery, but that of unavoidable famine." Expeditions like Soto's not only were Catholic, disorderly, and violent, they succumbed to the native ground: Indigenous people, Williams wrote, had informed Soto and his "unwelcome Company, golden lies, and miracles of Countreys farther distant, where they are likely to find small satisfaction for their covetousness or hunger."[47]

Williams's proposal provides crucial insight into seventeenth-century English ideas of southwestern expansion: establishing a permanent location and improving the land around it meant they could claim dominion. In the process Englishmen would confer upon Native polities English notions of religion, property, society, gender, and culture.[48] It would benefit both the invaders and the invaded, they believed, and because it was Protestant it would be far more benign than the Catholic alternative employed by Soto and other Spanish conquistadores.[49] Given what they would gain, Indigenous people could not (and would not) complain about English extension.[50]

Williams's imagined path to empire was obliterated by two fundamental realities. First, it failed to concede the extent to which Native southerners manipulated the English as expertly as they did the Spanish. Second, Williams's proposed garrisons simply could not serve as central points of trade and diplomacy. Historian Michael McDonnell has noted that distant European outposts in North America "were only one among many sites of meeting, encounter, and community" for Indigenous polities.[51] It is a point well taken: so far from extending English empire, Williams's proposal at best would only tenuously place a few Europeans in Native country. If they really wanted to expand, they would have to gain the approval of polities such as the then-coalescing Cherokee people.

At any rate, well-willer and Edward Williams never saw the Carolana patent come to fruition, and the restoration of Charles II in 1660 led to a new scheme of exploitation. In 1663 Charles established Carolina, a proprietary colony that would stretch from the tiny "Countie of Albemarle" near Virginia to the doorstep of La Florida, and from Atlantic to Pacific.[52] Its first seven years were marked by religious dissent, nascent tobacco growth, some hog farming, a brief effort to establish a settlement near modern-day Wilmington, North Carolina, and an utterly impractical "Fundamental Constitutions of Carolina" written by John Locke.[53] The colony's fortunes changed rapidly after 1670, however, when a group of Barbadian planters settled what they called Charles Town. The resulting shockwaves drastically affected Indigenous and European populations alike.

If the first eighty-five years of the English western presence was little more than a hypothetical flight into the unknown, Charles Town settlers expanded the Edenic boosterism and ethnocentric hubris that framed it. In 1672, for example, William Talbot proclaimed to Carolina's proprietors that the "Apalatean Mountains stoop to your lordships Dominions, and lay open a Prospect into unlimited Empires."[54] That same year John Lederer repeated rumors dating to Juan Pardo's sixteenth-century expedition that Indian towns in the Appalachians were surrounded by "rich Commodities and minerals" and suggested that "if possessed by an ingenious and industrious people, [it] would be improved to vast advantages by Trade."[55] Agreed Thomas Ash, "It's supposed and generally believed, that the Apalatean mountains which lie far up within the Land, yields Ore both of Gold and Silver, that the Spaniards in their running searches of this Country saw it, but had not time to open them."[56] In 1698 and 1699 a Virginian called Richard Traunter described possible gold and silver deposits in the Appalachian foothills. He and five partners (some of whom had indirect connections to William III) received approval from the Board of Trade to locate the minerals.[57] A former *coureur de bois* called Jean Couture collaborated in Traunter's expeditions, an experience that no doubt informed his own schemes. By 1700 he was so convinced of silver deposits on the "Chauanons" River (the modern Cumberland) that he proposed that Carolina's government fund a mining enterprise.[58]

By that point, fantasies of copper, silver and gold had become secondary reasons for Carolinian interest in trans-Appalachia. Far more potentially profitable were the developing trades in deerskins and Indigenous slaves, the consequence of which was a phenomenon that anthropologist Robbie Ethridge has described as the "Mississippian Shatter Zone."[59] Before 1539, she reminds us, chiefdoms drawing from Mississippian culture (which at its zenith spread from Cahokia in modern Illinois to modern Georgia, and from parts of the Ohio valley to areas west of the Mississippi) lived in a "heterogeneous world composed of dozens of polities, albeit with many cultural, social, and economic traits in common." These polities rose and fell based on warfare, ecological circumstances, and resource alteration, among other reasons. Archaeologists call it a process of "cycling," and it created an overall stability in Mississippian North America that began to break down after Hernando de Soto's 1539 arrival on the continent.[60]

The shatter zone phenomenon accelerated after 1670 when Charles Town traders began systematically to offer commodities to the Native South, in payment for which they would take deerskins and Indigenous slaves. (As noted earlier, both trades were abetted by Native willingness to procure and sell to English buyers.) Within a few decades everyone from Charles Town merchants to traveling English traders to Native southerners and Ohio valley polities were affected by the Atlantic-wide markets for these two commodities. They brought profit to a few but encouraged significant adaptation in Indigenous hunting styles and lifeways. They made credit and debt both more inflexible and an increasingly necessary aspect of day-to-day encounters between Natives and newcomers. And as a result, they generally heightened inter-Indigenous tensions across trans-Appalachia while imperiling relationships between the Native South, Carolina, and Virginia.[61]

Devastating enough on their own, the combination of the "skin" trades provided vectors necessary to catalyze demographically catastrophic disease epidemics.[62] Estimates by historians Peter Wood and Alan Gallay have indicated that as much as half of the Native South's population loss between 1685 and 1715 came from the slave trade, while the other half came from the diseases it projected.[63] Ethridge quantifies its impact another way: approximately 1,700 Natives a year were taken by English-sponsored slavers in an era when a simple Mississippian chiefdom had a population of somewhere between 2,000 and 5,000.[64] As deerskin and slave trading took hold they "shattered" chiefdoms of all sizes, leading remnant populations to begin coalescing into new polities.[65] Building political identities in the face of these forces became one of the most crucial issues in Native trans-Appalachia.

In addition to hastening a shatter zone, the two "skin" trades had a less fully explored consequence: mobility, already wide-ranging, became even more critical in the Native South and Ohio valley, the result of which, as noted in the introduction, was enhanced inter-Indigenous interaction beyond the understanding of English observers. Paradoxically, then, sporadic English extension circa 1670 strengthened the trans-Appalachian native ground. But if this evolving fast-paced reality was Native-driven, it had another consequence: it brought the English imperial imagination into contact with French visions of trans-Appalachian expansion. The resulting paranoia dovetailed with broader Franco-British conflicts then unfolding to frame narratives of European expansion in North America for decades to come.

THE FRENCH INVASION OF TRANS-APPALACHIA

At nearly the same moment the English invaded the Powhatan Chiefdom, the French moved into the Kaniatarowanenneh valley to the north—and with them came the roots of a French western imagination.[66] Jamestown was barely a year old when King Henri IV authorized Samuel de Champlain to establish Quebec. Thereafter the French slowly moved up the valley (which they rechristened St. Lawrence) toward the Great Lakes. Wanting both souls and beaver pelts, this first wave of French invaders pursued relationships with the Montagnais, Abenakis, Algonkins, and particularly Wendats.

Haudenosaunee incursions into Wendake (Huronia) in the late 1640s and 1650s, however, forced the French to consider alternatives.[67] It became clear that systematic access to the profitable furs of the *pays d'en haut* (literally, the "upper country"; the region surrounding the Great Lakes) would require negotiation with the Anishnaabeg generally and the Odawas in particular. The latter's location near the straits between Lakes Michigan and Huron, along with their extended kinship networks, placed them in a geopolitical position from which they easily could "manipulate relations with newcomers, including Europeans, to their advantage."[68] Subsequent alliances revealed Odawa mastery over the French—the latter traveled to Michilimackinac for diplomatic purposes, after all, not vice versa. Nor were these alliances a guarantee of stability, formed as they were between specific Native towns and individual traders rather than two overarching polities. As a practical matter, the Anishnaabeg engaged in considerable commerce, diplomacy, and warfare to which New France was not privy. Like their English counterparts, in other words, French interests perpetually suffered from unsettling deficiencies in knowledge and control.

Also like the English, their geopolitical ignorance both receded and expanded in the second half of the seventeenth century. They certainly became more aware of the complex dynamics of the *pays d'en haut*, but French missionaries and fur traders drifted into terra incognita when they descended into the Mississippi and Ohio valleys. Nor did they fully comprehend the complexity of inter-Indigenous interaction in the region. On the one hand, an increasing Anishnaabeg presence in the *pays des Illinois* was matched by the movement of polities such as the Peorias, Kaskaskias, and Cahokias towards Michilimackinac "to carry away hatchets and kettles, guns, and other articles."[69] On the other hand, these same Illinois polities by 1670 had become important trade links between the cis- and trans-Mississippi worlds. In effect, then, the small French presence found itself in a "confluence" of east-west Indigenous webs in addition to those running north-south from Michilimackinac to Illinois.[70] Bison and European goods were the centerpieces of regional economic activity, and Native willingness to exploit these resources made them opportunistic and powerful.[71]

Adding to French headaches was the perception that English Charles Town represented a serious challenge. As he established a post at Kaskaskia in 1680, for example, Robert de La Salle encouraged greater exploration of (and jurisdictional claims in) trans-Appalachia to counter his conviction that the English threatened French commerce. His fear grew out of an emerging awareness of trans-Appalachian riparian realities, even if the geography was vague and the river names were not yet established in the European mind. "The river on which the Chickasaw live," he insisted, "has its source near Carolina . . . 300 leagues to the east of the river Colbert [Mississippi]." In reaching out to the Chickasaws the English could easily "come by ship to the Illinois, to the Miami, and close to the Baye de Puans and the country of the Sioux, and secure thereby a great portion of our trade."[72] In 1682 he argued that by means of east-to-west "River Trade with the Illinois, Miamis, Nadouessians and other savages, [the English could] spoil for ever our Commerce."[73] To secure the illusion of French jurisdictional control, La Salle even planted a lead plate declaring "ownership" near the bottom end of the Mississippi River.[74]

The slave trade made the English Carolinian presence more aggravating, not the least reason being the availability of potentially willing partners. They may have traded both north and west for bison and European commodities, but by the late seventeenth century some Illinois polities had added trans-Mississippi slave raiding to their endeavors.[75] It came at roughly the same moment that the Chickasaws began slaving in Choctaw and Quapaw towns in the southern Mississippi valley. Anecdotal evidence suggests that Overhill Cherokees were beginning to raid the *pays des Illinois* for slaves as well. It was enough to catalyze a high level of French paranoia. In 1694, for example, Henri Tonti expressed concern that "some of the English from Carolina have settled on a branch stream, running into the Ohio which itself falls into the Mississippi."[76] Five years later Pierre Le Moyne d'Iberville observed darkly that the English were trading with Chickasaws for "toe-buckskins and Indian slaves."[77] When in 1700 South Carolina governor Joseph Blake sent an expedition down the Tennessee River, ostensibly to divert trade from New France to Charles Town, d'Iberville recommended closing

La Belle Rivière to the English entirely.[78] He also authorized a "reverse reconnaissance of the Tennessee River" through which Frenchmen eventually "found portage to the Savannah river system and made their way to Charles Town."[79] A Frenchman known as Sauvole described that expedition, pointing out that two men called "Bellefeuille and Soton" came down the "Ouabache" and continued on what seemed a natural path to the Tennessee and thence to Carolina. Along the way they made note of Chickasaw settlements near the mouth of the Tennessee, "around a hundred and forty leagues from the Miciscipi." In one of them, they observed, "there is an Englishman established to trade in slaves, as they are among numerous other nations."[80]

The potential damage was not lost on d'Iberville. Dismissing the possibility that Indigenous societies might act for reasons independent of Europeans, he proclaimed "English mercenaries" were sparking hostile Indian raids and "advancing the territorial boundaries of Carolina."[81] He worried that New France's recent refusal to allow *coureurs de bois* either to trade furs in Montreal or to bring them down the Mississippi would lead them to "the route now opened by the Ohio and Tennessee rivers, and carry their peltry to the English."[82] The idea of fortifying the lower Ohio and the Wabash valley also began to resonate. As early as 1700 d'Iberville insisted the French should establish a post on the "Ouabache" and compel Native polities to trade there (or, after 1712, with the Odawas near Detroit).[83] Motivated by similar concerns, the Sieur de Vincennes tried to "induce the Ouiatanons to remove to the lower Ouabache to serve as a protection against the Southern Indians."[84] Geopolitical paranoia (both imagined and legitimate) convinced one Messeur du Vergier that "it is . . . necessary to have a post on the River Ouabache where the English appear desirous to push forward." He thus made a specific appeal to "the commandant of [New France] to place there a body of troops to occupy first this territory and prevent the English from penetrating there."[85] An anonymous Frenchman elaborated in 1722: "There are two large rivers which flow together forming a point," he observed, "where it will be necessary to make an establishment, and indeed to build a fort. One of these rivers takes its rise in the direction of Carolina, and bears the name of the

[Cherokee] tribe, and the other comes from the direction of the great lake of the Illinois. The land between the two is most excellent for an establishment."[86]

The Tennessee corridor, in short, had become a visible element in fin de siècle French trans-Appalachian calculations—it was a means "by which comes the Canadians from Detroit to the Illinois" on one end, and "where one goes to Carolina" on the other.[87] And crucially, French interests increasingly associated the corridor with the Cherokees. Around 1700 Charles Juchereau de St. Denys settled a trade post at the mouth of the "Riviere des Cheraquis" to "augment the recent establishment of French power in the lower Mississippi; . . . counter encroachments by way of the Ohio, Tennessee, and Cumberland Rivers; . . . [and to align] Indigenous interests with the French to the extent of making them allies."[88] During the Yamasee War the French feared the Tennessee River as a location from "which the Cherokee descend when they go to war in the Illinois."[89] In 1721 Pierre de Charlevoix expressed concern that the Wabash valley was too exposed and demanded a garrisoned fortification to "keep the Indians in awe, especially the Cherokees, who are the most numerous nation on this continent."[90] Four years later Jean Baptiste LeMoyne, Sieur de Bienville, wanted further French action. The newly conceptualized Fort Vincennes simply was not enough to deter the Cherokee presence, he feared, which came "by way of the Ohio, Cumberland, and Tennessee Rivers."[91]

Trans-Appalachia and the Evolution of Euro-Cherokee Diplomacy

Just as English slaving and commodity trading produced French paranoia, so the small wave of voyageurs, *coureurs de bois*, and Jesuit missionaries between 1670 and 1715 convinced Carolinians that their interests were in danger. As early as 1690 Carolina's proprietors warned that the colony needed more systematic law and order lest "the countrey . . . be over run by either Indians or ffrench."[92] In 1701 the latter seemed so numerous that Southern Carolina governor James Moore wrote "[whether] war or peace we are sure to be always in danger and under the trouble and charge of keeping out guards."[93] He then pointed to broader conspiratorial forces shaping British North America by comparing Carolina's predicament to regions further north. "To put you in mind of the French of Canada's neighborhood to the Inhabitants of New England," he suggested, "is to say enough on the subject." Agreed Price Hughes, no one in Carolina should forget the "barbarities" perpetrated by the French upon New Englanders.[94] In 1712 Carolina's commissioners of the Indian trade went so far as to require traders when "among the Indians to enquire into the State of our Enemies, the French and Spaniards."[95] It is an important statement: in effect, the government deputized these people to engage in quasi-diplomacy and intelligence gathering.

Cognizance of the possibilities of the Tennessee corridor added another layer of British concern. An anonymous writer in the *London Post* noted in 1700 that a presence in the region would "considerably enlarge the Trade in those parts, by means of the Ohio River, which falls into the Spirito Sancto [Mississippi] and supplies them by a water carriage from Charles's Town in Carolina, except only a small Portage."[96] A few years later a man called Daniel Coxe similarly observed that the Tennessee River "comes from the south-east, and its heads are among the mountains, which separate this country from Carolina, and is the great road of the traders from thence to the Meschacebe, and intermediate places."[97] Tapping into such a potentially useful region, however, would require ever increasing vigilance lest the French come to control it first.

Early eighteenth-century paranoia became more pervasive because of the outbreak of the War of the Spanish Succession. As its name implies, the conflict broke out after the death of King Carlos II in 1700. Carlos had been a Habsburg, the family controlling the throne since the creation of Spain in 1469. Unfortunately for them, French (and Bourbon) King Louis XIV knew his grandson Philip had a strong claim and pulled out all the stops to put him on that throne—much to the chagrin not only of the Habsburgs but also of Queen Anne of England. It mattered to her government for two reasons. First, a Bourbon monarch created the potential for a combined Spanish and French empire that would become a formidable rival. Second, and perhaps more importantly, such a Catholic behemoth represented a clear and present danger to the English commitment to spreading the Protestant interest around the world.[98]

The details of monarchical succession in Europe meant little to anyone living in the American South, but the war's impact was evident everywhere around them. In 1704, for example, Carolinians led by James Moore used it as a pretext to raid Guales and other Spanish Missions Indians in Florida.[99] Two years later Charles Town residents suffered through a French naval attack, which many locals connected to the recently established Mobile settlement in "Louisiana." To Carolinians, Queen Anne's government had to challenge this growing French menace. And crucial to this impending confrontation was something the English had for a century generally failed to accomplish: they would have to cultivate meaningful Indigenous connections. It was more than just a recommendation for those living in the precariously situated Carolina colony—it represented an existential imperative. As Carolinian John Stewart put it in 1712 to William Legge, First Lord Dartmouth, "Whether we or france have the most war Like and Numerous body" of Indians would determine who "Commands all North America."[100]

Concomitant—and dizzying—efforts to secure trans-Appalachian allies illuminate European paranoia over their geopolitical weakness. Circa Queen Anne's War the map stood thus in the European mind: along the lower Mississippi the *petit* nations seemed to have thrown their support to the French, as had the Choctaws. The Mvskoke-speaking towns the British increasingly called "Creeks" seemed more divided. And in the *pays des Illinois* and Wabash valley, Twightwees, Kickapoos, Mascoutens, Peorias, Kaskaskias, and Cahokias seemed "French." British interests at this point would have suggested that their only "reliable" allies in trans-Appalachia were the Chickasaws then raiding Choctaws and Quawpaws for slaves to sell to Charles Town.[101] That polity's population was declining, however, which meant that it might not be possible for them to serve as a long-term trans-Appalachian partner.[102] To stabilize and protect their western interests, Carolinians increasingly turned toward establishing connections with the Lower, Middle, Out, Valley, and—particularly—Overhill Cherokees.[103]

By 1715 the newly proclaimed British Empire was coming to place serious value in exploiting Cherokees' extended reach. It certainly could stabilize affairs on the eastern seaboard, which in light of conflicts with Tuscaroras (1711) and Yamasees (1715) was no small thing. But for some British imperialists, allying with the Cherokees could offer another benefit: if they could be restrained, an alliance could serve as a means by which to unlock trans-Appalachian jurisdiction. Such an alliance would be far easier said than done.

CHAPTER 2

(De-)Constructing an Anglo-Cherokee Chain of Friendship, 1700–1730

In 1708 South Carolina Indian commissioner Thomas Nairne laid out a proposal for checking French "aggression" in trans-Appalachia. In language reminiscent of the Spanish Requerimiento two centuries earlier, he called for inviting "by fair means all [Indians] that would accept of our friendship, upon the Terms of Subjecting themselves to our government and removeing into our territory." The newly established British Empire would have to destroy Indigenous groups rejecting the invitation, he suggested, so that the French could not "raise an Indian Army to Disturb us or our Allies." Thereafter, he believed, laying waste to the lower Mississippi valley would divert upper valley trade to South Carolina via "factories, Setled on the [Tennessee] River."[1]

Fueled as it was by paranoia related to Queen Anne's War, Nairne's proposal illuminates just how seriously Carolinians took the perceived French threat from the Great Lakes, *pays des Illinois*, and Ohio valley. Regardless of the poverty and ineffectual nature of French settlements at that point, Nairne foresaw a noose tightening around South Carolina's neck—and by extension around the emerging empire. His plan for addressing the threat, however, was a nonstarter. Hubris-filled threats notwithstanding, turn-of-the-century Carolina sat precariously balanced between a European Atlantic and an Indigenous continent.[2] That Carolinians had commodities worth pursuing was a major reason why Native polities interacted with them, but most colonial leadership understood that aggressive assertions of authority in the west could threaten already fragile Anglo-Indigenous networks.[3] Cultivating alliances—not destroying them—would be essential.

Overhill Cherokees and their geopolitical reach were central to this complex moment in continental history.[4] As Queen Anne's War and subsequent Franco-British tensions—abetted by conflicts with the Tuscaroras and Yamasees—provoked ever-greater conspiracy theories, Carolinians came to see such an alliance as crucial. Not only would it help to stabilize affairs on the eastern seaboard, for many imperial-minded leaders the alliance could unlock the trans-Appalachian jurisdiction imagined by Nairne without the violent upheaval that came with his proposal. As long as the British could maintain Cherokees as subjects, so the thinking went, any area they might claim automatically became an extension of the empire.

The pursuit of a Cherokee alliance culminated in a delegation's visit to London in 1730. In the subsequent treaty, the empire purported to make an Overhill headman the leader of the Cherokee "nation," and proclaimed that said nation had accepted British dominion through a "Chain of Friendship." The problem: such an alliance required both political subordination and commercial exclusivity.[5] And although residents of the five Cherokee regions appreciated the abundance and quality of British goods, no leader accepted either precondition. On the contrary, political commitment to town and region remained strong, while the Iroquoian idea of the two-way relationship defined their trade practices.[6]

More fundamentally, the harder Britons worked to secure an alliance, the clearer it became that Overhill (and to a degree Valley) Cherokees would determine the validity of Britain's imagined western empire. They certainly used the Tennessee River to slave raid and to challenge French interests in the Ohio and Wabash valleys when it was in their interest to do so. They did not stop negotiating with Indigenous polities outside the purview of British interests, however, nor did they relinquish the power to negotiate with the French, whether at Fort Toulouse (after 1717) or in the *pays des Illinois*. Further complicating imagined imperial extension was a perpetual diplomatic problem for anyone wanting a singular, subordinate Cherokee Nation: British interests could not offer the same singular entity in return. Given the newness of the empire in the early eighteenth century, colonial cohesion did not exist anymore than did inter-Cherokee cohesion. They, too, were coalescing, and competition over diplomacy and trade—particularly between South Carolina, Virginia, and eventually Georgia—upended Anglo-Cherokee stability for decades before and after the 1730 treaty. (See appendix A for the text of the treaty and the Cherokee responses.)

This chapter explores more deeply the trans-Appalachian contexts for what has become known as the Anglo-Cherokee Chain of Friendship. As with chapter 1, it frames British North American concerns with Native realities, paying particular attention to issues embedded in Cherokee regional variations, the Overhill rejection of European ideas of diplomatic and commercial unity and exclusivity, and the inability of British interests to secure their own intercolonial unity.

Chestowee, Tugaloo, and Cherokee Regional Variations

Carolina's leaders were anxious in December 1715. Since 1702 they had stared down French and Spanish western threats, attacks on Charles Town, a war with Tuscaroras, and, beginning in April 1715, an explosive confrontation with Yamasees.[7] According to Francis Yonge nearly four hundred Carolinians died in that conflict, along "with many . . . Slaves, and great numbers of Cattle." The violence—combined with the danger to which South Carolina was exposed "by being a Frontier, to the French and Spaniards"—so appalled Yonge that in 1719 he would advocate for the transfer of colonial authority from the proprietors to the Crown.[8]

Yamasee attacks had slowed by December, but Carolinians nevertheless maintained good reasons to send Col. Maurice Moore and four hundred militiamen to the Lower Cherokee town of Tugaloo. Securing an alliance obviously was the major objective, with Carolinians hoping Lower Cherokees would do for the Yamasee conflict what they seemed to have done for the Tuscarora War four years earlier.[9] Time was of the essence, however, because of the intensity of the perceived competition for Cherokee attention. In addition to the Carolinians, Yamasees themselves were keen to secure their neighbor's support. And at roughly the same moment Colonel Moore and his troops arrived in Tugaloo, a delegation of Cowetas appeared as well. Having no formal connection to South Carolina, they too wanted to convince the Cherokees to join them.

A lot was at stake, in short, in December 1715. A well-established narrative explains the outcome of the negotiations: the Cherokees rejected Yamasee overtures and sided with Carolina, after which they rejected Mvskokc appeals by murdering the Coweta diplomats.[10] In the short term, this Anglo-Cherokee agreement became a turning point in the Yamasee War. "By siding with the Carolinians rather than the Yamasees, Creeks, and their allies," observes historian Steven Hahn, "the Cherokees . . . foreclosed the possibility of sustaining a truly pan-Indian revolt, and their regional influence seems to have had a ripple effect of convincing smaller tribes in the Carolina piedmont to make peace with the colony."[11] In the longer term, as John Savry observed in 1728, the decision to kill the Cowetas catalyzed "a continual war" wherein Cherokee "wives and children have been Killed or taken away Slaves."[12] As that conflict unfolded the Aniyunwiya increasingly blamed the Carolinians, expressing particular frustration that the colony broke promises by cultivating a Lower Creek relationship. True or not, according to William Hatton, the Cherokees were convinced that the British would forsake them for Mvskokes as soon as they "had gotten all the skins out of their Nation."[13] They found it bitterly ironic. After all, they informed Hatton, it was on South Carolina's account that the Cherokees had attacked the Cowetas in the first place.[14] At Tugaloo Carolinians had promised to stand with Cherokees "against their Enemies, but since [then] they have made friends with the Creeks and stand fast by them in spight of all arguments." They were further convinced, according to Hatton, that the British provided greater trade to the Creeks "by far then ever we did them otherwise they would not come and destroy so many Charikees as they do."[15] It was a critical lesson for all Cherokee regions: Carolinians could not maintain the reciprocal relationship necessary for Indigenous diplomacy to work, a fact that significantly complicated a long-term alliance.[16] Creek-Cherokee confrontations would continue (off and on) for the next several decades, in the process directly shaping the Anglo-Cherokee relationship—whether the British understood that point or not.[17]

As well known as this narrative has become, a closer look at processes of coalescence suggests that this early Anglo-Cherokee "alliance" was complex and limited mostly to the Lower towns. Even as the influential Tugaloo headman the Conjuror (also known as Charite Hagey) informed Colonel Moore that "He and ye English was all one," and that his subordinates would not wage war upon Carolina, he also explained that Yamasees "were his ancient people" and that he would only fight Shawnees, Yuchis, and Apalachees.[18] It was hardly a ringing commitment to unity, nor did it hint at interregional Cherokee alliance. Carolinians may not immediately have understood the latter point, but it took little time to manifest in front of them. In February 1716/17, for example, Indian trade commissioners begged Theophilus Hastings for intelligence on whether the Conjuror and a Valley headman called Caesar had agreed to side with the British, there having been "no great Understanding between them" prior to that point.[19] In 1717 the commissioners asked Hootlebayau (also known as Warrior of Tugaloo) why Valley and Overhill towns were reluctant to deal with Carolinians. He responded that "he knows not what Reason the upper People have for not dealing with the white Men, or what their Talk is, being unacquainted."[20] That same year they asked (unnamed) headmen why Quanasees [a Valley town] and Tellicos [an Overhill town] were acting so "inofficiously" towards White traders.[21] Specifically, they wanted to know why "the Quanasee and Tunese People did not assist" burdeners from the Lower towns in carrying deerskins to Charles Town. The headmen answered vaguely that "the Tunese and Quanase People . . . were gone out to War" before explaining that the missing burdeners would not appear until Carolinians fulfilled their own obligations. They would have to settle permanently "four white Men . . . in their Towns, for the better supplying them with Goods." [22]

Put simply, the Overhill and Valley towns felt no natural connection to Carolina. And given that they filtered it through their own lens of trade and reciprocity, whatever relationship did exist required consistent attention.[23] Carolina's leaders were frustrated and flummoxed by independent Native decision-making, however, over time coming to fear that the westernmost Cherokees had succumbed to European pressures from their periphery. John Savry made the point most explicitly in 1728. The British, he mused, simply could not rely on any Cherokees except those from the Lower towns. They alone, he insisted, had not been "corrupted by the Crown of France or Spain."[24]

Such paranoia was facilitated by regional tensions within Cherokee country. In 1716, for example, the Conjuror informed Theophilus Hastings that the Spanish had infiltrated the Overhill towns. He pointed to a "Spaniard of Movela" who was such an accomplished "Linguister" that he had influenced Indigenous affairs at least since 1700. Hastings was unequivocal on the Conjuror's intelligence: it would "hereafter prove of ill Consequence to this Government by [the Spaniard's] Influence over those Indians, if not removed."[25] The construction of French Fort Toulouse in 1717 further complicated the situation. Erected at the forks of the Coosa and Tallapoosa Rivers in "upper" Creek country after a failed British effort to do the same, Carolinians saw it as a violation of the 1713 Franco-British Treaty of Utrecht. (More on this point below.) Not only did it threaten their access to Overhill towns, it also economically separated the Cherokee regions by giving western towns another trading option. In so doing, it further opened the door for French influence in trans-Appalachia, thereby endangering Carolina's western borders.[26] Rumors of French and Spanish encroachment were so ubiquitous that they contributed to the British decision in 1718 to shore up Cherokee Lower town support by constructing Fort Congaree.[27]

Scholars also can tease tensions out of the Conjuror's willingness to confront Yuchis. In 1713, Cherokees (from different regions) had joined Charles Town traders Alexander Longe and Eleazar Wiggan in an attack on the Yuchi town of Chestowee. Carolina's trade commissioners left behind a reasonable, if basic, outline of the affair, but key issues—ranging from the precise location of Chestowee to a full-throated explanation for why it occurred— remain elusive.[28] According to several eyewitnesses, Longe instigated the attack out of a desire for revenge. Statements to the commission further reveal that Caesar was at the heart of the conspiracy, as was an Overhill known to the British as Flint.[29] Still another Cherokee man named Partridge (region of origin unclear) seemed to have had intimate knowledge of the affair.

The raid devastated Chestowee, a point that frustrated Carolina's leadership because of the existence of a perceived Anglo-Yuchi alliance. In its aftermath, then, the commissioners wanted answers that were difficult to obtain. Cherokees blamed the English. The English blamed Cherokees. Even though the commissioners relied on his testimony, Partridge conveniently was out hunting during the attack and could only provide hearsay—a common tactic in the world of Indigenous diplomacy. At any rate, the commissioners ultimately blamed and punished Longe and Wiggan (albeit lightly) for instigating the affair, and historians have accepted their verdict. Even so, barebones records lead to unresolved issues. Why, for example, did Caesar insist on attacking Chestowee before the Green Corn Ceremony? If Partridge was absent for the raid, why would the commissioners rely on his testimony? And what are we to make of the fleeting glimpse of an important inter-Indigenous diplomatic tool—Anetso, or the Ball Game, which Cherokees indicated they would use as a ruse for "cutting off" Chestowee?[30] These questions suggest that a Native explanation for the attack might diverge from the Charles Town version. One speculative path for addressing them sheds further light on regional Cherokee distinctions (and connects with the Tennessee corridor to boot).

It is important to note that the Chestowee raid divided Valley and Overhill towns on the one hand from Lower towns on the other. Trade commissioners recorded the claim that Flint and Caesar promised to move on Chestowee regardless of Carolina's support. The Conjuror was much more reluctant, however—even if he informed Colonel Moore two years later of his willingness to attack Yuchis. The situation becomes more curious when contextualized with paranoia that trans-Appalachian French interests lurked behind the affair. In 1712 a man called Richard Gower reported to the trade commissioners that Yuchis "were going from their settlement and itt was thought were going to the French."[31] The commissioners did not buy that rumor, but they did seem to embrace another concern:

the Overhills—not the Yuchis—maintained the French connection. A year later, while questioning Alexander Longe about Yuchi commerce, the commissioners insisted that he "enquire to what Place the French were designed to carry their Goods because we suspect they might have a design to tamper with the Charikees."[32] In effect, they deputized Longe to engage in quasi-espionage. They did the same with William Hatton in 1718, informing him not only that he needed to get "Indians to assist you in building Forts at your Trading Houses" but also that he was to "miss no Opportunity of giving the Governour what Advices you can of your Proceedings."[33]

Meanwhile, both Benjamin Clea and James Douglas warned that "French Indians" were frequently seen along the Hiwassee River—the location of the Overhill town of Euphase and the likely location of Chestowee.[34] Archeologist Brett Riggs points to the implications of their paranoid conviction: as the westernmost settlement on the Cherokee frontier, he observes, Chestowee was "an outlier that would have absorbed the brunt of raids from Louisiana or Illinois."[35] Riggs offers another tantalizing detail. In the 1940s, he observes, archeologist Joseph Bauxar associated "Chestowee with 'Tongoria' (var. of Taogaria, the Illinois term for Yuchi), a settlement near the mouth of the Hiwassee River indicated by the 1717 Vermale and 1718 de l'Isle French maps."[36] Given that the British considered Yuchis allies, that "foreign enemies infested" Euphase Town, and that Overhill towns generally engaged French interests at Toulouse and in the *pays des Illinois,* is it possible that the attack stemmed in part from Overhill frustration that Yuchis unnecessarily interfered with "French influence among the Cherokees"?[37] Regardless, the fact that Overhill and Valley towns diverged from others on "Yuchi policy" indicates they were willing to challenge smaller Indigenous polities, that they dismissed the idea of Cherokee unity, and that they understood Carolina's alliance building efforts on their own terms.

Historian William Ramsey has pointed to yet another crucial issue with western implications: that the Chestowee attack was connected to slave raiding.[38] In his testimony to the commissioners, Partridge observed that Longe and Wiggan boasted "there would be a brave Parcel of Slaves if Chestowe were cut off."[39] James Douglas lent credence to the observation by noting that Yuchis "killed their own

People in the War House to prevent their falling into the Hands of the Cherikees."[40] Other developments bear the hallmarks of slave raiding, not the least of which was the decision by trade commissioners to release detained Yuchis "with all convenient Speed" and to forbid English traders from demanding payment for them.[41] Partridge further intimated that Overhill and Valley towns maintained separate slaving interests when he observed that Flint and Caesar were loath to "acquaint the Lower Townes with their Design because they shoold not come in with them for a Share."[42]

Slavery casts a contextual shadow over the 1715 Tugaloo gathering as well.[43] Within six months of its conclusion, the trade commission ordered new "Brands, Locks, Bolts, Shackles, and such Necessaries as are wanting . . . to secure the Publick's Goods, and Slaves when brought in [by] the Charikees."[44] In June 1717 the commissioners recorded that Theophilus Hastings "together with a certain Number of Charikee Burdeners" would shortly appear "with several Slaves and Skins." They brought a massive haul with them: 901 dressed deerskins, 56 raw deerskins, 30 beaver skins, and 21 "Indian slaves," one of whom was "bought formerly of Indian Cesar, for a Horse."[45] In November that year John Fancourt petitioned to take possession of "an Indian Slave Woman purchased for the publick Account in the Charikees," along with three other slaves offered by the burdeners. He requested that Caesar receive "two Yards Duffields . . . for his Service in taking care of the slaves."[46]

Sources suggest that at least some of these slaves could have come via the Tennessee corridor. As early as 1702, the French voyageurs Bellefeuille and Soton described "an Englishman established to trade in slaves" near the mouth of the Tennessee River.[47] Roughly a decade later the Conjuror informed Col. George Chicken that an expedition of fifty Cherokees was "about 4 day jorney down" the Tennessee in search of Cahokias. Chicken subsequently reported that this party engaged "Conowes" and Cahokias along with a delegation of "16 frinch men," ultimately taking "all ther women and cheldern slaves."[48] Contemporary French sources also reported that raid, while a 1717 account further identified men from Quanasee and Tellico along the Wabash in search of "Nottoways, Senecas, and Caskaskias."[49] (The raid produced rampant paranoia in Carolina that a counterplot against Cherokees existed "by the Notawaugees, Senecas, and Cahokies, and several other Nations combined," which they feared would take place early in 1718.)[50] Overhill (and Valley) sightings and confrontations were common enough by 1721 that Pierre de Charlevoix believed France needed to fortify the Wabash valley "to keep the Cherokees in awe."[51] In 1725 Jean Baptiste LeMoyne, Sieur de Bienville, renewed the call to action. Neither New France nor Louisiana, he insisted, were doing enough to deter Cherokee raids "which seemed to come by way of the Ohio, Cumberland, and Tennessee Rivers."[52] Illinois polities would describe the Overhills as slavers for decades thereafter.[53] Their raiding no doubt connects with two other realities: that there already was a lively slave exchange in the *pays des Illinois*—particularly at Caskaskia, where "more than half the slaves enumerated in the villages of the Illinois Country resided";[54] and that Illinois polities were known occasionally to enslave Cherokees. According to historian Carl Ekberg, at least one Cherokee was identified as a slave in the region (at St. Genevieve) between 1719 and 1785.[55]

CHEROKEES AND EMPIRE IN THE BRITISH IMAGINATION

Properly contextualized, the events at Tugaloo and Chestowee offer an impressive window into the complex evolution of Cherokee regional distinctions, not to mention the influence of Native trans-Appalachian affairs on the sense of existential danger felt by early eighteenth-century Carolinians. As a practical matter, they also explain why the colony felt compelled to pursue Indian affairs as delicately as possible—even if slave trading continued for at least another fifteen years after the Yamasee War.[56] Instructions in 1711 from Carolina's trade commissioners provide a case in point. "Your Behaviour [must] be such towards the Indians that they may have no Reason or Grounds of Complaint," they declared, whether because of severity of treatment or because horses and livestock destroyed Native farm plots. In fact, the commission insisted, it probably would be best not to "give them any Offence on any Account whatsoever."[57] In 1716 it further demanded that traders supply guns to Cherokees regardless of legal restrictions because it was "of the highest Consequence not to disoblige these People."⁵⁸ Instructions to a slave trader called William Waties sheds light on Carolinian sensitivity from another angle. In December 1716 Waties was informed that he had to mark Indian slaves "by Powder or other Means, and not branded with the Iron Mark."⁵⁹ Branding, it would seem, was too permanent—it served as a visible reminder of aggression that easily could undermine fragile Anglo-Indigenous networks.

Maintaining these networks was particularly crucial in light of the tensions plaguing the Franco-British relationship after 1715. Between 1712 and 1714 the British Empire negotiated separate Treaties of Utrecht with Spain and France, thereby officially concluding the War of the Spanish Succession. The central agreements of the two treaties were that Britain would recognize the legitimacy of the Bourbon claim to the Spanish throne, but in exchange the French and Spanish monarchs permanently had to remove themselves from one another's lines of succession (making it impossible for them to establish a single Catholic Bourbon polity). Most other Utrecht mandates focused on European affairs, although North American concerns did emerge out of the conversation. In particular, Article XV of the Franco-British treaty spelled out that French Canadians would cease their "hinderance or molestation" both of the Haudenosaunee and any "other natives of America" who were subjects of (or friends to) British dominion. In return, Britain agreed they and their North American colonists would "behave themselves peaceably towards the Americans who are subjects or friends to France." The two further agreed that Indigenous people could trade with either European polity "without any molestation or hinderance" by the other.⁶⁰

Both parties almost immediately violated the spirit of Article XV, in the process exacerbating already palpable colonial fear and paranoia. British North American leaders concluded, in fact, that evolving Franco-British tensions had dangerous implications. In the North two examples drove their thinking: the conviction that the French were pursuing a Haudenosaunee alliance by building a fort at Niagara, in Seneca territory, and the fear that a Jesuit priest named Sebastian Rale was fomenting Wabanaki attacks on the New England frontier.⁶¹ The peril, the Board of Trade told Thomas Pelham-Holles, First Duke of Newcastle, grew out of the fact that such affronts kept

North America on a quasi-war footing, and battles with Indigenous groups inherently were "more difficult than if the French were our declared enemies." The board explained further: in this scenario colonials perpetually had to confront what they called the "sculking" way of war rather than having it out on an open battlefield, costing the empire unnecessary loss of blood and treasure.[62] Britons, it would seem, had no control over Indigenous North America.

A "Gentleman of America" reminded the British public that it was more than merely a northern problem. Colonists had to remain vigilant, he insisted, lest the French also "penetrate . . . Virginia and Carolina."[63] Fort Toulouse served as the southern "Niagara." It was a location, claimed John Savry, from which French agents discouraged Native southerners "from the commerce of any other person Whatsoever in trade or otherwise."[64] Anglican minister Francis Varnod put the problem in spiritual terms. A member of the Society for the Propagation of the Gospel in Foreign Parts, Varnod wrote in 1724 that French priests were traveling as many as four times yearly to Creek and Cherokee countries. He believed that these missionaries were capable of converting entire towns, which put the British Protestant interest at a serious disadvantage.[65]

Such behavior clearly violated Article XV and demanded more systematic monitoring by the British Empire. At the least, the government would need to fortify the southern colonies' "Inland Frontier" and formally "ascertain Boundarys."[66] For men like Savry and Varnod, the next step would be to confront the problem at Toulouse. Doing nothing simply was not an option—that would lead inexorably to French-inspired Indian assaults on South Carolina.[67] Others were more sanguine, hoping that the Overhill towns would block, as Thomas Nairne had put it, "any Incursions which Either the Illinois or any other French Indians may think of making into Carolina."[68] Agreed the Board of Trade, because Cherokees inhabited "a long Ridge of Mountains call'd Apalache . . . it wou'd be for his Majesty's Service that some small Forts shou'd likewise be built among them for the Encouragement of our Security."[69]

But if they provided a defensive bulwark for the colony, a long-term relationship could provide an offensive opportunity. Given their population of 10,379 in 1721, idealistic Britons like Virginia governor Alexander Spotswood and Member of Parliament (and Privy Councilor) Martin Bladen imagined that the Cherokee Nation (singular) could serve as a southern counterpart to the Haudenosaunee—a "subordinate" Indigenous polity that could project and secure British dominion across trans-Appalachia.[70] It was a heady proposition that made the Aniyunwiya potentially crucial to British North American policy. But to set the plan in motion, the empire needed to overcome a problem: the five Cherokee regions had no central representative entity such as the Onondaga Council Fire around which to build a one-to-one relationship.[71]

Given their experiences over the previous two decades, it is no surprise that imperial interests would tackle the dilemma directly. As early as 1721 the Board of Trade suggested that sending delegations to London could lead both to "the securing of the Natives in Your Majesty's Interest, and to the enlargement of your Frontiers in America."[72] In 1725, meanwhile, Carolina sent Indian Affairs superintendent George Chicken on a tour of Lower, Middle, and Overhill towns. Playing off Tennessee corridor complexities at each stop, Chicken warned that "ffrench Indians" were coming up the Tennessee River "with a design to destroy your People." He expressed hope that they would unify and go to "Warr with all Indians in Amity with the French."[73] He further encouraged Cherokees to gather as a single nation at a central location to enhance the growth and stability of the Anglo-Cherokee relationship.[74] Lest it seem that they were not willing to do their part, Chicken announced that the British would offer protection to the nation; he chastised unlicensed traders and warned others by letter that he had authorized Cherokees to shoot British animals "seen in their Cornfields destroying their Corn or doing them any such damages as they heretofore done."[75] Much to his chagrin, Cherokees were less than receptive. An Overhill "king" put it perhaps most clearly, explaining that his "people would work as they pleased and go to Warr when they pleased, notwithstanding his saying all he could to them." The Overhills, he declared, would not be malleable "like White Men." For that matter, they "have their own way of Warring and . . . it would be good if the English would let them alone and see what they will do themselves and by that means they may grow better."[76]

Five years later a curious fellow known as Alexander Cuming again attempted to centralize "the nation." A Scottish baronet and so-called explorer, Cuming traveled through Cherokee country alongside trader Ludovick Grant to demand that the five regions "'bring full power' to elect [one] 'emperor' of the Cherokee nation."[77] To facilitate the process he unilaterally declared Moytoy of Tellico the "Emperor over the whole" and demanded that town leaders in all other regions answer to Moytoy for "the conduct of their people." Not to do so would have dire consequences, he implied: they would "become no people, if they violated their promise and obedience."[78]

At the Middle town of Nequassee Cuming extended a fascinating offer: Why not appoint a Cherokee delegation to come with him to London?[79] After serious deliberation, according to a young Overhill man called Oukanekah—later known as Attakullakulla, or Little Carpenter to the British—seven delegates agreed.[80] George Chicken and interpreter Robert Bunning also joined the group.[81] As they embarked the delegation made it clear that their mission would be limited, whatever Cuming may have hoped (or projected). When asked if they carried "any message to deliver from the Nation," Attakullakulla explicitly stated that they "were only going to see England for our own pleasure." He was adamant that no one had proposed the Cherokees give up land—nor would any Cherokee agree to do so.[82]

IMAGINED NATIONS, INTERNATIONAL DELEGATIONS, AND CHAINS OF FRIENDSHIP

Imperial officials ignored such candor. In light of the London conference, they chose to mislead government and the public alike, declaring that the delegation assented to subject their nation (singular) "to the British Government and laws."[83] For good or for ill, it has defined the Anglo-Cherokee narrative ever since.[84] The formal diplomatic exchange occurred after weeks of entertainment, first at Windsor Castle then in London. Once the Cherokees were at Westminster, representatives of the Board of Trade explained the core reason for the visit: they required the Cherokees to pay "homage to his Britanick Majesty George 2d as subjects of the crown to Great

Britain."[85] According to representatives Martin Bladen, James Brudanell, and Paul Dominique, in two subsequent negotiations the board presented proposals that ultimately obtained the "Answer and full Consent . . . of the Indian Chiefs of the Cherrokee Nation."[86] Known as the 1730 Treaty of Whitehall, or Articles of Friendship, the articles reveal the British vision for a trans-Appalachian empire. Assuming Moytoy as the head of the nation, the articles required his diplomats symbolically to lay his "Crown," along with "Scalps of enemies and Feathers of Glory," at the feet of an accepting George II.[87] That achieved, George informed "the Great Nation of Cherokees" that the articles amounted to a "Chain of Friendship" fastened directly "to His own Breast." He encouraged the delegation to fasten the other end to Moytoy, and from there "to the Breasts of your old Wise Men, your Capts and all your People, never more to be broken or made loose." This Chain of Friendship, George declared, was "like the Sun; That as there are no Spots or Blackness in the Sun, so is there not any Rust of Foulness in this Chain." [88] His affection for the Cherokee Nation, said the King, was equal to his "People and His Children . . . on all sides of the Great Mountains," meaning that henceforth Cherokees' "Friends are His Friends; and Their Enemies are His Enemies."[89]

According to historian Alden Vaughan, the articles "promised nothing on Britain's part except friendship," even as they seemed to benefit South Carolina and the empire immensely.[90] Particularly important (from the idealized British perspective) was that the Cherokee Nation would have to "treat the English as Brethren of the same Family," always prepared to fight White men or Indians when called upon by the South Carolina governor. On this point the empire was firm, whatever its obligations under Article XV of the Treaty of Utrecht. Cherokees were not to accept "trade with the White Men of any other Nation but the English, nor permit White Men of any other Nation to build any Forts, Cabins, or plant Corn amongst them or near to any of the Indian Towns, or upon the Lands wch belong to the Great King."[91] Once agreed, a unified Cherokee Nation would then become central to an imagined empire sweeping from the Atlantic to the Mississippi River valley.[92]

There is an irony in imperial efforts at Cherokee consolidation: the British could offer nothing close to a unified polity in return, a point that had bedeviled Anglo-Indigenous diplomacy since the formation of the empire in 1706–7. Because it was a new entity in 1730, there was no more cohesion in Britain's North American districts than in the five Cherokee regions. Tensions between Virginia, South Carolina, and Georgia are instructive in this matter. As the self-proclaimed southern representative of the British Empire, South Carolinians insisted that they control major Native southern affairs. The colony demanded that the Aniyunwiya trade exclusively through them and seemed perpetually frustrated by Virginia's (and subsequently Georgia's) encroachment.[93] In 1715, for example, George Chicken complained that Governor Spotswood of Virginia undermined South Carolina's authority by providing Cherokees with coats, guns, blankets, and promises of greater trade.[94] William Hatton grew livid because Virginia's goods in the Overhill towns sold "much Cheaper than those from Carolina." He added that Virginians brought large numbers of horses for their Overhill trade, the consequence of which was that they did not impose the onerous task of burdening skins to Williamsburg.[95] Such antics were detrimental to Carolina's commercial interests, Hatton warned, but they also were potentially lethal to the colony's population. He explained further: on the one hand, Cherokee towns not only rolled out the welcome mat for Virginians, they also taunted Carolinians with "the hatefull News ... that the Virginians was very good, and had brought 'em abundance of Goods and Sold 'em at such and such prices."[96] On the other hand, Hatton observed, Virginians were whispering to various Lower Cherokee leaders that South Carolina was behind Mvskoke attacks on their towns, in violation of the Tugaloo claims of alliance. Given the violent realities of the recent Yamasee War, the Cherokee conviction of the truth of Carolina's abandonment could lead to renewed attacks.[97] By 1720 Carolina's leadership was fed up, complaining to the Board of Trade that Virginians were doing "all they can to draw the Indians from us." They mused that they would need perhaps to extend prohibitions on "foreign" trade to include their British neighbors to the north.[98] Virginia, it seemed, represented a problem nearly as great as France or Spain.

South Carolina's problems with Virginia continued into the 1730s (and well beyond). In 1734 Gov. Robert Johnson informed the Board of Trade that Cherokee demands for lower prices directly challenged Carolina trader viability, but he explained that "it is the Virginians under selling the Traders of this Province that occasions their Insolence to us, and would oblige us to Sell Cheaper than we can afford."[99] Johnson felt compelled to halt trade to force Cherokees to modify their demands, and he hoped that the board in turn would stop Virginia's unfortunate commercial behavior.[100] Without support on this point from London, however, his blockade of British goods would be meaningless.

Fortifying Overhill country became an extension of Britain's obligation to Carolina. The ink was hardly dry on the 1730 agreement, for example, when Governor Johnson informed the board it would need to help with the construction of "a Fort on the Frontier of the Cherokee Nation, for fear the French should do the same and bring over [those] Nations into their Interest."[101] The South Carolina Assembly was even more adamant in a 1734 petition to George II: "The Expence of our Safety [must come from] Your Majesty either for Men, or Money."[102] Eight years later the assembly again demanded imperial financing for a fort, particularly in light of the fact that the Overhills "are the only Indian Nation who can be a Barrier for this Province against the Incroachments of the French on the Northwestward Frontier."[103] Carolina would struggle to fortify the region for the next two decades. Along the way Charles Town leaders grew frustrated by imperial and local unwillingness to spend, exasperated and scared by their inability to control affairs, and angered by Virginia's continued willingness to interfere with what Carolinians believed was their rightful place at the head of the Anglo-Cherokee relationship.

Georgia made things worse. In 1736 Georgians authorized a statute requiring nonresidents to obtain a license before trading with Indians within the colony's claimed boundaries. South Carolina strongly opposed the law, particularly as it related to the Cherokees. Lt. Gov. Thomas Broughton reminded the Board of Trade that South

Carolina had already tried such a law to keep Virginians out of Cherokee towns, but that "her late Majesty Queen Anne was pleased to disallow" it.[104] He insisted that Georgia violated the British Constitution by obliging South Carolinians "to submit to the Laws of a Society of which they are not members, and to whom in their Corporate Capacity they have no sort of relation." Although he acknowledged that "the Laws of Georgia must be observed within the Limits of Georgia," the colony had no authority to obstruct "the Subjects of any other Colony, from a free and open Trade" with Cherokees.[105]

Broughton believed that the Georgia law unethically bound Cherokee regions as well. He relayed the South Carolina Assembly's belief that "the Indians [are] a free and independent People, who have neither by Conquest, Cession, or Compact, become the Subjects of any Prince in Europe."[106] Pointedly reinterpreting the Articles of Friendship in a manner more aligned with Aniyunwiya interpretations, Broughton insisted "that His Majesty . . . esteemed them the Friends and Allies of his People in America, and not as subjects to the Crown of Great Britain." Taken to its logical conclusion, Broughton's position conferred upon Cherokees the same recognition of sovereignty owed to any foreign power. As free and independent polities, the Cherokees could not be restricted in their trade by Georgia without damaging imperial interests.[107]

Broughton's admission of Indigenous sovereignty is stunning, even if politically convenient. Two decades later southern Indian superintendent Edmond Atkin again acknowledged Native sovereignty when he informed Upper Creeks, Chickasaws, and Choctaws that George II had no interest in taking their land. "He would rather stand by you," Atkin stated, "to hinder any body also from taking them from you . . . for you are a free People, & he does not want to make Slaves of you." Virginian Richard Bland went further in 1764, conceding that American Indians were never "conquered." On the contrary, they continued with "their native laws and customs, as savage as they are, in as full an extent as they did before the English settled upon their continent." Tellingly, he declared that Indians could not lose their "natural privileges by conquest." His fellow colonials and their descendants would put that declaration to the test over the next several decades and centuries.[108]

Despite these myriad complexities, British officials nevertheless exulted over their success in the 1730 negotiations. The Articles of Friendship, they announced, were so successful that even "the small Expence his Majesty has been at, upon this Occasion, is well laid out for his Service, and for the Interest of his People in Carolina."[109] Only positive developments could occur from that point, they thought. And much to the relief of British Carolinians, Overhills did seem to respond. They agreed to renew the Chain of Friendship in 1733, for example, and unquestionably increased their presence across trans-Appalachia. For the next two decades they acquired vital intelligence for the British, seemed to harass French trade, and generally convinced officials in Louisiana and New France that Cherokees represented a palpable threat to *their* long-term North American interests.[110]

CHEROKEE NATIONS AND THE CHAIN OF FRIENDSHIP

Cherokees, too, recognized the significance of the 1730 agreement. As historian Tyler Boulware has rightly noted, the articles "marked a watershed in Cherokee political history," not the least consequence of which was "the intensification of interregional communication and connectedness."[111] The question is: Of what exactly is this watershed moment made? Whatever the British Empire and its colonial representatives may have perceived, the Aniyunwiya filtered the Chain of Friendship through the lens of very different realities. According to Attakullakulla in the 1750s, the articles never meant more to the delegation than that the British would "assist us in our wars against our Ennemies [and that] We would assist them against their Ennemies." He was firm in limiting the parameters of the "treaty"—the delegation did not agree to an exclusive relationship, did not agree to come together in a singular nation, and certainly did not accede to subordination and land cession.[112] It is true that he made these statements two decades after the fact, but Ludovick Grant made a similar point in 1731 upon the delegation's return from London. Observing that not one word was spoken "about their Surrendering their Country," he also laid bare a major distinction between the Cherokee interpretation of the articles and the Board of Trade's: if the latter insisted that a deal had been struck, the former only saw "a written paper or Parchment . . . the title of which is Articles proposed or proposals made by the Lords of Trade to the Cherokees." Linguistically, a proposal was a far cry from an alliance.[113]

Other evidence lends support to Attakullakulla's 1750s statements. In a declaration at Whitehall, the Cherokee delegation had insisted that "The Crown of our Nation is different from that which the Great King George wears." Although they promised to carry "the Chain of Friendship . . . to our People," they were clear that Moytoy was not (and could not be) the accepted "king" of the Cherokees.[114] Subsequent behaviors reinforce the point, as each regional town cluster continued after 1730 to operate independently—with clear and growing but not unbreakable political, economic, and diplomatic links between them. The Overhills also demanded continual "brightening" and could firmly reject the treaty when necessary. In 1734, for example, merely one year after they had publicly agreed to a "brightening," a Tellico council both rejected the articles and "rebuked it signers." Several of those "signers" subsequently renounced their connection to it.[115]

Historian Leanne Simpson has observed that Indigenous treaty-making is deeply rooted in their own "worldviews, language, knowledge systems, and political cultures." Contra European definitions, "They were governed by the common indigenous ethics of justice, peace, respect, reciprocity, and accountability. Indigenous people understood these agreements in terms of relationship, and renewal processes were paramount in maintaining these international agreements."[116] The Articles of Friendship perfectly illustrate Simpson's observations. If the British thought the written agreement led to a long-term relationship lacking "rust or foulness," Overhill councils insisted that it required both renewal and a unified British voice. Virginians undermining Carolinians undermining Georgians simply was not conducive to such consistency. Moreover, the claim by George II that Cherokee "Friends are His Friends; and Their Enemies are His Enemies" no doubt provoked skepticism given the previous fourteen years' perception that the British had forsaken the Aniyunwiya in favor of Mvskokes. For that matter, the British were willing to invoke that obligation only so long as Europeans were the target. South Carolina's Indian Trade Commission made the point in 1718, at the height of post–Yamasee War paranoia. "We are resolved to stand by the Charikees," they told Theophilus Hastings, "if the French should attack them, but shall not intermeddle, if none go but Indians."[117] Reciprocity and accountability this was not, regardless of perspective.

A directly related point: the British audience did not fully grasp the two-way nature of diplomacy and trade within the Cherokee regions. Because exclusivity was not part of their calculation, a British agreement did not ipso facto preclude Overhills from approaching, trading, or negotiating with the French at Forts Toulouse, Chartres (constructed in Illinois c. 1720), or Vincennes (constructed in the Wabash valley c. 1731–32). They lived, understood, and operated within the context of Indigenous commercial and ethical guidelines regardless of whether the Europeans found it inscrutable, unscrupulous, or inconsistent.

Complicating the Chain of Friendship still further was the fact that the Haudenosaunee both regularly attacked (mostly) Lower Cherokee towns and encouraged Mvskoke men to do the same.[118] Inasmuch as they hoped to establish similar relationships with the "two" Iroquoian-speaking polities, the British could do little about the fact that they seemed perpetually in conflict. It was a measurable point of weakness in the imagined British North American empire, perhaps dovetailing with the Cherokee conviction since 1716 that Carolina, too, had encouraged Creek attacks on their towns. And topping it off was the ubiquitous, multilayered cacophony of general British North American diplomacy. Imperial-level mandates might have called for an Iroquois-Cherokee reconciliation, but New York and South Carolina directives could easily complicate or even countermand them. Virginia, Georgia, and Pennsylvania, meanwhile, were more than willing to interfere with imperial policy if their leaders felt it was beneficial to do so.

The above circumstances combined with the more important, *Indigenous* reality of the moment: neither the Aniyunwiya nor the Haudenosaunee were willing to march "in step with the beat of the British drum." Although they "tried reproachment," they also struggled to meet "the demands of their own societies and cultures" and thus went through decades of diplomatic and military contestation affecting trans-Appalachia.[119] Dispute over a boundary at the Great Kanawha River provides an excellent example. By midcentury Cherokees believed that the outer range of their hunting territories extended to the mouth of the Kanawha, which empties into the northern Ohio River in modern-day West Virginia. Between there and the mouth of the Tennessee was their territory, Cherokee polities believed—a claim directly challenged by Haudenosaunee perceptions that their boundaries extended across the same space (to say nothing of claims by Shawnees, other coalescing Ohio valley polities, or the Anishnaabeg).[120] Tensions remained palpable over this border throughout midcentury and would explicitly cause problems in 1768 when the British Empire tried to renegotiate boundaries at the Congresses of Hard Labour and Fort Stanwix.[121]

As important as they were, then, the 1730 Articles of Friendship were built upon remarkable fictions: neither imperial, Carolinian, Virginian, nor Georgian authority could subordinate Cherokees or establish a (viable) singular nation. Neither could any of them assert jurisdiction over the area encompassing the Tennessee corridor (euphemistically claimed by the "Great King George") without the support of their Overhill allies.[122] Whatever British Carolinians' perceptions, the Overhills traveled the corridor for myriad reasons other than to support imagined imperial obligations. In this world, the British were on the periphery.

Yet if they lacked control, British North Americans nevertheless perceived great benefit both from the Chain of Friendship and from the fact that the Overhills notably increased their trans-Appalachian visibility after 1730. By 1754 their extended presence was so common that, as South Carolina governor James Glen put it, "There never passes one year that the Cherokees do not take a Boat or two belonging to the French on the Mississippi and destroy most of the Crew."[123] Carolinians by that point imagined the *pays des Illinois* to be part of British North America, in large measure because of their fictitious ownership of the Tennessee corridor. It is to the mid-eighteenth-century Overhill presence in this corridor that we now turn.

CHAPTER 3

Cherokees, Europeans, and the Tennessee Corridor, 1730–1750

South Carolina's neighborhood seemed deeply troubled in 1734. In addition to four hundred soldiers garrisoned at St. Augustine, the assembly explained in a petition to King George II, Spanish authorities also maintained "several other small Settlements and Garrisons near the Appallatchys." Distressingly, the Spanish seemed poised to use those locations to exploit "several Nations of Indians living under their Subjection." Further west lurked even more menacing problems: in addition to having expanded their presence at Toulouse, reports indicated that the French had established "several other Forts and Garrisons; some not above three hundred Miles distant" from South Carolina. To cap it off, since the conclusion of Queen Anne's War the French had increased "their Strength and Traffic" at New Orleans and erected "many Forts and Garrisons on both Sides of [the Mississippi] River for several hundred miles up the same."[1] These developments represented clear violations of Article XV of the Treaty of Utrecht. Even more so than the Spanish (who did not agree a similar article in their 1713 treaty with Britain), it seemed obvious that the French intended these outposts to manipulate Indigenous polities beyond the reach of British control.

South Carolina's fears were complemented by French and Spanish challenges across the broader western Atlantic theater. Even as the British Empire struck the Chain of Friendship with Cherokees, metropolitan officials debated the best means by which to counter the growing influence of French West Indian sugar plantations. Production there not only seemed to surpass all others, French planters also proved willing to dump their wares on the North American market—thereby undercutting British sugar interests and upending mercantilist policies.[2] Meanwhile, in 1734 one Capt. Robert Jenkins, a smuggler, lost an ear to the Spanish as punishment for practicing his trade. For an emerging war hawk faction in Parliament, attacking Spanish ports and seizing shipping around the Caribbean provided a meaningful form of reprisal. In 1739 Parliament ordered the Royal Navy to attack, the result of which was a successful capture by Admiral Edward Vernon of the seaport of Porto Bello (Panama). His success, historians typically insist, inflamed British patriotism and strengthened transatlantic bonds by convincing Anglo-Americans they had a stake "in a joint enterprise, both Protestant and free."[3]

Carolinian officials would have agreed to a point. They certainly recognized close bonds between London and its colonies, but they would have stressed the importance of imperial defensive obligations, surrounded and thoroughly outgunned as they seemed to be across their neighborhood. A general regional war, they feared, would produce existential threats to the Protestant interest, imperial stability in Europe, and, more locally, to a profitable colonial contributor to the Exchequer.[4] Given Carolina's "utmost importance to the general Trade and Traffick of America," the Assembly insisted upon heightened defensive initiatives from London.[5]

If obviously framed in imperial terms, South Carolina's paranoia makes no sense without anchoring it in Native trans-Appalachia. Lieutenant Governor James Glen perhaps best encapsulated the reality in 1748. "The concerns of this Country are so closely connected and Interwoven with Indian Affairs," he wrote, and "so great a Branch of our trade and the safety of the Province depend so much upon preserving their Friendship that it would be unaccountable Indolence and Stupidness" for colonial governors not to seek greater insight into trans-Appalachian goings-on.[6] His predecessor, William Bull, agreed but added a more specific observation: the Overhill Cherokees were crucial to accessing the Tennessee corridor, and thereby to framing British western realities. He made the point rather emphatically in 1741 when he observed that Carolina's "dependence on the Cherokee Indians as a barrier against the designs and encroachments of the French is very great."[7] He was similarly clear in a missive to the Lords of Trade. "Notwithstanding our present flourishing condition by the Increase of our Inhabitants & Trade, & the Ships of War ordered by His Majesty for the protection of the same," he wrote, "the Safety and welfare of this province depends in a great measure on the Friendship of our Indian Allies, the most numerous of whom are the Cherokees consisting of about 3000 men living to the Northwest" of Charles Town.[8]

French Louisiana felt similar pressures, except in reverse. Chronically underfunded in the 1730s and 1740s, they watched with unease as Versailles focused on other French western Atlantic outposts and complained that irregular access to trade goods eroded Native alliances.[9] Their most pressing concerns lay closer to their settlements at Mobile and New Orleans, of course, but they were bewildered by the contingency of interactions at outposts as geographically varied as Forts Toulouse, Tombecbe, Arkansas, Chartres, and Ouiatenon. And given that they claimed the Ohio valley as part of *their* colonial jurisdiction, they also recognized the danger inherent in Native southern projections across trans-Appalachia.

This fact reflects another point on which the French would have agreed with their British adversaries: Overhill activities in the Tennessee corridor formed an important element in setting the parameters of their trans-Appalachian interests. Louisiana officials expressed frustration that Overhills used the Tennessee River to challenge commerce and Franco-Indigenous alliances in the *pays des Illinois* and the Ohio valley. Convinced that South Carolina lurked behind these activities, they sought stronger fortifications, particularly along the Wabash. At the same time, they pushed to improve relations with Overhill towns, an effort that accelerated as the Anglo-Spanish War of Jenkins' Ear folded into the War of the Austrian Succession in the 1740s. Coinciding with ever more palpable Anglo-Cherokee instability, French endeavors by 1750 seemed (to them) to open the real possibility of a formal alliance.

That perception was incorrect, and a cursory glance at trans-Appalachian realities explains why—the more the Overhills used the Tennessee corridor, the more they encountered, challenged, and negotiated with Indigenous societies dealing with similar geopolitical pressures.[10] These encounters were the real drivers of Euro–North American fears in this period. Mechanisms such as the Anglo-Cherokee Chain of Friendship or enhanced Franco-Overhill diplomacy (culminating in a 1756 treaty, as will be discussed in chapter 4) were supposed to serve as means by which to glean insight into such complexities, and on some level they did work. Much to Euro-American chagrin, however, they did not work well enough. Overhill leaders consistently challenged alliances, rejecting them when necessary, demanding regular diplomatic renewal on *their* terms, filtering intelligence through the lens of *their* realities, and casting aside the insistence upon economic and diplomatic exclusivity.[11]

In short, between 1730 and 1750 the expanded Overhill Cherokee presence in the Tennessee corridor directly shaped European western imaginations. This fact manifested most clearly in fear and paranoia over inter-Indigenous interactions to which Europeans were only sporadically privy. It also emerged, however, in responses to individuals such as Christian Priber, Cornelius Docherty, James Maxwell, and the Overhill headman Attakullakulla.

French Instability in Indigenous Trans-Appalachia

As with their Carolina counterparts, the French found it difficult to wrap their minds around the fact that Indigenous polities could act independently of European direction. It is no surprise, then, that news of the 1730 Anglo-Cherokee Chain of Friendship set off alarm bells in Louisiana. Having already dealt with decades of Overhill challenges, French officials saw the accord as another example of British aggression. Of immediate concern were rumors that Carolina officials had convinced Overhills to settle on the Wabash to disrupt commerce between the lower Ohio River and New Orleans.[12] If true, it would have both violated Article XV of the Treaty of Utrecht and challenged what appeared to many observers to be a stable world of commercial growth and Native collaboration. Historian Robert Morrisey has shown that in this period Illinois and its environs in fact seemed "quite prosperous, producing up to eight hundred thousand livres of flour in a year, becoming an indispensable supplier of food for Louisiana."[13] The supply line became all the more imperative in the 1740s given the dearth of support from France itself, where "resources were bound up in continental wars and French shipping began to be preyed upon by British privateers."[14]

Louisiana governor Étienne Perier feared an interconnected but potentially bigger consequence to Cherokee settlement on the Wabash: it would coincide with the construction of British forts on the Tennessee River, from which British forces could sever communication between Louisiana and New France.[15] And if that happened, warned Louis Juchereau de St. Denis, commandant at Natchitotches in 1731, farewell to meaningful Franco-Native collaboration. It could potentially become an existential danger. British extension along the Tennessee and Wabash Rivers, he believed, would position them better "to get hold of the Province of Louisiana than by any other place." Even if only rumors, it was imperative both to put more troops in Illinois and to construct stronger fortifications.[16] A decade later Louisiana governor Pierre François de Rigaud Vaudreuil renewed the demand for imperial action.[17] In addition to the Wabash, however, he believed the *French* would need to fortify the Rivière des Cherakis [the Tennessee] "to control the Cherokees, watch the English, and insure safe navigation" of the Tennessee corridor.[18] That the government was so reluctant to do so seemed to leave French trans-Appalachian interests perpetually in a state of danger.

At the core of French vulnerability lay inter-Indigenous realities rather than British-driven conspiracies. By the 1730s opportunities in the *pays des Illinois* were enough to draw everyone's attention.[19] It is not surprising that Overhills (among other Native southerners) would assert their presence in such an environment—potentially contributing to it via commodities from South Carolina and Virginia—regardless of coincidences like the Anglo-Cherokee Chain of Friendship.[20] And once one digs beneath the ethnocentric conviction of British conspiracies, at base level inter-Indigenous encounters drove the trans-Appalachian events about which the French were so concerned. In 1737, for example, the French were surprised to hear that Kickapoos and Mascoutens wanted to "expel" Cherokees (and Chickasaws) from the lower Ohio valley, while they regularly heard reports such as Antoine Bonnefoy's that Tellico men were preparing to go "to war against the Ouatanons."[21] In 1738, the governor of New France, Charles de la Boische, Marquis de Beauharnois, expressed frustration that Overhills and Wendats had agreed upon a diplomatic arrangement about which the French knew very little. Much to his puzzlement, the agreement had led Great Lakes Anishnaabeg to send a group of fighters toward the Wabash and Ohio valleys to attack the Cherokee delegation.[22] The situation no doubt produced more befuddlement when French observers reported that the Wendats were aware of Anishnaabeg efforts and got to the Cherokees first, in the process helping to coordinate a joint counteroffensive.[23] Beauharnois feared such activity negatively affected French stability but could do little to stop them over the next few years. And that fear, observed governor Vaudreuil in 1743, meant that "hostility between Indian nations must be considered when planning for the welfare" of Louisiana.[24]

A major byproduct of these inter-Indigenous encounters was that French interests could (and did) get caught in the crossfire. In 1738, for example, a party of "Cherake savages" took French prisoners from the Ohio valley to Overhill country, as did another raiding party a year later.[25] In 1741, meanwhile, Bonnefoy described an ambush by nearly eighty "Cherakis" on a convoy near the mouth of the Wabash. He expressed displeasure that they unloaded the French vessels "with the exception of the iron and three kegs of rum," before sending the convoy to "the River of the Cherakis, which leads up to the villages of those savages."[26] Observers suggested that the violence was not because of the French themselves. A diarist known as "Canelle," for example, was convinced that Overhills wanted peace but attacked French interests "because the French Indians are hostile."[27] From that perspective, relief seemed to emerge in 1742 with news that Cherokees had agreed to a "peace treaty with most Canadian nations." And yet the diplomatic path proved nowhere near clear of obstacles. That same year French observers reported that the Anishnaabeg were preparing to launch an expedition to Catawba country when the latter ambushed them, perhaps with Wendat support. At that same moment Cherokees and Catawbas were negotiating with the Haudenosaunee regarding a cessation of hostilities between those three polities. Still other reports suggested that the Overhills were again on the point of attacking the Ouiatanons in the Wabash valley.[28]

Equally ominously, the Overhills appeared to have joined Shawnees in a defense of Chickasaws, a potentially big problem in light of the so-called Natchez Rebellion.[29] In 1729 the Natchez had launched a major initiative against French planters near their territory. A well-established historiographical narrative explains what happened next: the Natchez could not sustain the momentum, and angry French settlers subsequently called in their alliance with Choctaws to put the Natchez to flight.[30] At first they went to Chickasaw country, but pressure soon came from Choctaws and the French for the Chickasaws to expel them. According to Chickasaws, Choctaws were not alone in applying pressure. A 1736 delegation, for example, informed Georgia governor James Oglethorpe that the "Tomolohaws (commonly called Ilonois), Nawtowees, and Wiantonoo [Ouiatanon] . . . with the French have just now fallen upon us. 700 men came into our towns twice, but have not killed us all. The French have Forts in all of these Nations and keep them always in readiness to send against us."[31]

Such pressure drew in the Overhills because it pushed Natchez refugees to depart Chickasaw towns for Overhill and Creek countries. This migration annoyed the French, but they could do little about it, as the Comte de Maurepas understood. In a 1742 letter to Vaudreuil, he made reference to unnamed "misfortunes that beset the French last Year at the Mouth of the River Ouabache of which it is said the Cherakees were the Authors." Louis XV, Maurepas declared, therefore ordered Vaudreuil to take immediate measures to put a "stop as soon as possible to the Invasions of these Savages into that Colonie." It was all the more important, he said, because if the Cherokee Nation, "Numerous of itself & always sure of being assisted by the [Chickasaws] & those from Natchez who it is said have taken Refuge among them, should be once accustomed to these incursions, it will be a difficult matter to reestablish the tranquility of that Country."[32]

One can only imagine the conversations between remnant Natchez and the Overhills. Certainly it is curious, for example, that at approximately this moment the French received reports of potential strikes by Overhills on the Ouiatanons, not to mention other locations along the Wabash and in the *pays des Illinois*.[33] No amount of French diplomacy and trade could put them in a position to understand and control encounters like those with the Natchez, or such as those between Overhills-Wendats, Overhills-Chickasaws, or Overhills-Shawnees.[34] Yet in spite of such helplessness, French leadership ploughed forward with the belief that greater fortification efforts would strengthen their hand. To this end, in 1742 the Piankeshaws—themselves relative newcomers to the region and regularly identified as a potential Cherokee target—allegedly "granted the French a large tract along the Wabash River."[35] A petition to Louis XV a year later relayed news that the Aniyunwiya were "trying to negotiate a peace with Canada through the Shawnees and Hurons," and insisted on a lower Ohio fort to protect communications between Louisiana and Canada, "control the Cherokees," and insure safe passage on the Wabash. (Vaudreuil made a similar request two years later.)[36] Roland-Michel Barrin de la Galissonière, governor of New France from 1747 to 1749, expressed hope that Versailles would supply enough capital to maintain "Several forts and 200 men at least in garrison on the [lower Ohio], especially toward its outlet into the Mississippi."[37]

Another opportunity presented itself through these potential fortifications: What would happen if France could undermine the perceived Anglo-Cherokee alliance? Although clearly a misreading of tea leaves, it was not an unreasonable question to ask given the stream of intelligence the French received. In 1740 an Okfuskee trader called Willy, for example, described a gathering at Fort Toulouse of "upper and Lower Creeks and Chelokees (or stinking Linguas) to the number of five hundred men" who seemed to embrace a French speech about how Louis XV "valued their Friendship [and] how ready he was to let them have Arms Amunition Strong Liquor &c."[38] Thereafter the Cherokees embarked upon a raid against an unnamed British post, only to be stopped by the Creek Mico Wolf before they could take anything. A group of Okchoys informed Willy that "some of the Stinking Linguas" subsequently went to Mobile for extended conversations with the French.[39]

Individual experiences such as Antoine Bonnefoy's further reinforced a perceived diplomatic opening. In 1741 he was captured on the Wabash and taken to Overhill country, but his treatment revealed curiosity instead of hostility. He seemed in fact to undergo a ritual adoption, suggesting that the Overhills symbolically welcomed the French to Chota and Tellico.[40] Thereafter, according to Bonnefoy, Overhill townsfolk asked him "in what manner they could appease the French and bring them to their place to trade."[41] The question indicates that they were probing Bonnefoy to learn more about French diplomatic prowess. Could they broker inter-Indigenous diplomacy in a way South Carolina, Virginia, Georgia, and the British seemingly could not? And would they put an end to their own contradictory behaviors? Such outreach certainly fit tactics rooted in Native diplomatic commitments to "justice, peace, respect, reciprocity, and accountability."[42] The French response was nuanced (and reinforces the lack of singular nationhood amongst the Aniyunwiya to boot). Indeed, Louisiana developed two policies simultaneously: they both encouraged Shawnees and Upper Creeks to facilitate Franco-Overhill trade and urged Lower Creeks to wage war upon Lower Cherokee towns to prevent them from mobilizing on Britain's behalf.[43] For his part, Bonnefoy worked to secure the Overhills by emphasizing the quality (if not the quantity) of French commodities over British alternatives.[44]

This seemingly promising opening with the Overhills was even more important given the mid-1740s drift of European affairs. By 1745 the War of Jenkins' Ear was bogged down in stalemate, but Britain and France had gone to war over whether Maria Theresa should inherit the throne of the Austrian Empire. Few interest groups in North America necessarily cared about that, but as with Queen Anne's War four decades earlier the ripple effect of King George's War (as it was known in British North America) was huge. Scholars tend to focus on events in New England and Canada, which is understandable given contemporary praise for William Shirley's successful siege of Louisbourg in 1745.[45] It should come as no surprise, however, that Native trans-Appalachia loomed large in French Louisiana (as well as the British South). Perhaps Vaudreuil put it most clearly when he informed Versailles that it was "of infinite consequence, to acquire the Management of English Indian Allies; and then project a Scheme of forming an Alliance with the Chicasaws & Cherokees."[46] As regards the latter, he observed, the French should "propose to them the permitting a Fort & Settlement in their Country on the River Cherokee, to Stop the progress of the English there, and to secure the Navigation of the River Ouabasch."[47] In 1747 Vaudreuil encouraged Chickasaws, Creeks, and Shawnees to travel to Chota, "the Mother Town of the Upper Cherokees," to meet with the latter and "induce . . . raids on [British] settlements."[48] An obvious side benefit was the possibility of opening a French trading post in the region. (For the first time, that is, since Charles Juchareau's turn-of-the-eighteenth-century post at the mouth of the Tennessee, or the early-eighteenth-century effort at "French Lick" on what is now the Cumberland River.)[49]

French efforts at developing Native trade networks ran up against the perpetual problem of a lack of supply. Yet as legitimate a concern as that was, scholars must not overemphasize trade as the exclusive feature of Euro-Indigenous alliance building. To do so minimizes the importance of nonexclusive relationships in the Native world, which in Cherokee terms has the consequence of encouraging excessively Anglo-centric narratives. Certainly, many contemporaries believed that trade and diplomacy were more complicated than Cherokees simply playing European powers off one another. In 1751 South Carolina governor James Glen suggested to New York governor George Clinton that "to one unacquainted with Indian Affairs, the designs of the French may seem dark and doubtful, their projects improbable, and their views very distant." A closer look, however, suggested to him that the totality of rumors and intelligence was reasonably accurate. The French were metaphorically all over the Overhill country, and their influence waxed and waned depending upon circumstances beyond the availability of trade goods.[50] Given the number of directions from which European commodities could enter the Tennessee corridor, French shortages in and of themselves could not ipso facto serve as diplomatic deal breakers.[51]

Alliance-building no doubt also was aided by serendipitous developments such as Bonnefoy's conversations in the Overhill towns and by the efforts of men such as Antoine Lantagnac. In 1745 Lantagnac claimed to have been captured by Chickasaws and sent to Charles Town before setting up a licensed trade post in Overhill country. He later explained to Louis Billouart, Chevalier de Kerlérec, that he could have returned to Fort Toulouse but chose to spend the next ten years cultivating relations "and discovering how the English controlled their Indians."[52] As we shall see, Lantagnac's connection to Overhill country would make him useful to Louisiana in the 1760s.

Fear and Loathing in Charles Town

The French certainly did not have a monopoly on paranoid overreach. At the same moment in 1738 that the Wendats and the Overhills flummoxed New Orleans and New France, South Carolina governor William Bull warned the Board of Trade that a Franco-Indigenous army of 205 had left Montreal to attack "some Indians Scituated near a branch of the Missisipi River in Amity with His Majestys Subjects."[53] He understood that the Chickasaws were the primary targets (most likely because of the aftermath of the Natchez War) but believed that greater danger lay in Overhill country, where the "French have for a long time wanted an opportunity to get an Interest."[54] No army actually materialized in the Tennessee corridor, but when rumors of a Franco-Indigenous army reemerged, the assembly framed it as an exclusively "Cherokee" issue (and given the alleged army's western point of origin, an Overhill issue in particular). They also projected their fears of imperial warfare in the Atlantic world onto Native trans-Appalachia—whether that world worried about European affairs or not. A 1742 petition to George II from the South Carolina Assembly illustrates the point: the Overhills "have several Enemies to withstand" and had become so worried by the French and their Native allies that they "in the most Earnest & pressing manner Implored your Majestys Protection."[55]

Scholars traditionally would interpret that statement as evidence of Cherokee reliance on British Carolina. Maybe. One point was certainly undeniable: the Aniyunwiya did in fact face "several enemies" that were nearly exclusively Indigenous and ranged across both cis- and trans-Appalachia. Arguably their most formidable adversaries were the Mvskokes and the Haudenosaunee, although the lack of singular Cherokee (or Creek) nationhood complicates the point quite a bit. At times Upper Creeks and Overhill Cherokees worked together reasonably smoothly, for example, even as Lower Creeks and Lower Cherokees went to war.[56] In the 1750s the Creek mico the Mortar even established a town on the edge of Overhill country, allegedly with the intention of "swaying" the region into allying with French Louisiana.[57]

Historians have probed Creek-Cherokee encounters in vivid detail, but the midcentury Cherokee-Haudenosaunee relationship is worth exploring further. By the 1730s the Haudenosaunee influenced a swath of territory stretching from the *pays des Illinois* to the Atlantic seaboard, and from the St. Lawrence River valley to the Native South. During this period the Tuscaroras were in the midst of migrating from (what is now) North Carolina to the upper reaches of the Delaware River valley, in the process becoming the Sixth Nation to join the Onondaga Council Fire. That migration seemed to have had an impact on a number of levels, both in terms of Haudenosaunee encounters in the Native South and in terms of their soft power in influencing British policy. A striking example of the latter draws from their willingness to lend legitimacy to the Walking Purchase of 1737. In making themselves the arbiters of land along the Delaware River, they agreed that Pennsylvania officials could seize territory the size of Rhode Island from Lenapes.[58] The problem: at no time had the Five/Six Nations subdued Lenapes, nor had they established a realistic claim to the land they sanctioned giving away. Approving the Walking Purchase indicates that they were thinking about the Covenant Chain relationship with Britain, yes, but it also suggests they were thinking in terms of Indigenous geopolitics. By playing along with Pennsylvania they could both lay claim to Lenape space near to where Tuscaroras were settling and increase their perceived power by making Lenapes into "Props of the Longhouse."[59]

The Haudenosaunee looked to project similar metaphorical power into other cis-Mississippi regions of the continent, whether with Shawnees and others in the upper Ohio valley, Catawbas further south, or the polities in the *pays des Illinois*.[60] The Aniyunwiya also were part of this power projection, although the complexity of their relationship with the Haudenosaunee clouds that projection. To be sure, Europeans had observed tensions between the two Iroquoian-speaking groups from the earliest moments of the eighteenth century. By the 1750s the Six Nations suggested openly that they had been warring with Cherokees "ever since we were created."[61] An abundance of evidence reveals their willingness to engage in mourning wars in Cherokee country, no doubt a serious source of tension between the two. Moreover, Cherokees reported that their adversaries to the "Norward" were all too happy to encourage Mvskoke enmity towards Aniyunwiya towns in the decades after the 1715–16 events at Tugaloo.[62] The Tuscarora migration of the 1720s–40s adds still another layer of complexity. Historiographically, it is a settled narrative that Cherokee intervention in 1711 was important to the resolution of the Tuscarora War. It is impossible now to explore the logic of that intervention, but—as it was with Yuchis in light of the Chestowee raid—it no doubt would have remained part of Tuscarora memory as they migrated towards the Delaware valley. And that in turn must have affected Haudenosaunee relationships across Aniyunwiya country.

On one point this narrative is incomplete, however, avoiding as it does a major question to emerge out of the available records: Did the Haudenosaunee see Cherokees as peers or as Props of the Longhouse? Anecdotally, the answer seems to be both—it merely depends upon *where* one chooses to examine. On the one hand, the Six Nations seemed to think of Lower Cherokees more in subordinate terms—a community worthy of raiding in mourning wars to restore population in Iroquoia. On the other hand, Valley and Overhill towns seemed to maintain a different status. Senecas regularly were reported moving through Overhill country in both confrontational and nonconfrontational ways as they traveled to negotiate with Mvskokes and Shawnees.[63] Passing references suggest fascinating possibilities—such as British trader Ludovick Grant's comment to James Glen regarding nine "Northward Indians who have lived some Years Over the Hills and almost naturalized."[64] (More on this point in chapter 4.) That they were peers, so to speak, also draws out of tensions over a major point of trans-Appalachian geopolitics:

Who maintained (imagined) Native jurisdiction over large swaths of the Ohio valley? Neither the British nor the French had anything to say on the matter, even if they idealistically both claimed the valley for themselves.

A good snapshot of Cherokee-Haudenosaunee complexity draws from the early 1740s and helps to explain why South Carolina formally tried to brighten the Cherokee Chain of Friendship in 1745. Having been unable to stop the confrontations for decades, in June 1742 Carolina's leadership was relieved to learn that the Six Nations and the Cherokees were preparing to meet the following "spring to exchange prisoners and negotiate peace." A few months later Charles Town learned that "an Indian from the Southward of the Charikee Nation" had traveled to Seneca country and declared that Cherokees wanted to "live in peace and friendship." The unnamed Cherokee so effectively cleared the diplomatic path that Senecas suggested "there shall be no hindrance for the future from going and coming that way to transact Publick affairs." The Cherokee man, they informed New York governor George Clark, even had become a Haudenosaunee sachem—not an uncommon development in the world of Indigenous diplomacy.[65]

It ultimately did not work out, and by 1745 Cherokee-Iroquois tensions seemed to European observers to be as palpable as ever. When combined with the expanding War of the Austrian Succession and heightened perceived French pressures in the Tennessee corridor, it convinced Carolinians that the Chain of Friendship needed serious help.[66] In April that year 131 Aniyunwiya delegates arrived in Charles Town "to strengthen and confirm the ancient friendship and Union" between the polities. Channeling the language of 1730, Gov. James Glen expressed hope that "the Chain of Friendship by which we [are] linked together be for ever bright and clear like the Sun . . . or without Spots and Clouds; may it [remain] firm, fixed and immoveable like your native Mountains."[67] For his part, Glen considered the congress a success and subsequently informed the Duke of Newcastle he would "send the Emperor of the Cherokees' crown to England by the next ship so that it may be laid at His Majesty's feet."[68] Reality soon forced him to abandon such an optimistic appraisal. According to the South Carolina

Assembly, by 1746 "Cherokee friendship" was once again "very precarious."[69] It was utterly confusing, too. The Overhills seemed duplicitous, dangerous, incapable of peace with the Haudenosaunee, and in danger of falling into the pocket of the French.

To the Overhills, however, the 1745 congress was no doubt an example of same song, second verse. Unable to understand the real complexity of Indigenous diplomacy, Glen made the same mistakes as his predecessors in the 1720s and 1730s. He, too, attempted to create a singular Cherokee Nation under the control of one ruler.[70] As in 1730, he insisted that Cherokees hand over both Whites and Natives accused of murder and theft for British justice rather than subjecting them to Cherokee legal customs.[71] And as in 1730, Glen insisted that Cherokees not only "come at my Call against the common Enemies," but that they "not suffer any Agents or Emissaries, either French or Indians, to come amongst you to withdraw you from your Duty and to alienate your Hearts from this Government."[72]

To Cherokee diplomats such demands revealed remarkable (and sustained) inconsistency. As usual, the British wanted them to forsake crucial elements of their lifeways while only sporadically holding White criminals to account for depredations in Native country.[73] Nor could the Carolinians offer the same unity they were demanding of the Aniyunwiya, perpetually plagued as they were by interference from Virginia and Georgia. Contemporaneous negotiations between Cherokees, Catawbas, and the Six Nations illustrate just how torturous the diplomatic process could be. In 1741 "the Virginia Warrior brought a message from the Governour of Virginia to the Cherokee Nation relating to a peace with the Six Nations with a Belt of Wampum." Overhill leaders sent the message to Carolina governor William Bull along with a clear expression of their desire "to be at peace with the Six Nations." To make it official, however, Carolina—not Virginia—would need to send "Beads and also a Pipe and a White Flag which we took from the French in a Fight last Winter with an Eagle's Tail . . . to the Six Nations as a Token of the Cherokees' acceptance and Confirmation of the Peace."[74] More simply, placing the British on the same page with inter-Indigenous interests required working with Charles Town, Williamsburg, occasionally Savannah, and, more distant to Native southerners, Albany. It had to have been exhausting; certainly, it undermined the reciprocal consistency required of Indigenous diplomacy. It is worth noting that the Virginia Warrior's wampum belt went to Chota, where it remained—an indication that the Overhills put great store in the negotiation even if Williamsburg and Charles Town misunderstood it.

Perhaps, then, there is a more accurate way to interpret the South Carolina Assembly's 1742 insistence that Cherokees were "imploring imperial protection": that their negotiators, exasperated by Virginian, South Carolinian, and Georgian in-fighting, wanted to interact directly with the monarch. It was their right, after all, as sovereign polities with a record of having traveled to London for formal diplomatic negotiations. The idea would form an important part of the Anglo-Cherokee conversation in the 1750s.[75]

Of Mines and Paradise

Individual activities further frustrated Cherokee negotiators, reinforced regional variations, and exacerbated British North American paranoia in this period. In 1743, for example, traders Cornelius Docherty and James Maxwell went public with their plan to exploit silver mines in the Valley town region. Stimulated by centuries of Spanish and French rumors—not to mention conversations between the Earl of Shaftsbury and Henry Woodward in the 1670s and expeditions by Richard Traunter in 1698–99—they attempted to purchase thirty thousand acres from the Valley towns and subsequently sent a request to Whitehall for confirmation of the title.[76] Framing it through the lens of French conspiracy, the two men also petitioned George II that their trading operations had for years been threatened by "the Danger of a French settlement there."[77] As loyal Britons they had "used their utmost endeavours to prevent any communication" between Valley towns and French operatives. At one point they claimed even to have stopped "a Deputation [of] the Chief Men of the Nation [from] going to the French settlements in Order to conclude a treaty . . . by representing to them that the French had it not in their Power to furnish them with so good Commoditys and at such easy rates as their Old Allies."[78] Imperial sanction of their mining project, they believed, would tie "the bond of Friendship more fast" while at the same time preventing that "design long entertained by the French of getting footing amongst the Cherokees."[79]

South Carolina's leadership saw it rather differently: Docherty's and Maxwell's bald-faced land grab violated the 1730 Chain of Friendship and destabilized Carolina's western periphery at an already dangerous moment. At stake was a fundamental principle of Native sovereignty. Cherokees, observed the assembly, had "always claimed the property of the Lands on which they and their ancestors have been settled for a time immemorial." Said ownership had "never been controverted by Your Majestys Gov^{rs} in any of the said Treatys," which were *sine qua nons* for Carolina's security. Put simply, Cherokees relied "upon a Strict adherence to these terms as well as the other articles contained in the said Treatys . . . to continue in strict Amity and Friendship with Your Majestys Subjects of this Province."[80]

In acting contrary to the 1730 treaty, Maxwell and Docherty seemed about to inflict major damage on the safety and stability of South Carolina. And one need look no further than the Yamasee War to see how consequential that could be, explained the legislature. The "enormitys and abuses committed by but a very few white persons" before 1715, it insisted, "occasioned a heavy War which cost this Your Province much blood and Treasure the doleful effects whereof we severely feel to this day." Besides, noted legislators, unchecked pursuit of silver might divert colonial attention from the rice trade, the result of which would be to undermine the empire generally.[81] It was from "a just sense thereof and to prevent as much as possible the like Mischief" that they insisted the empire put an end to the mining venture.[82] Governor Bull added yet another dimension to the argument: South Carolina simply did not have the manpower to deal with a breakdown in relations. To the Lords of Trade he explained that the colony faced grave danger "without the assistance of a greater number of British Forces than this Province at present is able to raise."[83] Much to the relief of southern colonial officials, nothing came of this silver mine venture.

Maxwell and Docherty were particularly problematic because their shenanigans coincided with the activities of perhaps the most enigmatic person to plague the British South in the 1730s and 1740s: Christian Priber. German by birth, Priber arrived in South Carolina (via England) around 1733, entered Cherokee country by 1736, and had settled in the Overhill town of Tellico by 1739, ostensibly to build a Christian utopian "paradise."[84] According to several witnesses he became close to "Emperor" Moytoy, perhaps even marrying the headman's niece.[85] On the surface, his behavior was simple to explain. Contemporary observers insisted that he upended expectations of civil behavior because he so "ate, drank, slept, danced, dressed, and painted himself, with the Indians . . . that it was not easy to distinguish him from the natives."[86] At one point, according to British Carolinians, Priber even came to see himself as Moytoy's "prime minister."[87]

That conviction provides an opening to rethink the Priber enigma: he was a visible reminder of the peripheral nature of the British to western affairs at a moment when everything seemed to spiral beyond their control. One of Priber's biggest crimes, for example, was that he encouraged Overhill leadership to disregard the Chain of Friendship and treat the French and British equally. (Overhills, of course, would say that Priber could not influence their long-standing diplomatic rejection of exclusive relationships.)[88] Moreover, he represented a clear and present danger to another of Carolina's complex realities: African slavery. According to Georgia governor James Oglethorpe, Priber's real mission was "to settle a Town . . . of fugitive English, French, Germans and Negroes, and they were to take particularly under Protection, the runaway Negroes of the English."[89] Coming on the heels of the Stono slave rebellion, such behavior was intolerable. It represented a flagrant violation of the Chain of Friendship, too, in that Cherokees were supposed to serve as an African slave patrol.[90]

On some level, Priber's activities are reminiscent of Alexander Longe's a few decades earlier. Longe had first come to the attention of Carolina leadership when he seemingly convinced Cherokees not to side with Tuscaroras in 1711, at the height of the Tuscarora War. Only a few years later he interfered in colonial and imperial diplomacy by encouraging Overhills to attack Yuchis at Chestowee.[91] His willingness to use Aniyunwiya connections in such a manner put the colony in harm's way, a crime exacerbated by the broader fear and paranoia associated with Queen Anne's War. Thirty years later—and again with the Overhills—Priber seemed to threaten colonial safety at a moment when Carolina's world seemed in danger of breaking down. Consider: rumors of westward and northward Indian invasions were swirling, not to mention possible Franco-Indigenous armies, thereby suggesting that the French were taking "Considerable Steps towards their grand design in Surrounding the British Colonies."[92] Catawbas, Cherokees, and the Six Nations, meanwhile, were struggling to negotiate a peace that directly affected British North American well-being.[93] Maxwell and Docherty were threatening further to upend Carolina's periphery. And to top it off, in 1742 the Spanish launched an invasion of St Simon's Island, Georgia. Amidst this confusion it is hardly surprising that William Bull would implore the empire to dispatch three independent companies to "the Frontiers of this Province to protect & secure the Inhabitants in the cultivation of their Lands as well as the Trade with the Indians."[94]

That same year Bull also sent an expedition to extricate Priber from Overhill country. It did not go as planned. The expressions of sovereignty and control offered by Overhill leadership are stunning. For one thing, Tellicos explained to expedition leader Joseph Fox, "the Country was their own [and] they might do in it what they thought proper." If that meant receiving "any person and giv[ing] him Protection," then so be it—they "would permit none others to force him away." Anyone who even tried to do so in their estimation "deserved punishment."[95] Hardly an acceptance of British legal norms, whatever their perceived obligations under the Chain of Friendship. (And perhaps a reason for their restatement in the 1745 congress?) Trader James Adair later quoted a Cherokee speaker he called "the warrior" (possibly Moytoy) as saying that because Priber "was not accused of having done any ill to the English, before he came to the Cheerake, his crime must consist in loving the Cheerake." To this man Carolina's decision "to send one of their angry beloved men to enslave him ... confirmed all those honest speeches Priber had often spoken to the present great war chieftains, old beloved men, and warriors of each class."[96] Another Overhill speaker told Fox to "inform his superiors, that the [Overhills] were as desirous as the English to continue a friendly union with each other, as 'freemen and equals.'" They suggested, though, that it would be in the British interest to "send no more of those bad papers to their country, on any account; nor to reckon them so base, as to allow any of their honest friends to be taken out of their arms, and carried into slavery."[97] It took another three years for Carolina finally to capture Priber, and when they did it was not because of Overhill interference. In 1745 he traveled to Fort Toulouse with the idea that he would go from there to Mobile to parlay with Louisiana officials. Along the way, however, he was apprehended by Mvskokes who seemed alarmed by Franco-Cherokee rapprochement.[98]

A third individual offers even more tantalizing insight into the Overhills and trans-Appalachia at mid-century: Attakullakulla. In 1753 he inserted himself into Governor Glen's consciousness after twenty years of focusing primarily on inter-Indigenous affairs—including a stretch of several years during King George's War when he was a captive in Odawa country. In June of that year Carolina captured and imprisoned six Shawnees from the town of Wakatomica traveling across the periphery of the colony.[99] When questioned they initially claimed to have been Cherokees looking for Yuchis—perhaps drawing a connection to the memory of the Chestowee raid. That alibi broke down under scrutiny, however, at which point they claimed they were looking for a French trader called Peter Chartier and a Shawnee town in Alabama country. Further complicating the moment, according to the *London Public Advertiser*, was that the Shawnee men were well-armed with "guns of the French make, with rifled Barrels," and carried with them "a bit of Black Wampum, Cords for tying Slaves when made prisoners, a cross of silver, and several bracelets of the Same metal."[100] The cords fit with their eventual "admission" to Glen that they were looking for Catawbas to take prisoner—but also suggests something else might have been afoot given that they went straight past Catawba country without taking a single captive. When asked, they pointedly refused to reveal their actual numbers, claimed to have gotten lost ("we lost the path for there were so many paths that we did not know which to take"), and at one point declared that alcohol fueled their actions.[101]

The following month Governor Glen negotiated with delegations representing the Overhill and Lower towns, both of whom wanted to free the six Shawnee prisoners. On July 7 he was taken aback when Attakullakulla aggressively stepped into the fray. Prior to this encounter Glen had only occasionally come across Little Carpenter, but on this day the latter completely knocked the former off his guard. Asserting authority as a member of the 1730 London delegation, he reframed the Chain of Friendship three different times to suit his purposes. He also implied strongly that Cherokees knew where to find other sources for European commodities and threatened a rupture with Carolina should Glen refuse to release the Shawnees. Glen scolded Attakullakulla for acting like a "boy." Fortunately for him the Keowee headman Skiagunsta agreed. (Perhaps because he did not want to interfere with the ongoing construction of Fort Prince George?) Cooler heads prevailed, and the two Cherokee delegations agreed that the Chain of Friendship remained unbroken. The story for the six Shawnees did not end so peaceably, as three managed to escape and lay "waste to frontier settlements as they made their way back to Wakatomaka."[102] The potential consequences were huge—particularly in light of 1754 events such as the breaking of the Anglo-Haudenosaunee covenant chain or the British disaster at Fort Necessity. In 1754 Overhill headman Kanagatoga (also called Connecorte and known to the British as Old Hopp) explained to Ludovick Grant that recent "Northward" attacks on Lower Cherokee towns had occurred because "these Cherrockees . . . when in Charles Town, did not procure the Freedom of the Savannahs from your Excellency and send them home."[103] He understood perhaps better than anyone that such inter-Indigenous encounters could cause a "chain of interrelated and allied towns [to] mobilize for war against the British."[104] For his part, Glen could only watch "with horror as Indian towns, from Alabama to New York, learned of Glen's ill-treatment of the Shawnee prisoners."[105]

Historians tend to argue that Attakullakulla was an extremely complex man, willing to entertain French overtures but ultimately remaining within the pro-British camp. From the perspective of Native country, however, he was neither pro-British nor pro-French. He was pro-Overhill, and his behavior offers an individual snapshot into the forces shaping trans-Appalachia at midcentury. He employed Indigenous understandings of diplomacy, rejected ideas of either commercial or diplomatic exclusivity, and seemed ever willing to negotiate with Louisiana, Virginia, and Carolina. He maintained connections to other major players in the Tennessee corridor, including Odawas and Shawnees. (His mother could well have been Shawnee, and he certainly spent significant time in Shawnee country.) And from 1753 onward the Carpenter would play a major role in Anglo-Cherokee affairs.

One final observation. Careful attention to the moment reveals curious parallels between the Aniyunwiya situation circa 1718 and the "Shawnee prisoner" moment of 1753. In 1718 Carolinians established a factory at Congaree amidst complaints of inadequate and corrupt trade. Moreover, tensions were palpable between Lower town leaders and their Valley-Overhill counterparts (in particular, Charite Hagey and Caesar). In 1753 the British established a fort and trading post at Keowee amidst complaints of inadequate and corrupt trade. The Overhills wanted a fortification as well, but South Carolina balked even as Virginia went to work constructing one. Moreover, tensions were palpable between the Lower towns and the Overhill towns (in particular, Little Carpenter and Skiagunsta). In both moments, that the Aniyunwiya controlled the conversation is nearly self-evident. In both moments rumors swirled of plots to undermine Cherokees and the British from the northward and westward—both European and Indigenous. And in both moments Virginia's presence seemed ubiquitous.

After three decades it is hardly any wonder that the Overhills would distrust the British as much as their Yamasee War era predecessors.

Continuing War in Trans-Appalachia

King George's War ended with the 1748 Treaty of Aix-la-Chappelle, but given the level of rumor and paranoia it would have been hard to tell in trans-Appalachia. In January 1748–49 the French government sent a coded message to Louisiana governor Pierre François de Rigaud Vaudreuil and New France governor Charles de la Boische, Marquis de la Galissonière, that the British Parliament soon would debate whether to establish colonies "in various parts of North America which are uncultivated and to which will be transported families from already-established colonies." Louis XV commanded Vaudreuil to "do the same from the Louisiana side in order to prevent" such an establishment. Subsequently, twenty-four companies were ordered to deploy throughout Louisiana, with several appearing to head for the *pays des Illinois*.[106] Later that year Pierre Joseph Céleron de Blainville embarked upon a journey down the Ohio River both to "secure" French claims (by placing lead plates of ownership along the riverbed) and to cultivate stronger Native alliances.[107] Along the way his expedition encountered a number of British traders, a frustration reinforcing the legitimacy of the warnings emanating from Versailles. By 1751 irritation over those encounters—not to mention incessant rumors of British settlements "near the Ilinois, either on the Ohio, the River Cherokee, or elsewhere"—led to instructions to "oppose them with open force."[108] To the south, the French took measures to improve the structure at Fort Tolouse.[109] To the east, they extended fortifications off Lake Erie, culminating in the 1754 establishment of Fort Duquesne at the Forks of the Ohio (modern Pittsburgh, Pennsylvania).

In September that year Vaudreuil left Louisiana to become governor of New France, but his replacement, Louis Billouart, Chevalier de Kerlérec, continued to advocate for expanded fortification along the lower Ohio. He believed it would serve multiple purposes. It would protect lines of communication between Louisiana and New France, for example, which was no small detail in light of rumors of British settlements or of events such as the 1752 inter-Indigenous confrontation often mislabeled a 'French attack' on the Twightwee (Miami) town of Pickawillany.[110] Kerlérec could neither see nor understand the implications of inter-Indigenous engagement, but given the pervasiveness of British interference and of ambiguous encounters such as Pickawillany, he intuited that lower

Valley fortifications would be essential to securing Louisiana. Doubly so when one considered that new fortifications would also "afford the colony protection . . . against the incursions that the Chickasaws and the Cherokees very frequently make on the river." Equally important, as we have seen, he believed lower Valley forts would serve as a means by which commercially to infiltrate Aniyunwiya country.[111]

Despite persistent shortfalls in money and manpower, Louisiana somewhat made good. In 1755 Attakullakulla revealed to Charles Town that "the French were building a Fort near the mouth of a River that runs into Tennessee River & on which . . . the Shawanese live [the Cumberland]." Only a twenty-four-day journey from the Overhill towns, this location, he suggested to Charles Town, had "a great many Guns Ammunition & Provisions."[112] He exaggerated both the state of construction and the availability of supplies (for that matter, he may have conflated it with developments at Fort Chartres), but he was hardly the only witness to French development along the lower river. British Chickasaw agent Jerome Courtonne confirmed it when he reported "that the French were determined to Build a Fort somewhere about the Fork of [Ohio] & the Cherokee River."[113] A very rickety Fort Massac, as it eventually became known, opened in 1757 at precisely that location. For Kerlérec it was a potential tipping point—a "favorable moment [through which] the *Shawnees* and the *Cherokees* might perhaps decide to protect our workers and oppose with certain success the incursions [of] the English."[114] Franco-Overhill interaction only accelerated from there, culminating in a 1756 treaty through which the French agreed to increase trade while Overhills agreed to abandon the British.

Carolina's responses to French trans-Appalachian maneuvering illuminates how, in the European mind, Indigenous affairs had become so inextricably woven into their own that confrontation in one realm could spark war in the other. It represented an existential danger that had been deeply ingrained in the South Carolina psyche since the Yamasee War. James Glen alluded to this fear in 1744 when he informed the Board of Trade that the people most experienced in the "Affairs of this Country have always dreaded a French War from an apprehension that an Indian one would be the consequence of it." Since his arrival in 1744 he had "carefully attended to Indian Affairs and taken much pains" to avoid such a catastrophe.[115] His success in this regard was an illusion, as events in the 1750s would make vividly clear.

CHAPTER 4

Of Fortifications and Chains of Friendship, 1750–1759

In July 1754 Gov. James Glen of South Carolina received news from his Virginia counterpart, Robert Dinwiddie, that a confrontation had occurred between George Washington's militia and French forces (with their Native allies) near the Forks of the Ohio River. He was appalled that Dinwiddie had written "these remarkable Words 'The French have got the Advantage by Capitulation.'"[1] Such a defeat, he feared, could have wide-ranging consequences for the British North American empire. At the least, he warned Sir Thomas Robinson, Secretary of State for the Southern Department, this "small Spark may kindle a great Fire, and . . . if the Flame bursts out all the Water in the Ohio will not be able to extinguish it."[2]

Glen's Ohio valley–based fears were echoed up and down the imperial hierarchy, with Cherokees assuming a notable position in the conversations. MP Thomas Potter, for example, proclaimed in the Commons that French success would surely lead to the unraveling of Britain's Indigenous alliances. "The forts they have erected," he observed, "and those they propose to erect . . . will make [them] absolute masters of all our friendly Indians: the Six Nations, the Cherokees, the Creeks, in short, all the Indian nations upon the back of our Settlement, from Georgia to Nova Scotia."[3] From South Carolina Edmond Atkin warned that trans-Appalachia was dangerous because it combined northern and southern fears of French alliances "with those of the Six united Nations and other Indians who live upon the Waters of the Ohio, on the back of Pensilvania, Maryland, and Virginia; and with the Cherokees on the back of Carolina."[4]

Atkin extended the danger to the Tennessee corridor. By securing communications "between Canada and Louisiana by way of the River Wabash," he noted, the French had put themselves in a position to control the Tennessee, Ohio, "and other Rivers that run from the Eastward into the Same."[5] Cherokee trader Ludovick Grant was even more specific, his rhetoric reflecting both paranoia and the importance of Overhill friendship. "It is not to be doubted," he told Glen, that if the Overhill towns shift loyalty "the French with those Indians would soon settle these famous back Rivers to which at present these Indians Over the Hills are the only Hindrance."[6] When combined with Attakullakulla's and Jerome Courtonne's intelligence regarding what would become Fort Massac, it seemed to Carolina's leaders that the French were dangerously close to reigning supreme in trans-Appalachia.

Paranoia or not, for Carolinians the empire needed to spare "neither . . . Blood nor Treasure to prevent" such a catastrophe.[7] Charles Pinckney elaborated to the Board of Trade in 1754: should the French "enfort themselves" in Overhill territory, he feared, they would turn Chickasaws, Creeks, and ultimately all other Cherokee regions against the British. In the process they would cut off "our trade and intercourse with all the Indians" and place Augusta, Savannah, and Charles Town within easy striking distance. Such a scenario not only would lead to the destruction of out settlements, Pinckney emphasized, it also would encourage slaves "to rise in rebellion against us" and force planters to flee to "the Towns on the Sea Coast." From there, it would take only a nudge to push South Carolina (and Georgia) "into the Sea."[8]

As the Seven Years' War unfolded in North America, in short, Overhill Cherokees and events in the Tennessee corridor loomed large. The empire would need to take two courses of action. First, it would need to do more to secure Anglo-Cherokee friendship.[9] Second—and directly related—it would need to secure the Overhill towns "from any Invasion of their Enemies" by systematically sending them arms and ammunition and by constructing fortifications.[10]

From the Overhill perspective, Carolina's handwringing looked remarkably similar to the previous four decades of empty rhetoric.

Perpetual dithering over fortifications, they felt, translated as indifference to the white path of diplomacy—and justified the wisdom of pursuing multiple avenues of alliance and resource acquisition. Their leaders certainly seemed to work within the context of the Chain of Friendship, accepting (on their terms) the 1755 Saluda treaty and encouraging as they did the construction both of a Virginia fort and eventually of Fort Loudoun. Yet they did not hide their deep frustration with inconsistent commercial, diplomatic, and military policies. Nor did they embrace the singular definition of nationhood their British neighbors demanded but could not offer in return. Even as they engaged in trade and diplomacy with Virginia and Carolina, the Overhills also cultivated a "strong, bright chain" with the French, culminating in a 1756 treaty of alliance.[11] (See appendix B for the text of the treaty and the Cherokees' responses.)

This chapter uses a trans-Appalachian lens to explore these complexities, in the process both connecting with and moving beyond prevailing scholarship. Over the past several decades historians have studied 1750s Anglo-Cherokee relationships in detail. Observations about fortifications, trade, and friendship are sophisticated and learned, but over time scholars have come to overlook trans-Appalachian realities, regional identity, and the extent to which the Overhills controlled Carolina's "door to the Ohio valley"—and thus how they represented a key element of Britain's (and France's) imagined North American empires. By emphasizing the Overhill connection to trans-Appalachia, the chapter zeroes in on other motivators at the heart of Overhill decision making: Native alliances (particularly with Shawnees) as well as consistent Indigenous peril from the *pays des Illinois* and the Ohio valley, which threatened war and challenged access to trade goods at a moment when those seemed increasingly difficult to acquire from Carolina, Virginia, or French sources. Westward problems in the 1750s foreshadowed what for the Overhills would remain a concern for at least the next two decades.[12] And that in turn would have major implications for British North America in the last third of the eighteenth century.

Exploring South Carolina's Fortification and Unity Problems

Given broader continental events in 1754 and 1755—as well as the long-standing perception that the Overhills protected South Carolina's "northwestward" flank—it is hardly surprising that Governor Glen would call for another congress to knock the rust off the Chain of Friendship. (A nice secondary purpose was to acquire thousands of acres between the Wateree and Savannah Rivers.)[13] He initially requested that it take place in Charles Town, but when confronted with Cherokee reluctance to travel that far, he agreed to hold it halfway between there and Chota, at Saluda Creek.[14]

At the subsequent gathering Glen insisted to five hundred Cherokee delegates that the British Empire was committed to them despite decades of diplomatic and commercial inconsistency, intercolonial squabbling, kneejerk reactions to rumors, and misfires on fortifications. Invoking the language of the 1730 agreement, he explained that George II held the same "tender Affection for the Cherokee Nation that Parents have for their Children." The king, he said, had commanded him "to love and cherish them, to supply their Wants, to help to defend them against their Enemies, and to protect their Country against the French." Glen also asked the Overhills to let him know if "the French [make] a Settlement any where upon Tannessie River." In such an event he would "send Warriours to your Assistance, to drive them back to their own Country, and to build a fort there for all that Country is yours."[15] To Attakullakulla he was even more explicit, explaining that the British wanted to protect "not [only] the Land which you live on, but all the Lands on each Side down Tennessie River as far as Mississippi, and all from Tennessie to the Ohio."[16]

Glen, in other words, was anxious to stabilize Cherokee friendship and offered more extended military help as a lure for achieving it. Left unsaid was the imagined meaning behind such language: if the Tennessee valley was demonstrably Cherokee territory, and if Cherokees were in alliance with the empire, then British actions would extend imperial sovereignty accordingly. Out of Overhill earshot Glen even suggested that the British should "build two Forts at the Confluence of [the] three Rivers, one on the Neck of Land betwixt Tennessee and Ohio, and the other betwixt Ohio and Ouabash."[17] Ludovick Grant concurred, adding that a fort garrisoned with a regiment "would command these Rivers and all the Country, and absolutely cut off communication between Canada and Louisiana, for a single Canoo could neither go down Tennessee, the Ohio, or the Ouabash, nor pass up without Leave." In the event of formal war with France, Grant believed, such a fort would disrupt "New Orleans and their Trade which depend in a great measure upon the supplies of Flour and other Things that [come] down the Mississippi from [Illinois]."[18]

Skeptics would have pointed out that the pursuit of western fortifications was anything but a new idea. As early as 1720, recall, the Board of Trade had emphasized the necessity of building "some small Forts among [the Cherokees] for the Encouragement of our Security."[19] The ink was hardly dry on the 1730 accords before South Carolina governor Robert Johnson called for the construction of "a Fort on the Frontier of the Cherokee Nation, for fear the French should do the same and bring over [those] Nations into their Interest."[20] (The South Carolina Assembly was unwavering that "the Expence of our Safety [must come from] Your Majesty either for Men, or Money."[21]) In 1748 Glen petitioned Westminster to fund some type of fortification, to which the Board of Trade responded by directing him to pursue a treaty with Cherokees "for such a Quantity of Land as may be necessary for building a Fort to keep the French from coming amongst them, and in such Place as will most effectually Answer the purposes thereof."[22]

By 1752 Glen partially had what he wanted: with Board of Trade support the colonial assembly approved £3,000 (Carolina currency) for the construction of what became Fort Prince George at the Lower town of Keowee (in modern-day Pickens County, South Carolina).[23] The problem was that the Lower towns already seemed to maintain a stable friendship with Britain, but the Overhills were demonstrably different. To secure both the Chain of Friendship and South Carolina's western border, Ludovick Grant explained, and thus to extend imagined British sovereignty, Carolina had little choice but to fortify "over the Hills."[24] The good news for Carolinians was that the Board of Trade agreed, authorizing a second Cherokee fort in 1754 and even calling for Virginia to help defray costs.[25]

Alas for Glen, opposition from local and regional interests challenged his vision of friendship and western extension. The colonies, it seemed, lacked the unity even to proclaim a systematic British presence very far into the mountains, much less to secure the Tennessee corridor. Perhaps nothing illuminates the point quite as sufficiently as the problems associated with the oft-proposed but slow-to-be-built Overhill fort. Its absence ensured that Carolina would remain on the margins of trans-Appalachian affairs and encouraged perceptions of insufficient trade and "protection"—issues periodically complicated (as in 1734 and 1751) by Carolina's decisions to shut down commerce entirely. Although historians can overplay Cherokee economic dependence, it is difficult to overstate the *perceptual* impact of embargos such as these. In 1755 Ludovick Grant spelled it out: the Cherokees themselves, he informed Glen, "especially those over the Mountains, are in the same State they were in [in 1730], as they themselves confessed, when they gave up themselves and their Lands to the King."[26] It is not hard to read between the lines. Despite remonstrances to the contrary, Carolina had repeatedly violated the reciprocal commercial and diplomatic obligations the Overhills required, thereby destabilizing the Chain of Friendship.[27]

As it had since the 1710s, South Carolina blamed Virginia (and Georgia) for these failures.[28] Convinced they were the southern representatives of the British Empire, South Carolinians long had insisted that they drive economic, military, and diplomatic initiatives in the Native South and were deeply frustrated when Virginia and Georgia encroached upon Cherokee affairs. At one point, recall, the colony's leadership even suggested categorizing Virginia as a foreign power to exclude them from Cherokee country.[29] Robert Dinwiddie complicated the situation in the 1750s by insisting to imperial leadership that Virginia should maintain separate connections to the Cherokees.[30] Even more troubling, Dinwiddie also decided his colony needed its own Overhill fort. Although no one manned it, said fort served as yet another example of confused and confusing British policy.[31] (To be fair, the South Carolina fort eventually known as

Loudoun would perform only marginally better.) Despite their persistent demand for an artificially singular Cherokee Nation, the British were utterly incapable of speaking with one voice.

For his part, Glen believed greater imperial oversight of Native affairs could both solve the cycle of intercolonial frustration and help secure the Chain of Friendship. Historians typically attribute this interest to the governor's personal ambitions.[32] Fair enough—although that alone does not explain the full measure of his actions given his paranoia over trans-Appalachian threats. As early as the 1745 Cherokee congress, he expressed the opinion that more unified commercial and diplomatic efforts were crucial, while his opposition to people like Docherty, Maxwell, and Priber spoke to his willingness to frame local squabbles in imperial terms. By 1750, moreover, he had initiated correspondence with New York's leadership to encourage solidarity between what he felt were the two hubs of Anglo-Indigenous diplomacy. A unified voice, he insisted, could serve imperial western interests far better than the extant cacophony of thirteen separate policies. To New York governor George Clinton he expressed an "extreme desire" for the two to agree that nothing "can be more for his Majestys Service, and for the welfare and safety of his Provinces upon this Continent than an Union of Councils amongst the several Governours, upon Indian affairs."[33] In 1754 he explained to Thomas Robinson that "if the Provinces [could] enter into a Confederacy . . . it is probable that when the French see that we are proceeding regularly and unanimously, that is with united Councils, they will be too wise to measure their Strength with ours, well knowing that such a Combat must prove very unequal."[34]

Empire, fortifications, and friendship, in short, were at the heart of Glen's agenda as he initiated the conversation at Saluda Creek in 1755. And after serious negotiations, he and his compatriots had reason to think they might have succeeded in restoring luster to the Chain of Friendship.[35] As the congress wound down, the Cherokee delegates seemed to make a big concession by laying earth from a small pouch at the feet of the governor, with the idea that it go to George II as a symbol of their acknowledgment that "he was the owner of all their lands and waters."[36] Thereafter Kanagatoga and Attakullakulla traveled the Cherokee regions to explain the treaty, an effort that historians have used to describe Saluda as a "decisive" moment in securing an alliance "necessary for Carolina to compete, particularly with rival Virginia, for engagement in the trans-Appalachian west."[37]

Other observers were less certain. Edmond Atkin, for one, explained to the Board of Trade that it is "a great absurdity to imagine that either the French or ourselves can maintain an interest and Influence, more especially among the Inland Nations, barely by the possession of Forts, without being at the same time possess'd of their Affections."[38] Young British officer John Stuart made much the same point. When a July 1757 supply train arrived at Fort Loudoun without "one Shilling's worth of goods," Attakullakulla told Stuart that he felt "in Some measure ill used." Stuart in turned warned Glen's gubernatorial replacement William Lyttelton that he would need to send "an Immediate Supply of Powder & ball and Such other things as are necessary to fill them for their hunting Grounds." The alternative, he feared, was that "every forgery from the French" and Shawnees would solidify perceptions that they could acquire them elsewhere.[39]

Other colonial leaders tended to agree with Stuart. When in 1754 Dinwiddie reached out to the Overhills to reinforce Virginia's weak trade lines, Kanagatoga wondered why the governor had not also sent "ammunition and war utensils . . . according to Promise." Without them, he explained, "neither he nor his People could make powder, and bullets, and other Things they very much wanted." He sarcastically observed that "Paper alone, meaning the Letters, would not defend them from their Enemies either at Home or abroad."[40] Two years later Attakullakulla welcomed the construction of a Virginia fort out of a conviction that South Carolina had stopped most trade and refused to build its own fort. He found that Carolina's behavior directly violated both the Saluda treaty and longer-standing agreements. In 1730, after all, "the Great King our Father, told me, that we should mutually assist each other," but Governor Glen had "forfeited his Word."[41]

South Carolina neither upheld reciprocal obligations as required in Native diplomacy nor supported the Cherokee conviction that they and the colonies were equal brothers.[42] Virginia fared little better, however. As Little Carpenter scolded at a 1756 joint congress with the Catawbas, for years "our Brethren of Virginia have declined a trade with us . . . [even though] The King Our Father, when I was in England, assured me that we Should be constantly supplied with Goods."[43] A year or two earlier he had insisted that Virginians transmit this message to George II, "who we doubt not is quite ignorant of our Circumstances, and will relieve us, as soon as he is acquainted with them."[44] That the relief still was not forthcoming explained Overhill reluctance to engage with Dinwiddie's colony. A group of Overhill headmen remarked that they had "always promised you the help of [our] Young Men [and would] have been as good as [our] promises had you sent men here as I thought you would have done long before this." Their rebuke was stunning. "When you agreed to build this Fort you then promised us a trade from Virginia," they observed. But now it appeared that "you have no Value for us or you would not have forgot us so long as you have."[45] The Overhills would not act until the Virginians upheld *their* promises, a fact Attakullakulla made explicit when he informed them that he had "a Hatchet ready, but we hope our Friends will not expect us to take it up, till we have a place of Safety for our Wives and Children."[46]

Both Virginia and Carolina were disappointing allies, and this deficit seriously challenged whatever luster Glen thought he may have added to the Chain of Friendship at Saluda. From that perspective alone it is hardly surprising that people like Andrew Lewis would perceive "equivocating Arguments to Avoyd Sending" troops to attack the French in the unfolding European war.[47] Lewis's autumn 1756 observations offer solid insight into the situation. Commissioned by Virginia to build its fort, he reported that Overhills leaders were friendly only so long as he did not demand that they "fulfil their Promise of sending their Warriors with me to the Assistance of Virginia." He described how Attakullakulla received a steady stream of secret messages from both Shawnees and Fort Toulouse despite "their many promises to acquaint me with Everything they heard or knew."[48] It synched with other anti-British communications of which he was aware between the French, Shawnees, and "the Great Town of Tellico." Overhill folk even seemed to favor constructing "a French Fort in their Towns, and the Head Men in

General approve of the same."[49] Taken together, it indicated to Lewis that they were "Greater Friends to the French Over the Hills then to the English."[50] Approximately six months later David Ochterlong warned General Loudoun that "Severall parties of Catawba, Cherokee, and Tuscarora Indians, have passed by Williamsburgh, on their Way to the Frontiers." He explained that "the Cherokees have behaved in such a Manner, as to give Grounds for believing that They intend us no Good; Nay Mr Atkins who is here, goes so far, as to say, that he expects hourly to hear, of their having struck a stroke upon the Frontier Inhabitants, and gone off."[51]

The 1756 Franco-Overhill Treaty and Its Potential Impact

Underpinning Overhill frustrations were the twin realities of regional identity and nonexclusive trade and diplomacy. It meant that they saw no contradiction in simultaneously traveling east to attend the Saluda congress and west to negotiate with French Louisiana. As early as 1754 Kerlérec had informed ministre de la marine Jean Baptiste de Machault D'Arnouville of a "proposal for an alliance that the Great Chief of the Cherokees (Attakullakulla) had made."[52] Two years later twenty-five Overhill men, primarily from Tellico (including Kanagatoga and Oconostota, the latter also known as Mankiller or Great Warrior of Tellico), arrived at Fort Toulouse to negotiate further. Five emissaries then proceeded to New Orleans, where they informed Kerlérec that "the English have a Bad Heart." They announced that their mission was "to request the peace in the name of and on the part of the whole nation" and to establish a chain stretching from New Orleans to Chota.[53] That language is telling—by connecting to Chota, the delegates symbolically declared that their "nation" was Overhill country, an identity they subsequently embedded in offers to "strike at [the British] and chase them beyond the mountains."[54] They were willing to cleanse their towns of Carolina and Virginia interests, in other words, but a removal from the other settlement areas was not within their mandate.[55] To this end, in December 1756 Ostenaco (known to the British as Jud's Friend) acknowledged that the Overhill towns seemed to have joined the French but that the other regions probably would not.[56]

Regional distinctions emerge through other examples at roughly this same moment, perhaps most notably through interactions with the Haudenosaunee and the Shawnees. In 1755 Kanagatoga (and others) informed a "northward" delegation "that if they wanted War they should not come against any of the seven Towns over the Hills, but that it was what they would with the rest."[57] The Six Nations subsequently reported to newly minted Indian superintendents William Johnson and Edmond Atkin that "the Seven Towns of the Cherokees living on the North side of the Mountains are . . . our Friends." They simultaneously (and unconvincingly) warned that "the lowest three Towns are in the French Interest—they live about half a days running distance from the lowest of the Seven Towns of the Cherokees who are in our Interest."[58] Further reinforcing the regional distinctions was a 1758 delegation of Cherokees to Onondaga, which offered "a White Belt with one black Row of Wampum in the middle signifying the Road and 3 Figures of Men, signifying Sir Wm Johnson & the 6 Nations, and the Kohy and Tsyoody [Keowee and Chota] Nations."[59] In 1759, meanwhile, Lower town headman Tiftoe (Tistoe, also known as the Wolf of Keowee) identified himself to non-Cherokee Natives as a member of the Keowee Nation.[60]

If the proposed French chain did not extend beyond Chota, however, the delegation certainly was open to offering that Overhill connection. In return for more systematic trade, they promised they would "bury their cassetête [war club] and faithfully prevent that any warrior of their nation be found in any party of enemies who strike against the French." Negotiations culminated in a treaty of alliance (see appendix B), which if implemented could have brought the Overhills into direct confrontation with the British as early as 1757.[61] Not surprisingly, the French used the treaty to push for military assistance. In Article 7 Kerlérec insisted that the Overhills "command [British garrisons] to depart the nation, and if they will not do it willingly, to constrain them to do it by force." He further insisted that they would need to destroy "the identified magazine that the English come to build in their lands"—an obvious allusion to the

Virginia and Carolina forts. Kerlérec even hoped that military support would extend to Native trans-Appalachian affairs that had fallen perpetually beyond the French ability to control. In Article 5 he requested that the Overhills "make war on the Chickasaw who have always had ill-made spirits and who are always the declared enemies of the French and the Red Men befriended by and allied with the French." Perhaps not surprisingly, the Overhills refused. (The Lower towns eventually seemed to do so, however.)[62]

Overhill delegates responded by consenting in principle to "force the English . . . to retire from their nation" and to "destroy the house by force that they had already built there."[63] They also agreed they would no longer "permit the English to come despoil either their land or their rivers in order to do ill to the French."[64] It could not have been lost on anyone that keeping the English out of "their rivers" meant rejecting British visions of imagined empire along the Tennessee corridor. All that was needed, they insisted, was the implementation of French obligations: more systematic lines of trade from New Orleans, Mobile, and Fort Toulouse. In Article 10 Kerlérec had agreed he would "take care to send to [Fort Toulouse] powder, bullets, war clubs, logging saws, flint, and vermilion to reward the valor of the Cherokee warriors, and the attachment that the nation will prove to have for the French." To this promise he could have added, Old Ceasar of Chatuga later suggested, that supplies also would come up the Tennessee River from Illinois.[65]

The negotiations seemed successful enough that, like Ostenaco, a woman known as Oninaa (English name Nancy Butler) warned Fort Loudoun that Kanagatoga was encouraging Overhill towns to accept "treaties and alliances with the French and attack the garrison at Fort Loudoun."[66] Kerlérec had a major problem, however: he lacked access to the plethora of supplies he was promising, which meant he would have to stall. He thus placed conditions on the diplomatic and commercial exchange, announcing that he would send goods only after he had "learned that the nation has chased from its lands all the English and . . . declared war on them by a valorous and magnificent action." Article 4, moreover, required that an Overhill delegation travel to Montreal to obtain New France governor

Vaudreuil's approval before the treaty fully could come into effect. The Overhills responded in equally nuanced fashion. They had marked, they said, "the promise [Kerlérec] had made to them to send to the Post of the Alibamoux . . . the war materiel they needed."[67] In Article 9 they pointedly "added that they hoped they would not lack after the Great Chief of the North had mixed his words with" Kerlérec's. Including Montreal in the conversation was sensible, in other words, which meant that some delay in formally securing the alliance was inevitable.[68] Even so, the Overhills would need immediate supplies before they would move against British interests.[69]

Kerlérec certainly understood such caution. Requests for supplies "seemed to be fair to me," he told d'Arnouville, "because if they reject the English and devote themselves to us, they have the right to make sure that we will provide for what they were getting from the English, especially their indispensable needs." He insisted that Versailles drastically improve their commercial endeavors, commenting that the alternative would be an Overhill conviction "that French people are so poor that they only have local goods."[70] More pointedly, he asked d'Arnouville "what would be the significance . . . of an alliance that would not be sustained and supported by all the assistance that the Cherokees would have a right to expect of us?"[71]

In retrospect, of course, the Franco-Overhill Articles of Friendship never worked to the satisfaction of either side.[72] Nor are they indicative of any meaningful shift on the part of the Overhills, particularly given the nonexclusive ideas embedded in Native diplomacy and trade. They do, however, offer an interesting avenue for rethinking prevailing narratives of the Cherokee experience in the mid-eighteenth century. They shed different light on British observations of French loyalties, offer an intriguing avenue for thinking about Overhill interactions with Fort Massac, and potentially explain Overhill reluctance to supply troops to march on Fort Duquesne in 1758.[73] They also suggest that the Overhills had a model for attacking British fortifications nearly four years before the 1760 siege of Fort Loudoun. It is perhaps not unreasonable partially to interpret the Anglo-Cherokee War through the lens of this treaty. (More on that point in chapter 5.)

The Overhills, Indigenous Interactions, and the Westward Problem

As intriguing as it is, the above narrative needs to address an elephant in the room: inter-Indigenous issues tended to shape European actions in 1750s trans-Appalachia, not vice versa. [74] It was the case whether Europeans understood it or not. One of the more well-known examples stems from the 1752 confrontation at Pickawillany. Historians have described the affair as a continental turning point, arguing that it set in motion a chain of events leading to the Seven Years' War. Fair enough, although a closer inspection of the moment reveals that it was not French dominated. On the contrary, it was orchestrated by the Anishnaabeg and was the first of a series of upper Ohio valley encounters in which Native polities pursued agendas of their own. That they happened to overlap with Franco-British concerns was on many levels coincidental.[75] Certainly the Twightwees thought of it in Native terms when they described the situation to Robert Dinwiddie. Two hundred and forty "fighting Men," they explained, had "sent us wampum, & a fine French Coat, in Token of Peace & Good-will, just to deceive and draw our people out a Hunting." Thereafter, they said, this force fell upon the "more weak & defenseless Part" of the town. Crucially, "there was but two French Men . . . among the Indians in Time of Battle."[76]

A less well known but similarly critical snapshot from the upper Ohio valley helps to illuminate Dinwiddie's decision to reach out to the Overhills in 1754. Inter-Indigenous developments were on his mind because a group of Chickasaws and one Cherokee had recently killed a Mohawk delegation along the Ohio River.[77] The murders threatened to ignite a war between the Haudenosaunee and elements of the Native South at a moment when Mohawks had already declared the Covenant Chain broken, Fort Necessity had proven a disaster for Virginians, and Carolina was struggling to renew the Chain of Friendship with Cherokees. At the very least, Dinwiddie feared, a Native war would destroy the fragile relationship his colony maintained with the Overhills. James Glen, fearing larger impacts, reached out to Onondaga to inform them that the "Mohawks who were sent to assist the Catawbas, Creeks, and Cherokees along the Ohio were killed by mistake."[78] Better to get out in front of the problem before British southern interests were crushed.

Dinwiddie's (and Glen's) fears speak to the fact that complexity in trans-Appalachia was more than European empires wanted to negotiate. Instead, they emphasized western expansion through Edenic imagery, idealized cartography, imagined boundaries, cultural and technological superiority, and claims of sovereignty that only they embraced. They deeply embedded such (deliberate?) obtuseness in the epistolary record, lulling subsequent generations into assuming that Franco-British confrontation was the driving force of midcentury affairs in North America. In this narrative Indigenous people were somewhat unidimensional, dangerous actors in the North American theater of a global war, relegated to playing Europeans off one another to secure some level of (diminishing) agency.

The reality was far more complicated. To complete the complex portrait suggested by the Saluda agreement or the Franco-Overhill treaty, then, it is critical to explore how western issues may have shaped them. The oft-mentioned association between the Overhills and some Shawnee towns offers an initial launching point. If it is true that the two nations maintained an uneven, sometimes violent relationship, it is also fair to say that neither group should be pinned to monolithic labels. Just as Cherokees maintained five regional variations, so Shawnees, "the greatest travelers in America," were divided into settlements lacking a singular national identity, economic interest, or diplomatic policy.[79] In Cherokee terms, it meant that Shawnees might show hostility toward the Lower towns (and vice versa) while simultaneously reaching out to the Overhills. In 1746, for example, a Frenchman in Mvskoke country described a negotiation "both on the upper part of the [Ohio] river and in the lands of the Wabash" in which "twelve Shawnees had come to confirm [the peace] also with all the nations," including the Cherokees. When the twelve subsequently traveled to Choctaw country they explained that "they had just made peace with the Cherokees."[80] In 1752, meanwhile, Briton William Trent described six Cherokees entering a Shawnee town near the Ohio and Alleghany Rivers and hoisting "a Suit of French Colours" first given to Shawnee sachem Nucheconner.[81] Trent saw the display "as an Affront to His Majesty the King of Great Britain" and announced he "coud hear no Councils under them."[82] He subsequently noted that the six Cherokees informed Shawnee leadership that "fourteen hundred of our Men will be here in about two months, to live amongst you for we can live no longer in our own Country. For the English are angry, & refuse to supply us with Powder & Lead, because they say we kill their traders."[83] Overhills also seem to have allowed reciprocal access to Overhill country, in one case even allegedly allowing them to build "a new Town, near Telliquo."[84] Attakullakulla's impassioned defense of imprisoned Shawnees in 1753 sheds yet further (if indirect) light on this complex relationship.

As the Seven Years' War unfolded in North America, and as both the French and British attempted to secure their Overhill relationship, so too did the Shawnees.[85] In 1756 reports from French spies indicated that Shawnee leaders were making "very moving speeches" to persuade Overhill towns "to take their stand on their side." In addition to potential conversations regarding spiritual renewal, these speeches no doubt led (at least in part) to joint decisions regarding geopolitical issues. Kerlérec, for one, pointed to such an outcome when he described how the two polities had agreed to travel together to Quebec to "negotiate ... peace with M. de Vaudreuil."[86] In 1757 George Croghan, Edmond Atkin, and George Washington heard from a French ensign that Fort Duquesne shortly expected to receive "a great body of Indians to the number of 1500 composed of the Illinois, upper Cherokees and Creeks."[87] He may have exaggerated the number, but his observation that Overhills were visiting the forks of the Ohio was supported by other eyewitnesses. At roughly that same moment, for example, a Seneca man named Rosa (also called Silver Heels) confirmed to Sir William Johnson that a Cherokee delegation of ten *had* in fact "arrived at Fort du Quesne to an Invitation from the French."[88] The Overhills, it seemed, were conversing with Lenapes and Shawnees inside the fort at the same moment that Britons were pressuring Cherokee regions to lay siege to it. Still more inter-Indigenous pressure came in 1758, when the Overhills heard from "a deputation of Northern Indians who proudly reported that they had entirely defeated the English Army ... [and] invited the Cherokees to join with them to drive the colonists into the 'salt water.'"[89]

As fleeting as they are, these snapshots reveal a meaningful connection between a so-called British ally and a polity commonly identified as a British enemy in the era of the Seven Years' War. Problematic in and of itself, such a relationship would have represented (from the British perspective) an affront to the 1730 Chain of Friendship or the 1755 Saluda agreement. It undoubtedly shaped how the Overhills thought about continental affairs at least as much as—if not more than—the offers (or threats) they received from the British and French. And they dovetail with another point of Overhill-Shawnee commonality: both had to deal with additional pressure from further west in trans-Appalachia. By the 1730s the Shawnees had developed notable rivalries with Illinois and Wabash valley polities, in fact. Their confrontations only became more intensive in the 1750s and 1760s, as the Illinois and Miami "along the Wabash were 'seeking to avenge themselves for the inroads that the Shawnees have been making in recent years.'"[90]

So it was with the Overhills as well. In 1754 Ludovick Grant reported that the Overhills had executed a captive identified only as an "Over the Lake Indian." Apparently, the man "had killed a beloved Woman" near Chota before fleeing the area. An "alarmed" Overhill expedition pursued and captured him, but before his death he warned that an army of combined "red and white" fighters were "inforting themselves on the Tennessee River." Their intention was "to come against Chotte and cut it off because that Town ... was always killing their Indians and taking their white Men who were Traders."[91] His warning resonated so much, Grant said, that Overhill leaders sent requests to the "Valey People to repair over the Hills with all Expedition to their Assistance against a great Body of Enemy who as they were informed were approaching their Towns." "Iwassee, Canoste, and Little Telequa" were asked to report to "Great Terequa," while "the long-Savanna People, Noewee, Tomatly, Cheawee, [and] Nantarialy" were to go to Chota.[92]

Such pressures seemed to escalate over time. At the 1756 Cherokee-Catawba conference Attakullakulla reminded Virginians that their new fort was crucial because "the Upper Towns . . . are as much exposed to the incursions of the French and Indians as your Frontier inhabitants."[93] Later that year he left "with a dozen more Warriours for Wawbache," and although the British thought the expedition was going "to wait there for French Boats" it is just as likely that something else was afoot.[94] After all, the Wabash valley was the home of Ouiatanons, Weas, and Twightwees, three polities the Overhills had been confronting for decades. Nor were they shy about informing the British of the extant state of war out west. In 1757, for example, Oconostota told Raymond Demere he intended to "go to War against the French and their Indians called the Tewateways [Twightwees] by Land, that they live upon a Branch of the Mississippi."[95] Given the previous year's Franco-Overhill negotiations, one cannot help but suspect that the French were not Oconostota's target. (On the contrary, he probably was telling the British what they wanted to hear within the context of the Chain of Friendship.) A year later he and Attakullakulla appeared at Fort Loudoun with a "female Twightwee prisoner," in the process revealing that the state of war continued unabated.[96] Other intelligence sources confirmed that Kaskaskias, Illinois, and "Miamies or Twightwees, who live between the Ouabasche and Misscippi" had become hindered by "frequent interruptions from the Cherrockees and Chickesaws."[97]

The confrontation went in both directions. In 1757, for example, Raymond Demere reported that a party of Ouiatanons had killed Overhills along the Tennessee River.[98] In March 1758 Attakullakulla explained that because "we are in open War" with Miamis, he was certain that their parties soon would arrive in Overhill country.[99] He was vindicated when, around that same moment, Paul Demere described "a Party of Tweektwees, twelve in Number" that had come within forty miles of Fort Loudoun, intent upon attacking local residents at the first opportunity.[100] The "Head Man of Talico," meanwhile, "sent a Party of young Fellows of his Town against a Gang of French Indians that were discovered in that Neighbourhood."[101] In November that year Kanagatoga announced that several Overhills had been "killed on the Path, [and] had been scalped by Tweektwees." The offending Miamis had since departed for the Ohio valley, but Old Hopp hoped that "two Gangs" heading toward Fort Massac might catch them.[102] It is not clear whether they actually did so, although Demere later acquired three "Twightwee scalps" from Ostenaco and Oconostota.[103] The latter explained that their excursion had gone a "great way up La Belle Riviere," where they found the enemy surveilling "the Bateaux that went to Fort Du Quene." His sortie ultimately engaged these "scouts" in a firefight in which "they killed three, and wounded another on the arm, who made his Escape tho followed very close."[104]

These vivid if fleeting accounts of Overhill-Miami warfare in the Tennessee corridor—in combination with the better-known Cherokee-Creek confrontations to the south and west of Overhill country—illuminate that Native explanations existed for the ways in which Cherokees responded to the British and the French in the 1750s.[105] They offer another angle for understanding Overhill frustration over inconsistency of British (both Virginian and Carolinian) supply lines, why embargoes would elicit metaphorical charges of nakedness and starvation, and why the Franco-Overhill negotiations mattered. They also highlight that the Overhills pursued their own agenda in the Tennessee corridor (and trans-Appalachia more broadly), even if their interests did overlap or dovetail with European desires.

The British position in North America took a turn for the better vis-à-vis the French in late 1758 and 1759. In November the French garrison at Duquesne finally was forced to abandon and destroy the fort, after which the British constructed Fort Pitt. They followed that success with a 1759 victory on the Plains of Abraham outside Quebec City, which gave the Royal Navy control of the St. Lawrence River and placed Montreal squarely within British sights. That city would fall in 1760, forcing New France to capitulate and effectively securing British mastery over European affairs in the northeastern part of the continent.[106]

The two victories were particularly worrisome for Louisiana. If it was as yet unconquered, its leaders nevertheless feared an imminent British attack in the lower Ohio valley via both La Belle Rivière and the Tennessee corridor. A soldier known as Silhouette articulated it well: "The English," he wrote in his diary, "could move from Carolina against the lower part of [Louisiana], and attack the upper part by the Ohio River" with impunity. He thought it would lead to the construction of forts "at the junction of the Ohio and Wabash, or at that of the Ohio with the Mississippi." Governor Kerlérec believed that these construction projects in time would lead to permanent British settlements and create a staging ground from which to assault New Orleans.[107] Even as Kerlérec sent orders to encourage "different bands of Indians and Frenchmen along La Belle Riviere in order to observe the maneuvers of the English," he worried that an invasion was only a matter of time.[108]

Such an elaborate strategy would hinge upon the extent to which Britain's Cherokee allies agreed to go along with it, however. And although men such as Gen. John Forbes suggested they could convince them (along with Chickasaws) to "attack the Ennemy on the Mississippi," others were not so sure it would work.[109] Observers in Charles Town, in fact, might have suggested that the empire's relationship with the Overhills was in dire straits. It is to a closer examination of that moment that we now turn.

CHAPTER 5

The Overhills and the Limits of the European Imperial Imagination after 1759

In 1760 war broke out between the Cherokees and British Carolinians, and it was unquestionably a pivotal moment for both sets of people.[1] Afterward it became clear that the combination of war and smallpox had notably diminished the Cherokee population, leading many to abandon the Lower and Middle towns and begin to consolidate farther west. As they did so, an ever-growing stream of Euro–South Carolinians filled the void. They and their counterparts from Virginia, North Carolina, and Georgia became more visible in trans-Appalachia as well. Best known from this early stage of western invasion were so-called long hunters such as Daniel Boone, but his and others' activities went beyond hunting game animals to include land surveying.[2] Merely one such example was John Campbell, "a very early pioneer of Southwestern Virginia," who crossed the mountains and all boundary lines to explore "the valley of the Holston [demonstrably Overhill territory] as early as 1764, and purchase an ancient survey, where he and his father and his family afterwards settled."[3]

While perhaps not the most pressing issue facing Overhill country at that moment, people like Boone and Campbell certainly were exasperating. And coinciding as it did with the conclusion of the Seven Years' War, this Euro-American invasion forced the British Empire to confront the dissonance between global victory and the reality that Native polities controlled trans-Appalachia. Southern Indian superintendent John Stuart summarized the emerging problem in 1765: "I beg Leave to observe," he wrote to Board of Trade secretary John Pownall, "that the far Extension of Our Boundaries backwards by approaching too near the Indian Nations will expose us to perpetual Broils. The Inhabitants of those back Countries are in general the lowest & worst Part of the People, and as they & the Indians live in perpetual Jealousy & dread of each other, so their rooted Hatred for each other is reciprocal."[4] Such tension would provide a powerful catalyst in the 1760s and early 1770s for debate between colonial and imperial interests over the nature, meaning, and future of the British North American empire.

The Anglo-Cherokee War (and its aftermath) had a notable effect in Cherokee country for still other reasons. For one thing, the intraregional Cherokee migrations resulting from the conflict produced an increasingly visible sense of singular nationhood—even if spiritual renewal movements tempered national identity formation with a sense of something broader.[5] For another, the demise of New France in 1761 and the cartographical removal after 1763 of the entire French North American presence seemed to end what had been a regular source of trade and diplomatic negotiation in the Overhill region. Combined, eastern encroachment, internal migrations, and shifting Euro-North American dynamics unquestionably put the Aniyunwiya at a crossroads.

Historians have described this crossroads quite well, supported as they are by the explosion of extant British source material dating to this period. Yet while persuasive, the narrative is incomplete because it tends not to incorporate the impact of broader trans-Appalachian pressures. Notably, for example, French Louisiana was far less removed circa the Anglo-Cherokee War (and thereafter) than their cartographical erasure would suggest. More fundamentally, that war was one of two fronts on which the Overhills had to engage: in addition to the British, in 1760 and 1761 they also had to deal with Indigenous tensions to their west. And while the Anglo-Cherokee War itself ended in 1761, the latter confrontations did not. They shaped Native and newcomer interests alike, ensuring that the Cherokees would continue to play an important role in British visions of western empire.

Starting with the Anglo-Cherokee War, this chapter explores the freneticism defining trans-Appalachia in the 1760s and early 1770s.

It contextualizes that conflict with French diplomacy and Native complexities before describing how, after its conclusion, the Overhills continued to struggle with westward polities (particularly in the Tennessee corridor). Such powerful western dynamics ensured that, so far from entering into a period of declension, the Aniyunwiya would remain where they had been since the 1670s: a crucial player in an Indigenous trans-Appalachia beyond Euro-American control.

Anglo-Cherokee Hostilities: The View from the West

Modern scholars generally agree with James Adair's assertion that Carolinians bore most of the blame for the Anglo-Cherokee conflict. "We forced the Cheerake to become our bitter enemies," he explained, "by a long train of wrong measures, the consequences of which were severely felt by a number of high assessed, ruined, and bleeding innocents."[6] Given the thorough nature of the literature there is no need to provide a blow-by-blow account of the war itself.[7] One unavoidable notation, of course, was its extensive impact upon Cherokee country. As Adair suggested, the Aniyunwiya faced widespread death, devastation, and unjust captivity. Entire towns were burned. Crop fields were destroyed.

Smallpox made the situation worse. Since the (probable) first outbreak of the disease in 1696, Cherokees had done everything in their power proactively to deal with it.[8] Despite their best efforts, however, another outbreak occurred at Fort Prince George in late 1759 that afflicted Overhill diplomats held hostage at the fort, radiated outward into the Lower towns, and spread widely from there.[9] Formal Anglo-Cherokee hostilities in 1760 exacerbated the situation, turning "what might have been a controllable outbreak into an epidemiological nightmare."[10] The result was a stunning decline in population. According to one modern estimate, by 1775 the Cherokees were reduced to "perhaps 3,000 warriors (about 12,000 people)."[11] Adding to the death and destruction was dislocation: the Lower and Middle towns depopulated because of the war, with many people migrating further west (particularly to the Overhill region). And as that happened, British colonial settlers moved into the vacuum, raising the curtain on what would evolve into decades of tension between the Cherokees and their Euro-American counterparts.[12]

Yet for all that devastation and encroachment, the Cherokee situation was more complex than contemporary British sources might suggest. Most notably, neither of the war's two major Carolinian expeditions (in 1760 and 1761) proceeded beyond the Lower and Middle towns before they ran out of provisions and energy.[13] As a practical matter, it meant that towns such as Estatoe and Keowee were attacked but that Overhill towns generally were spared.[14] Had Cherokee military interests maintained better supplies of war materiel, James Adair (perhaps hyperbolically) suggested that "twice the number of troops could not have defeated them."[15] South Carolina governor William Lyttelton inadvertently supported that conviction of Cherokee military prowess when he offered his opinion that the British army would need to take "extreme courses" to ward off Cherokee success.[16]

Moreover, if the Anglo-Cherokee War was fundamentally a cis-Appalachian conflict, it would be a mistake not to consider it through the lens of the complexities that challenged Overhill country from its west. In some ways, the Anglo-Cherokee War is one manifestation of the events making trans-Appalachia a hot-zone of Atlantic world geopolitics between 1754 and 1815.[17] The long-standing issues animating the conflict certainly had several western roots, after all, which remained unsettled after the peace in 1761. And within two years similar problems would lead to the more well-known Pontiac's War to the north of the Ohio River. An astute observer might note that many of the same Indigenous players were involved in both conflicts. At any rate, two issues particularly provide trans-Appalachian context for the war: Franco-Overhill interactions via Fort Massac (and thus the Tennessee corridor) and the 1756 Franco-Overhill treaty.

Although unimpressive as an actual installation, Louisiana governor Kerlérec long had supported Fort Massac out of a conviction that it would help to establish "known and honest traders . . . charged with keeping warehouses always well stocked with everything that would be necessary and over whose conduct the commandant would be in a position to keep close watch." He hoped these supplies would connect French Illinois to the Overhill towns via the Tennessee River, with ideal side benefits that Massac could serve as both a "check to the Southern Indians" and as a gathering and launching point for attacks on Carolina.[18] Ten years later British captain Harry Gordon more clearly articulated why Kerlérec would have thought this way, in the process shedding light on the Native forces giving shape to the region. The location of Massac, he wrote in his journal, "is a good one, no where Commanded from, nor can the Retreat of the Garrison (a Consideration in the Indian Countries) ever be cut off; The River being, from the Entrance of that called the Cherokee, from 7 to 800 Yards wide. It will in a political light hold the Ballance between the Cherokee and Wabash Indians, as it favors the Entrance of the former, across the Ohio into the latter's Country, and covers their Retreat from it, and there is no proper Spot for a Post nearer the Cherokee River above, or the Mississippi below, but this, as the grounds on the Banks of the Ohio, begin to be very low."[19] At any rate, Massac's walls were barely completed in 1756 before officer Charles Phillipe Aubry "left there a captain, a lieutenant, an ensign and a garrison sufficient to defend it, [and] departed with forty Frenchmen and as many savages to go along the Keraquis river to reconnoitre."[20]

To the ministre de la marine, Nicolas René Berryer, Comte de La Ferrière, Kerlérec revealed that his efforts with Massac and the Overhills were part of a broader plan to connect Native allies "in a continuous chain from fifty leagues to the northeast of the post of the Alabamas extending along the English settlements as far as the source of the river of the Cherokees." By adding detachments from the Arkansas post and from the *pays des Illinois*, he explained in 1758, he could have "four times as many Indians as M. de Vaudreuil" in New France. If equipped appropriately, this idealized force, Kerlérec believed, would have "irretrievably ruined" most of the British South, thereby freeing Vaudreuil "to occupy himself usefully elsewhere."[21]

For their part, Overhill leaders used Massac to tweak British noses almost from the moment it opened. In 1757 Kanagatoga informed South Carolina governor William Lyttelton that proper Carolinian supply lines would have ensured that the Overhills "cut off [Massac] as soon as possible"—something they no longer seemed inclined to accomplish. Given their war with Miamis, Attakullakulla approached Fort Loudoun with a demand for greater assistance to the Overhill towns and was scornful of how little the garrison agreed to provide. He suggested to John Stuart that "perhaps many of his people might approve of the French Coming so near them and think thar designes good."[22] These statements came on top of warnings from Old Caesar of Chatuga, who in 1756 (shortly after the conclusion of the Franco-Overhill treaty negotiations) floated the rumor that a large body of Indians was about to send "a letter to Captain Demere [at Fort Loudoun] proposing an Armistace between Carolina and Louisiana, [so] that Virginia and the Northward Collonys may carry on the War as they have done." It would be in South Carolina's interest to consider the proposal, he recommended, particularly given that the French planned "to Come up [the Tennessee] River with a Number of Boats, from Fort Cuskuskia or Ilionois."[23] Although he did not "know what their Design may be" he imagined that they would "bring a Body of Troops to Join those that are to Come from the Southward and perhaps to bring Great Guns [of] War to the Stores &c." Already, he suggested, the French had agreed "to send Sixty pack horses Loaded with Ammunition and presents."[24] The implication was clear: go along with the armistice or face an attack from the west.

Beyond these paranoia-inducing rumors and warnings were observations such as John Charles Vian's that Fort Massac represented the tip of a French trans-Appalachian iceberg. "Towards Canada there is a village 50 Leagues from [Massac]," he reported, "with a small fort defended by Militia called de Cass. Six Leagues farther on is a large town called New Chartres with a Stone Fort but vastly strong garrisoned by a Major and 150 soldiers. Many Inhabitants and Indians make much Wine and raise all Kind of Grain there." Only a little beyond Chartres, Vian observed, one would encounter "a Fort called Le Couahchos [sic] with an Officer and 21 Soldiers, many inhabitants and Indians." Another unnamed fort was only "Forty leagues beyond that," he explained. And on it went—Vian ultimately took his report all the way to the Great Lakes. His point: while Massac might be little other than rotting wood, a vast

Illinois network seemed to exist into which the French could tap. It placed British North America in a precarious position. Battles in the north and northeast, it seemed, now were combined with a potential trans-Appalachian and southern theater of the Seven Years' War.

The peril was serious enough that many officials embraced Northern Indian superintendent Sir William Johnson's fear that the French "are mustering as many Indians of the distant, and Neighbouring Indian Nations as possible, in order to make a Descent upon the Southern Provinces."[25] In 1755 and again in 1756 North Carolina passed statutes intended to "Contribute to the Defense against the French and Indians." At the same time a paranoid Gov. Arthur Dobbs declined to send troops north to support the British Army owing to the need to "secure our frontier, since the French were now at Liberty to send forces to the Ohio by the Lakes, and thereby enable their Indians to attack our frontiers."[26] William Lyttelton explained that Franco-Native alliances, in combination with a presumed French naval attack upon Charles Town, might utterly destabilize the already fragile British South.[27] Virginia governor Robert Dinwiddie was more specific in 1757, proclaiming that the combination of Franco-Creek alliance, Franco-Overhill rapprochement, and successes elsewhere in North America left him with little doubt "that the French wou'd attack some of the Southern Colonies by Force from the Mississippi & a Sea Armament, & I dreaded that of So Carolina to be the Place they wou'd probably attack."[28] A year later the North Carolina government lent support to South Carolina via legislation noting that its neighbor "is threatened with a formidable Invasion from the French and Indians in their Interest and Alliance and our own Frontier much exposed in this time of War."[29]

The 1756 Franco-Overhill treaty further illuminates trans-Appalachian contexts for the Anglo-Cherokee War. By 1758 Kerlérec had grown cautiously optimistic of the possibilities presented by the treaty, a sentiment he extended both into the Native South and to his superiors at Versailles.[30] In late summer 1759, for example, French traders in the Mvskoke town of Oakchoi gave the Slave Catcher of Chota (and several other Overhills) "a large belt of Wampum that was strong with white beads of each Side & black & white in the Middle & said that the white beads on Each Side, denoted the

Clear path between Cherokees & the Albamy Fort [Toulouse], & likewise to Fort Lassumption [Massac] & that the black beads Sett forth the bad Intentions the white people at Fort Loudoun had against the Cherokee Nation."[31] As the British invaded Cherokee country the following year, Kerlérec informed his superiors that the Overhills were making "the strongest protestations of their friendship, preference, and loyalty to the French."[32] He explained that embassies "in the name of the Cherokees (who previously had sent me wampum belts to seek an alliance with us and to ask us for assistance) ask us to furnish them the trade goods that they cannot obtain from the English, whom they have abandoned because of us." In line with James Adair's assessment of Cherokee strength, he wrote that "they are calling upon me for the assistance in munitions of war," which, along with other commodities, the French had been "promising them for four years."[33] Inadvertently, he also illuminated the fact that the Overhills controlled the parameters of the negotiations in much the same way that they did with the British—they were expressing alarm, he warned his superiors, that Louisiana was not living up to its treaty obligations. If Kerlérec did not soon act, "they would see themselves forced, in making their peace with the English, to abandon us." In such circumstances, they would not have the ability "to answer for their warriors and perhaps for themselves."[34] Now was the time, if ever, for the French to live up to their promises.

Kerlérec never could offer meaningful support, but it suited his geopolitical interests to bluff. He informed the Overhills that they had not yet received systematic supplies because they had not secured an exclusive relationship with Louisiana as required by the treaty. Adding to French frustrations was the fact that some Cherokees had falsely informed the British that Louisiana could not trade appropriately, and "furthermore . . . that the French are destroyed, the cities are taken, and the spindles are burned."[35] It was a demonstrable lie, he insisted, and violated the Overhills' obligation of securing the nation to the French alliance. Live up to your commitments, he told the Overhills, and he would "not refrain from going to war against" Carolina.[36] Kerlérec subsequently sent Antoine Lantagnac to Chota, where he offered goods, soldiers, and cannons to induce a siege of Fort Prince George.[37] He demanded that the ministre de la marine step up support in light of the August 1760 Overhill capture of Fort Loudoun, noting that a distribution chain already was in place because of Lantagnac's (along with two unnamed Mvskoke headmen's) established links there.[38] In February 1761 he made Oconostota a "captain and great medal chief of all the detachments which shall go to war against the enemy and in the service of the French Nation." All French officers, he declared, would have "to regard and treat the said Okana-Stoté as a faithful ally devoted to the service of the French Nation."[39] Even as the British and the Cherokees pursued détente in 1761, Étienne François, Duc de Choiseul, congratulated Kerlérec "for inciting the Cherokees to fight the English, even though the French have not been able to provide all their needs."[40]

Nor did the French presence disappear from Overhill country and the Tennessee corridor after the Anglo-Cherokee War concluded. In 1762 Kerlérec reached out to "the Cherokees, Choctaws, Abekas, Alibamos, and other [Southern] Indian nations" to distribute supplies. He further ordered Lantagnac to "bring him ... six respected Cherokees ... to New Orleans." His explicit purpose, he stated, was "to discuss ways of protecting the Illinois by destroying all the English establishments in that area."[41] Such efforts convinced both General Sir Jeffrey Amherst and Sir William Johnson that, far from retreat, the French actually were *enhancing* their presence along the Tennessee corridor.[42] Henry Timberlake supplemented this paranoia with the observation that the Overhills remained "much attached to the French, who have the prudence, by familiar politeness (which costs but little, and often does a great deal) and conforming themselves to their ways and temper, to conciliate the inclinations of almost all the Indians they are acquainted with, while the pride of our officers often disgusts them."[43]

Two other (interrelated) observations are in order. First, in light of the loss of Fort Duquesne (1758) and Montreal (1760), a cynic might suggest that the French desperately wanted to play the Overhills off the British, other Cherokee regions, and conceivably even other Native polities to secure their position on the continent—precisely the opposite of the trope that Indigenous people maintained their agency by playing off the European powers. Second, Overhill

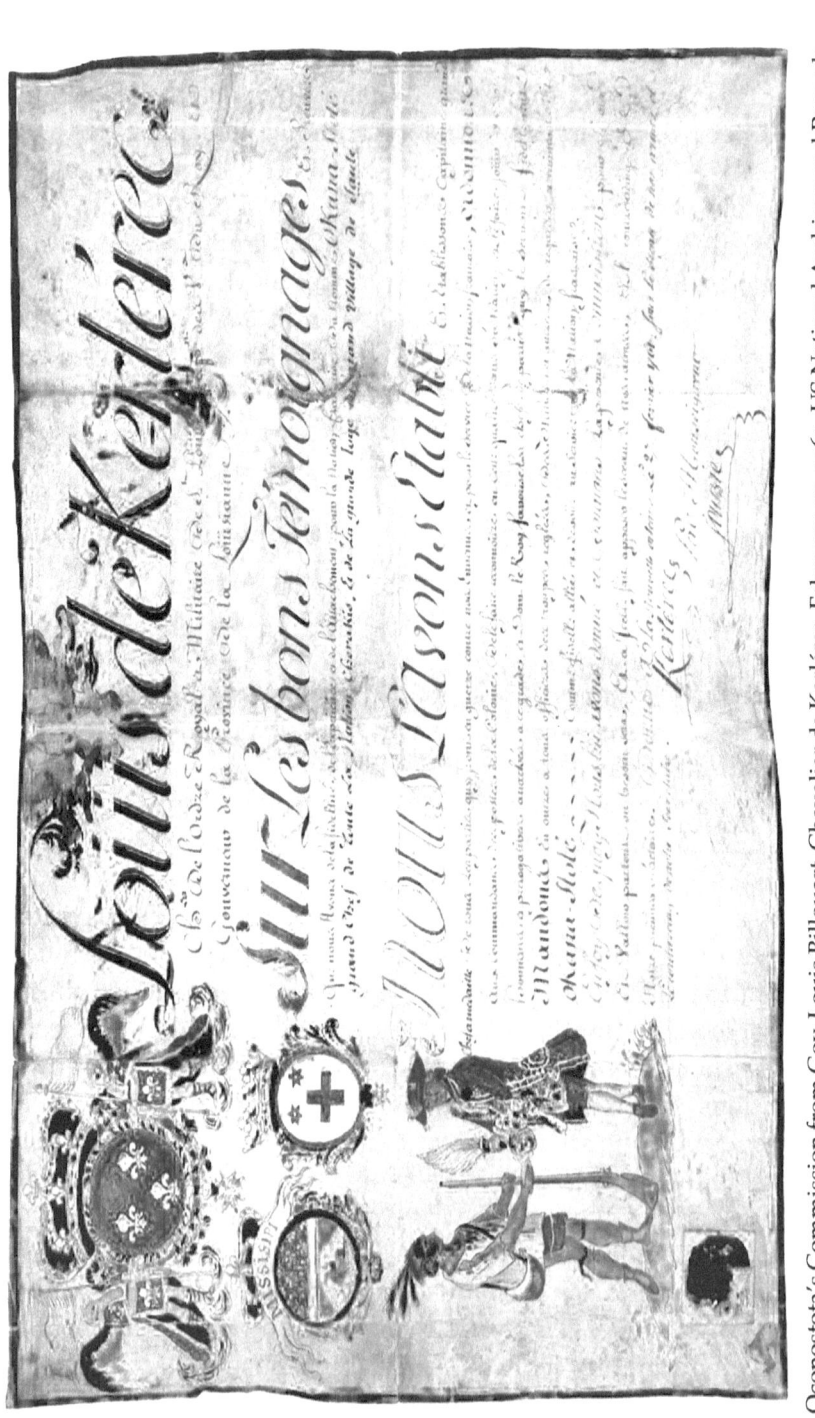

Oconostota's Commission from Gov. Louis Billouart, Chevalier de Kerlérec, February 27, 1761. US National Archives and Records Administration.

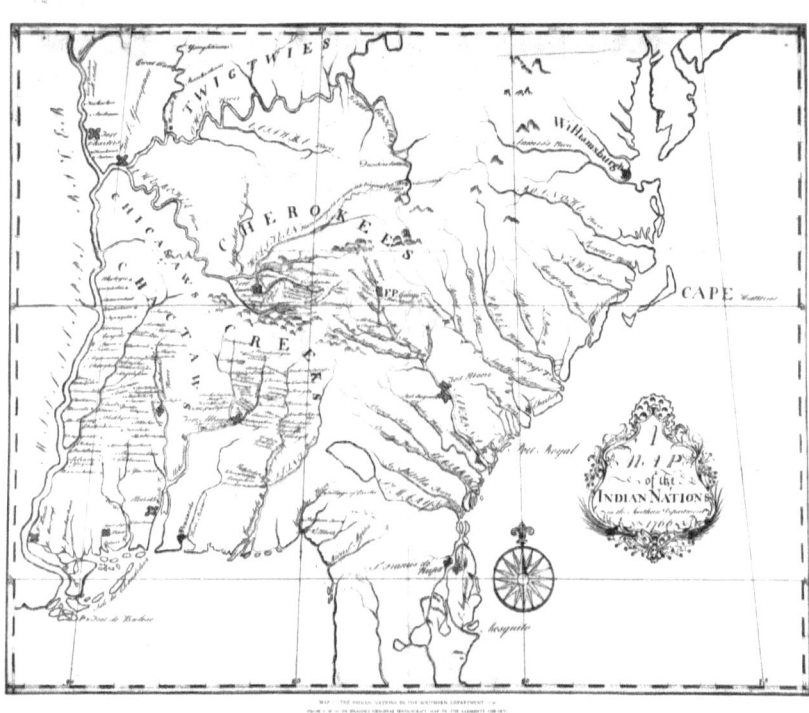

A map of the Indian nations in the Southern Department, 1766, with Cherokees and Twightwees prominently displayed. WCL Image Bank, https://quod.lib.umich.edu /w/wc11ic/x-562/wc1000665.

connections to Louisiana provide a concrete example of how Native agendas could overlap with European initiatives. As noted in chapter 4, in this period the Overhills engaged in tense encounters with Twightwees, Mascoutens, Anishnaabeg, and other westward polities. Reaching out to Louisiana could well have served as a way for them to acquire help in brokering a Native armistice. It certainly would fit with multiple extant (if fleeting) snapshots of inter-Indigenous diplomacy taking place in that moment. In 1760 William Lyttelton's temporary replacement as South Carolina governor, William Bull II, warned General Amherst that the Overhills were reaching out to the French and their "Indians for assistance" in the war with Carolina.[44] If successful, he wrote, these efforts could free the Overhills to focus more systematically on the British conflict.

And that, in turn, could provoke "a general Southern Indian war" that might cost the empire both Carolina and Georgia.[45]

Other leaders agreed, hoping to undermine Overhill-westward détente before it negatively affected the colonies. In December 1760 Deputy Northern Indian Superintendent George Croghan explicitly attempted to influence the Anglo-Cherokee War by encouraging Odawas (along with Wyandots and Potawatamis) to fight rather than accept Overhill diplomatic outreach. "If they want diversion after the Fateague of Hunting," he wrote of Odawa men, "there is your Natural Enemy's the Cherokees, with whome you have been long at War."[46] A year later he gloated that "the Cherokees, are Natural Enemies of the Western Indians that the French will not get any Nation that lives on the Ohio; or the Lakes; from the Illanois Upwards, to Join the Cherokees."[47] He was apparently unaware that at that same moment a man called Pierre Roubaud was reporting to William Johnson of an inter-Indigenous council at Kahnawake on the St. Lawrence River. "The subject of those Councils was upon Speeches brought to them from the Ohio by some Ottawawas & even by the Cherokees from Carolina," he explained. "These Speeches are to reunite all the Indians in the same Sentiment."[48] Only a few years thereafter Southern Indian Superintendent John Stuart warned Gen. Thomas Gage that an Illinois delegation was in New Orleans to see whether Kerlérec could "mediate between them & the Cherokees to procure them a peace."[49]

In the end, Overhill-westward détente proved elusive, and the impact of their continued confrontations would reverberate for at least the next two decades. It would be a mistake, however, to ignore the potential influence of these conflicts and negotiations—not to mention Fort Massac and the 1756 Franco-Overhill treaty—on the Overhill approach to the war with Carolina. If the fate of the trans-Appalachian west was the great problem of North American (and perhaps Atlantic) history from 1754 to 1815, then that conflict—and the Overhills more specifically—were critical elements of the struggle. [50]

Cherokees and Trans-Appalachia after 1761

After two years of violence South Carolina readily went along when Cherokee leaders pursued a resolution to their conflict. In the resulting 1761 treaty both sides agreed to exchange captives and to establish a formal boundary separating Aniyunwiya country from their colonial neighbors. (The location of that line placed a sizeable amount of Lower town territory in South Carolina.)[51] Thereafter the Anglo-Cherokee relationship was on some level restored. A year later, the British Empire even welcomed a Cherokee delegation to London to symbolize the rejuvenation of the Chain of Friendship.[52]

Several issues lurked behind South Carolina's agreement to end the war, but two stand out. First, imperial accountants increasingly concluded that continuing it would be expensive—to the tune of at least £100,000 Sterling, according to the new South Carolina governor Thomas Boone.[53] Given that the imperial debt had jumped from £73 million to at least £137 million because of the Seven Years' War, many at the Exchequer were loath to add more.[54] Second, and directly related, was the dawning comprehension that trans-Appalachia remained well beyond Britain's ability to control, whatever the perceived implications of the global victory over the French. It stymied long-imagined continental extensions, called into question the structural integrity of the empire in North America, and ensured that the Overhills would remain an important element of British western calculations.

The experiences of Lt. Thomas Morris offer an indirect but excellent entryway for illustrating this latter point. In August 1764 Morris embarked on a mission from Point aux Cedrés on Lake Erie both to proclaim British control over the *pays des Illinois* and to appeal for peace with the polities involved in Pontiac's War. Within days he became acutely aware that both missions were likely to fail. Long before the expedition could reach La Belle Rivière, unhappy Odawas and Twightwees diverted it to towns along the Maumee River. Once there, Odawa sachem Pontiac proclaimed to Morris not only that "the English were liars" but that "his father (the french king) was not crushed (rubbing one hand over ye other) as they said." He then presented Morris a letter "full of the most improbable falshoods" that the French Empire continued to encourage westward nations to block the extension of British jurisdiction in the Ohio valley. A few days later, in a powerful display of performative symbolism, an unnamed Miami sachem dressed in a British uniform acquired from Sir William Johnson before informing Morris that they could not trust the English. Meanwhile, an unnamed Mohawk absconded with the expedition's supplies, while Shawnees and Lenapes urged Miami leaders to execute the British agent before he could proceed further.[55]

All told, Morris spent roughly three weeks in the upper Ohio valley. When not fearing the imminence of his death, he described an Indigenous world of remarkable pace and complexity. Illinois polities such as the Kickapoos entered and left the area, no doubt taking their observations of Morris's expedition to their leadership. It would have been reinforced by Odawas loyal to Pontiac, who themselves spent significant time in the *pays des Illinois*. Shawnees and Lenapes departed for Ouiatanon on the Wabash to encourage Weas to kill the English expedition. Others left to negotiate with St. Joseph's River Potawatamis.

Shortly after Morris finally was released and returned to Detroit, Ensign Gavin Cochrane reported from Overhill country that the French at Fort Massac were "very Assiduous in sending for different tribes of Indians in their Alliance to whom they gave talks, ammunition, guns, flints, tomahawks, & knives, desiring them to go to War against the English & their allies, to kill all & not trouble them with prisoners."[56] The intelligence came from an Overhill man recently at Massac and seemed to confirm what Pontiac had boasted to Morris. It also confirmed newly appointed commander in chief Thomas Gage's suspicion that "the French at the Ilinois" were furnishing Lenapes and Shawnees with a "Considerable Quantity" of arms and ammunition.[57] The combination convinced Gage that trans-Appalachian confrontations could extend into the foreseeable future.

That Cochrane's intelligence came from Overhill country, however, suggested that Cherokees could offer a solution to the dilemma. It was not a new idea. Only a year before, Gage had thought of the

Aniyunwiya as good candidates to serve "as mediators in taking possession of Illinois" when an expedition under Maj. Arthur Loftus left New Orleans with that mandate. (In a pattern of futility repeated by Morris, Loftus quickly gave up due to Indigenous challenges and rumors of opposition from Louisiana's government.[58]) In 1764 Gage again invoked the idea by ordering Southern Indian Superintendent John Stuart to inquire whether "it may be possible to engage the Cherokees perhaps, to Seize the Persons & Goods of [French] Traders, as they go up the Ohio."[59] "Understanding that Nation extends [to the mouth of the Ohio]," and that they were "almost the only Indians who trade at Fort Massiac," Gage felt confident that if they were offered the appropriate gifts and diplomacy, the Overhills could help.[60] An important British benefit would be that it might short-circuit potential collaborations between the combatants then engaging the British army north of the Ohio River and their perceived Overhill allies. Agreeing with William Johnson that Shawnees in particular "have some connections with ye Cherokees [and] will probably fly to them" for safe harbor, he ordered Stuart "to represent to the Cherokees, that the Retreat it's Reported, they have promised to the Shawnese, is a Breach of Friendship with us."[61] Failure in this regard, he feared, could well translate into "Eternal broils with the Twigtwees, Shawnese, Ottawas, and the rest of the Western Tribes."[62]

Gage seemed to have fallen victim to the same logic that had negatively affected William Lyttelton, James Glen, William Bull, and others going back to the 1730s—that the subjecthood implied by the Chain of Friendship translated into exclusive alliance and support.[63] His willingness to tap into trans-Appalachian geopolitical complexity placed the British even more at the mercy of regional tensions such as those affecting Loftus and Morris and which had framed Overhill activities for decades.[64] Merely a few examples illuminate the situation. In 1762 George Croghan reported that Weas had left Ouiatanon "to fight the Cherokees."[65] A year later unnamed western Natives asked the British for paint, "Powder & Ball and some Knives, as they are all Going to War against our Enemies the Cherokees."[66] And in 1764—only a few months before the Morris expedition was diverted to the area, in fact—Henry Gladwyn reported that towns along the Maumee River "are all Going to War against our Enemies the Cherokees."[67] In early 1765, meanwhile, a French informant called Lagautrais reported that Potowatamis had "killed 21 Charaqui" in Illinois and feared that open war could result.[68] Later that year Philip Pittman informed Maj. Robert Farmar in Overhill country that he planned "to engage 12 or 14 [Overhills] to proceed with me to the Illinois falling down the Cherokee River." He hoped his guides would be willing to "carry with them the white Colours in order to talk with the Illinois." If successful, he planned to remain there for the winter and establish British jurisdiction; otherwise, he would "drive down the Mississippi with the Current."[69]

Nothing came of his efforts, but it did not stop further British attempts. That same year another expedition, this time led by Alexander Fraser, attempted to establish British jurisdiction in the *pays des Illinois*. Yet again Cherokee issues interfered. Upon arriving, for example, Fraser was met by skeptical unnamed Natives who forced him to explain that he was "an English Chief come to acquaint their Nation that the Shawanese, Delaware, and all the Nations on the Ohio had made Peace." The response was telling: "They said it was very well, that they thought we had been Cherokees."[70] Like Morris and Loftus before him, Fraser's expedition did not secure British jurisdiction. (He even was warned by the Native representatives that any subsequent Briton in Illinois could face execution.) Not long thereafter another group led by George Croghan arrived from Fort Pitt. Kickapoos and Mascoutens explained to him that the French "had warned them that the English were leagued with the Cherokees, bent on enslaving all Illinois people and on taking Indian land." These men even "said that they had mistaken Croghan's Shawnee and Delaware escorts for invading Cherokees."[71] In December 1765, meanwhile, Gage learned that an Overhill raiding party had just returned from "war against the Wabash and Twightwee."[72]

The problems continued for the rest of the decade. In 1766 Attakullakulla informed John Stuart that the Overhills were "at war" with Twightwees, Ouiatanons, and Kickapoos, reporting that young Overhill men had just returned from "war in Illinois with a scalp."[73] Chota headman Kittagusta (known by the British as the Prince of

Chota) explained further at that year's congress at Fort Prince George: "Our enemies," he revealed, have "attacked us this year in all parts of our Country in greater Numbers & more frequent than we have ever known."[74] English Overhill agent Alexander Cameron described one such confrontation between an unnamed group and "a hunting Party of the Cherokees down the Tenassie." In that event four of the attackers had died, along with three Cherokees "& several wounded on both sides." Although the Overhills had been vastly outnumbered, Cameron explained that they protected themselves by securing a blockhouse constructed by Attakullakulla the previous winter "for his own defense in his hunting Camp."[75] For his part, Kittagusta felt these reports were crucial for Stuart to understand not just because "their Hatchets . . . are very Sharp" but also because they "have been lifted up against White as well as Red Men in our Nation."[76]

Aniyunwiya-Haudenosaunee diplomacy offers still further insight into trans-Appalachian freneticism. As noted in earlier chapters, the two Iroquoian-speaking groups had maintained a tense relationship for most of the eighteenth century, and a key issue revolved around *Indigenous* notions of jurisdictional boundaries. The Haudenosaunee had long claimed control over the Ohio valley and *pays des Illinois* and were displeased that Overhill influences overlapped. By the 1760s the Cherokees particularly—if implicitly—challenged Iroquois claims to a swath of territory between the Great Kanawha and Tennessee Rivers.[77] The Haudenosaunee insisted that it belonged to them by right of conquest and flatly rejected the Cherokee claim that it formed part of their extended hunting grounds.[78] Despite William Johnson's assurances to the contrary, they could not have been happy when the British Empire informed Cherokees that Six Nations "claims have not been Suffered to extend beyond the Conhoway and its Confluence with the Ohio."[79] Working through these two competing contentions factored directly into the 1768 land cession negotiations at Fort Stanwix, New York, and Hard Labor, South Carolina.[80]

By 1766, however, the Aniyunwiya and the Haudenosaunee seemed to have a common problem in the form of the westward polities. Six Nations claims to jurisdiction over the Ohio valley implied that westward groups were subordinate to them within the Covenant Chain—and had no say, for example, in the land cession to which the Haudenosaunee agreed at Fort Stanwix. Kaskaskias, Kickapoos, Cahokias, Mascoutens, Miamis, Weas, Shawnees, and Lenapes thought otherwise and worked hard to achieve a greater level of intertribal cooperation at the expense of their Native "uncles."[81] It was increasingly clear to Onondaga that they could not control their supposed subordinates, and their power was at stake. Despite disagreements relative to the Kanawha and Tennessee Rivers, they agreed to a peace when Cherokees reached out to them. Explained Oconostota in 1768, the two polities had "buried the Hatchet and cleared the path of every thorn and obstacle that rendered it bad; some of the Northern Warriors are now at Chote sitting upon a White Seat."[82] William Johnson provided a telling description of the Haudenosaunee satisfaction with the alliance. "I must say," he wrote to George Croghan, "I never See the Six Nations so hearty in any thing, as in this Peace."[83] Less than a year later Cherokees traveled to Iroquoia to encourage their new allies "to join their Arms with yours against Several Tribes of Western & Southern Indians Enemies to both."[84]

With the Haudenosaunee issue (momentarily) settled by 1768, Oconostota informed John Stuart that westward polities represented the major Indian threat to Overhill country. They had "shut their Ears to the Talks of their Father Sir William Johnson," he explained at the Hard Labor congress, "and continue to strike us." Like Kittagusta two years earlier, Oconostota observed that "it is not us alone who they strike the white people's blood runs as well as ours they make no distinction." Only a few days before the congress at Hard Labor, in fact, "they killd a great man of our Nation and a white Trader near Great Telico." He finished with a rhetorical flourish: "Father," he said, "I am much beaten by those Western Indians the Piankashaws, Youghtanous, Twightwees, Kickapous, Meamis, Otowawas and other western Nations [and] you are struck by them also." Although he had agreed once before to "Sit still whilst a peace was Negotiating with them," now was the time for aggressive action.[85]

Stuart understood quite well that western polities "were in an Hostile State with us, as well as [Cherokees], [an opinion] Confirmed by Intelligence of their Behavior on the Ohio, and at the Illinois."[86] Thus, he recommended that Oconostota go on the offensive (albeit without direct British military support—yet another example of the pattern established at Tugaloo in 1715). Although William Johnson might have something to say because of his "jurisdiction over the western nations," Stuart nevertheless advised that Cherokees could not "remain passive and Suffer your people and Traders to be killed with Impunity."[87] Overhill leaders did not need another invitation. At a congress at Congarees, South Carolina, in 1770, Oconostota informed Stuart that they had sent parties to attack "Piankashaws and other Western Tribes." Stuart responded positively and reinforced his delight at the Cherokee-Haudenosaunee alliance, telling Oconostota that "You are certainly right to strengthen Yourselves by Joining with the Northern Indians against them."[88]

The British hoped to use Haudenosaunee-Cherokee diplomacy to threaten Illinois and Wabash valley polities and improve their chances of stabilizing trans-Appalachia. In 1769 Lt. John Wilkins explained to a gathering at Vincennes that the British had too long "endured the evil actions of a number of his ill disposed Children." They were tired, he said, of "their bad Conduct toward their Fathers in many different parts of the Country & particular . . . on the Wabash & Ohio Rivers." He informed his audience that Iroquois, Shawnees, and Lenapes "as well as the Cherokees & Chikesaws to the Southward, are now but one People with their Fathers the English."[89] He then delivered an ultimatum: rein in westward warriors and give immediate evidence of having done so. Otherwise, the British would interpret it "as an open Declaration of War, and shall directly send an Account thereof to the great King your Father, and to all the Indians with whom We are in Friendship, all of whom are now ready to join us in Extirpating you from the face of the Earth."[90] If unaware of the evolving efforts to construct a pan-Indian identity that undermined such threats, Wilkins and his military commanders did understand that they were in no position to make them—and trans-Appalachian polities knew it. When they called the bluff, the British could do little about it.

Western Problems Meet Eastern Corruption

Exacerbating the British trans-Appalachian headache was increasingly rapid, mostly uncontrolled land surveying, speculation, and settlement on the part of Euro-American colonists. If the empire was ill-equipped to deal with inter-Indigenous complexities, it certainly did not want its subjects exacerbating the situation. That conviction led the government in October 1763 to establish a colonial boundary loosely corresponding to the crest of the Appalachian Mountains.[91] That line, said a Royal Proclamation, Anglo-Americans could not cross until the "Royal Pleasure be known." Colonial officials also would have to halt private land sales, cease issuing trans-Appalachian land grants, and ensure that Indians "not be molested or disturbed in the Possession of such Parts of our Dominions and Territories as, having been ceded or purchased by us, are reserved to them, or any of them, as their Hunting Grounds."[92] It was a temporary fix, but this proclamation meant for the colonies to operate within imperial parameters. Any subsequent expansion would have to follow protocols, the most important of which was that land could only transfer from Indigenous to European ownership through formal congresses. According to the *Oxford English Dictionary*, a congress is a "formal meeting or assembly of delegates or representatives for the discussion or settlement of some question; *spec.* (in politics) of envoys, deputies, or plenipotentiaries representing sovereign states, or of sovereigns themselves, for the settlement of international affairs."[93] By acknowledging the congressional nature of the encounter, the British Empire conceded the fact of Indigenous sovereignty.

Colonial surveyors and speculators powerfully disliked such restraint, pinning their right to land in the philosophy of men such as John Locke and Emmer de Vattel. "The savages of North America had no right to appropriate all that vast continent to themselves," Vattel had written in the *Law of Nations*, "and since they were unable to inhabit the whole of those regions, other nations might without injustice settle in some parts of them, provided they left the natives a sufficiency of land."[94] Taking that insistence to heart, Anglo-American surveyors, speculators, and squatters dismissed the diplomatic complexities of Native sovereignty and undermined the ministry's policies almost as soon as they became aware of them. In addition to the protocols established in the proclamation, colonials cast aside obligations required by congresses at Augusta, Georgia (1763), Fort Stanwix, New York (1768), Hard Labor, South Carolina (1768), and Lochaber, South Carolina (1770), among others.

Government was exasperated by such behavior, as a set of instructions from George III to North Carolina governor William Tryon illustrates: "Indians," it observed, "make great Complaints that Settlements have been made and Possession taken of Lands the Property of which they have by Treaties reserved to themselves." Particularly galling to His Majesty's government was that the "Chief Officers of Our said Colonies, regardless of the Duty they Owe to Us and of the Welfare and Security of Our Colonies, have Countenanced such unjust Claims and Pretensions by passing Grants of the Lands so pretended to have been purchased of the Indians." Such blatant violations of the 1763 proclamation would have "fatal Effects [and] would attend to a Discontent amongst the Indians in the present situation of Affairs," Tryon was informed. The government was unequivocal on the point. "Upon all Occasions," it instructed, "support and protect the said Indians in their just Rights and Possessions, and keep Inviolable the Treaties and Compacts which have been Entered into with them."[95] To translate: colonies had to respect the rule of law and stop exacerbating a western situation already beyond British control.[96]

To drive home the point further, the ministry instructed that neither Tryon nor any other official in North Carolina "upon any pretence whatever upon pain of Our highest Displeasure, and of being forthwith removed from Your or his Office, pass any Grant or Grants to any Persons whatever of any Lands within or adjacent to the Territories possessed or occupied by the said Indians or the Property or Possession of which has at any Time been reserved to or claimed by them." The colony also would have to proclaim publicly that squatters would be removed from Indigenous land, and so that no misunderstandings would arise, North Carolina would have to publicize "amongst the several Tribes of Indians living within the [Province] to the End that Our Royal Will and Pleasure in the Premises may be made known, and that the Indians may be apprized of Our determined Resolution to support them in their just Rights."[97]

It did not help. Patterns of corruption became so predictable that Native diplomats explicitly called out the British government over it. In 1768, for example, the Haudenosaunee informed Sir William Johnson that although he represented "a Government and Laws[,] you don't prevent [land fraud]." They found it ironic: "You often tell us we don't restrain our people, and that you do so with yours," they observed, but "your Words differ more from your Actions than ours do."[98] If an empire built on written laws could not make its "people do what they are desired [and] prevent all this, and if they wont let us alone you should shake them by the head." Or perhaps, suggested the delegates, the government had "no Mind to hinder them?" If that was the case, they could do it on behalf of the British. After all, Haudenosaunee "Legs are long and our Sight is good, that we can see a great way thro the Woods; We can see the Blood you have spilled and the Fences you have made, and surely it is but right that we should punish those who have done us all this Mischief."[99]

The Six Nations further expressed dismay on behalf of their Cherokee allies, noting that provincial boundary lines "have surrounded and stifled them."[100] The Aniyunwiya agreed wholeheartedly. Exasperated by Euro-American indifference to formally negotiated boundaries, Oconostota declared at the 1768 Hard Labour congress that Cherokees would agree once more to new lines. Thereafter, however, he would personally "dig a ditch" over which Whites could no longer pass.[101] John Stuart was on board with this metaphorical action, promising Cherokees that after the boundaries were finalized, "you may rest satisfied that none of his Majesty's Subjects shall with Impunity violate the Treaty now entered into by invading your Rights."[102]

Two years later he had to admit the hollowness of that declaration. Virginians were undermining the Hard Labour boundary, and Stuart was outraged. "His Majesty's instructions render it my Duty to Endeavour to see justice done you," he insisted to the Cherokees, "and his Express orders prevent my Ratifying any other Boundary Line, than what he has been pleased to point out. I have humbly submitted to His Majesty's Ministers my Sentiments on the pretensions of the province of Virginia, and wait for further Instructions which as soon as I receive shall be Communicated to you in the mean Time the Line agreed upon at Hard Labour the 14 October 1768 remains valid & is the true Boundary."[103] Stuart was equally frustrated with Cherokees, however: by the 1770s some Cherokee leaders had begun selling land directly to individual colonists, which violated the 1763 Proclamation, was contrary to the spirit of the Congress of Hard Labour, and rendered "ineffectual the orders given by the King to prevent Encroachment on your Hunting Grounds." Cherokees, Stuart insisted, should deal only with imperial authority—not the provinces or locals. Otherwise, "if irregular people who settle on such Lands by your permission behave ill you are not to Complain or to expect any Redress from us."[104]

Oconostota did not disagree but blamed "Virginians" for coveting land at the expense of fairness and diplomatic balance. "They are always renewing their Demands, and are never satisfied," he observed. And despite their promises, they never followed through on sharing "their Bounty." The remedy, he suggested, was for the empire to retake control of the diplomatic ground.[105] Its representatives, after all, remembered imperial obligations, while "the Virginians pretend to have forgotten what was said at Augusta and agreed upon at Hard Labour."[106] Overhill leaders added another layer to colonial corruption at a 1776 meeting with Stuart's brother Henry. "They said that when Mr Cameron ran the line of Virginia," observed Stuart, "there were people who had set themselves down on this side of the Boundary Line; they were ordered to remove off but they begged as their crops were then on the ground that they might be allowed to reap them and that they would certainly remove the Spring following." When spring came, "some of them went away but others and more people came in their room [and decided] to stay on the land, they pretend that they purchased it."[107]

For his part, General Gage was sympathetic to such complaints. "I am sorry you find Reason every where to complain of the fraudulent and bad Practices of the Traders, which I wish was in my Power to remedy," he wrote to John Stuart in 1772.

I have heard of those Complaints as long as I have heared of America, and tho' various schemes have been formed to put the Trade under proper Restrictions, the old Complaints continue, and I despair of seeing it upon a good Footing. You have had much Trouble as well as Sir Willm Johnson in settling the Boundarys throughout the Continent and a large Sum it has Cost the Government. . . . The People in some Places have already passed the Boundarys, the Indians Complain of their Building and planting beyond the Line, and they talk of making Purchases of considerable Extent of the Indians beyond the Limits fixed in 1768.[108]

By 1774 eastern encroachment had only gotten worse. Even as Parliament was responding to the Boston Tea Party, Virginians attempted to assert control over undeniably Indigenous land at the confluence of the Great Kanawha and Ohio Rivers. Gage believed the (predictable) subsequent conflict—known as Lord Dunmore's War and which included Cherokee fighters—was nearly criminal.[109] Mere months before Lexington and Concord, he insisted to Shawnees and Lenapes that it "was Intirely a War with [Virginia, and] that none of the Kings troops had appeared against them." He also proclaimed that "his Majesty was not pleased with the Virginians for what they had done."[110] Frustrations increased when word leaked that Virginian Richard Henderson's Transylvania Company appeared to have "purchased" twenty-seven thousand square miles of the southern Ohio valley from Cherokees.[111] A few years later Cherokee headman the Old Tassel informed U.S. commissioners that Henderson was a "liar" who had forged Cherokee names on the deeds to the purchase.[112] Although Virginia, North Carolina, and the British Empire rejected this Transylvania Purchase, the damage was done.

Trans-Appalachia, in short, remained far outside of British control after 1761, new cartography and imagined imperial extension notwithstanding. Perhaps Thomas Gage best illuminated this reality. "Upon the whole," he wrote James Grant in autumn 1764, "as Matters now stand, the Consent and good Will of the Indians is the best and only Security we can have for settleing" the region.[113] In such an environment the British Empire needed the Aniyunwiya. Despite the devastations associated with the Anglo-Cherokee War, then, the Overhills between 1761 and 1774 largely remained where they had been for the previous century: a crucial element of an Indigenous world that shaped the parameters of European empire in North America.

Yet if they did not necessarily enter a period of declension, the internal dynamics of Cherokee life certainly became far more complex after 1761. The declining Cherokee population found itself dividing along generational lines. Identities began to shift, as regional consolidation brought ever-stronger ideas of a singular Nation. Even as the South Carolina conflict encouraged that sense of consolidated nationalism, an evolving spiritual renewal movement pushed some Cherokees to start thinking in pan-Indigenous ways. The resulting buildup of internal tensions eventually exploded in the Chickamauga split of 1776. That story is complicated and in desperate need of more systematic research.[114] Inter-Indigenous trans-Appalachian encounters between 1774 and 1800 also need closer examination, with a particular eye toward understanding the Native world as an important topic in and of itself. Not every revolutionary-era western encounter, after all, included Europeans or Euro-Americans. Whether Cherokee or Chickamauga, both groups continued to embark on trading, spiritual, diplomatic, and military expeditions in the Tennessee corridor.[115]

The ultimate fate of the Cherokee people and of Indigenous trans-Appalachia was far from settled in 1774.[116] But if that was true, it is also fair to say that the onset of the War of American Independence forced a shift in the way Native polities understood themselves, not to mention how they related to one another, to European polities, and to this emerging new creature, the American.[117] A brief overview of these matters provides a fitting place to conclude this study.

Epilogue

Cherokees, Trans-Appalachia, and the Era of the American Revolution, 1774–1800

It is fair to say that the War of American Independence had a substantive impact on trans-Appalachia in general and the Aniyunwiya more specifically. If they felt they were peripheral to what seemed like a European "family squabble," the conflict nevertheless unleashed forces that both made them "Principals in this War," as British trader Alexander Cameron warned, and upended at least a century of Native-newcomer protocol.[1] In particular, the rebellion set in motion what historian Eric Hinderaker has described as an empire of liberty—a political experiment rooted in land acquisition and that cared little for Indigenous alliance building as pursued by the British, French, or Spanish.[2] By 1774, the failure of British authority to control colonists (and after 1776, the lack of any meaningful effort to do so by the new Republic) allowed an increasing number of Euro-Americans to survey, claim, sell, and squat on trans-Appalachian land, regardless of title, Native approval, or geopolitical realities.

In the area along the Tennessee corridor these endeavors became remarkably unscrupulous and violent. Edenic mythology notwithstanding, the region now known as Kentucky became infamous in the late 1770s and 1780s for bloody confrontations between Euro-Americans and Native polities. In the U.S. territory south of the Ohio River (now the state of Tennessee), the state department estimated that as of 1791 a White population of only 35,698 (28,649 in the eastern part of the territory, 7,049 in the Cumberland River settlements to the west) had claimed all but three hundred thousand acres—a realization that significantly limited the new government's perceived ability to reduce its crushing debt burden.[3] The Cherokee leader Bloody Fellow put an Indigenous spin on the situation in 1792 when he informed territorial governor William Blount that the Washington administration had asked Cherokees not to wage war against Whites in the territory, and that in return, settlers "should not encroach on our land. But in place of that they are daily encroaching and building on our land; this is not what [we] had agreed upon."[4] Agent James Seagrove reinforced the point when he informed the government that Native attacks near the Cumberland settlements were occurring "on lands that never have been sold, or ceded by the Indians; that those people have repeatedly been ordered off by the Indians, but will not go."[5]

Seagrove and Bloody Fellow illuminate that in the emerging empire of liberty the Aniyunwiya were less a polity with which to negotiate than an adversary to overcome—violently, if necessary.[6] In the first two years of the war alone, Patriot militias "tramped through . . . the Tennessee Valley, leaving smoking ruins and burned cornfields behind them."[7] Partially, such carnage was associated with efforts to find Loyalists fleeing into Native country.[8] Partially, it was retribution for perceived Cherokee aggression against Patriot interests in Virginia and the Carolinas. Either way, the violence became a powerful means by which to procure large swaths of land. In the Treaty of DeWitt's Corner (1777) the Cherokees ceded roughly one million acres to South Carolina to stem Patriot aggression. (Notably, they also agreed to hand over White captives and to cease taking horses. More on that point below.) Later that year, they ceded another four million acres to North Carolina and Virginia via the Treaty of Long Island of the Holston.[9]

The two land cessions came on top of the frustration associated with the 27,000 square miles claimed by Richard Henderson's Transylvania Company in 1775, and at a moment when Cherokees already were rethinking national identity, dealing with spiritual renewal movements, and debating how pan-Indigenous alliance building connected to both.[10] As early as 1770 John Stuart had pointed to attempts by westward polities "to form a general confederacy of all the southern nations to recover and maintain possession of their lands." Creeks, Chickasaws, and Choctaws, he said, had chosen not "to accede as they did not think themselves aggrieved in that respect." The Cherokees, however, took a softer line. Ongoing confrontations with Illinois and Wabash polities made it impossible at that moment "to declare their concurrence," but they *were* willing to receive "from the deputies a painted hatchet which remained ... until the present distracted state of America has afforded such an opportunity as they wished for."[11] By 1777 outrage over land grabs suggested to many younger and spiritually awakened Cherokees that that opportunity had arrived, making it increasingly difficult for older Cherokee leaders to maintain control.[12] That spring a split occurred, as hundreds of people led by Dragging Canoe left the Cherokee towns to settle on Chickamauga Creek. Soon known as the Chickamaugas, this group's bolder anti-Patriot stance added a notable western layer to the Revolutionary era. Dragging Canoe (and his supporters) would engage in "repeated attacks ... upon the settlements west of the Appalachians" between 1778 and 1796.[13]

Indigenous Trans-Appalachia in the Era of the Revolution

Yet if violent and divisive, the Revolution did not cause Cherokees to spiral inexorably into an era of irrelevance. As had been the case for Englishmen in the 1630s and 1640s, the small stations that began to dot the Tennessee corridor—from which surveyors, speculators, and settlers projected their presence—did little more than tenuously place these people in demonstrably Native country, where *Native* issues remained most resonant.[14] Sometimes those concerns related to European affairs; sometimes they did not; and sometimes the two overlapped. In 1778 and 1779, for example, Cherokees expressed a willingness to accommodate British requests for help at Fort Vincennes, with the ulterior motive that it would put them in closer contact with Illinois and Wabash polities.[15] Moreover, as historian Kathleen DuVal has suggested, by the 1790s many Cherokees were coming to view the Osages as a threat at least as great as (if not greater than) the fragile new republic.[16]

Events at or near Vincennes reveal another notable issue: that pan-Indigenous efforts at alliance building seemed on some level to cause an abatement in confrontations between the Overhills and westward polities. In 1776, while discussing the possibility of confederation at Chota, a deputation of fourteen Mohawks, Ottawas, Shawnees, and Lenapes announced "that now all the Nations of Indians were at peace with one another; that they had sent messengers to the Oubash to the Tribes there to secure their friendship, and that they would not trouble the Cherokees any more."[17] Two years later John Stuart and Fort Vincennes commander Henry Hamilton called for a gathering of Odawas, Wyandots, Shawnees, Senecas, Lenapes, Potawatamis, and Cherokees to assemble at the mouth of the Tennessee River both to support Loyalists traveling the Ohio River and to attack Patriot interests along the Virginia and Pennsylvania frontiers (among other reasons).[18] In January 1779 rumors floated that "Cherokees, Chickasaws, Choctaws, and Alibamos plan to send out four parties this spring—one towards Kaskaskia to attack the rebels, one to the Ohio to assist the Shawnees, one to visit Ft. Vincennes and make peace with the Wabash Indians, and one to the mouth of the Cherokee River to intercept rebel boats."[19] The situation so concerned Patriot leaders that George Rogers Clark was sent to disrupt the rumored gathering.[20] His invasion, and subsequent capture of Fort Vincennes, may have provided Patriots with a western victory, but it did nothing to stop Cherokee and Chickamauga cooperation with westward polities.[21] By 1787 some Chickamaugas had even left "Tennessee" to settle in Miamitown, in the heart of what had been a center of anti-Overhill sentiment for most of the eighteenth century.[22] Inter-Indigenous negotiations outside the purview of European and Euro-American witnesses would continue to frame life in trans-Appalachia and the Tennessee corridor for decades thereafter. A Spanish report circa 1796 illuminates the point, noting that negotiators could expect encounters in Kentucky with "the Chickasaws, Choctaws, Yuchis, Catawbas, Delawares, Mingoes, Wyandots, Six Nations, Shawnees, Chippewas, Hurons, Tawas (Odawa), Mawmees (Miamis), Piankeshaws, Vermillions, Wabash, Kickapoos, Osage, Kaskaskias, Illinois, Potawatamies, and the Sioux." Spanish officials would need to understand, however, that the "Cherokees are the most important tribe that live near Kentucky, and the Chickamaugas (one branch of the Cherokees) have numerous towns close to Kentucky."[23]

Responses to the Transylvania Purchase and to the 1777 treaties further illuminate Cherokee power in the extended Revolutionary era. In 1785 Chief Old Tassel informed U.S. commissioners that Richard Henderson was a "liar" who had forged names on the Transylvania land deeds.[24] An aggressive pushback is hardly surprising in such circumstances, and it ensured that, except for a brief reduction in violence in 1789 and 1790, Cherokees and Chickamaugas would aggressively assert their autonomy and power against Euro-American invasion.[25] The Treaty of DeWitt's corner is similarly revealing. Circa 1830, Cherokee leaders articulated that that treaty offered a clear recognition of the Nation's sovereignty by the new republic. Echoing Attakullakulla's responses to the Chain of Friendship seven decades earlier, the author Outalassi insisted in an 1829 issue of the *Cherokee Phoenix* that the treaty conferred upon South Carolina neither "a title to the soil or sovereignty of the Cherokee country." On the contrary, he explained, it had "been a treaty of *Peace*; and not of *cession*, [and that the commission's mandate was] to '*conclude a peace with the Cherokee Nation, upon such terms as may be just and equitable.*'"[26] Recognition of Cherokee sovereignty suggested that it was impossible for the state to transfer title to that land to anyone else—a crucial issue in the era when removal was intensely debated.[27]

Another revelation contained in the treaty comes through its requirement that Cherokees cease trading in horses. That never happened, but it offers insight into broader economic issues suggested earlier in this monograph: informal markets at the continent's riparian "confluence" did not go away in the 1770s, 1780s, or 1790s.[28] In 1778 and 1779, recall, Cherokees traveled towards Fort Vincennes because it put them in a position to interact with Illinois and Wabash polities.[29] Cumberland River settler James Robertson pointed out circa 1787 that "for some years past a trade has been carried on by some Frenchmen from the Wabash to the Indians on the Tennessee."[30] Only a year later, according to nineteenth-century historian J. G. M. Ramsay, Cherokees and Creeks halted a confrontation in what is now east Tennessee because they had acquired more goods than they could carry away for resale.[31]

Horses were perhaps the most valuable commodity in the Native South. In 1785 White settlers in East Tennessee reported that Cherokees were more focused on taking horses than engaging in battle.[32] Four years later so many horses were taken from the Cumberland River settlements that residents complained to the new George Washington administration about their "considerable" losses.[33] In 1791 those same settlers reported another round of horse theft and demanded that the administration do something to stop it.[34] In 1792 James White complained that Creeks "took from me the remains of a large stock of horses, into which I had turned much of my property. The rest they had plundered before."[35] The broader horse trade was so lucrative that in 1794 Governor Blount condemned Euro-American participants at "Swannano, North Carolina, Ocunnee Mountain, South Carolina, and Tugelo, Georgia" and demanded that the Washington administration "divide a company of Foederal Troops into three parts & station [them] at well chosen spots upon the Indian boundary near each of those places."[36]

Perhaps the Creek leader Alexander McGillivray best summarized trans-Appalachia in the era of the American Revolution. In 1785 he explained to West Florida governor Arturo O'Neill that "the whole continent is in confusion." For him, the solution was for "the three [European] kings [to] Settle the matter by dividing America between them."[37] Although no one else accepted this eventuality, there is no doubt that chaotic negotiations were developing between Natives, Anglo-Americans, the British, and the Spanish. It reinforces that trans-Appalachia was a hot zone defining the late eighteenth-century North American experience.[38] For historian François Furstenberg this fact led to existential questions for Natives, European empires, and American settlers alike: Would the region "become a permanent Native American country? Would it fall to some distant European power? Or, perhaps the most unlikely scenario of all, would it join with the United States?"[39]

More extensive research would illuminate the dynamic interplay of internal and inter-Indigenous issues with the external pressures associated with this hot zone. For now, it is enough to remember that the Revolution did not break the Cherokees. The ultimate fate of the Nation (and of Indigenous trans-Appalachia) was far from clear in 1776, 1783, or, for that matter, even 1815. And as nuanced and compelling as is the standard narrative of seventeenth- and eighteenth-century Cherokee history, it nevertheless cedes too much power to European ideas of dominance, jurisdictional control, and nationhood. Between 1670 and 1774, and into the era of the American Revolution, Euro-Americans misinterpreted political and diplomatic cues to overcome their limited practical reach, and North American historical (and cartographical) representations have suffered as a result. Properly framed and interpreted, Overhill (and Cherokee) trans-Appalachian experiences offer a powerful tool by which to rethink the centrality of Indigenous polities to the narrative of continental development.

APPENDIX A

Transcription of the 1730 Anglo-Cherokee Treaty and Cherokee Responses Thereto

Articles of Friendship & Commerce Cherokee Nation in South Carolina & His Majestey's Order, on Monday the 7th Day of September 1730.

WHEREAS You Scayagusta Oukah, Chief of the Town of Tassetsa;—You Scalelasken Ketagusta;—You Tethtove;—You Clogoillah;—You Colannah;—You Oucounacou;—have been deputed by Moytoy of Telliko, with the Consent and Approbation of the Whole Nation of the Cherokee Indians, at a general Meeting at Nikossen the 3d of April 1730 to attend Sr Alexander Cuming Bart to Great Britain, where you have seen the Great King George at whose Feet the said Sr Alexander Cuming, by express Authority for that Purpose from the said Moytoy and all the Cherokee People, has laid the Crown of your Nation, with the Scalps of your Enemies and Feathers of Glory, at His Majesty's Feet, in Token of your Obedience. Now the King of Great Britain, bearing love in His Heart to the powerful [ ] great Nation of the Cherokee Indians [ ] good Children and Subjects, His Maj[esty] has empowered us to treat with you and accordingly we now speak to you [ ] if the whole Nation of Cherokees, the Old Men, Young Men, Wives and Chil[dren] were all present, And you are to underst[and] the Words we speak as the Words of [the] Great King our Master, whom you [have] seen; And we shall understand the Words which you speak to us as the Words of all your People, with open and true Hearts to the Great King. And thereupon we give Fo[ ] Pieces of striped Duffles.

Hear then the Words of the Great King, whom you have seen, and who [has] commanded us to tell you, That the English every where on all Sides of the great Mountains and Lakes are His People and His Children, whom He loves; That their Friends are His Friends, and their Enemies are His Enemies; That He takes it kindly that the great Nation of Cherokees have sent you hither a great way, to brighten the Chain of Friendship [ ] People; That the Chain of Friendship between Him and the Cherokee Indians, is like the Sun, which both [ ] and of the English; That as there are no Spots or Blackness in the Sun, so is there not any Rust or Foulness in this Chain; And as the Great King has fastened one end of it to His own Breast, He desires you will carry the other end of the Chain, and fasten it well to the Breast of Moytoy of Telliko, and to the Breasts of your old Wise Men, your Cap^{ts} and all your People, never more to be broken or made loose; And hereupon we give Two Pieces of Blue Cloth.

The Great King and the Cherokee Indians, being thus fastned together by the Chain of Friendship, He has ordered His People & Children the English in Carolina, to trade with the Indians, and to furnish them with all manner of Goods that they want, and to make haste to build Houses, and to plant Corn, from Charles Town towards the Town o the Cherokees, behind the great Mountains, for He desires that the Indians and the English may live together as the Children of one Family, whereof the Great King is a kind and loving Father, And as the King has given His Land on both Sides of the great Mountains to His own Children the English, so He now gives to the Cherokee Indians the Priviledge of living where the please; And hereupon we give One Piece of Red Cloth.

The great Nation of Cherokees being now the Children of the Great King of Great Britain, and He their Father, the Cherokees must treat the English as Brethren of the same Family, and must be always ready, at the Governor's command, to fight against any Nation— whether they be White Men or Indians, who shall dare to molest or hurt the English; And hereupon we give Twenty Guns.

The Nation of the Cherokees shall on their Part take Care to keep the trading Path clean, and that there be no Blood in the Path where the English white Men tread, even tho' they should be accompany'd by any other People with whom the Cherokees are at War; Whereupon we give Four Hundred Pounds Weight of Gunpowder.

That the Cherokees shall not suffer their People to trade with the White Men of any other Nation but the English, nor permit White Men of any other Nation to build any Forts, Cabins, or plant Corn amongst them or near to any of the Indian Towns, or upon the Lands wch belong to the Great King; and if any such Attempt shall be made, you must acquaint the English Governor therewith and do whatever he directs in order to maintain and defend the Great King's Right to the Country of Carolina; Whereupon we give Five Hundred Pounds Weight of Swan Shott and Five Hundred Pounds Weight of Bullets.

That if any Negroe Slaves shall run away into the Woods from their English Masters, the Cherokee Indians shall endeavour to apprehend them, and either bring them back to the Plantation from whence they run away, or to the Governor, and for every Negroe so apprehended and brought back, the Indian who brings him shall receive a Gun and a Match Coat; Whereupon we give A Box of Vermillion, Ten Thousand Gun Flints, and Six Dozen of Hatchets.

That if by any accidental Misfortune it should happen, that an English Man should kill an Indian, the King or great Man of the Cherokees shall first complain to the English Governor, and the Man who did it, shall be punished by the English Law as if he had kill'd an English Man, and in like manner if an Indian kills an English Man, the Indian who did it, shall be delivered up to the Governor and be punished by the same English Law, as if he was an English Man, Whereupon we give Twelve Dozen of Spring Knives, Four Dozen of Brass Kettles and Ten Dozen of Belts.

You are to understand all that we have now said, to be the Words of the Great King, whom you have seen, and as a Token that His Heart is open and true to His Children and Subjects the Cherokees and to all their People, He gives His hand in this Belt, which He desires may be kept and shewn to all your People ad to their Children, and Childrens Children, to confirm what is now spoken, and to bind this

Agreement of Peace of Friendship betwixt the English and the Cherokees, as long as the Mountains and Rivers shall last, or the Sun Shine; Whereupon we give This Belt of Wampum.

Septr 30th 1730

Board of Trade.

Treaty wth the Cherokee Indians

Answer of the Indian Chiefs of the Cherokee Nation the 9th day of Septem^r 1730, to the Propositions made to them, in behalf of His Majesty, by the Board of Trade, on the 7th day of the Same Month.

We are come hither from a dark Mountainous Place, where nothing but darkness is to be found; but are now in a place where there is light. There was a person in our Country with Us, he gave Us a Yellow token of Warlike Honour, that is left with Moytoy of Telliko; And as Wariors, we received it; He came to Us like a Warrior from you, a Man he was, his talk was upright, and the token he left, preserves his Memory amongst us.

We look upon you as if the Great King George was present; And We love you, as representing the Great King, and shall Dye in the Same way of thinking.

The Crown of Our Nation is different from that which the Great King George wears, and from that which We Saw in the Tower; But to Us it is all one, an[d] the Chain of Friendship Shall be carried to Our People.

We look upon the Great King George as the Sun, and as Our Father; and upon Our Selves as his Children; For tho' We are red, and you white, yet Our Hands and Hearts are join'd together.

When We shall have acquainted Our People with what We have Seen, Our Children from Generation to Generation will always remember it.

In War We Shall always be as one with you; The Great King George's Enemies Shall be Our Enemies; His People and Ours Shall be always o[ne] and dye together.

We came hither naked and poor, as the Worm out of the Earth, but you have every thing; and We that have nothing must love you, and can never break the Chain of Friendship that is between Us.

Here stands the Governor of Carolina, whom We know; This Small Rope which we Shew you, is all We have to bind our Slaves with, and may be broken; but you have Iron Chains for yours. However if we catch your Slaves, We Shall bind them as well as We can, and deliver them to Our friends again and have no pay for it.

We have looked round for the Person that was in Our Country, he is not here, however We must Say, that he talked uprightly to Us, and We shall never forget him.

Your white People may very Safely build Houses near Us, We Shall hurt nothing that belongs to them, for We are the Children of one Father the Great King, and Shall live and Dye together.

Then laying down his Feathers upon the Table, he added; This is our way of Talking, which is the Same to Us, as your letters in the Book, are to you; And to you, beloved Men, We deliver these Feathers, in confirmation of all We have Said, and of Our Agreement to your Articles.

Memorand[m]   That in further Proof of their Agreement they did afterwards Sign the Articles which had been proposed to them by the Lords Commissioners for Trade and Plantations.

Answer of the Cherokee Indians to the Propositions Made to them by the Board

In ye Board of Trade's Lett[rs] of Septr 30th 1730.

Source: National Archives, Kew, UK, CO 5 4 1D.

APPENDIX B

Transcription and Translation of the 1756 Franco-Cherokee Treaty of Friendship

[1]

Chérakis

Articles et conditions préliminaire de Paix entre les françois et la nation *Chérakis* proposés par M. de Kerlérec Gouverneur de la Louisianne aux Chefs et considerés que la ditte nation a deputé et envoyé a la Nouvelle Orléans pour luy demander la ditte Paix et l'Etablissment d'une traité chex eux pour fournir a leur besoins.

ARTICLE 1.

Les deputés Chérakis ont promis au nom de toute leur nation de se conformer exactement au present article.

Les Chérakis doivent promettre de bonne foy d'enterrer leur cassetête et d'empêcher fidellement qu'aucun guerrier de leur nation se trouve dans aucun party d'ennemis qui frapent sur le françois.

ARTICLE 2.

Les deputés ont promis de ramener nos prisonniers qu'ils ont dit etre soldats et deserteurs

Mr. de Kerlérec grand chef des françois de la Partie du Sud et Pere commun des hommes rouge

de Illinois a condition neanmoins qu'il ne leur seroit fait aucun mal, et persistant dans cette demande M. de Kerlérec leur a accordé leur grace sous le bon plaisir de S. M. en exigeant de son bonté qu'a l'avenir ils arreteroient et remettroient tous ceux qui tomberoient entre leurs mains et les rendroient a nôtre discretion et sans aucun conditions ce qu'ils ont forméllément promis.

Ont repondû qu'ils étoient énvoyer pour demander la paix au nom et de la part de toute la nation

Ont promis de se conformer au contenû du présent article et d'envoyer des deputés a M. de Vaudreüil grand chef du nord des leurs rétour dans la nation, et M. de Kerlérec leur a remis en consequence le jour de leur depart une lettre pour ce Genéral.

du même continent demande la réstitution des prisonniers françois qui sont aux *Chérakis* au nombre d'une fille et de quatre soldats dont deux doivent être de rétour de La Virginie et se sont sans dessein. bien entendû cependant que si il survenoit quelques difficultés de la part du grand chef du nord pour la paix (ce qu'il ne prévoit pas) les dits Prisonniers seront sensés traités de bonne foy, et payés la Valeur ordinaire des Prisonniers a titre de rançon.

ARTICLE 3.
Que cette Paix ne peut avoir lieu avec une partie des *Chérakis* a moins que ce ne soit avec toute la nation entiere.

ARTICLE 4.
Que quatre chefs des plus notables et autant de considerés de la nation *Chérakis* partiront aussitot que les deputés icy presens seront de rétour a leur Village, pour Montréal ou Québec dans l'un ou l'autre de ces deux on sera (M. de Vaudreuil) auquel ils porteront la même parolle de Paix et telle qu'ils l'ont portée au chef de guerre françois des Alibamoux, et a M. de Kerlérec Gouverneur de la Louisianne qui les chargera

d'une lettre pour M. de Vaudreüil en bonne parolle pour laquelle il expliquera les demarches des *Chérakis* pour parvenir a la paix qu'ils desirent.

ARTICLE 5.

Les deputés ont représenté qu'ils comptent que les Tchikachas se réünisont a eux pour fraper sur les anglois qu'en ce cas ils ne leur feroient pas la guerre mais que s'ils refusoient de prendre leur cassetête contre les anglois qui veulent s'emparer de leur terre ils etoient des hommes et savoient le qu'ils devoient faire.

Que les *Chérakis* feront la guerre aux Tchikachas qui ont toûjours eû l'esprit mal fait et qui sont de tout têmps les ennemis declarés des françois et des hommes rouges amis et alliés des françois.

ARTICLE 6.

Ont repondû que les anglois avoient le Cour mauvais, et que les regardant comme leurs ennemis et ceux des françois ils frapperent sur eux, et les chasseroient au dela des montagnes.

Les anglois n'ayant declaré la guerre aux françois que parce que les françois veulent protéger et deffendre les hommes rouges, leurs enfants, freres, et alliés, les *Chérakis* doivent regarder les anglois comme leurs ennemis d'autant plus qu'ils ont eux mêmes tout à craindre des anglois qui ne proposent de battir des forts sur leur terre que pour s'en emparer plus facilement et les rendre esclaves, eux, leurs femmes, et leurs enfants, ainsi que leurs vieillards.

Ont repondû et promis qu'a leur arrivé chez eux ils forceroient les anglois qui s'y trouveront a de retirer de leur nation et détruiroient la maison de force qu'ils y ont deja batté et ne permettront jamais qu'ils y fassent des forts ni des batteaux pour gatter leurs rivieres

Ont repondû que devenûs les enfants des françois ils ne permettront jamais que les anglois viennent gatter leur terre ni leurs rivieres pour faire du mal aux françois aujoûrd'huy, leurs freres, et leurs alliés et que des leurs retour a leur village ils vont aller en guerre et fraper sur les anglois.

ARTICLE 7.

Que les *Chérakis* detruiront au rétour de leurs deputés icy présens et portant de parolle, le magazin cerné que les anglois viennent d'établir chez eux pour servir de depot a l'artillerie, aux munitions, ferrures, et outiles qu'ils y ont deja envoyé pour la construction des forts, et des batteaux qu'ils projettent.

Que quand aux 19. soldats et un sargent anglois qui tiennent garrison dans ce fort pour la garde de ce depot, les *Chérakis* doivent et seront tenûs de les sommer de sortir de la nation, et s'ils ne le font de gré ils les y contraindront par la force; aprés quoy les *Chérakis* ne souffriront aucune entreprise sur leurs terres, et encore moins d'y etablir aucun fort, mais repousseront en frapant sur les anglois toutes celles qu'ils pourroient tenter contre les françois.

ARTICLE 8.

Aprés cette declaration faite aux anglois de la part des *Chérakis*, les Chérakis doivent des ce moment regarder les anglois comme leur ennemis, et repousser par la hache et le cassetête la moindre entreprise qu'ils voudroient faire sur leur nation, soit en y faisant passer des troupes ou autrement; et pour donner aux françois des preuves de leur attachement, les *Chérakis* doivent former et faire sortir des partis frequens contre les anglois pour fraper sur eux puis qu'ils ont juré la destruction des hommes rouges, et celle des françois leurs amis et leurs alliés.

ARTICLE 9.

Les deputés cherakis ont repondu qu'ils etoient contens de la bonne reception que leur avoit fait. M. de Kerlérec leur Pere, et des promesses qu'il leur fait par le présent article pour leur procurer les marchandises necessaires pour eux, leurs femmes, et leurs enfants; et ont ajoutté qu'ils esperoient quelle ne leurs manqueroient pas aprés que le g.[grand] chef du nord auroit mêlé sa parolle avec la sienne.

Mr. Kerlérec grand chef de la nouvelle orléans Pere commun des hommes rouges du même continent promet aux *Chérakis*, si la Paix se termine, comme il l'espere, de prendre tous les arrangemens convénables pour fournir a la traite de la nation le plus abondamment qu'il sera possible.

Mais les *Chérakis* doivent faire attention que devenant aujoûrd'huy les enfans des françois ils en augmentent le nombre; et qu'une augmentation d'enfans demande aussy une augmentation de marchandises. Qu'il fait par consequent du têmps et qu'ils prennent patience pour que leur Pere commun fasse venir d'audéla du grand lac celles qui feront necessaires pour leurs besoins.

Ont repondû a M. de Kerlérec qu'ils voyoient bien par la Promesse qu'il leur fait d'envoyer en attendant la reponse du grand chef du Canada au Poste des Alibamoux des marchandises de guerre pour leur besoins qu'il etoit un bon Pere et ont promis de s'en servir fortement contra ses ennemies, et les leurs qui sont les anglois.

Ont promis que quand on etablira la traite chez eux ils empêcheront qu'il ne soit fait aucune insulte ni aucun tort aux traiteurs françois, et de faire escorter les convois(?) de marchandises par de bons guerriers quand ils en seront requis.

Les deputés ont repondu a M. de Kerlérec qu'il sera bon qu'il fasse annoncer comme il le leur promet a tous les hommes rouges amis

ARTICLE 10.

Qu'en attendant la reponce et le consentément de M. de Vaudreuil grand chef du nord pour la dite Paix, M. de Kerlérec aura neanmoins soin d'envoyer au poste des Alibamoux de la poudre, des Balles, Cassetêtes, des couteaux bucherons, des pierres a fusil [flint], et du vermillon pour recompenser la valleur des guerriers *Chérakis*, et l'attachement que cette nation prouvera avoir pour les françois, mais ce ne sera qu'aprés qu'il aura apris quelle aura chassé de chez elle tous les anglois et quelle leur aura declaré la guerre par une action de valleur et d'eclat.

ARTICLE 11.

Quand la paix entre les *Chérakis* et les françois sera terminé la nation Chérakis s'engage et promet d'accompagner et escorter les françois qui iront porter leurs besoins, par un nombre convénable de bons guerriers s'ils en sont requis, le tout au moyen du payement dont la nation sera convenüe de gré a gré avec les traiteurs françois.

ARTICLE 12.

Quand aux differentes nations des hommes rouges de ce Continent alliés, enfans, et amis des françois; particulierement leurs des françois, que les **Chérakis** ont retrouvé l'esprit et etoient devenûs comme eux les enfans, et les alliés des françois en ajouttant qu'ils alloient partis pour declarer la guerre aux anglois, et venger par leur teste la mort de leurs freres qu'ils ont tué; et ont prié en même têmps M. de Kerlérec leur Pere d'ecrire une forte parolle a M. de Vaudreüil pour que celle qu'ils vont luy porter ne tombe pas a terre, et afin qu'il oublie comme luy leurs egaremens puis qu'ils veulent toûjours tenir la main du françois qui est bon et qui a le coin(?) bien fait.

anciens amis les Tchaktas et Alibamoux, M. de Kerlérec leur grand chef promet de faire tout ce de qui dependra de luy pour quelles ecouttent la parolle qu'il va leur fair porter, qui sera de n'avoir qu'une même hache pour fraper sur les anglois qu'un même cassetête, et une même micoüenne que les Chérakis. M. de Kerlérec leur pere commun des hommes rouges de la partie du sud promet au surplus aux **Chérakis** d'ecrire en leur faveur a M. de Vaudreuil grand chef de la partie du nord; et afin que ce grand chef ecoutte favorablement la parolle qu'ils doivent luy faire porter, et qu'il ratifie la paix qu'ils demandent, il luy fera connoitre que la nation Chérakis a toujours bien traité les prissoniers quelle a fait sur les françois.

Tous les douze articles Préliminaires de Paix cy dessus enoncés et proposés par M. de Kerlérec Gouverneur de la Louisianne; et qui ont été bien expliqués et duement interpréttés aux **Chérakis**, et auxquels les dits Chérakis ont hautement acquiessé; seront neanmoins remis a la decision a M. de Vaudreüil Gouverneur General de la nouvelle france pour y étre par luy ajoutté ou diminué ainsi qu'il le jugera a propos pour le bien du service du Roy. Les dits articles ne devant avoir lieu qu'autant qu'il jugera que les interets de la partie du nord de la nouvelle france et ceux de celle cy pourront se consilier pour la ratification de celle paix proposée.

Fait et arretté par nous Gouverneur pour le Roy dans nôtre hotel du Gouvernment a la nouvelle Orléans le 23 novembre 1756. Signé

Kerlérec, et ont aussy signé comme présens et commandés pour se trouvér aux assemblée tenües a ce sujet, Belille major, Derneviüe, Duvergé, volant Gasmond, Lavergne, Raquel, le Bretton, Boudouin jesuitte, Dorville, Dutillet, Chabert, Grandmaison, Chr.[Chévalier?] Makarty, neyon, Trudo, Marquis, St. Martin, Duplessis, Vaugine, et monin.

Se certifie avoir interpretté en termes clairs et intelligibles, les douze articles Préliminaires de Paix cy dessus proposés par M. de Kerlérec Gouverneur aux deputés Cherakis comme aussy fidellement rendu les reponses faites par les dits deputiés qui sont telles qu'ils les ont faites a costé dessus dites articles, en foy dequoy j'ay signé le present.

A la nouvelle orléans le 23 novembre 1756. Signé:

[Translation]*

[1]

Cherokee

Articles and conditions preliminary to Peace between the French and the **Cherokee** Nation proposed by M. de Kerlérec, Governor of Louisiana, to the Chiefs and ambassadors [considerés] that the said nation has deputed and sent to New Orleans in order to request of him the said Peace and Establishment of a treaty between them to furnish their needs.

ARTICLE 1.

The Cherokee deputies have promised in the name of their whole nation to conform exactly to the present article.

The Cherokee must promise in good faith to bury their cassetête and faithfully prevent that any warrior of their nation be found in any party of enemies who strike against the French.

---

*Translation by G. Matt Adkins on behalf of the author.

The deputies have promised to return our prisoners who they have said are soldiers and deserters from Illinois on condition nevertheless that no evil come to them, and persisting in this request, M. de Kerlérec has granted to them their grace under the good pleasure of His Majesty in calling upon his goodness that in the future they will arrest and deliver back all those who fall into their hands and yield to our discretion and without any conditions this that they have formally promised.

Responded that they were sent to request the peace in the name of and on the part of the whole nation.

Have promised to conform to the contents of the present article and to send deputies to M. de Vaudreüil, Great Chief of the North, upon their return into the nation, and M. de Kerlérec has remitted to them in consequence, on the day of their departure, a letter for this General.

ARTICLE 2.

Mr. de Kerlérec, Great Chief of the French of the South and Common Father of the Red Men of the same continent, requests the restitution of the French prisoners held by the **Cherokee** to the number of one girl and four soldiers of which two must be returned to Virginia and are [held] without purpose. Naturally, however, if there occurred some difficulties on the part of the Great Chief of the North for the Peace (which he does not foresee), the said prisoners will suppose themselves to be treated in good faith and paid the ordinary value of prisoners as a ransom.

ARTICLE 3.

That this Peace cannot take place with a part of the **Cherokee** unless it be with the whole entire nation.

ARTICLE 4.

That four of the most notable chiefs and as many of the notables of the **Cherokee** nation will depart, as soon as the deputies here present have returned to their village, for Montréal or Québec, in the one or the other of which will be M. de Vaudreüil, to which they will carry the same words of Peace such as they have carried to the French war chief of the Alibamoux, and to M. de Kerlérec, Governor of Louisiana, who will charge them with a letter for M. de Vaudreüil in good speech by which he will explain the steps taken by the **Cherokee** to reach the peace that they desire.

ARTICLE 5.

The deputies have explained that they expect that the Chickasaw will unite with them to strike the English, that in this case they will not make war upon them [the Chickasaw] but that if they refuse to take up their war club [cassetête] against the English who want to seize their land, they are men and know what they must do.

That the Cherokee will make war on the Chickasaw who have always had ill-made spirits and who are always the declared enemies of the French and the Red Men befriended by and allied with the French.

ARTICLE 6.

Responded that the English have a Bad Heart, and that regarding them as their enemies and as those of the French, they will strike at them, and chase them beyond the mountains.

The English having declared war on the French only because the French want to protect and defend the Red Men, their children, brothers, and allies, the **Cherokee** must regard the English as their enemies since they themselves have everything to fear of the English who propose to build forts on their land in order to seize them more easily and make them slaves—them, their women, their children, and even their old ones.

Responded and promised that at their arrival home they would force the English who were there to retire from their nation and would destroy the house by force that they had already built there and would not ever permit them to build either forts or boats to despoil their rivers.

Responded that having become the children of the French, they will never permit the English to come despoil either their land or their rivers in order to do ill to the French, today their brothers and their allies, and that as soon as they return to their village,

ARTICLE 7.
That the Cherokee will destroy, upon the return of their deputies here present and carrying the words, the identified magazine that the English come to build in their lands, to serve as a depot for artillery, munitions, fittings, and tools that they have already sent there for the construction of the projected forts and boats.

That when 19 soldiers and an English sergeant who garrison this fort take guard in this depot, the **Cherokee** must and will be required to command them to depart the nation, and if they will not do it willingly, to constrain them to do it by force; after which the **Cherokee** will not suffer any enterprise upon their lands, and even less the establishment there of any fort, but will repulse, by striking at the English, all that they could attempt against the French.

ARTICLE 8.
After this declaration made to the English on the part of the **Cherokee**, the Cherokee must from that moment on regard the English as their enemies, and repel by the axe and the war club [cassetête] the least venture that they would like to make on the nation, be it in

they will go make war and strike at the English.

The Cherokee deputies responded that they were content with the good reception that M. de Kerlérec, their Father, had made for them, and the promises that he had made them by the present article for procuring the merchandise necessary for them, their women, and their children; and have added that they hoped they would not lack after the Great Chief of the North had mixed his words with his [Kerlérec's] own.

Responded to M. de Kerlérec that they saw well by the promise that he had made to them to send to the Post of the Alibamoux, while awaiting the response of the Great Chief of Canada, the war materiel they needed, that he was a good Father. And they promised to

having troops pass through or otherwise; and in order to give to the French proofs of their attachment, the **Cherokee** must form war parties and sortie frequently against the English in order to strike at them since they have sworn the destruction of the Red Men and their friends and allies, the French.

ARTICLE 9.

Mr. Kerlérec, Great Chief of New Orleans, Common Father of the Red Men of the same continent, promises to the **Cherokee**, if the Peace treaty is completed, as he hopes it is, to make all the arrangements suitable to provide for the most abundant trade for the nation that will be possible.

ARTICLE 10.

While awaiting the response and consent of M. de Vaureuil, Great Chief of the North, for the said Peace, M. de Kerlérec will meanwhile take care to send to the post of the Alibamoux powder, bullets, war clubs, logging saws, flint, and vermilion to reward the valor of the **Cherokee** warriors, serve themselves well of it against his enemies and theirs, who are the English.

Have promised that when trade is established between them, they will prevent any insult or injury to the French traders, and will have the merchandise convoys escorted by good warriors when it is required of them.

The deputies have responded to M. de Kerlérec that it will be good that he has announced as he has promised to all the red men who are friends and allies of the French, that the **Cherokee** have rediscovered spirit and have become, as they, the children and the allies of the French, adding that they will go out to declare war on the English, and take vengeance on their heads for the deaths of

and the attachment that the nation will prove to have for the French, but this will only be after he has learned that the nation has chased from its lands all the English and has declared war on them by a valorous and magnificent action.

ARTICLE 11.

When the peace between the **Cherokee** and the French is finalized the Cherokee nation commits and promises to accompany and escort the French who will transport their goods, by an appropriate number of warriors if it is required of them, all as a means of payment to which the nation will consent by mutual agreement with the French traders.

ARTICLE 12.

As for the different nations of red men of this continent, allies, children, and friends of the French, particularly their ancient friends the Choctaw and Alibamu, M. de Kerlérec their great chief promises to do everything that depends on him to make heard the words that he will give them to carry, who will have the same axe for striking the English, the same warclub, and even the same micoüenne as the their brothers whom they [the English] have killed; and have at the same time prevailed upon M. de Kerlérec, their Father, to write strong words to M. de Vaudreüil in order that this that they will carry to him falls not to the earth, and so that he forgets their errors since they want forever to hold the hand of the French who are good and who have done well [illegible?].

Cherokee. M. de Kerlérec, their common father of the red men of the southern territory promises in addition to the **Cherokee** to write in their favor to M. de Vaudreuil, great chief of the northern territory; and so that this great chief hears favorably the words that they must take to him, and so that he ratifies the peace that they request, he [Kerlérec] will make him [Vaudreuil] understand that the Cherokee nation has always treated well the prisoners that they have taken of the French.

All twelve articles Preliminary to Peace enunciated and proposed above by M. de Kerlérec, Governor of Louisiana; and which have been explained and duly interpreted to the **Cherokee**, and to which the said Cherokee have above agreed; will be nevertheless remitted to the decision of M. de Vaudreüil, Governor General of New France, to be appended or reduced by him as he will judge appropriate for the good of the service to the King. The said articles having to take effect only so much as he will judge that the interests of the northern part of New France and those of this one accord for the ratification of the proposed peace.

Made and ordered by us, Governor for the King, in our Governor's residence, at New Orleans the 23rd of November 1756. Signed Kerlérec, and also signed as present and ordered to be in attendance at the meeting held on this subject, Belille major, Derneviüe, Duvergé, volant(?) Gasmond, Lavergne, Raquel, le Bretton, Boudouin jesuitte, Dorville, Dutillet, Chabert, Grandmaison, Chr.[Chévalier?] Makarty, neyon, Trudo, Marquis, St. Martin, Duplessis, Vaugine, et monin.

This certifies that the twelve articles Preliminary to Peace above proposed by M. de Kerlérec, Governor, have been interpreted in terms clear and intelligible to the Cherokee deputies, and also that the responses made by the said deputies are faithfully rendered such as they have made them alongside the above said article, in witness whereof I have signed this.

New Orleans the 23rd November 1756. Signed:

Source: William Lyttelton Papers, WCL

Abbreviations

AMDC   Adam Matthew Digital Collection, Colonial America, http://www.colonialamerica.amdigital.co.uk

CDFA   Cherokee Documents in Foreign Archives, Hunter Library, Western Carolina University (microfilm collection)

CO 5   Original correspondence between the British government and the governments of the American colonies, National Archives, Kew, UK

CSRNC   *Colonial and State Records of North Carolina*, Documenting the American South, https://docsouth.unc.edu/csr/

DRIA   *Colonial Records of South Carolina: Documents Relating to Indian Affairs*, followed by volume number, ed. William McDowell

GCDFA   *A Guide to Cherokee Documents in Foreign Archives*

ISHSP   Illinois State Historical Society Publications

JCIT   *Journals of the Commissioners of the Indian Trade, September 20, 1710–August 29, 1718*, ed. William McDowell

MPA   *Mississippi Provincial Archives*, followed by volume number, ed. Patricia Galloway et al.

PGW   *Papers of George Washington*, Colonial Series, followed volume number

SWJP   *Papers of Sir William Johnson*, followed by volume number, ed. James Sullivan

WCL   William Clements Library, University of Michigan

Notes

INTRODUCTION

1. The original, unlabeled deerskin map has been lost to history. Fortunately, the British drew an exact replica (applying labels) in 1725. My interpretation of this map draws from Gregory A. Waselkov, "Indian Maps of the Colonial Southeast," in Wood, Waselkov, and Hatley, *Powhatan's Mantle*, 324–29. See also Cashin, *Guardians of the Valley*, xvi; and Ray, "Interpreting Native Trans-Appalachia." See also Anderson, "Rediscovering Native North America," 478–505.

2. Contemporary Britons identified the following polities as "westward": Piankeshaws, Mascoutens, Twightwees (Miamis), Peorias, Kaskaskias, Shawnees, Lenapes, and Anishnaabeg. In 1750 South Carolina governor James Glen defined "northward Indians" as falling under the "general Name of Nottaweegas, & they are sometimes called Senecas. . . . Besides the Five Nations, there are . . . the Susquehannah and Virginia Indians." Glen to George Clinton, July 7, 1750, George Clinton Papers, Series I, Box 4, Folder 2, William Clements Library, University of Michigan (hereafter cited as WCL).

3. Fanni Mingo personifies this mobility—he was Chickasaw, a polity primarily located in modern Mississippi, but was part of a smaller group that for a time settled near Fort Moore in modern South Carolina. Waselkov, "Indian Maps of the Colonial Southeast," 324–29; Cashin, *Guardians of the Valley*, xvi.

4. Language here draws from email correspondence between the author and Gregory Waselkov, July 5, 2022.

5. Warren, *Worlds the Shawnees Made*; DuVal, *Native Ground*.

6. Neal L. Trubowitz, "Native Americans and French on the Central Wabash," in Walthall and Emerson, *Calumet and Fleur-De-Lis*, 243, 246. According to Trubowitz, Mascoutens arrived around Ouiatenon in the 1740s (254). Scholars should understand the critical role played by the Haudenosaunee (the Five and Six Nations) in trans-Appalachia generally and in the Southeast specifically, where for their own reasons they confronted Cherokees in the Appalachians and along the Wabash. See

also Sleeper-Smith, *Indigenous Prosperity and American Conquest*. For more on the Haudenosaunee in the west, see Hinderaker, *Elusive Empires*; and Ray, "Indians, Europeans, and the Struggle for Empire in Eighteenth Century North America," in Frentzos and Thompson, *The Routledge Handbook of American Military and Diplomatic History: The Colonial Period to 1877*, 53–60; and Theda Perdue, "Cherokee Relations with the Iroquois in the Eighteenth Century," in Richter and Merrell, *Beyond the Covenant Chain*, 135–50. Other important recent scholarship on the Iroquois includes Parmenter, *Edge of the Woods*; Preston, *Texture of Contact*; Brandau, "Your Fyre Shall Burn No More"; Richter, *Ordeal of the Longhouse*; Dennis, *Cultivating a Landscape of Peace*; Jennings, *Ambiguous Iroquois Empire*; and Jordan, *Seneca Restoration*.

7. Warren and Noe, "The Greatest Travellers in America," in Ethridge and Shuck-Hall, *Mapping the Mississippi Shatter Zone*, 163–87; Penelope Drooker, "The Ohio Valley 1550–1750: Patterns of Sociopolitical Coalescence and Dispersal," in Ethridge and Hudson, *Transformation of the Southeastern Indians*, 115–34. See also Lakomäki, *Gathering Together*, 46, 49–50.

8. If, as archeologist Christopher Rodning has argued, "center places are manifested in many forms, and at many scales . . . in the broader Cherokee cultural landscape," then Overhill country itself was in many ways a center place in a broader Cherokee world. Rodning, *Center Places and Cherokee Towns*, 25.

9. Glen to Thomas Robinson, undated, 1754, in McDowell, *Colonial Records of South Carolina: Documents Relating to Indian Affairs*, vol. 1, May 21, 1750–August 7, 1754, 536 (hereafter cited as *DRIA* followed by volume number). Agreed British trader James Adair, the Tennessee "runs through the middle and upper parts of the Cheerake nation, about a north-west course—and joining other rivers, they empty themselves into the great Missisippi." Adair, *History of the American Indians*, 251.

10. "Charles Town in America, July 17," *Gentleman's Magazine* 25 (October 1755), 470, American Antiquarian Society Historical Periodicals Collection: Series 1.

11. Historian Fred Anderson describes the Haudenosaunee as an eighteenth-century empire in *Crucible of War*.

12. Text taken and paraphrased from Ray, "Cherokees, Empire, and the Tennessee Corridor in the British Imagination, 1670–1730," in Ray, *Before the Volunteer State*, 35–64.

13. Covenant Chain "is the name given to the complex system of alliances between the Haudenosaunee (also known as the Six Nations and Iroquois League) and Anglo-American colonies originating in the early 17th century." The first such chain was forged between the Dutch and the Mohawks. The then–Five Nations transferred it to the English after the latter claimed the colony of New Netherlands, *Canadian Encyclopedia* online, s.v. "Covenant Chain," by Cornelius Jaenen, last edited August 2015, https://www.thecanadianencyclopedia.ca/en/article/covenant-chain. See also Parmenter, *Edge of the Woods*; Richter, *Ordeal of the Longhouse*; Jennings, *Ambiguous Iroquois Empire*; and Merrill and Richter, *Beyond the Covenant Chain*. The English came to believe that the chain both subordinated the Haudenosaunee to their interests and made them the exclusive European contact of the

Haudenosaunee. They reinforced this "fact" of Iroquois subordination in the Treaty of Utrecht. The British also believed that the Haudenosaunee had conquered all Native polities between Iroquoia and the Mississippi. Those lands by right of conquest belonged to the Haudenosaunee, and the Treaty of Utrecht asserted that the Iroquois and their country were expressly under the dominion of the English Crown. For more on this point, see, for example, Benjamin Franklin, "Observations on the late and present Conduct of the French," (Boston, 1755), 3–4, in *The Works of Benjamin Franklin*, vol. 10, 561, http://galenet.galegroup.com/servlet/Sabin?af=RN&ae=CY110400812&srchtp=a&ste=14.

14. Brudanell, Bladen, and Pelham to the Duke of Newcastle, August 20, 1730, Cherokee Documents in Foreign Archives, Hunter Library, Western Carolina University (hereafter cited as CDFA).

15. North Carolina governor Arthur Dobbs put it even more explicitly thirty years later. The Haudenosaunee, he informed the Board of Trade, claimed everything "from the falls on the Ohio to the Mississippi on the South side of the Ohio our allies the Cherokees claim a Right and dispute it much higher of the South side with the six Nations." This Cherokee right, he felt, also gave North Carolina and the British "a claim to these." Dobbs to Board of Trade, December 26, 1755, *Colonial and State Records of North Carolina*, vol. 5, 464, https://docsouth.unc.edu/csr/index.php/document/csr05-0183#p5-464 (hereafter cited as *CSRNC*, followed by volume and page number). Eric Hinderaker describes the importance of "imagined" European empires from the perspective of the northeast in *Elusive Empires*.

16. Historian Linda Colley has observed that British identity increasingly entailed celebrating the British nation, culture, and commitment to liberty. It came to mean Protestantism, as Britons saw themselves as leaders in the worldwide struggle with Catholicism and with France. It also meant development of overseas empire and a shared identity, not just among the elite but throughout the empire. North Americans adopted this identity and consistently measured themselves against "what England had achieved." Indeed, as Jack Greene has noted, eighteenth-century North Americans thought of themselves as "demonstrably British." See Colley, *Britons: Forging the Nation*; Marshall, introduction to *Oxford History of the British Empire*, vol. 2, 12; and Greene, *Pursuits of Happiness*, 175. For more on British North American identity, see McConville, *The King's Three Faces*; Canny and Pagden, *Colonial Identity in the Atlantic World*; Mancke and Shammas, *Creation of the British Atlantic World*. For more on the religious implications of British identity, at least in New England, see Kidd, *The Protestant Interest*. See also Thompson, *Britain, Hanover, and the Protestant Interest*.

17. An excellent early example of this position draws from Francis Yonge's insistence on the rectitude of transferring power over South Carolina from proprietary to royal. In that internal power struggle, both sides saw the Yamasee War and its aftermath as a moment wherein their political opponents had abandoned the colony to the French, Spanish, and their Indigenous allies. Both sides appealed to the Crown for resolution, and both sides saw the empire as the necessary tool for future

defense of Carolina. Yonge also laid it out clearly when he pointed out that the empire would need to send military force "sufficient to Protect . . . Subjects; [otherwise] this Valuable Province in all Probability will be lost." Yonge, *Narrative of the Proceedings of the People of South-Carolina*.

18. Scholars can connect this idea with John Murrin's observations in "A Roof Without Walls: The Perils of American National Identity," in Beeman, Botein, and Carter, *Beyond Confederation*, 333–48. See also Hendrickson, *Peace Pact*; and Hendrickson, "The First Union: Nationalism vs. Internationalism in the American Revolution," in Onuf and Gould, *Empire and Nation*, 35–53.

19. Anderson and Lewis, eds., *Guide to Cherokee Documents in Foreign Archives*, 56 (hereafter cited as *GCDFA*).

20. Perier to Maurepas, March 25, 1731, in *MPA* 4:75. See also Morgan, *Land of Big Rivers*; Ekberg, *French Roots in the Illinois Country*; Engelbert and Teasdale, *French and Indians in the Heart of North America*; Morrisey, *Empire by Collaboration*; Lee, *Masters of the Middle Waters*; and Teasdale, *Fruits of Perseverance*.

21. *MPA* 4:74.

22. French actions (such as they were) were part of a broad initiative to secure Indigenous alliances and stabilize French North America as France and Britain careened from one imperial contest to another. The British and the French engaged in "a cycle of imperial confrontation from 1689 to 1815," with only periodic (and incomplete) breaks. See Taylor, *American Colonies*, 421.

23. "Strong, bright, chain" comes from Boulware, *Deconstructing the Cherokee Nation*, 75.

24. Put simply, Indigenous trans-Appalachia directly affected how the British Empire addressed issues of land, taxation, and the consolidation of imperial power. It suggests that perhaps the roots of the American Revolution are planted in Indigenous realities. For more on this point see Ray, "Indigenous Roots of the American Revolution."

25. For that matter, what was a "nation" in the eighteenth century? According to the *Oxford English Dictionary*, eighteenth-century Europeans thought of an Indigenous nation as a collective within a "territory occupied by such a people." Nineteenth-century Anglican missionary Samuel Johnson defined it as "people distinguished from other people." Quoted in Fried, *Notion of Tribe*, 9.

26. The seven Cherokee clans are: Blue or Panther; Long Hair or Wind; Bird; Paint; Deer; Wild Potato or Bear (or Raccoon or Blind Savannah); and Wolf; see Marcelina Reed, *Seven Clans of the Cherokee Society*. Historiography of the early Cherokee experience is voluminous. See, for example, Hudson, *Southeastern Indians*; Rodning, *Center Places and Cherokee Towns*; Marcoux, *Pox, Empire, Shackles, and Hides*; Boulware, *Deconstructing the Cherokee Nation*; Kelton, *Cherokee Medicine*; Tortora, *Carolina in Crisis*; Hatley, *Dividing Paths*; Thornton, *The Cherokees*; Perdue, *Cherokee Women*; King, *The Cherokee Nation*; Corkran, *The Cherokee Frontier*; Oliphant, *Peace and War on the Anglo-Cherokee Frontier*; and Reynolds, *Cherokee Struggle to Maintain Identity*.

27. Adair, *History of the American Indians*, 248. See also Smithers, "Our Hands and Hearts Are Joined Together."

28. Mooney, "Cherokee River Cult," 1. Another crucial point, as Theresa Smith has noted of the Ojibwe: "Myth is the inherently meaningful memory of a people spoken in the form of a symbolic narrative. It both defines and reflects reality and possibility in the world." *Island of the Anishnaabeg*, 20.

29. Gragson and Bolstad, "Local Analysis of Early Eighteenth-Century Cherokee Settlement," 437–38.

30. Hudson, *Knights of Spain*, 188. See also Hudson, *Southeastern Indians*.

31. Continuing, Rodning notes that "towns were groups of households who shared a common identity and a set of ritual practices and civic responsibilities." *Center Places and Cherokee Towns*, xii, 6; Hatley, *Dividing Paths*, 6. See also Kelton, *Cherokee Medicine*, 35.

32. Rodning, "Reconstructing the Coalescence of Cherokee Communities in Southern Appalachia," in Ethridge and Hudson, *Transformation of the Southeastern Indians*, 155.

33. Boulware, *Deconstructing the Cherokee Nation*.

34. Parmenter, *Edge of the Woods*, 24.

35. For more systematic discussion of this phenomenon in other regions, see DeLay, *The War of a Thousand Deserts*; and Hämäläinen, *Comanche Empire*. One possible avenue for commercial acquisition has a more gendered element: a growing body of scholarship in the mid-Atlantic suggests "collusion" between "colonial and aboriginal women," including smuggling activities that "in some cases persisted for decades." Some of these women were part of "trading parties," but several others "arrived as intermediaries in the trade with other natives." Waterman and Noel, "Not Confined to the Village Clearings," 44, 47.

36. "SECTION 6TH. OF THE CHARACTER OF THE ILINOIS; OF THEIR HABITS AND CUSTOMS; AND OF THE ESTEEM THAT THEY HAVE FOR THE CALUMET, OR TOBACCO-PIPE, AND OF THE DANCE THEY PERFORM IN ITS HONOR," in *The Jesuit Relations*, vol. 59, *Lower Canada Illinois Ottawas 1667–1669*, ed. Reuben Gold Thwaites, 25–26, http://moses.creighton.edu/kripke/jesuitrelations/.

37. Raudot, "Memoir," in Kinietz, *Indians of the Western Great Lakes, 1615–1760*, 404.

38. Liette, Pierre [de] (d. 1729), 1940, *Memorial concerning the Illinois Country* [manuscript]: [1940?], Newberry Library, Ayer MS 3237, online at American Indian Histories and Cultures, http://www.aihc.amdigital.co.uk/Documents/Details/Ayer_MS_3237. See also the estate inventory of Jacques Bourdon, as noted in Ekberg, *Stealing Indian Women*, 34.

39. William Bull to Jeffrey Amherst, March 13, 1761, Amherst Papers, War Office 34/35, Fols. 191–92. For more on horse trading, see, for example, Boulware, "'Skilful Jockies' and 'Good Sadlers': Native Americans and Horses in the Southeastern Borderlands" in Frank and Crothers, *Borderland Narratives*, 68–95; and Ray, *Middle Tennessee*.

40. Liette, *Memorial concerning the Illinois Country*, 178–81. The "confluence" concept draws from Aron, *American Confluence*. See also McDonnell, *Masters of Empire*; and DuVal, *Native Ground*.

41. On slave trading in Illinois, see Morrisey, *Empire by Collaboration*; Rushforth, *Bonds of Alliance*; and Ekberg, *Stealing Indian Women*.

42. French traveler Jean-Bernard Bossu described Illinois as "one of the finest [lands] in the world; it supplies all the lower parts of Louisiana with flower [flour]. Its commerce consists in furs, lead, and salt. There are many salt springs, that attract the wild oxen, and the roe-bucks, which like the pastures around them very much. Their flesh and tongues are salted, and furnish another branch of commerce to New Orleans; and they cure hams, which equal those of Bayonne. The fruits are as fine as in France." Bossu, *Travels through That Part of North America Formerly Called Louisiana*, Letter 7, 127, John Carter Brown Library, Brown University.

43. Hatley, *Dividing Paths*, 45–46.

44. French sources point out quite well how ubiquitous were British goods in the Native South. A tiny sliver of examples can be found in *MPA* 4, documents 48, 50, 52, 67.

45. Deceptive Euro-Cherokee narratives speak to a more general academic conundrum: the lack of extant written sources to facilitate the study of political development in the postcontact Native world. It makes exploring identity formation difficult, to say nothing of how each evolving polity might have understood Western concepts such as sovereignty and power. The conundrum is made worse by the fact that scholars have tended to define "sovereign power" nearly exclusively as an outgrowth of Western philosophical traditions. Such restrictive standards reduce everything from the Aztec Empire to the Tascaluza Chiefdom to the Haudenosaunee to something less than Western nation-states. Political scientists typically have labelled them "primitive" or "premodern," supposing they lacked the sophistication to construct civil polities and therefore were unworthy of inclusion in the Western pantheon of political and economic supremacy. Historian Brian DeLay sheds light on the dilemma. "The all-too-common notion that nation-states are normative," he observes, "and that polities deviating from that norm are somehow politically incomplete necessarily misrepresents the workings of nonstate societies." *War of a Thousand Deserts*, xviii. Historian James Taylor Carson similarly warns scholars that "power ... ought not to be gauged in comparative geopolitical terms, for when a society produces outlooks and achieves outcomes comprehensible in terms of *its own* culture and not that of the politically or economically predominant other, then the society, the individuals, and the culture in question have power." *Searching for the Bright Path*, 6.

The irony, of course, is that early modern actors from Western polities hardly represented single "states" themselves. Moreover, they consistently—if begrudgingly—pointed to the sophistication of Indigenous politics, legal customs, and economies. Most famously, conquistadores (who certainly had not come to grips with the concept of the single nation-state of Spain in 1519) were overwhelmed by the complexity and reach of the Aztec Empire. In 1609 Henry Spelman described a number of Powhatan political, economic, and legal mechanisms, as did Jesuits amongst the Wendats, Montagnais, Illinois, Anishnaabeg, and Haudenosaunee. Between 1750 and 1850, as Pekka Hämäläinen has persuasively shown, Comanches "were an interregional power with imperial presence." Evidence is abundant, he writes, that as they expanded their authority, Comanches were able "to reduce Euro-American colonial regimes to building blocks of their own dominant position." *Comanche Empire*, 2, 3. DeLay agrees: if not for their ability to piggyback on Comanchería, the American invasion of Mexico in 1846 could have turned out *much* differently.

It is incumbent upon scholars, then, to think more carefully about how to explore Indigenous political identity. DeLay makes the point persuasively. "If one defines politics broadly," he insists, "not as a matrix of particular institutions, positions, or mechanisms, but rather as a process, one of establishing and pursuing public goals," then regardless of circumstances or philosophical background everyone in North America engaged in complex political behavior. *War of a Thousand Deserts*, 119. For more on this point, see, for example, Díaz del Castillo, *Conquest of New Spain*; Townsend, *Fifth Sun*; and Elliott, *Empires of the Atlantic World*. On Spelman, see Wright Haile, ed., *Jamestown Narratives*. See also Gallivan, *Powhatan Landscape*. For Jesuits, see *Jesuit Relations and Allied Documents,* ed. Reuben Gold Thwaites, http://moses.creighton.edu/kripke/jesuitrelations/.

46. Donald Fixico, "Teaching American Indian History Using the Medicine Way," in DeSanti and Ray, *Understanding and Teaching Native American History*, 276–77. See also Fixico, *Call for Change*.

Chapter 1

1. Mooney, *Myths of the Cherokee*, 239.
2. For more on Indigenous notions of time, see, for example, Perley, *Defying Maliseet Language Death*; Smith, *Island of the Anishnaabeg*; or Fixico, *American Indian Mind in a Linear World*. See also Basso, *Wisdom Sits in Places*.
3. Thornton, *The Cherokees: A Population History*, 1.
4. Hudson, *The Southeastern Indians*, 194. Pisgah-Quallah pottery is most prominent in "Cherokee" areas, he notes. The lack of historical and archaeological clarity on Cherokee origins in the Native South reinforces his point that Mississippian traditions expanded into the Southeast because of the diffusion of ideas but also because of the "intrusive movements of people out from the Mississippi valley" (82).
5. Hudson, *Knights of Spain*, 194.
6. Warren, *Worlds the Shawnees Made*, 48–49. Anecdotally, that they may originally have lived so near Iroquoia provides a plausible explanation for their linguistic dialects.

7. Evidence for the Mvskoke argument is Red Clay State Park in modern Bradley County, Tennessee. Interpreted today as a Cherokee site and with a clear connection to the Trail of Tears, Creeks nevertheless suggest that Red Clay is their territory. For more on this point see Kelton, *Cherokee Medicine*, 44.

8. For more on Joara, see Hudson, ed, *Juan Pardo Expeditions*; and Moore, Beck, and Rodning, "Joara and Fort San Juan."

9. Kelton, *Cherokee Medicine*, 33. For more on Catawbas, see Fitts, *Fit for War*; Merrell, *Indians' New World*; Bauer, *Becoming Catawba*; and Heath, "Catawba Militarism."

10. According to Hudson, early Cherokee-speaking people "were more specifically located in the mountains and high foothills" than most of their descendants. He continued: "It appears that their wider political and perhaps cultural alliances were with the paramount chiefdom of Cofitachequi." *Southeastern Indians*, 193–94. According to Kelton, Soto's and Juan Pardo's chroniclers provide good evidence "that at least some sixteenth-century Cherokees resided in settlements north and east of their later location." Kelton, *Cherokee Medicine*, 35.

11. Kelton, *Cherokee Medicine*, 33.

12. Ibid., 35.

13. According to Kelton, these settlements included people who "once lived along the Nolichucky, where Pardo visited Tanasqui." Ibid., 33.

14. They certainly were willing to do so in the aftermath of the 1713 raid on the Yuchi town of Chestowee, as well as the Natchez War of 1729. Hudson, *Knights of Spain*, 436. See chapter 2 in this work for more on the Chestowee raid. See also Brett Riggs, "Reconsidering Chestowee: The 1713 Raid in Regional Perspective," in Jackson, *Yuchi Indian Histories before the Removal Era*, 43–71. On the Natchez War, see Milne, *Natchez Country*; Ellis, "Natchez War Revisited," 441–72; and Usner, *Indians and Settlers in a Frontier Exchange Economy*.

15. On linguistic diversity, see Hudson, *Knights of Spain*, 188. See also Christopher Rodning, "Reconstructing the Coalescence of Cherokee Communities in Southern Appalachia," in Ethridge and Hudson, *Transformation of the Southeastern Indians*, 155; and Rodning, *Center Places and Cherokee Towns*.

16. Thornton, *The Cherokees: A Population History*, 11.

17. Marcoux, *Pox, Empire, Shackles, and Hides*, chs. 3–6.

18. Hatley, *Dividing Paths*, 13.

19. Thornton, *The Cherokees: A Population History*, 11. See also Robbie Ethridge, "The European Invasion and the Transformation of the Indians of Tennessee," in Ray, *Before the Volunteer State*, 3–34.

20. Rodning explains that "leaders of towns were spokespersons for their communities, but their status did not grant them power over people in other towns. Different towns likely formed alliances with each other in different situations, but there were not paramount chiefs that ruled whole groups of towns." "Reconstructing the Coalescence of Cherokee Communities," in Ethridge and Hudson,

Transformation of the Southeastern Indians, 155. Regarding seventeenth-century Cherokee isolation from the English, see Marcoux, *Pox, Empire, Shackles, and Hides*, 38–50.

21. Specifically, if his numbers were correct, it would "make from the first introduction of fire arms, and the first trade, 155 years [from 1826] . . . and this account is, perhaps, as nearly correct as the tradition admits of." Charles Hicks to John Ross, May 4, 1826, in Ross, *Papers of Chief John Ross*, 1:117. On the report from Virginia, see Hatley, *Dividing Paths*, 253–54.

22. Waselkov, "Seventeenth-Century Trade in the Colonial Southeast," 118–19.

23. Kelton, *Epidemics and Enslavement*. For more on Indian slavery, see Reséndez, *The Other Slavery*; Gallay, *Indian Slave Trade*; Ethridge and Shuck-Hall, *Mapping the Mississippian Shatter Zone*; Ray, "Constructing a Discourse of Indigenous Slavery"; Shefveland, *Anglo-Native Virginia*; Negrin, "Possessing Native Women and Children"; and Wood, *Black Majority*. For Indian slavery in New France and Illinois, see Rushforth, *Bonds of Alliance*; and Ekberg, *Stealing Native Women*. For Native slavery in New England, see Newell, *Brethren by Nature*; and Fisher, "Dangerous Designes."

24. *Vacuum domicilium* translates as "vacant land." For more on this concept, see, for example, Greer, *Property and Dispossession*; Corcoran, "John Locke on Native Right," 225–50; and Williams, *American Indian in Western Legal Thought*. For contemporary ideas of the concept, see John Winthrop, "Reasons to be Considered for Justifying the Settlement of New England," in Mancall, *Envisioning America*; and Vattel, *Law of Nations*.

25. "Invasion of America" comes from Jennings, *Invasion of America*.

26. Harriot, *A Briefe and True Report of the New Found Land of Virginia*; and Ralph Lane, "Discourse on the First Colony," in Quinn, *Roanoke Voyages*, 1:255–94. For more on the Roanoke experience, see Oberg, *Head in Edward Nugent's Hand*; Rountree, *Manteo's World*; and Horn, *A Kingdom Strange*. In 1672 John Lederer continued the tradition regarding the South Sea when he wrote to the Lords Proprietors that "the Indian Ocean does stretch an Arm or Bay from *California* into the Continent as far as the *Apalatean* Mountains, answerable to the Gulfs of *Florida* and *Mexico* on this side." "Discoveries of John Lederer," 23.

27. "The First Charter of Virginia, April 10, 1606," Avalon Project, Yale Law School, http://avalon.law.yale.edu/17th_century/va01.asp. The historiography of the English invasion of the Chesapeake is voluminous. More recent examples include Townsend, *Pocahontas and the Powhatan Dilemma*; Kelso, *Jamestown: The Buried Truth*; Horn, *A Land as God Made It*; Rountree, *Pocahontas, Powhatan, Opechancanough*; Kupperman, *The Jamestown Project*; and Musselwhite, Mancall, and Horn, *Virginia 1619*.

28. Kupperman, *Pocahontas and the English Boys*, 56.

29. Pope, *Virginia's God Be Thanked*, 13.

30. Pory was a member of Parliament (1605–11), secretary of the Virginia Colony (1619–21), and speaker of the 1619 Virginia House of Burgesses. Powell, "John

Pory," *Dictionary of North Carolina Biography*, https://ncpedia.org/biography/pory-john. See also Powell, *John Pory, 1572–1636*.

31. Pory's description reflects the English interest in exploiting North America for mercantilist purposes. For other views on the matter, see Richard Hakluyt the Elder, Hakluyt the Younger, and Walter Raleigh. Scholars can find a good introductory overview in Peter Mancall's edited volume *Envisioning America*.

32. Pope, *Virginia's God Be Thanked*, 13. For more on the impact of rumors, see Dowd, *Groundless: Rumors, Legends, and Hoaxes*. On Pory's expedition, see Powell, "Carolana and the Incomparable Roanoke," 2–3.

33. "Sir Robert Heath's Patent 5 Charles 1st; October 30, 1629," Avalon Project, Yale Law School, http://avalon.law.yale.edu/17th_century/heath.asp.

34. For a brief description of the origins and evolution of Carolana, see Lindley S. Butler, "Carolana" in the *Encyclopedia of North Carolina*, https://www.ncpedia.org/carolana.

35. Lefler, "Description of 'Carolana' by a 'Well-Willer,'" 104.

36. *Virgo Triumphant*, quoted in Powell, "Carolana and the Incomparable Roanoke," 13.

37. According to Williams, in Carolana was "a kinde of a Red Sand falling with a streame issuing from a Mountaine, which being washed in a sive, and set upon the fire speedily, melts and becomes some Copper." Williams, *Virgo Triumphant*, 17, Huntington Library.

38. Ibid., 18.

39. Ibid.

40. Hudson, *Knights of Spain*, 174.

41. For more on the Hernando de Soto and Juan Pardo entradas, see Hudson, *Knights of Spain*; Clayton, *De Soto Chronicles*; and Hudson and Hoffman, *Juan Pardo Expeditions*.

42. "Ralph Lane's Discourse on the First Colony," in Quinn, *The Roanoke Voyages*, 1:255–94; Oberg, *Head in Edward Nugent's Hand*; Rountree, *Powhatan Indians of Virginia*; and Gallivan, *Powhatan Landscape*.

43. DuVal, *Native Ground*, 9. Scholars can compare the Native ground concept with White, *The Middle Ground*.

44. Excellent examples of English Carolinians succumbing to the Native ground appear only a few decades later. In 1674 Henry Woodward wrote that the "Chorakae Indians" inhabited "western branches" of the Savannah River and were hostile to Carolina's slave-raiding partners, the Westos. Specifically, he noted that "Savanas" (Shawnees) had warned him "that the Cussetaws, Checsaws and Chiokees intended to come downe and fight" the Westos. No such action occurred, which indicates Westos and Savannahs actively manipulated English efforts for their own ends. They certainly shaped Woodward's understanding of polities like "Cherokees"—they were hostile to Westo interests, and thus by proxy to the English. That same year Abraham Wood offered a different interpretation of Cherokee affairs, pointing out that the Lower towns seemed welcoming to Carolinians. Much

as Edward Williams suggested of the Spanish, Wood gives direct evidence of the Native ground while also providing a fleeting seventeenth-century glimpse of the mobile trans-Appalachian world eventually illuminated by Fanni Mingo. Further down the Tennessee River, he was told, were "many nations of Indians . . . which [the Cherokee] are at warre withe." War? Possibly. Engaged in extensive interaction about which Europeans knew little? Absolutely. And most likely, the Cherokee representatives in these inter-Indigenous activities drew from the Overhill towns. Henry Woodward, "A Faithfull Relation of my Westoe Voyage, By Henry Woodward, 1674," in Shelley, *Narratives of Early Carolina*, 133–34. Abraham Wood to John Richards, August 22, 1674, in Williams, *Early Travels in the Tennessee Country*, 27–28. Archeologist Charles Heath offers another avenue of insight when he notes that Charles Town traders encouraged trade in guns and ammunition with Catawba towns "perhaps as early as the mid-1670s." "Catawba Militarism," 83. It would be more than a little surprising if they did not extend a bit further and contact Lower Cherokees as well. See also Ethridge, *From Chicaza to Chickasaw*, ch. 3 (esp. 113). For more on Westos, see Bowne, *Westo Indians*; and Maureen Meyers, "From Refugees to Slave Traders: The Transformation of the Westo Indians," in Ethridge and Shuck-Hall, *Mapping the Mississippian Shatter Zone*. As we shall see, rumors of inter-Indigenous warfare would drive Europeans into spirals of paranoia for the next century.

45. In the 1650s Virginians briefly recognized that land usurpation had been a major cause of the preceding twenty years of confrontation. Tobacco fields had expanded at near exponential rates, and by the 1650s Burgesses were receiving numerous complaints touching on the "wrong done to the Indians, in takeing away their land and forceing them into such narrow streights and places that they cannot subsist either by planting or hunting." Circumstances meant that "Indians may be justly driven to despaire & to attempt some desperate course for themselves." Even as the Burgesses addressed the problem, it continued to receive petitions that "manie English doe still intrench upon the said Indian's land, which this Assembly [conceives] to be contrary to justice, and the true intent of the English plantation in this country." *Hening's Statutes*, March 1657–8–9th of Commonwealth, Act LXXII, 467–68. And what was the true intent of the colony? Efforts "whereby the Indians might by all just and faire waies be reduced to civillity and the true worship of God." For more on this point, see Ray, "Constructing a Discourse of Indigenous Slavery," 19–39; Shefveland, *Anglo-Native Virginia*; and Negrin, "Possessing Native Women and Children."

46. Williams, *Virgo Triumphant*, 37.

47. Ibid.

48. In the sixteenth century Englishmen defined civility as "civil order; orderliness in a state or a region; absence of anarchy and disorder; civil organization and government." In other words, civility was a necessary precondition for the expansion of dominion. Definitions come from *Oxford English Dictionary Online*, http://www.oed.com.ezproxy.lib.apsu.edu/view/Entry/33581?redirectedFrom=civility#eid.

49. Oberg, *Dominion and Civility*; and Oberg, *Head in Edward Nugent's Hand*. Important English western visionaries included Richard Hakluyt (the Elder), "Inducements to the Liking of the Voyage Intended towards Virginia in 40. And 42. Degrees," in Quinn and Quinn, *New American World*, 3:64–69; Richard Hakluyt (the Younger), "A particular discourse concerning the greate necessitie and manifold comodyties that are like to grow to this realme of Englande by the Westerne discoveries lately attempted," in ibid., 71–123; and Harriot, *A Briefe and True Report of the New Found Land of Virginia*.

50. For more on this type of argument, see George Peckham, "A True Reporte of the Late Discoveries and Possession, Taken in the Right of the Crown of Englande," in Mancall, *Envisioning America*, 62–70.

51. McDonnell, *Masters of Empire*, 14.

52. The original dimensions of Carolina are available in the Charter of Carolina, March 24, 1663, Avalon Project, Yale Law School, https://avalon.law.yale.edu/17th_century/nc01.asp.

53. For more on the early settlement of what would become North Carolina, see Gallay, *Indian Slave Trade*; B. Wood, *This Remote Part of the World*; Roper, *Conceiving Carolina*; La Vere, *The Tuscarora War*; and McIlvenna, *A Very Mutinous People*.

54. Talbot's introduction in Lederer, "The Discoveries of John Lederer," Sabin Americana, http://galenet.galegroup.com/servlet/Sabin?af=RN&ae=CY102149844&srchtp=a&ste=14.

55. Ibid., 16. Archeologists are unsure of Sara's exact location, although it appears to have been somewhere along the Dan River in modern Virginia. See Ethridge, *From Chicaza to Chickasaw*, 106.

56. Ash, "Carolina," 79–80.

57. Traunter, *Travels of Richard Traunter*, xiii–xiv.

58. For more on Couture, see *Travels of Richard Traunter*, esp. 65–68; and M. de Sauvole, *The Journal of Sauvole*, 54. As late as 1775 James Adair continued to endorse the legend: "The Cheerake mountains," he insisted, would produce "as great quantities of gold and silver, as Peru and Mexico, in proportion to their situation with the equator." Similarly, he insisted that silver mines near the remains of British Fort Loudoun "are so rich, that by digging about ten yards deep, some desperate vagrants found at sundry times, so much rich ore, as to enable them to counterfeit dollars to a great amount; a horse load of which was detected in passing for the purchase of negroes, at Augusta." *History of the American Indians*, 255.

59. Ethridge and Shuck-Hall, *Mapping the Mississippian Shatter Zone*. See also Ethridge, *From Chicaza to Chickasaw*; and Beck, *Chiefdoms, Collapse, and Coalescence*.

60. Ethridge, introduction to *Mapping the Mississippian Shatter Zone*, 1–3. The slave trade became particularly crucial to the economic growth of southern Carolina: it both brought a workforce to the colony and provided capital by supplying labor to New England and to the West Indies. Gallay, *Indian Slave Trade*, 7. See also Wood, *Black Majority*; and Ray, "Constructing a Discourse of Indigenous Slavery."

61. Ramsey, *The Yamasee War*. For more on merchant profit, see Bossy, "Godin & Co.," 96–131.

62. Rejecting the "virgin soil" thesis, Paul Kelton has observed that "vectors" were necessary for diseases such as smallpox to spread in any systematic way. Those vectors were not present in the Native South, he argues, until the advent of slave trading. Kelton, *Epidemics and Enslavement*. See also Kelton, *Cherokee Medicine*; and Edwards and Kelton, "Germs, Genocides, and America's Indigenous Peoples," 52–76. For more on the virgin soil thesis, see Crosby, *The Columbian Exchange*.

63. Ethridge, introduction to *Mapping the Mississippian Shatter Zone*, 14. See also Gallay, *Indian Slave Trade*; and Peter Wood, "The Changing Population of the Colonial South: An Overview by Race and Region, 1685–1790," in Wood, Waselkov, and Hatley, *Powhatan's Mantle*, 35–103.

64. Ethridge, *From Chicaza to Chickasaw*, 15.

65. By 1730 the Natchez were for all intents and purposes the last Mississippian chiefdom, although they succumbed to a combined French-Choctaw invasion that year. See Ellis, "Natchez War Revisited"; Milne, *Natchez Country*; and Usner, *Indians, Settlers, and Slaves*. See also Smyth, "Uncovering an Unknown Diaspora."

66. It never was as profitable as other French imperial pursuits in the seventeenth century. For more on this point, see Pritchard, *In Search of Empire*. See also Eccles, *France in America*; and McShea, *Apostles of Empire*.

67. For more on Haudenosaunee-Wendat confrontations, see Parmenter, *Edge of the Woods*; and Havard, *Great Peace of Montreal*. See also Lozier, *Flesh Reborn*; and Richter, *Ordeal of the Longhouse*.

68. McDonnell, *Masters of Empire*, 17.

69. Ibid., 39.

70. Historian Stephen Aron describes this region as an "American confluence" in *American Confluence*. The late sixteenth-century in-migration of Algonquian speakers from the Lake Erie area set in motion significant out-migration on the part of previous inhabitants: Oneotas went west, for example, while Quapaws went south to the Arkansas River valley. DuVal, *Native Ground*. Stephen Warren reminds us, moreover, that Fort Ancient cultures broke up between 1650 and 1680 and went in multiple directions, only to return to the Ohio valley in the early eighteenth century. In effect, the "Illinois" newcomers were the first wave of "colonizers" in the region. See Morrisey, *Empire by Collaboration*. For Shawnees, see Warren, *Worlds the Shawnees Made*.

71. Bison herds also were relatively new to the Illinois prairies, but they were abundant and potentially useful in multiple ways. Hunting them required greater "organization and scale," however, the result of which was that the Illinois people established a "more unified and cohesive society than was typical of Algonquians and pre-bison Oneota." Morrisey, *Empire by Collaboration*, 23. See also Kenneth Tankersley, "Bison Exploitation by Late Fort Ancient Peoples."

72. La Salle on the Illinois Country, 1680, published in Pease, *French Foundations*, 6–7; Morrissey, *Empire by Collaboration*, 46.

73. "The Journal of De La Salle (1682)," in Williams, *Early Travels in the Tennessee Country*, 50.

74. Morrisey, *Empire by Collaboration*, 46.

75. For more on this point, see Rushforth, *Bonds of Alliance*; Morrisey, *Empire by Collaboration*; and Lee, *Masters of the Middle Waters*.

76. Williams, *Early Travels in the Tennessee Country*, 94.

77. Crane, *The Southern Frontier*, 44.

78. Ibid.

79. Hatley, *Dividing Paths*, 21.

80. Sauvole, *Journal of Sauvole*, 52–53. Fifty years later British maps would continue to identify Chickasaw towns near the mouth of the Tennessee. See, for example, the 1757 "John Stuart" map, William Henry Lyttelton Papers, WCL.

81. Ethridge, *From Chicaza to Chickasaw*, 195.

82. Crane, "Tennessee River as the Road to Carolina," 14. Similarly, Sauvole feared that the Tennessee route would give "these vagabonds and rebels" access to better fur prices, which would ensure that they would not return to New France or Louisiana. For him, "It is absolutely a matter of consequence to put order into it." *Journal of Sauvole*, 53.

83. Phillips, "Vincennes in Its Relation to French Colonial Policy," 311–13.

84. Standard historiography suggests that Vincennes ultimately convinced Piankeshaws to settle in the Wabash valley. Given the demonstrable lack of control on the part of the French, it is more likely that Piankeshaws settled there for geopolitical reasons of their own. See Dunn, "Mission to the Ouabache," 281.

85. "Mémoire pour M. du Vergier, Directeur Ordonnateur de la Colonie de la Louisiane, concernant les différents opérations . . . ," in Dunn, "Mission to the Ouabache," 320.

86. Marginalia in "Instruction sommaire pour achever en peu de temps un solide etablissement dans la Louisiane, dirigée par le Sr. Drouot de Valdeterre, Capitaine Reformé au regiment du Prince de Pons, cydevant Commandant L'isle Dauphine et les Biloxy dans la Louisiane," in Dunn, "Mission to the Ouabache," 325.

87. Memoires et Documents, Amerique, MD Amerique, vol. 1: 1712–1725, *GCDFA*.

88. Fortier, "New Light on Fort Massac," in McDermott, *Frenchmen and French Ways*, 57; Phillips, "Vincennes in Its Relation to French Colonial Policy," 315.

89. Memoires et Documents, Amerique, MD Amerique, vol. 1: 1712–1725, *GCDFA*.

90. "Father Pierre de Charlevoix's Journal (1721)," in Williams, *Early Travels in the Tennessee Country*, 86.

91. Phillips, "Vincennes in Its Relation to French Colonial Policy," 317.

92. Craven to Andrew Purcevall (Correspondence, 1690/18/10), CO_5_288_039, AMDC.

93. Crane, *The Southern Frontier*, 74–75.

94. Ibid., 74–75, 101–2. See also Lepore, *Name of War*; Pulsipher, *Subjects Unto the Same King*; and Kidd, *The Protestant Interest*.

95. McDowell, ed., *Journals of the Commissioners of the Indian Trade*, September 20, 1710–August 29, 1718, 33. This rule illustrates an important point: Spain also animated the collective mind of the Carolina colony. See Crane, *The Southern Frontier*; Gallay, *Indian Slave Trade*; and Ethridge, *From Chicaza to Chickasaw*.

96. *London Post*, January 26–29, 1700–January 29, 1700. Seventeenth- and Eighteenth-Century Burney Newspapers Collection, accessed December 27, 2021, link.gale.com/apps/doc/Z2001389584/BBCN?u=unihull&sid=bookmark-BBCN&xid=74fa898.

97. Coxe, "A Description of the English Province of Carolina, By the Spaniards called Florida, and by the French La Louisiane," in B. F. French, *Historical collections of Louisiana: Embracing many rare and valuable documents relating to the natural, civil and political history of that state*, vol. 2, 229, 256–57, Sabin Americana, http://galenet.galegroup.com/servlet/Sabin?af=RN&ae=CY107803302&srchtp=a&ste=14. Coxe was referring to a proposed attempt to reestablish "Carolana," which represents another way of thinking about the British imperial imagination at the turn of the eighteenth century. According to Coxe, Carolana was situated west of "Carolina," had the Mississippi running down the middle of it and encompassed all connections with the Ohio and Wabash Rivers. Coxe insisted that "the timely possession and due improvement [of such a colony] may be more beneficial to [the English] than all the other colonies they are at present possessed of; besides that they will thereby secure forever all the rest of our plantations upon the continent of America." In the 1720s Parliament upheld Coxe's claim to Carolana, but nothing ever was done to implement such a grandiose experiment. See also Craven to Andrew Purcevall, CO_5_288_039, AMDC.

98. For more on Queen Anne's War, see Lockyer, *Habsburg and Bourbon Europe*; and Speck, *Birth of Britain*.

99. For more on the Carolinian raids on La Florida, see Dubcovsky, *Informed Power*; Dubcovsky, "All of Us Will Have to Pay"; and Gallay, *Indian Slave Trade*. More general overviews of this issue in this period include Ethridge, *From Chicaza to Chickasaw*; Oatis, *A Colonial Complex*; and Beck, *Chiefdoms, Collapse, and Coalescence*.

100. A letter from Mr. [John] [Stewart] of Carolina to the Lord Dartmouth (Correspondence), CO_5_9_017, AMDC. Stewart's focus on the Gulf Coast led him to insist that the British ally with the Mvskoke-speaking people then coalescing into what Europeans called Choctaws. Divided into three settlement regions with unique (if overlapping) political/economic interests, their towns controlled French trade into the interior. For Choctaws, see Galloway, *Choctaw Genesis*; Carson, *Searching for the Bright Path*; Usner, *Indians, Settlers, and Slaves*; and Patricia Galloway, "Choctaws at the Border of the Shatter Zone: Spheres of Exchange and Spheres of Social Value," in Ethridge and Shuck-Hall, *Mapping the Mississippian Shatter Zone*.

101. See, for example, Ethridge, *From Chicaza to Chickasaw*; Crane, *The Southern Frontier*; Gallay, *Indian Slave Trade*; and Ramsey, *The Yamasee War*.

102. Paul Kelton estimates that Chickasaws "lost over fifty percent of their populations between 1696 and 1715" due to disease and slave raiding. Kelton,

"Shattered and Infected: Epidemics and the Origins of the Yamasee War, 1696–1715," in Ethridge and Shuck-Hall, *Mapping the Mississippian Shatter Zone*, 312.

103. Gallay puts it this way: "If Carolina could control Cherokee access to English goods, they believed, the English would have the power to restrain the Cherokee." *Indian Slave Trade*, 144. See also Ethridge, "The European Invasion and the Transformation of the Indians of Tennessee," in Ray, *Before the Volunteer State*. Early imperial visionaries seemed to grasp this reality more than did local interests. In 1690, for example, James Moore's efforts both to find the fabled "Spanish" mines and to trade with the Lower Cherokees produced significant political headaches in Charles Town. Conflicting reports make it difficult to know what he and his ilk were doing, but suffice it to say that it was problematic enough for the proprietors to weigh in. "Some of the Inhabitants of Carolina," they unhappily wrote in 1691, "have without any war first proclaimed by the Grand Council or authority from the Government fallen upon the Cherokee Indians In an hostile maner and murdred Severall of them." Such behavior clearly put the safety of the colony at risk.

For those thinking in terms of empire, it also had much broader implications. In addition to destabilizing Charles Town politics, noted proprietary interests, Moore's expedition threatened the peace of "Virginia and other [of] their Ma^{tys} good subjects." It represents a major diplomatic red flag: even as they struggled to stabilize their presence on the continent, different colonies were coming to see themselves as central components of English western expansion. To the north, New York saw itself as mission critical because of its Covenant Chain agreement with the Haudenosaunee. Below the Ohio River it was much murkier—both South Carolina and Virginia believed they were the only proper hub for imperial Indigenous affairs. Both claimed to have the best interests of the emerging empire in mind; both acted for local advantage; and both thoroughly frustrated the evolving coalescent societies in the Native South. Crane, *The Southern Frontier*, 9; Bossy, "Godin & Co.," 110. Proprietors to Seth Sothell, James Colleton, Thomas Smith, Joseph Blake, and Bernard Skinking (Correspondence), CO_5_288_039, AMDC. See also, Traunter, *Travels of Richard Traunter*. Gallay has rightly contextualized Moore's expedition as indicative of powerful internecine machinations between the proprietors and those who wanted greater local control. To see it, one need look no further than the fact that Moore—the primary arbiter of trouble—later became governor of the colony. Gallay, *Indian Slave Trade*, 135–61.

CHAPTER 2

1. Nairne, *Nairne's Muskhogean Journals*, 74. For the text of the Requerimiento, see the National Humanities Center, American Beginnings, https://nationalhumanitiescenter.org/pds/amerbegin/contact/text7/requirement.pdf.

2. Fernand Braudel provided an apt description of European hubris while explaining late sixteenth-century Spanish and Austrian power: the elite were, he

observed, "despite their illusions, more acted upon than actors." Braudel, *La Méditerranée et le Monde Méditerranéen*, 19. For more on the complexity of the early eighteenth-century Atlantic, see Weaver, *Red Atlantic*.

3. Ramsey, *The Yamasee War*. Stephen Oatis describes this broader neighborhood as a colonial complex of interests in *A Colonial Complex*. The neighborhood concept draws from James Lewis, *American Union and the Problem of Neighborhood*.

4. Perhaps not surprising given their geographic location along the "Ridge of Mountains call'd Apalache," and the fact that they were "the only barier or Lyne between the ffrench and us." John Savry Declaration, September 18, 1728, CO_5_1337_Part1_040, AMDC (hereafter cited as Savry Declaration). In 1708 Nairne had explained that a stable Cherokee alliance could block "any Incursions which Either the Illinois or any other French Indians may think of making into Carolina." Nairne to Charles Spencer, Earl of Sunderland, July 10, 1708, in *Nairne's Muskhogean Journals*, 76.

5. Commercial exclusivity drew out of prevailing mercantilist economic theory of the period. For more on mercantilism, as well as its application to the emerging British Empire, see Stern and Wennerlind, *Mercantilism Reimagined*. See also Hancock, *Citizens of the World*.

6. The phrase "town and region" comes from Boulware, *Deconstructing the Cherokee Nation*.

7. For more on the Tuscarora War, see La Vere, *The Tuscarora War*. On the Yamasee War, see Ramsey, *The Yamasee War*; Kelton, *Epidemics and Enslavement*; Oatis, *A Colonial Complex*; Gallay, *Indian Slave Trade*; Ethridge and Shuck-Hall, *Mapping the Mississippian Shatter Zone*; and Steven C. Hahn, "The Long Yamasee War: Reflections on Yamasee Conflict in the Eighteenth Century," in Bossy and Gallay, *The Yamasee Indians*.

8. Yonge, *Narrative of the Proceedings of the People of South-Carolina*, 7, 8.

9. Optimistic Carolinians believed Cherokees would reprise their Tuscarora War role and drive Yamasees "entirely from their Towns and Settlements." Orders and Letters of the lords proprietors of Carolina relating to . . . the outbreak of the Yamasee War, CO_5_390_014, AMDC.

10. Hahn, "Long Yamasee War," in Bossy and Gallay, *The Yamasee Indians*, 194. See also Savry Declaration.

11. Hahn, "Long Yamasee War," in Bossy and Gallay, *The Yamasee Indians*, 194–95.

12. Savry Declaration. It certainly did not help that South Carolina pursued an alliance with Lower Creeks as well. Several Cherokee observers expressed serious concern over it. See McDowell, *Journals of the Commissioners of the Indian Trade* (hereafter cited as *JCIT*).

13. Vassar, "Some Short Remarkes on the Indian Trade in the Charikees,"416 (hereafter cited as "Some Short Remarkes").

14. Cherokees noted that their 1716 attack on Mvskokes at Tugaloo had depended "upon the promise of the White People to supply [Cherokees] plentyfully with what they wanted but especially Amunition." Vassar, "Some Short Remarkes," 420–21.

15. Ibid. Ten years thereafter John Savry revealed that Cherokees "have told me that if it had not been to save the white people they would have been at peace and quietness" since 1716. Savry Declaration.

16. For more on the importance of reciprocity in Indigenous diplomacy, see Simpson, "Looking After Gdoo-naaganinaa."

17. For more on Creek-Cherokee conflicts in the eighteenth century, see, for example, Boulware, *Deconstructing the Cherokee Nation*; Marcoux, *Pox, Empire, Shackles, and Hides*; Boulware, "'It seems like coming into our Houses': Challenges to Cherokee Hunting Grounds, 1750–1775," in Ray, *Before the Volunteer State*, 65–82; Hatley, *Dividing Paths*; Piker, *Four Deaths of Acorn Whistler*; Piker, *Okfuskee*; and Hahn, *Invention of the Creek Nation*.

18. Chicken, "Journal of the March of the Carolinians," *Year Book—1894, City of Charleston*, 330–31, Internet Archive, http://archive.org/details/yearbookcityofchoounse_6 (hereafter cited as Chicken, "Journal").

19. Commission to Hastings, February 27, 1716/17, *JCIT*, 168.

20. Ibid., 149–50.

21. They particularly wanted to know why these two towns were "refusing to supply them with Provision or Necessaries, or building, or repairing Trading Houses." Meeting of the Board of Indian Commissioners, December 2, 1717, *JCIT*, 236–37.

22. Ibid. It was more extensive an answer than they could get from Charite Hagey, who merely stated that "he was unwilling to treat of that Matter" but would do so "when Cesar and Partridge do." *JCIT*, 151.

23. Hatley, *Dividing Paths*, 26. A good example draws from Tugaloo in 1716, when the Valley man called Caesar informed the British that his town would not fight unilaterally—the English would have to join them in any attack on Mvskokes. When the English stalled on the matter, Cherokee diplomats accused them of "two talks" before eventually resolving "to go to war with there short knives in their hands & with what ammunition they had by them if not suplyed by ye English." Hatley, *Dividing Paths*, 26. The English decision to rush out of Tugaloo after the assault on Cowetas (without supporting Cherokee endeavors) no doubt reinforced to Overhill and Valley towns the rectitude of independent decision making and nonexclusive commercial activity. Chicken, "Journal," 342–43; Hatley, *Dividing Paths*, 24–26; Boulware, *Deconstructing the Cherokee Nation*, 39–40.

24. No one, he hoped, could mistake his warning: "Once they came into friendship with the ffrench [Cherokees] then would be as slaves and no more ffree people." Savry Declaration. Such paranoia had percolated for decades, of course. In 1710 a Carolinian called John Stewart had lamented (quite unrealistically) to Queen Anne herself that the French maintained somewhere around four thousand Cherokee supporters. Stewart to Queen Anne, March 10, 1710/11, AC C13C/2, CDFA.

25. Hastings to the Commissioners, November 22, 1716, *JCIT*, 127.

26. Thomas, *Fort Toulouse*, 9–11. A few decades later Frenchman Jean-Bernard Bossu described the situation thus: "The Allibamons offered, in 1714, to build upon

their ground, and at their expence, a fort, which was afterwards called Fort Toulouse, and they introduced the French to it. M. de Bienville, was then governor, went to take possession of it in the King's name. . . . They never would permit the English to do the like; they pay no regard to the menaces of the King of England; every Cacique or chief of a village thinks himself a sovereign, who only depends upon the Master of life, or the Great Spirit." Bossu, *Travels Through that Part of North America Formerly Called Louisiana*, Letter 16, 254–55, John Carter Brown Library, Brown University.

27. Fort Congaree was established on the Congaree River in what is now Lexington County, South Carolina. For more on that fort, see Stewart and Cobb, "Fort Congaree."

28. Archeologist Brett Riggs suggests that Chestowee's location was most likely near the Overhill town of Euphase. Riggs, "Reconsidering Chestowee: The 1713 Raid in Regional Perspective," in Jackson, *Yuchi Indian Histories*, 60–61.

29. Caesar's background is elusive, but it seems that he once was a slave. By the time of the Chestowee raid he had acquired a measure of political and diplomatic power, which suggests that he could have been born into another Indigenous polity, captured, enslaved, and ultimately adopted by Valley Cherokees. For more on Caesar, see Riggs, "Reconsidering Chestowee," in Jackson, *Yuchi Indian Histories*; and *JCIT*.

30. For more on modern Cherokee understandings of the Ball Game, see Zogry, *Anetso*, and Fogelson, "The Ballgame Cycle."

31. Board of Commissioners Meeting, May 14, 1712, *JCIT*, 24.

32. Indian Commissioners to Alexander Longe, May 14, 1713, *JCIT*, 45.

33. Commissioners to William Hatton, July 19, 1718, *JCIT*, 312.

34. *JCIT*, 53–54.

35. Riggs, "Reconsidering Chestowee," in Jackson, *Yuchi Indian Histories*, 53.

36. Ibid., 47.

37. Ibid., 53.

38. Ramsey, *The Yamasee War*, 82–83.

39. *JCIT*, May 4, 1714, 53.

40. *JCIT*, 56.

41. Allies, it seems, were unenslaveable. *JCIT*, 55.

42. *JCIT*, 56.

43. In November 1716 the commission eased the rules on slaving, issuing instructions that "as to the tenth Article whereby you are restrained to buy no male Slaves of above fourteen Years of Age, you are now hereby left at your Liberty, to any Age not exceeding thirty Years." Minutes of the Board, November 23, 1716, *JCIT*, 129.

44. *JCIT*, 129.

45. Minutes of the Commission, June 7, 1717, *JCIT*, 186. The minutes also indicate that the commission "ordered that Speedy Care be taken, to purchase a sufficient Quantity of Provision, for feeding of the said Indian Burderners and Slaves."

46. Board Minutes, November 25, 27, 1717, *JCIT*, 232. Fancourt's situation is complex: his Native slave woman was taken from him by Yamasees in 1715 and later

was purchased by the Cherokee factor before selling at auction to one Charles Hill in June 1717. Fancourt wanted compensation, and the commissioners gave him thirty pounds. *JCIT*, 235. There may also have been slave trade connection with Chickasaws. In December 1717 the commissioners heard that Chickasaws came "from the Charikees, and they were pressing on us for a Trading House to be forthwith settled at a Town called Talasee, where they proposed to resort unto, with their Skins and Effects." Commission to Theophilus Hastings, January 16, 1717/18, *JCIT*, 238, 249.

47. Sauvole, *Journal*, 52–53.
48. Chicken, "Journal," 331.
49. *GCDFA*, 51, 55.
50. Minutes of Board Meeting, October 4, 1717, *JCIT*, 215. The specific timeframe for attack was "about five Moons hence."
51. Father Pierre de Charlevoix's Journal (1721), in Williams, *Early Travels in the Tennessee Country*, 86.
52. Phillips, "Vincennes in Its Relation to French Colonial Policy," 317.
53. By the 1750s, in fact, a Chota man was commonly called "Slave Catcher." The title could well have referred to runaway African slaves, but in this context it could have taken on additional meaning. Paul Demere to William Lyttelton, August 28, 1759; "Talk of the Indian Woman called the Buffalo Skin," August 1, 1759, both in the Lyttelton Papers, Box 11: June–August 1759, WCL. It is also important to keep in mind the role of slaves in eighteenth-century Cherokee social structure. Captured slaves who were not adopted into a clan suffered "social death" and represented the bottom of Cherokee society. According to Theda Perdue, this structure offered a means by which to validate the "common values" of a town. Perdue, *Slavery and the Evolution of Cherokee Society*, 18.
54. A 1725 French census identifies 66 Native slaves, which comprised thirteen percent of the French settlements in Illinois. Seven years later the number was 119, and by 1752 it was 149. Ekberg, *Stealing Indian Women*, 39, 41–43.
55. Ibid., 48.
56. For more on this seeming contradiction, see Gallay, *Indian Slave Trade*; and Oatis, *Colonial Complex*.
57. *JCIT*, 14–15. Instructions a year later similarly insisted that agents use their "utmost Endeavour to regulate the Lyves of the Traders, so that they give not the Indians Offence and Scandal." Agent Instructions, July 9, 1712, *JCIT*, 30.
58. Commissioners to the Governor, July 11, 1716, *JCIT*, 75. Cherokees in particular needed access to firearms, as Jessica Yirush Stern has observed. As the Yamasee conflict unfolded, she notes, "South Carolina Governor Robert Daniel cast aside legal restrictions by staging a gift-giving ceremony: a gun to the Cherokee, and an acceptance of ten beaver skins as a gift from the Cherokee." Stern, *Lives in Objects*, 1. According to archeologist Charles Heath, English interest in western expansion encouraged trade in guns and ammunition with Catawba towns, their satellite

allies, or subjects "perhaps as early as the mid-1670s." There is no reason to think the same situation did not exist for Cherokees. "Catawba Militarism," 83.

59. Commissioner Instructions to William Waties, December 10, 1716, *JCIT*, 137–38.

60. Documents relating to the building of a French fort on Indian land in breach of the [Treaty] of [Utrecht], CO_5_1085_Part2_021, AMDC. In its entirety Article XV reads: "The subjects of France inhabiting Canada, and others, shall hereafter give no hinderance or molestation to the five nations or cantons of Indians, subject to the dominion of Great Britain, nor to the other natives of America, who are friends to the same. In like manner, the subjects of Great Britain shall behave themselves peaceably towards the Americans who are subjects or friends to France; and on both sides they shall enjoy full liberty of going and coming on account of trade. As also the natives of those countries shall, with the same liberty, resort, as they please, to the British and French colonies, for promoting trade on one side and the other, without any molestation or hinderance, either on the part of the British subjects or of the French. But it is to be exactly and distinctly settled by commissaries, who are, and who ought to be accounted the subjects and friends of Britain or of France." Chalmers, *Collection of Treaties between Great Britain and Other Powers*, 1:340–90.

61. Ibid. For more on Father Rale, see Chmielewski, *The Spice of Popery*; and Kidd, *The Protestant Interest*. See also Saxine, *Properties of Empire*; and McShea, *Apostles of Empire*.

62. Letters concerning the interception of French letters, revealing their contravention of the [Treaty] of [Utrecht] by assisting the American Indians in the war against the British, CO_5/752_Part1_026, AMDC. Pelham-Holles (1693–1768) was a protégé of Robert Walpole, who is widely considered to have served as the first British prime minister. Newcastle himself would twice serve as prime minister. See Browning, "Holles, Thomas Pelham-, duke of Newcastle upon Tyne and first duke of Newcastle under Lyme," *Oxford Dictionary of National Biography* online, https://doi.org/10.1093/ref:odnb/21801. See also Anderson, *Crucible of War*. It reinforced a point made in an earlier report to the Board of Trade: that existential dangers were being perpetrated in North America "by the Neighbouring Indians at the instigation of the French and Spaniards." September 8, 1721, Report on the Plantations General, M. Bladen, J. Chetwyne, E. Ashe, P. Dominique, Records of the Board of Trade, vol. 45, Shelburne Papers, WCL.

63. Gentleman of America, "Some Considerations on the Consequences of the French Settling Colonies on the Mississippi," London, 1720, *Sabin Americana*, 26–27.

64. Savry Declaration.

65. 1724 Jul. 21: Francis Varnod, Dorchester, St. George's Parish, to the Secretary (SPG series A, vol. 18, 85; also copied as series B, vol. 4, 346–48), in George Williams, "Letters from the Clergy of the Anglican Church in South Carolina, c. 1696–1775." It was a message the British government heard in other contexts. As the war initially unfolded, the Rev. John Blair of North Carolina wrote that "having

missioners" in Indian country would greatly benefit the government. If the Church of England took no action it would be disastrous, however, "for if they shou'd once be brought over to a French Intrest . . . It wou'd be (if not to the utter ruin) to the Great prejudice of all the English Plantations on the Continent of America." John Blair's "Account of Mission," November 1704, in Cain, *Colonial Records of North Carolina*, vol. 10, 29. Twenty years later John Fordyce articulated the same concerns, writing that Queen Anne's War had made things precarious in his parish. He hoped that South Carolina governor James Glen's decision to send men to keep the French from converting Creeks and Cherokees would pay dividends before it was too late. October 1746: John Fordyce, Prince Frederick's Parish, to the Society (SPG series B, vol. 14, 239).

66. Carolina & Nova Scotia. Representation with a Draught of Instructions for a Governor of Carolina, appointed by the King & relating to the State of Defence of that Province & of Nova Scotia. August 30, 1720, CO 5 381 1D, Box 346, CDFA. Forward-looking Carolinians like John Stewart even had made explicit interregional connections. In a 1712 letter he informed William Legge, First Lord Dartmouth, that "the holding and keeping of the British Empire in America" should be a primary war objective. The Royal Navy would provide a central element of such a policy, Stewart suggested, but Indigenous allies would have to provide the keystone given the limited continental reach of the British. His advice: use the Royal Navy to secure Montreal and Nova Scotia and use Indigenous allies to evict the French from Mobile. A letter from Mr. [John] [Stewart] of Carolina to the Lord Dartmouth, CO_5_9_017, AMDC. Stewart's focus on the Gulf Coast led him to insist that the British ally with Choctaws.

67. Savry Declaration.

68. Thomas Nairne to Charles Spencer, Earl of Sunderland, July 10, 1708, *Nairne's Muskhogean Journals*, 76.

69. Carolina & Nova Scotia, August 30, 1720, CO 5 381 1D, Box 346, CDFA.

70. Spotswood described Cherokees as the "nearest to and most considerable Body of Indians on our Southern Frontier [and] the only Indians we ought to depend on to ballance the Northern Nations." Spotswood to the Board of Trade, February 1, 1719/20, CO 5 1318 428, CDFA. Population figure comes from Kelton, *Cherokee Medicine*, 24.

71. Many Carolinians framed it as a problem of trade. In July 1716, for example, the Indian commissioners informed newly appointed Cherokee factor Theophilus Hastings that "you must let the Upper Charikees have the half-Part of the Ammunition, and if you can prevail with the lower People, you may send up Half of the Strouds too; all in way of Trade. It is our Desire that when and as often as you send Burdeners to the Savano Town, that you get the upper and lower People to joyn and come together for their better Security." *JCIT*, 84. Hastings responded that the Cherokees put an end to that possibility rather quickly. Ibid., 123, 125.

72. More specifically, the board wrote "that it might be convenient to imitate the French in sending home some Chiefs of the most considerable Clanns or Nations;

to whom they take care to shew the Glory and Splendor of the French Nation in Europe; that the said Indians upon their return instill the greater Respect for them amongst their Countrymen." September 8, 1721, Report on the Plantations General, M. Bladen, J. Chetwyne, E. Ashe, P. Dominique, Records of the Board of Trade, vol. 45, Shelburne Papers, WCL.

73. Chicken, "Journal," in Mereness, *Travels in the American Colonies*, 107, 118.

74. Ibid., 162.

75. Ibid., 146, 158. For that matter, unlicensed traders could undermine empire: moving from town to town rather than staying in one place "in my Opinion is a great Detriment to the Trade and will in a little time (if care be not taken) Create great disputes and Quarrells among the Traders which will be Ill Examples to the Indians and my prove of Ill Consequence to the Country." Chicken, "Journal," in Mereness, *Travels in the American Colonies*, 107.

76. Ibid., 153–54.

77. Boulware, *Deconstructing the Cherokee Nation*, 47.

78. Ibid.

79. Specifically, he said that "he was soon going over the Great Water and if any of them would go with him to see England he would carry them." According to Attakullakulla, Cuming and Eleazar Wiggan subsequently cajoled Cherokee leadership to travel with him. Wiggan, it would seem, had long overcome whatever punishments he had received for his role in the Chestowee attack. "Historical Relation of Facts Delivered by Ludovick Grant," 57.

80. Timberlake, *Memoirs of Lt. Henry Timberlake*, xvii, 37. See also Vaughan, *Transatlantic Encounters*, 141.

81. Vaughan, *Transatlantic Encounters*, 137.

82. "Historical Relation of Facts Delivered by Ludovick Grant," 67.

83. Papers [manuscript]: 1734–67, Edward Ayer American Indian Studies Collection, MS 204, Newberry Library (hereafter cited as Ayer MS 204, Newberry Library).

84. Historian Tom Hatley has observed, for example, that the Treaty of 1730 was "the basis of relations between the tribe and colony until the 1760s." *Dividing Paths*, 27. See also Boulware, *Deconstructing the Cherokee Nation*, 48. The narrative was ubiquitous in the contemporary media as well. According to the *London Daily Journal*, for example, "Seven Kings, or Chiefs of the Chirakees Indians bordering upon Carolina, are come . . . to pay their Duty to his Majesty, and assure him of their Attachment to his Person and Government, etc." Quoted in Vaughan, *Transatlantic Encounters*, 137. It is worth noting that the 1730 delegation was at least the second to have visited London since 1700. The first—a 1710 visit of "Four Iroquois Kings"—established themes and protocols for Indigenous visits that would recur for the remainder of the century. Upon arriving the four kings were given tours of major sites around the city and participated in a number of fetes through which their hosts displayed their guests' uniqueness as "real live savages." The result was the amassing of rather large expenditures, which were only made larger by the expansive

inventory of gifts they took back to North America. Fullagar, *The Savage Visit*, 37. According to Fullagar, "The four Iroquois Kings stirred fresh levels of interest through the ways in which their reputed savagery resonated with problems regarding war, governance, and social order, which together may be defined in this period as the consequences of continued overseas expansion." Ibid., 38. For analysis of earlier Indigenous delegations in England, see Kupperman, *Indians and English*; and Oberg, *Head in Edward Nugent's Hand*. See also Fullagar, *Warrior, Voyager, and Artist*.

85. Ayer MS 204, Newberry Library. When Cherokees returned from their two-day deliberation, they deployed diplomatic rituals of speech and gift exchange, observes Alden Vaughan, including hyperbole that their English counterparts no doubt misunderstood: "When they arrived in Britain, their spokesman lamented, they were 'like Worms out of the Earth, naked,' but English officials 'had put fine clothes on their Backs.' While acknowledging that 'we are red and you are white,' what mattered, the Cherokees insisted, was that 'our hands and hearts are joined together.'" Vaughan, *Transatlantic Encounters*, 146.

86. Ayer MS 204, Newberry Library.

87. Cuming had earlier described making "the King of Tannassie declare his Obedience on his knee." "Journal of Alexander Cuming (1730)," in Williams, *Early Travels in the Tennessee Country*, 125.

88. "Articles of Friendship and Commerce with the Cherokee Nation in South Carolina," CO 5 4 1D, Public Record Office, UK, CDFA. Compare this passage with historian Timothy Shannon's observation of the situation in New York: "The British interpretation of the Covenant Chain is conveyed visually by the colonial seal of New York. On it, two Indian figures kneel before the king, presenting furs to their sovereign, who in return offers security and Christianity." Shannon, *Indians and Colonists at the Crossroads of Empire*, 21.

89. Crucially, George II also conceded that Cherokees would maintain "the Priviledge of living where they please." "Articles of Friendship and Commerce with the Cherokee Nation in South Carolina," CO 5 4 1D, CDFA.

90. Vaughan, *Transatlantic Encounters*, 146.

91. "Articles of Friendship and Commerce with the Cherokee Nation in South Carolina," CO 5 4 1D, CDFA. Cherokees also had to serve as an African slave patrol. Legally, the deaths of Englishman and Indians were to be tried in Carolina courts.

92. The Articles of Friendship obligated Cherokees to confirm that they would "maintain and defend the Great King's Right to the Country of Carolina" through exclusivity of trade and alliance. Ibid.

93. William Hatton insisted in 1717 that Virginians were interlopers taking advantage of Carolina's Yamasee War successes. Because they had assumed no risk, they should reap no reward. Vassar, "Some Short Remarkes," 406–7. Commissioners told the Conjuror, for example, that wrongs done to Cherokee laborers "occasioned by their choosing rather to deal with private persons, which, if they continue

to do, for the Future, will be out of our Power to prevent or making Restitution, but if his People would deal wholy with us and our Factors; for whatever Injury they received, they should be restored two-fold, and the Offenders severely punished." Board Meeting January 25, 1716/1717, *JCIT*, 152.

94. Chicken noted that Spotswood "promised them a Trade and that they were all still and queatt and would not come down aney more to fitte ye English, botte if they should then he would cotte them all." Chicken, "Journal," 330–31.

95. Vassar, "Some Short Remarkes," 406. Hatton specifically was commenting on the fact that Virginians were traveling through Catawba country "with 2 or 300 Horses loaded with goods . . . design'd [for] the Charikees to Trade."

96. Ibid., 406–7.

97. Specifically, he noted that Cherokees "have often been told so by the Virginians." Vassar, "Some Short Remarkes," 420–21.

98. The commission also believed that "when matters come to be better settled, we may also bring up and educate" Indian children more effectively than Virginians. Board to Meredith Hughes, April 27, 1717, *JCIT*, 176.

99. Robert Johnson to the Board of Trade, November 9, 1734, CO 5/363, South Carolina, Original Correspondence, Board of Trade, 1733–34, 14, CDFA.

100. Johnson described the situation thus: "The Young ungovernable fellows of the Cherokee Indians, but far from being the Generality of them have of late been very Insolent, they have threatened Sevrl of Our Traders to take their Lives away, if they did not Sell their goods cheaper than they can Afford, altho' Prices of all Sorts of goods are settled by agreement betwixt them and us, and they actually proceeded so far as to Seize a whole Store of Goods to the Value of 4 or £500 this Currency; Our Traders were so alarmed that they durst not go into their Towns again, and the General Assembly passed a Resolution that no Trade should be carried there, until they made Submission and promised Amendment; So the Trader was Intirely stopped from hence; In the mean time we had an Account that some Virginia Traders were on the Road carrying great Quantitys of Goods, Powder and Ball, which obliged us to send Orders to Stop them at the Catawba Nation till the Cherokees came down to make their Submission." Johnson to the Board of Trade, November 9, 1734, CO 5/363, South Carolina, Original Correspondence, Board of Trade, 1733–34, 14, CDFA.

101. Ibid., 16.

102. The assembly declared that the empire needed to build "some forts . . . among the Cherokees [to provide] cover to Your Majestys Subjects settl'd backwards in this Province, as also to those of the Colony of Georgia." Neither ever could "be effected by Your Majesty's Subjects of this province who in Conjunction with Georgia do not in the whole amount to more than three thousand and five hundred men." South Carolina Assembly's Petition to the King, April 9, 1734, CO 5/363, South Carolina Original Correspondence, Board of Trade, 1733–34, 105, CDFA.

103. At that moment, explained the assembly, the Franco-Indigenous army was "within a few days . . . of the Cherokees." South Carolina Assembly Petition to the King, June 3, 1742, CO 5/368, South Carolina Original Correspondence, Board of Trade, 1740–42, CDFA.

104. Broughton to the Board of Trade, August 6, 1736, CO 5/365, South Carolina Original Correspondence, Board of Trade, 1735–37, 142, CDFA.

105. Ibid., 143.

106. Ibid.

107. Ibid. See also "Some Observations on the Right of the Crown of Great Britain to the North West Continent of America," PRO CO 5 283 1-E 1D, CDFA.

108. Mr. Bull to the Duke of Newcastle, CO_5_388_Part1_069, AMDC; Edmond Atkin, Tuckabatchee Congress, July 9, 1759, Lyttelton Papers, Box 13, WCL; Bland, "The Colonel Dismounted," in Bailyn, *Pamphlets of the American Revolution*, 319. For more on Native polities and the narrative of American Revolution, see Ray, "Indigenous Roots of the American Revolution," in *Oxford Research Encyclopedia of American History*.

109. Dominique, Bladen, and Brudenell to the Duke of Newcastle, September 30, 1730, CO 5 381 1D, Box 346, CDFA.

110. Tortora, *Carolina in Crisis*, 20.

111. Boulware, *Deconstructing the Cherokee Nation*, 48.

112. "Historical Relation of Facts Delivered by Ludovick Grant," 68.

113. Ibid., 57–58.

114. Boulware, *Deconstructing the Cherokee Nation*, 48. In many ways Moytoy's lack of national power reflected the same problem felt by the Mvskoke mico Brim and Malatchi after him. For more on this point see Piker, *Four Deaths of Acorn Whistler*.

115. Tortora, *Carolina in Crisis*, 20.

116. Simpson, "Looking After Gdoo-naaganinaa," 29. Gregory Smithers observes that for Cherokees the ideals of reciprocity and communal responsibility grew out of the origins story of Selu and Kana'ti. Smithers, *Native Southerners*, 21. For the text of the narrative, see Mooney, *Myths of the Cherokee*, 242–49.

117. Commissioners to Theophilus Hastings, July 19, 1718, *JCIT*, 309.

118. For more on this point see, for example, Theda Perdue, "Cherokee Relations with the Iroquois in the Eighteenth Century," in Richter and Merrell, *Beyond the Covenant Chain*, 135–50; Gregory Evans Dowd, "'Insidious Friends': Gift Giving and the Cherokee-British Alliance in the Seven Years' War," in Cayton and Teute, *Contact Points*; and Warren and Noe, "The Greatest Travelers in America," in Ethridge and Shuck-Hall, *Mapping the Mississippian Shatter Zone*.

119. Perdue, "Cherokee Relations," in Richter and Merrell, *Beyond the Covenant Chain*, 135–50. See also Ray, "New Directions in Early Tennessee History."

120. North Carolina governor Arthur Dobbs described the situation in 1755. The Haudenosaunee, he informed the Board of Trade, claimed everything "from the

falls on the Ohio to the Mississippi on the South side of the Ohio our allies the Cherokees claim a Right and dispute it much higher of the South side with the six Nations." This Cherokee right, he felt, also gave North Carolina and the British "a claim to these." Dobbs to Board of Trade, December 26, 1755, *CSRNC*, vol. 5, 464, https://docsouth.unc.edu/csr/index.php/document/csr05-0183#p5-464.

121. For more on the 1768 congresses, see Campbell, *Speculators in Empire*; Ray, "'Our Concerns with Indians are now greatly extended': Cherokees, Westward Indians, and Interpreting the Quebec Act from the Ohio Valley, 1763–1774," in Furstenberg and Hubert, *Entangling the Quebec Act of 1774*; and Ray, "Indigenous Roots of the American Revolution." See also Calloway, *Scratch of a Pen*.

122. The king's imagined "right to the Country of Carolina" was extensive by 1730. The Board of Trade linked this right to the 1497 Sebastian Cabot expedition as well as to the Roanoke, Jamestown, and Carolana claims. Then there was the issue of Carolina itself. As William Bull put it in 1739, "The limits of the Charter granted by His late Majesty King Charles the Second to the Lords Proprietors of Carolina, Since Surrendered to His present Majesty, includes the Cherokees, and Your Grace best knows whether that is not a Sufficient Objection against the French's taking possession of Land by a Fort within the limits thereof. Doubtless the French will endeavor by all means to Accomplish this as soon as possible, as it will be such a Considerable Step towards their grand design of Surrounding the British Colonies." "Some Observations on the Right of the Crown of Great Britain to the North West Continent of America," PRO CO 5 283 1-E 1D, CDFA.

123. Glen to Thomas Robinson, 1754, *DRIA* 1:533.

CHAPTER 3

1. Indeed, feared the assembly, conflict with Spain could easily catalyze "an Incursion . . . upon Your Majestys Subjects, by the French, and the Indians." South Carolina Assembly's Petition to the King, April 9, 1734, CO 5/363, South Carolina, Original Correspondence, Board of Trade, 1733–34, 102, CDFA. Wildly inaccurate intelligence already indicated that Louisiana was employing five hundred "Woodrangers to keep their Neighbouring Indians in Subjection, and to prevent the distant ones from disturbing their Settlements." Ibid. Robert Johnson reinforced French paranoias later that year: "I am informed," he wrote, "that the French increase very fast at New Orleans, and are Extending their Limits by building Forts, so that His Majestys British Empire is America is more than one half Surrounded by the French from the Mouth of the Missisipy River to . . . that of St. Lawrence." Robert Johnson to the Board of Trade, November 9, 1734, CO 5/363, CDFA. South Carolina Original Correspondence, Board of Trade, 1733–34, 4–5, CDFA.

2. For more on this point, see, for example, Richard Sheridan, "The Formation of Caribbean Plantation Society, 1689–1748," and J. R. Ward, "The British West

Indies in the Age of Abolition, 1748–1815," both in *Oxford History of the British Empire*, 2:394–414, 418. See also Pritchard, *In Search of Empire*; and O'Shaughnessy, *An Empire Divided*, 62–64.

3. Elliott, *Empires of the Atlantic World*, 233. Historian Ian Steele observes that the capture of Porto Bello by Edward Vernon inflamed public patriotism to such a degree that it helped popularize the song "Rule Britannia" in 1740. As recently as the summer of 2020 the descendants of the British Empire have continued to debate the appropriateness of the song. See Steele, "The Anointed, the Appointed, and the Elected: Governance of the British Empire, 1689–1784," in *Oxford History of the British Empire*, 2:119. For twenty-first-century controversy over "Rule Britannia" and its representation of British colonialism, see BBC online, https://www.bbc.co.uk/news/entertainment-arts-53888209. For overviews of the War of Jenkins' Ear and King George's War, see Taylor, *American Colonies*; Anderson, *War of the Austrian Succession*; and Browning, *War of the Austrian Succession*.

4. According to British economist Alfred Young, Carolina rice brought as much as £1,000,000 per year to the Exchequer in the 1730s. See Taylor, *American Colonies*, 237.

5. South Carolina Assembly's Petition to the King, April 9, 1734, CO 5/363, South Carolina Original Correspondence, Board of Trade, 1733–34, 102, CDFA.

6. "James Glen's Answers to the Board of Trade, 1749," Shelburne Papers, vol. 45, WCL. In these answers he identified that South Carolina shared a boundary with North Carolina but explained that poor surveying had led to a dispute with North Carolina governor Arthur Dobbs over whether the boundary was at the Cape Fear River or the Pee Dee River. He also noted that Catawba country lay two hundred miles from Charles Town, the Lower Cherokee towns were three hundred miles to the northwest, the Chickasaws were eight hundred miles to the west, the Creeks five hundred miles, and the Choctaws "a little further" than the Chickasaws. Interestingly, Glen also believed that a contested boundary with Georgia meant that Spanish interests literally abutted South Carolina.

7. William Bull to George Clark, June 1741, CO_5_1094_Part2_027, AMDC.

8. William Bull to the Board of Trade, June 15, 1742, CO 5/368, South Carolina Original Correspondence, Board of Trade, 1740–42, CDFA.

9. For more on these points, see Usner, *Indians, Settlers, and Slaves*; and Pritchard, *In Search of Empire*.

10. Hovering over this mobile world was the claim of jurisdictional control by the Haudenosaunee. Remember that South Carolinians hoped the Chain of Friendship would establish the Aniyunwiya as the southern counterpart of the Six Nations, which only added another layer of inter-Indigenous complexity Europeans could not control.

11. Explained William Bull in 1739: "The French have for a long time wanted an opportunity to get an Interest among the Cherokees and build a Fort there. As this Army which the French now have on its March from Mountreal, will come down a branch of the Missipi River which runs near the Cherokees, they will probably

Endeavour to get consent of those people to build a Fort there which may Enable them to have a Considerable Influence in that Nation as they have already amongst the Upper Creeks by their Fort at Albamas." Mr. Bull to the Duke of Newcastle, October 5, 1739, CO_5_388_Part1_069, AMDC.

12. Recall that in 1731 alone Louisiana governor Étienne Perier estimated that at least "100,000 pounds of flour" would move between the two locations. Perier to Maurepas, March 25, 1731, in *MPA* 4:75. See also *GCDFA*, 56; Morgan, *Land of Big Rivers*; and Ekberg, *French Roots in the Illinois Country*.

13. Robert Morrissey notes that Franco-Indigenous collaboration created "a remarkably stable colonial culture. In Illinois, colonists, Indians, and slaves created large families and farm, featuring huge wheat fields, flour mills, and big herd of livestock." Morrissey, *Empire by Collaboration*, 7. See also Engelbert and Teasdale, *French and Indians in the Heart of North America*; and Lee, *Masters of the Middle Waters*.

14. Patricia Galloway, "Choctaw Factionalism and Civil War, 1746–1750," in Reeves, *Choctaw before Removal*, 79.

15. Ibid., 74. In 1747 Vaudreuil reported to the Comte de Maurepas of Cherokee activity in the Ohio valley and expressed frustration that Cherokees were providing Carolina and (and Virginia) with news "of the Wabash, where it is to be feared that [the British] may forestall us in establishing some fort which would cut us off from all communication from here to . . . Illinois and from [there] to Canada." Vaudreuil to Maurepas, April 8, 1747, Collections of the Illinois State Historical Library, vol. 29: Pease, *Illinois on the Eve of the Seven Years' War, 1747–1755*, 19–20. Hereafter cited as ISHSP 29.

16. Ibid. Perier: Fortify Illinois "with troops and forts of stone" as a show of strength; Jucheareau: At least four hundred men would be necessary to secure a French post on the Wabash. "From Memoire de M. de St. Denis commandant aux Natchitoches, du 30 Novembre 1731," in Dunn, *Mission to the Ouabache*, 296.

17. Vaudreuil reminded Louis XV that the Aniyunwiya were "a numerous nation in the direction of Carolina" well situated to challenge French interests along the Wabash. So worrisome was the situation to Vaudreuil that he drew up plans for fortifying the valley, which he would have implemented if not for explicit instructions not to do so. It was his hope that French leadership would reverse course and "authorize me, by the next vessel, to make this establishment, according to the plans which you have received." Vaudreuil to Louis XV, February 10, 1744, *MPA* 4:213–14. See also Letter of M. Vaudreuil, April 8, 1747, in Dunn, *Mission to the Ouabache*, 328.

18. AC C13A/28 General Correspondence, Louisiana: 1743–1745, Folios 49, 73, *GCDA*, 60.

19. Pierre de Liette, *Memorial concerning the Illinois Country* [manuscript]: [1940?], Newberry Library, Ayer MS 3237, available at American Indian Histories and Cultures online, http://www.aihc.amdigital.co.uk/Documents/Details/Ayer _MS_3237.

20. Ibid., 178–81.

21. *GCDFA*, 52; "Journal of Antoine Bonnefoy (1741–1742)," in Williams, *Early Travels in the Tennessee*, 150.

22. Anishnaabeg displeasure was problematic in and of itself: as historian Michael McDonnell has noted, Michilimackinac Odawas served as "masters of empire" in the Great Lakes. Incapable of controlling the parameters of exchange in this region, French strategists grew concerned (and befuddled) when Odawas began to move away from the straits between Lakes Huron and Michigan. *Masters of Empire*, 124.

23. *Historical Collections of the Michigan Pioneer and Historical Society*, vol. 34, 151–52. See also Edmunds, *The Potawatomis*, 41.

24. AC C13A/28 General Correspondence, Louisiana: 1743–45, Folios 49, 73, *GCDA*, 60. Louisiana commissary general Edmé Gatien Salmon spoke to the point from another angle in a 1742 letter to French ministre de la marine Jean-Frédéric Phélypeaux, First Comte de Maurepas. His colony would be in real trouble, he feared, if Aniyunwiya negotiators won over "the Choctaws or constrain them by force to enter into an alliance with them and leave our side." Salmon to Maurepas, February 13, 1742, *MPA* 4:194. Overlooking inter-Indigenous diplomatic efforts, French leadership ultimately reached the conclusion that Cherokees were using the Shawnees and Wendats "to negotiate a peace with Canada." Vaudreuil to Minister, July 29, 1743, AC C13A/28 General Correspondence, Louisiana, 1743–45, *GCDFA*, 60.

25. Ibid., 154.

26. "Journal of Antoine Bonnefoy," in Williams, *Early Travels in the Tennessee*, 149–51.

27. "Journal of Canelle," August 1742, AC C13A/27 General Correspondence, Louisiana, 1741–42, Folio 176, *GCDFA*, 59–60.

28. See, for example, December 3, 1742 "Copie de la déclaration du nommé Coussot, prisonier échappé des Cherokquis," AC C13A/27, Folio 182, CDFA.

29. "Journal of Canelle," *GCDFA*, 59–60.

30. For more on the Natchez Revolt, see Ellis, "Natchez War Revisited"; Smyth, ""Uncovering an Unknown Diaspora"; and Milne, *Natchez Country*. For more on Franco-Choctaw pressures, see Usner, *Indians, Settlers, and Slaves*; Galloway, "Choctaw Factionalism," in Reeves, *Choctaw before Removal*; and George Milne, "Picking up the Pieces: Natchez Coalescence in the Shatter Zone," in Ethridge and Shuck-Hall, *Mapping the Mississippian Shatter Zone*, 388–417.

31. "Chickesaws Indian talk," 1736/07/13, CO_5_655_Part2_009, AMDC.

32. Maurepas to Vaudreuil, October 27, 1742, Loudoun Papers, Box 23, Huntington Library.

33. It certainly was enough for French observers to fear that an inter-Indigenous trans-Appalachian war was imminent. See McDonnell, *Masters of Empire*, 128–29.

34. And the French knew it, even if they chose to frame it as British-induced, as did Vaudreuil in 1746 when he called for a French-procured "general Amnesty &

Alliance by the Mediation of the Shawanes, with the Cherokees, Catawbas, and Chicasaws." Letter to the Court dated 1746, in John Appy, "Some Facts Stated, that prove the French to have been the Agressors in North America, for four Years successively, before the English were obliged to take up arms in their own defense," 1756, Loudoun Americana, Box 57, #5177, Huntington Library.

35. Watson, *Buying America from the Indians*, 18.

36. AC C13A/28, General Correspondence, Louisiana: 1743–45, Folio 49, CDFA; *GCDFA*, 60. The 1745 petition is noted in Kerlérec to De Machault d'Arnouville, September 15, 1754, *MPA* 5:142–43.

37. ISHSP, vol. 29, 246–47. He further believed that there was a need to "fortify and increase the garrisons of all the neighboring posts of the Mississippi River." Ibid.

38. A. Willy to Captain Croft, May 10, 1740, CO 5/368, South Carolina Original Correspondence, Board of Trade, 1740–1742, CDFA.

39. Ibid.

40. Burial of hair in the town is particularly relevant. For more on this point, see Chambers, "Space, the Final Frontier?"

41. Bonnefoy wrote that he "told them that it would be necessary for them to send a calumet of peace to the nearest post; that I supposed that would be the post of the Alibamons [Fort Toulouse]." Only one issue got in the way: at that moment elements of the Cherokees and Lower Creeks were not on good terms. Overhill leaders acknowledged that "they had already been" to Toulouse, but they feared open war with the Lower Creek towns. "Journal of Antoine Bonnefoy," in Williams, *Early Travels in Tennessee Country*, 157. Bonnefoy's description shows how inter-Indigenous tensions could affect European alliances. Lower Creeks and Cherokees had been on hostile terms since the Cherokee peace with Carolina in 1716. An added problem was the fact that Lower Creeks received Iroquois messengers at a time of tension between elements of the Cherokees and the Iroquois. Appeasing Lower Creeks, in other words, might normalize trade relations with French Louisiana, but it would not solve potentially larger diplomatic and commercial tensions.

42. Simpson, "Looking After Gdoo-naaganinaa," 29.

43. For more on French approval of a Cherokee–Lower Creek confrontation, see Piker, *Four Deaths of Acorn Whistler*, 22.

44. Bonnefoy pointed out (successfully?) that a pound of French powder "had twice as much effect as a pound of the English." Waselkov, "French Colonial Trade in Upper Creek Country," in Walthall and Emerson, *Calumet and Fleur-De-Lys*, 41.

45. In 1745 William Shirley led an expedition out of Boston to capture the French fortress Louisbourg on Cape Breton Island. With the help of the Royal Navy, the venture was successful. Much to the chagrin of British North Americans, however, the empire returned it to France in the 1748 Treaty of Aix-la-Chappelle. For more on this sequence of events, see Sosin, "Louisbourg and the Peace of Aix-la-Chapelle," 516–35; and Anderson, *War of the Austrian Succession*.

46. Letter to the Court dated July 18, 1743, in John Appy, "Some Facts Stated," 1756, Loudoun Americana, Box 57, #5177, Huntington Library.

47. Building on forty years of recognition, Vaudreuil noted that the Wabash provided "the Rout of the Ilinois to Canada." Letter to the Court dated July 18, 1743, ibid.

48. *GCDFA*, 291; Vaudreuil to Maurepas, March 15, 1747, ISHSP, vol. 29: 8–9.

49. Charles Juchereau de St. Denys first settled a trade post at the future site of Fort Massac around 1700, suggesting that it would "augment the recent establishment of French power in the lower Mississippi." According to John Fortier, Juchereau believed his presence "would counter English encroachments by way of the Ohio, Tennessee, and Cumberland Rivers [and] would align the Indians with French interests to the extent of making them allies." In 1712 Jean Baptiste Bissot, Sieur de Vincennes, went to Miamis in the Wabash country; in 1718 his son would follow, as would eventually the fort that bears their name. In 1721 Pierre de Charlevoix pointed out that "a fort with a good garrison [on the Wabash] would keep the Indians in awe, especially the Cherokees." John B. Fortier, "New Light on Fort Massac," in McDermott, *Frenchmen and French Ways in the Mississippi Valley*, 57; Philips, "Vincennes in Its Relation to French Colonial Policy," 315; "Father Pierre de Charlevoix's Journal (1721)," in Williams, *Early Travels in Tennessee Country*, 86.

50. Glen to Clinton, May 21, 1751, George Clinton Papers, Series I, Box 4, Folder 8, WCL. See also Ray, "Cherokees and Franco-British Confrontation," 44.

51. Archeological evidence reveals that although they principally traded deerskins for gunpowder, lead balls, and trade shirts; in the 1740s French agents at Fort Toulouse offered silver commodities for the first time. Waselkov, "French Colonial Trade in Upper Creek Country," in Walthall and Emerson, *Calumet and Fleur-De-Lys*, 38–39.

52. See Lantagnac to Kerlérec, October 1, 1755, AC C13A/39, General Correspondence, Louisiana: 1755–57, CDFA; and the "Account of the Chevalier de Lantagnac," in Williams, *Early Travels in Tennessee Country*, 177–86. See also Boulware, *Deconstructing the Cherokee Nation*, 78–79; Gregory Waselkov, introduction to Thomas, *Fort Toulouse*, 31; and *MPA* 5:159–60, 161–65.

53. The expectation was that the force would be augmented "by other French & Indians on their March." Bull to the Board of Trade, March 20, 1740, CO 5/368, South Carolina Original Correspondence, Board of Trade, 1740–1742, CDFA.

54. Continuing: Given their inroads "among the Upper Creek Indians by their Fort at the Albamas," such an outcome could "prove fatal to this Province"—fatal to the province "by subduing those Indians or compelling them to forsake the British Interest & joyn the French against it." To get to the Chickasaws, after all, this Franco-Indigenous army would have to "come down a branch of the Missisipi which runs near the Cherokees [i.e., the Ohio]." From there they easily could persuade the Overhills to allow a fort along the Tennessee, the result of which would be "Considerable Influence in that Nation." Bull to the Board of Trade, March 20,

1740, CO 5/368, South Carolina Original Correspondence, Board of Trade, 1740–42, CDFA.

55. At that moment, explained the assembly, the Franco-Indigenous army was "within a few days . . . of the Cherokees." South Carolina Assembly Petition to the King, June 3, 1742, CO 5/368, South Carolina Original Correspondence, Board of Trade, 1740–1742, CDFA.

56. For more on this point, see Boulware, *Deconstructing the Cherokee Nation*; and Piker, *Four Deaths of Acorn Whistler*. See also Boulware, "It seems like coming into our Houses," in Ray, *Before the Volunteer State*.

57. See Ray, "Cherokees and Franco-British Confrontation."

58. For more on this moment, see Merrill, *Into the American Woods*. For more on the Walking Purchase, see Merritt, *At the Crossroads*; and Hinderaker, *Elusive Empires*.

59. Historian Peter Silver points to another issue with western ramifications. Because the Susquehanna River had long served as "the main corridor that Iroquois raiding parties followed southward, and their Catawba and Cherokee opponents northward," Pennsylvania negotiators tried as early as 1732 "to push this path, and the friction along it between European settlers and provision-seeking war parties, farther west." Silver, *Our Savage Neighbors*, 321n16.

60. For more on the idea of props of the longhouse, see Richter, *Ordeal of the Longhouse*. For more on Shawnees in this period, see John Bowes, "Shawnee Geography and the Tennessee Corridor in the Seventeenth and Eighteenth Centuries," in Ray, *Before the Volunteer State*; Spero, "Stout, Bold, Cunning"; Warren and Noe, "Greatest Travelers in America," in Ethridge and Shuck-Hall, *Mapping the Mississippian Shatter Zone*; and Warren, *Worlds the Shawnees Made*. For more on Six Nations power in the Ohio valley, see Hinderaker, *Elusive Empires*; and Richter, *Ordeal of the Longhouse*.

61. Calloway, *Indian World of George Washington*; Vaughan and Rosen, *Early American Indian Documents*, vol. 3, 640. Nineteenth-century accounts point to Iroquois raids upon Cherokee towns as early as 1710. See, Marcoux, *Pox, Empire, Shackles, and Hides*, 45.

62. A good example at midcentury is the possible role of Senecas in getting Mvskokes to attack a Cherokee delegation outside Charles Town in 1750, which challenged Malatchi's and other Creek headmen's political strength and ultimately led to the execution of Acorn Whistler. For more on this fascinating moment, see Piker, *Four Deaths of Acorn Whistler*.

63. The British tried to counter this influence, if only feebly. In 1731, for example, a Captain Wattis threatened to send Cherokees to attack Tuscaroras because of the extent to which the latter were taking Carolina "slaves." CO 5/364, South Carolina Original Correspondence, Board of Trade, 1731–35, Folio 172, CDFA.

64. Ludovick Grant to James Glen, July 22, 1754, *DRIA* 2:15.

65. Answer of the Six Nations to George Clark, June 16, 1742, CO 5/1094, Part 2. Governor William Bull on the peace treaty between Six Nations and Cherokees

and Catawbas: "This peace I apprehend to be very necessary to prevent the Indians in the British interest from weakening one another that they may be the better able to withstand the attempts of the French Indians." William Bull to the Lords of Trade, 1742/06/15, CO_5_368_024, AMDC.

66. To be fair, from time-to-time fears were fueled by legitimate developments. In 1742, for example, the Spanish *did* launch an attack on Georgia, which would have been more than enough to lend credence to fears of Franco-Indigenous armies marching out of Canada. For more see Taylor, *American Colonies*. See also Sweet, *Negotiating for Georgia*; and Juricek, *Colonial Georgia and the Creeks*.

67. *American Weekly Mercury* (Philadelphia), June 20–27, 1745, America's Historical Newspapers, https://www.nypl.org/research/collections/articles-databases/americas-historical-newspapers.

68. *GCDFA*, 272.

69. Ibid., 289.

70. To an unnamed headman Glen conferred "immediate Directions to you, as Emperor of the Cherokees . . . requiring all your people to obey you as their Ruler." *American Weekly Mercury*, June 20–27, 1745. Continuing, Glen proclaimed that "These Offices belong to you by Birth, you likewise hold them [?] a better Tenure, the Desire and Wishes of a willing people and lastly they will be confirmed to you by the Commission which I shall give you."

71. Ibid. In 1748 Glen threatened to cut off trade with Cherokees over accusations of murder but backed off when the latter assured him they had executed the perpetrator.

72. In return for such exclusivity, Glen promised that "the Traders that may be sent you be such as love your Nation, Men of Honesty and Probity who will not over reach or impose upon you; and if any still do it (upon your application to me) I will send others [in] their Room." *American Weekly Mercury*, June 20–27, 1745.

73. Kawashima, *Igniting King Philip's War*. See also Pulsipher, *Subjects unto the Same King*.

74. Conference with the Cherokee and Catawba Indians, June 1741, CO_5_1094_Part 2_027, CDFA.

75. For more on this point in another geopolitical context, see Pulsipher, *Subjects unto the Same King*.

76. For the conversation between Henry Woodward and the Earl of Shaftsbury, see Cooper, *The Shaftsbury Papers*.

77. CO 5/370, South Carolina Original Correspondence, Board of Trade, 1743–44, Folio 155, June 19, 1744. It probably was built upon early eighteenth-century French fantasies such as Jean Couture's to tap a silver vein along the Cumberland River. Around that same time South Carolina governor Joseph Blake sent Couture and a group of Carolinians down the Tennessee to the Ohio and Mississippi to divert trade from New France to Charles Town. See Crane, *Southern Frontier*, 44; and Hatley, *Dividing Paths*, 21.

78. Cornelius Docherty and James Maxwell Petition to the Board of Trade, 1744/06/27, CO_5_37_011, AMDC.

79. Ibid.

80. Ibid. Continuing: "That the French are so sensible of the strength of this Barrier as well as the many advantages accruing to the British Empire from the strict amity hitherto maintained with the Cherokees that they are daily endeavouring to weaken their Friendship with Your Majestys Subjects to draw them over to their particular interest and by these means to obtain a settlement amongst them which if not prevented may possibly be attended with Consequences very detrimental to Your Majestys American Dominions."

81. For more on the rice economy, see Coclanis, *Shadow of a Dream*; Wood, *Black Majority*; Edelson, *Plantation Enterprise*; and Olwell, *Masters, Slaves, and Subjects*.

82. Petition of the South Carolina Assembly to the Board of Trade, 1744/06/27, CO_5_37_011, AMDC.

83. William Bull to the Lords Commissioners, March 20, 1741, CO_5_368_01, AMDC.

84. Verner Crane described Priber as "a backwoods utopian who, in the fourth decade of the eighteenth century, imported into the American wilderness the most radical current European social and political philosophy." He also hypothesized that Priber was inspired to settle in Cherokee country by the 1730 visit of Cherokees to London. Crane, "Lost Utopia of the First American Frontier," 49, 53. See also Mellon, "Priber's Cherokee 'Kingdom of Paradise'"; and Bowne and Bowne, "Natives, Women, Debtors, and Slaves."

85. Dickson, "Judicial History of the Cherokee Nation," 8. Certainly other Europeans had married into Indigenous families as a means by which to expedite trade networks, so in many ways Priber was nothing new. For more on this point, see, for example, Inman, *Brothers and Friends*; LeMaster, *Brothers Born of One Mother*; Rindfleisch, *George Galphin's Intimate Empire*; or Hahn, *Life and Times of Mary Musgrove*.

86. Adair, *History of the American Indians*, 258.

87. Adair later described the Priber situation as one would describe European diplomatic affairs. "As it is too hard to struggle with the pope in Rome," he explained, so "a stranger could not miss to find it equally difficult to enter abruptly into a new emperor's court, and there seize his prime minister, by a foreign authority; especially when he could not support any charge of guilt against him." *History of the American Indians*, 259. Adair believed Priber was crucial to cementing the French connection: he lived in the Overhill towns "as a brother, only to preserve their liberties, by opening a water communication between them and New Orleans . . . and bring up a sufficient number of Frenchmen of proper skill to instruct them in the art of making gunpowder, the materials of which, he affirmed their lands abounded with." Ibid.

88. According to Ludovick Grant, Priber also "inculcated . . . into the minds of the Indians a great care & Jealousy for their Lands, and that they should keep the

English at a distance from them," even though Cherokees unequivocally fell under British geographic jurisdiction. "Historical Relation of Facts Delivered by Ludovick Grant," 59.

89. "Account of Christian Pryber's proceedings," April 22, 1743, CO_5_655_PART2_009, AMDC.

90. "Historical Relation of Facts Delivered by Ludovick Grant," 60. See also Account of Christian Pryber's proceedings, CO_5_655_Part2_009, AMDC; and Bowne and Bowne, "Natives, Women, Debtors, and Slaves," 67. For more on the Stono Rebellion, see Wood, *Black Majority*; and Hoffer, *Cry Liberty*. See also Berlin, *Many Thousands Gone*.

91. For more on this point, see Ramsey, *The Yamasee War*, 83–84. See also Riggs, "Reconsidering Chestowee," in Jackson, *Yuchi Indians before the Removal*, 43–72. For more on the Tuscarora War, see La Vere, *The Tuscarora War*.

92. William Bull to the Board of Trade, October 5, 1739, CO 5/367, South Carolina Original Correspondence, Board of Trade, 1739–40, CDFA. The legislature put it this way: because "the Subjects of the French King [have] extended their Possessions and Surrounded Your Dominions from Quebeck to the Mississippi River," the assembly had "great reason to apprehend if the said Mine should be worked up the utmost ill consequences not only from their numbers and the Several Nations of the Indians with them but even those whom we are too sensible they have often attempted to withdraw from Our friendship ever since they gained Possessions in their neighbourhood to prevent which this Your Province is at a very extraordinary annual charge and expense." Petition of the South Carolina Assembly to the Board of Trade, CO_5_37_011, AMDC. Indian trader James Adair later agreed that the French had sent Priber to Cherokee country "in order to seduce them from the British to the French interest." *History of the American Indians*, 258.

93. Having been unable to stop the confrontations for decades, in June 1742 Carolina's leadership was relieved to learn that the Six Nations and the Aniyunwiya were preparing to meet the following "spring to exchange prisoners and negotiate peace." Answer of the Six Nations to George Clark, June 16, 1742, CO_5_1094_Part2_034, AMDC. Governor William Bull on the peace treaty between Six Nations and Cherokees/Catawbas: "This peace I apprehend to be very necessary to prevent the Indians in the British interest from weakening one another that they may be the better able to withstand the attempts of the French Indians." William Bull to the Lords of Trade, CO_5_368_024, AMDC.

94. Ibid.

95. "Historical Relation of Facts Delivered by Ludovick Grant," 60–61.

96. Adair, *History of the American Indians*, 259.

97. Ibid., 260.

98. According to Ludovick Grant, Priber's arrest came none too soon. "If he had been permitted to have lived much longer in that Country," he wrote, Priber "would undoubtedly have drawn that nation over to the French Interest." "Historical Relation of Facts Delivered by Ludovick Grant," 61.

99. Warren, *Worlds the Shawnees Made*, 220.

100. "News." *London Public Advertiser*, August 30, 1753. Seventeenth- and Eighteenth-Century Burney Newspapers Collection, accessed December 27, 2021, link.gale.com/apps/doc/Z2001066025/BBCN?u=unihull&sid=bookmark-BBCN&xid=dd82d195. The author confirmed the news via three letters "which mention the number of forces to be 7000 Indians, and 1000 French Regulars, with all kinds of military Stores requisite for a March, or carrying on a siege." Ibid.

101. *DRIA* 1:421–55.

102. Warren, *Worlds the Shawnees Made*, 222. This entire exchange can be found in *DRIA* 1:421–55.

103. "Old Hopp attributes in it the "Occasion of the War to your Excellency in putting and detaining in Prison those Savanahs that on that Account the Savannah Nation had given Belts of Wampum to the Northward Towns in general." Ludovick Grant to James Glen, July 22, 1754, *DRIA* 2:19.

104. Warren, *Worlds the Shawnees Made*, 222.

105. Ibid.

106. Comte de Maurepas to Vaudreuil, January 2, 1749, in the Loudoun Papers, Huntington Library. According to Jean-Bernard Bossu, the ministre de la marine subsequently sent Vaudreuil "twenty-four companies of marines, to augment the forces in Louisiana," in addition to a number of "female recruits enlisted in France, who come to people these climates." Bossu continued that any soldier who chose "to marry these girls, get their dismission, and a certain number of acres of ground to cultivate: they get victuals from the King for three years together, and he makes them a present of half a pound of gun-powder, and two pounds of shot every month; of a gun, a hatchet, a pick-axe, and corn to sow their fields; with a cow, a calf, cocks & hens, &c." Bossu, *Travels Through that Part of North America Formerly Called Louisiana*, Letter 2, 21, John Carter Brown Library, Brown University.

107. "Lambing, Céleron's Journal," 335–423.

108. Instructions to Macarty, August 8, 1751, in John Appy, "Some Facts Stated," 1756, Loudoun Americana, Box 57, #5177, Huntington Library.

109. Thomas, *Fort Toulouse*, 42–60.

110. The standard narrative of events at Pickawillany is that by 1752 certain Twightwee (Miami) towns appeared to tire of French trade inconsistency, refusing to trade either with them—or notably to anyone who thinks about it—their Native allies. At this point the Miami mingo known as "La Demoiselle" invited the British to trade at Pickawillany. In 1751 the French raided the town, killing two Miamis and capturing two British traders. A year later the French brought Native allies and attacked again, using Miami women as shields to force town leaders to hand over British traders. Eventually they took five traders prisoner and killed La Demoiselle. Historians have described the Pickawillany affair as a continental turning point, arguing that it set in motion a chain of events leading to the Seven Years' War. Point taken, but historian Michael McDonnell reminds us that scholars tend to "lose sight of how much Native American" agendas drove trans-Appalachian experiences. In

this case, he explains, the attack was orchestrated by the Anishnaabeg and was the first of a series of 1750s confrontations in which Native polities implemented plans of their own. See McDonnell, *Masters of Empire*, 161. See also Merritt, *At the Crossroads*. Interestingly, the Overhills may have had a connection to the Pickawillany affair. Under interrogation, the six Shawnee prisoners made a fleeting reference to it. See Interrogation transcript, June 18, 1753, *DRIA* 1:423. For a very basic overview rooted in the traditional narrative, see Ohio History Connection online, accessed December 8, 2022, https://ohiohistorycentral.org/w/Pickawillany. Some text in this paragraph draws from Ray, "Rethinking Indigenous Power," 81–84.

111. *MPA* 5:142–43. According to Norman Caldwell, the French seemed to become so "obsessed with the idea of fortifying the mouth of the Tennessee" that they even had begun locating a "projected fort" on maps. Caldwell, "Fort Massac during the French and Indian War," 102–3.

112. Extract from Governor Glen's Talk with the Cherokees, December 6, 1755, Lyttelton Papers, WCL.

113. Courtonne, "A Journal kept by the Subscriber from his Departure from Augusta in the Province of Georgia for the Chickasaw Nation till his Return to the Same, July 18, 1755–April 23, 1756," in the Lyttleton Papers, Box 1, WCL.

114. Kerlérec to de Machault d'Arnouville, April 1, 1756, in *MPA* 5:169.

115. "James Glen's Answers to the Board of Trade, 1749," Shelburne Papers, vol. 45, WCL.

CHAPTER 4

1. James Glen to Thomas Robinson, 1754, *DRIA* 1:39.

2. Glen to Robinson, *DRIA* 1:532. Affairs seemingly became bleaker in July 1755 when Gen. Edward Braddock, commander in chief of British forces, was killed along with half his army while attempting to "reclaim" the Forks of the Ohio from the French and their allies. For more on Braddock's march, see Preston, *Braddock's Defeat*; Anderson, *Crucible of War*; Kelton, "British and Indian War"; Lengel, *General George Washington*; and Calloway, *Indian World of George Washington*.

3. Commons debate November 15, 1754, in *Proceedings and Debates of the British Parliaments Respecting North America*, vol. 1: *1754–1764*, 7. Agreed MP Henry Conway, French control of locations like the Forks of the Ohio would serve as a net "which, if drawn a little tighter, might shuffle us into the sea." Ibid., 3.

4. Jacobs, *Appalachian Indian Frontier*, 4. For more on British paranoia and the power of rumors in this moment, see Dowd, "Panic of 1751."

5. Jacobs, *Appalachian Indian Frontier*, 4. See also Robert Dinwiddie to James Glen, January 29, 1754, *DRIA* 1:473.

6. Ludovic Grant to Glen, July 22, 1754, *DRIA* 2:15–20.

7. James Glen to Thomas Robinson, n.d., *DRIA* 2:535–36. Virginia governor Robert Dinwiddie naively believed that the Twightwees (Miamis) had offered a

way out: not only did they intend to remove French forts, they also "have given us their consent to settle all the Lands on the south side of [the Ohio] river." Dinwiddie to James Glen, November 8, 1752, *DRIA* 1:360–61.

8. Charles Pinckney to the Board of Trade, June 27, 1754, quoted in Hamer, "Anglo-French Rivalry in the Cherokee Country," 305–6. See also the Edmond Atkin's Report of 1755, in Jacobs, *Appalachian Indian Frontier*, 6. These observations support Tom Hatley's argument that "the complexity and sometimes apparent chaos of Cherokee village politics forced the English and French to oversimplify as they struggled for measurable diplomatic results to include in year-end reports." *Dividing Paths*, 93.

9. Perhaps, Glen informed Attakullakulla, the king even might be "desireous of seeing some of your Head Men in England. Seven went about twenty Years ago and I think as many or more should go now." *DRIA* 1:519.

10. Ludovick Grant to Glen, April 29, 1755, *DRIA* 2:54. A year earlier Grant already had explained that the British should "spare no Pains or Expence to enable them to stand their ground." Grant to Glen, July 22, 1754, *DRIA* 2:15–20.

11. "Strong, bright, chain" comes from Boulware, *Deconstructing the Cherokee Nation*, 75.

12. In April 1776, for example, an "Illini" raiding party took nine pack animals from a train going from Saint Augustine to Chota. See Reynolds, *Cherokee Struggle to Maintain Identity*, 141.

13. As he put it to Secretary of State Robinson, earlier negotiations had "been productive of many good Consequences." James Glen to Thomas Robinson, August 1754, *DRIA* 1:537–38. A bonus was the fact that a new negotiation would serve to minimize the chaos that increasingly engulfed western Carolina. As Glen put it, "While they [are among the English] they will be a sort of Pledge [for the good behavior] of their People at Home, and when they return I know they will keep them firm to their Engagements." Ibid. Regarding land, see Reynolds, *Cherokee Struggle to Maintain Identity*, 59. The South Carolina Assembly had stipulated that as much land as possible between Ninety-Six and Keowee should be acquired from the Cherokees. Although it seems like a land grab, it makes some level of sense in context with Treaty of 1730. See also Calloway, *American Revolution in Indian Country*, 187.

14. Glen to the Board of Trade, CO 5/375, Folio 49, *GCDFA*, 245. Glen further noted his fear that the "French and Northern Indians have reportedly concluded a peace treaty with the Cherokees," and that the "Cherokees have avoided talking about the Overhill fort."

15. *DRIA* 1:519.

16. Ibid. In a 1754 letter to Catawba king Hagler, Glen asked for Catawba assistance "along the Ohio" and noted that he was requesting the same of Cherokees and Creeks. *GCDFA*, 245.

17. James Glen to Thomas Robinson, August 1754, *DRIA* 1:537–38.

18. Grant to Glen, August 20, 1755, *DRIA* 2:74.

19. "Carolina & Nova Scotia. Representation with a Draught of Instructions for a Governor of Carolina, appointed by the King & relating to the State of Defence of that Province & of Nova Scotia. August 30, 1720," CO 5/381 1D, Box 346, CDFA.

20. Robert Johnson to the Board of Trade, November 9, 1734, CO 5/363, South Carolina Original Correspondence, Board of Trade, 1733–34, 16, CDFA.

21. The assembly declared that the empire needed to build "some forts . . . among the Cherokees [to provide] cover to Your Majestys Subjects settl'd backwards in this Province, as also to those of the Colony of Georgia." Neither ever could "be effected by Your Majesty's Subjects of this province who in Conjunction with Georgia do not in the whole amount to more than three thousand and five hundred men." South Carolina Assembly's Petition to the King, April 9, 1734, CO 5/363, South Carolina Original Correspondence, Board of Trade, 1733–34, 105, CDFA.

22. CO 5 21 1D, British National Archives, microfilm in CDFA; Order in Council Instructions to James Glen, June 30, 1748, CO 5 21 1D, CDFA.

23. Oliphant, *Peace and War on the Anglo-Cherokee Frontier*, 12. See also Tortora, *Carolina in Crisis*; Boulware, *Deconstructing the Cherokee Nation*; Kelton, *Cherokee Medicine*; and Reynolds, *Cherokee Struggle to Maintain Identity*.

24. Grant to Glen, August 20, 1755, *DRIA* 2:75.

25. Oliphant, *Peace and War on the Anglo-Cherokee Frontier*, 13; Hamer, "Anglo-French Rivalry in the Cherokee Country," 306. In July 1754 Thomas Robinson informed Dinwiddie that "it is likewise His Majesty's Pleasure, you should concert with Mr Glen the GovR of South Carolina the necessary Measures for Securing the Cherokee Indians by a proper present & for obtaining forthwith their Permission for the building a Fort in their Country for which purposes You are hereby empowered to remit to Mr Glen such Sims out of the Money for which the £10,000 Credit is now given You as shall be so agreed between you and the said Governor." Robinson to Dinwiddie, July 5, 1754, Loudoun Papers, Box 11, #491, Huntington Library. A year later, according to Dinwiddie, Glen's "Assembly was to meet [at which time] he thinks they will grant 70,000 their curr'cy for H. M'y's Service, and on such Principles y't he can give his Consent to it. But in the mean Time desires me to send him 3,000 St'g to build a fort among the Cherokees." Dinwiddie to Arthur Dobbs, May 5, 1755, *CSRNC*, 5:401.

26. Grant to Glen, 29 April 1755, *DRIA* 2:54.

27. The perception in Overhill country was that the British were attempting to cut them off completely—a direct violation of the Chain of Friendship. Chota leader Cunneshote (known to the British as Standing Turkey), for example, informed missionary William Richardson that "he had given away all his Clothes when they danced & told their Exploits" in support of the British Empire. Much to his chagrin, however, he had received nothing for his services—an oversight that spoke to what he perceived as the shortcomings in Carolina's commitment to equal brotherhood. At another point Kanagatoga refused to talk to Richardson "for want of clothes." In that instance Richardson "took him a shirt in hopes it might have

some Influence upon him to give me a public hearing or at least dispose him to think well of Christianity for I told him we were told in it to clothe the Naked & feed the hungry which I should endeavor to do out of obedience to the Precepts." Kanagatoga was grateful but repeated that "he was in very great need had only one all in Raggs." William Richardson, "Report on Indian Mission, 1758–1759," William Richardson Davie Papers, 1758–1819, Folder 1, Southern Historical Collection, University of North Carolina at Chapel Hill (hereafter cited as "Richardson Journal").

Such admonitions took on layered meanings because of tensions in trans-Appalachia. As noted in earlier chapters, European sources offer tantalizing glimpses of how Spanish, French, and British commodities appeared in inter-Indigenous markets in the lower Ohio valley. As a result, by the 1750s the Overhills seemed capable of acquiring goods from a number of these sources rather than "officially sanctioned" trade from South Carolina, Virginia, or Georgia. It was a point to which Attakullakulla alluded during the 1753 conversation regarding Shawnee prisoners, but British officials saw evidence of it themselves—even if they did not piece together the broader puzzle or its implications. For all the Overhills' claims of nakedness and poverty, for example, Lt. Henry Timberlake observed in his journal that they had "many tools among them," not to mention guns, ammunition, and other European-made supplies. Timberlake, *Memoirs*, 32. In this milieu metaphorical, then, charges of "starvation and nakedness" take on multilayered meanings. "We call you the Elder Brother & it is the Duty of the Elder to clothe the younger," scolded Standing Turkey. "Richardson Journal." For notations of "the diplomatic language of poverty" in other contexts, see McDonnell, *Masters of Empire*, 208. For more on brotherhood issues, see LeMaster, *Brothers Born of One Mother*. A good example of source hubris: dismissing French power in light of Fort Duquesne, and misunderstanding the complexity of trans-Appalachian trade, Lyttelton explained that "the English are the only Nation that can furnish you, and are willing to continue to do it, if you do not prevent them by your own Faults. But if you do, you will remember my words and repent your Rashness when it is too late." Lyttelton to the Lower and Middle Cherokee Headmen and Warriours, *DRIA* 2:481.

28. Then there was the ever-present confusion associated with Virginia. Just as William Lyttelton was trying to tamp down on Cherokee "recalcitrance" in 1759 via trade embargoes, he also reached out to Virginia governor Fauquier to "take hostage a two-man Cherokee delegation which had gone to Williamsburg 'until the real intentions of the Cherokees are more fully known.'" The problem was that at that same moment, Fauquier had initiated efforts to reduce an explosion of violence between Cherokees and Virginia settlers. Lyttelton was no doubt horrified when he learned that Fauquier had made a deal: in return for an apology from Cherokees, he conceded that colonist behavior was shameful and treacherous and that he could not have stopped Cherokee revenge (an admission of the complexities of Native legal customs relative to British). Contra an embargo, Fauquier was

hoping to restore Cherokee-Virginia trade lines. Oliphant, *Peace and War on the Anglo-Cherokee Frontier*, 92.

29. Board to Meredith Hughes, April 27, 1717, *JCIT*, 176. See chapter 2 of this work.

30. See, for example, Robert Dinwiddie to General Loudoun, May 24, 1756, Box 26; Dinwiddie to William Shirley, March 13, 1756, Box 20; Dinwiddie to Thomas Robinson, Sept. 23, 1754, Box 11; and Robert D'Arcy (Lord Holdernesse) to Dinwiddie, August 28, 1753, Box 10, all in Loudoun Papers, Huntington Library. See also Adam Stephen to George Washington, November 7, 1755, in Abbot, *Papers of George Washington*, Colonial Series, vol. 2: *August 1755–April 1756*, 158–62 (hereafter cited as *PGW* followed by volume number).

31. The response of Lord Halifax to the Virginia fort is telling as regards colonial unity. "Mr Dinwiddie's Treaty with the Cherokees is an happy circumstance," he explained, "if well improv'd; and if Mr Glen had thought proper to obey the orders of the Crown for the erection of a Fort in their Country at the time he ought to have done, Mr Braddock's Life, and those of the many gallant officers, that perished with him, might probably have been Saved." Halifax to Loudoun, August 13, 1756, Loudoun Papers, Box 33, Huntington Library.

32. In his masterful study of the "four deaths" of a minor Creek mico known as Acorn Whistler, historian Joshua Piker has described James Glen as someone who "struggled to find a place" in the evolving British Empire. For Piker, centralizing Native affairs gave Glen the opportunity to carve out that place, although antipathy from the South Carolina Assembly, neighboring colonial governors, and even the Board of Trade crushed his hopes and produced a perception that he was a failed leader—an assessment persisting to the present. Put another way, for Glen centralization was an unsuccessful means by which to short-circuit local problems and enhance his personal power. It is a point well taken. Piker, *Four Deaths of Acorn Whistler*, 32.

33. Glen to Clinton, September 25, 1750, George Clinton Papers Folder 4, WCL.

34. Glen to Thomas Robinson, 1754, *DRIA* 1: 535–36. Glen's position reflects the position taken by Benjamin Franklin, who put forward this argument in the Albany congress at roughly the same moment. See Shannon, *Indians and Colonists at the Crossroads of Empire*.

35. As the Saluda congress wound down, Glen also suggested to delegates another option for overcoming intra- (and inter-) colonial barriers and securing a fort. Write directly to the king, he recommended, to formally acknowledge his sovereignty and request the construction of a Tennessee River fort. From there, the Overhills should ask the king "to put white Men Warriours in it, and Great Guns to defend you his Children, and to protect your Country which is his own." Cherokee delegates understood the symbolic implications of such action (and the subsequent Saluda agreement, for that matter) rather differently: it would guarantee that they would be "brothers with the people of Carolina," with one house covering all of them. "Governor Glen to the Head Men of the Upper Cherokees," in *DRIA* 1:519. These realities put a different spin on the performative symbolism of the bag

of earth, and prompt two major questions: Did it really mean what the translators believed it did? And did the handover mean *all* of the Cherokee regions?

36. "Charles Town in America, July 17," *Gentleman's Magazine* 25 (October 1755), 470.

37. Hatley, *Dividing Paths*, 78; Reynolds, *Cherokee Struggle to Maintain Identity*, 59.

38. Jacobs, *Edmond Atkins Report*, 9, quoted in Dowd, "Gift Giving and the Cherokee British Alliance," 127n18.

39. John Stuart to Lyttelton, July 23, 1757, Lyttelton Papers, Box 5, WCL.

40. Ludovick Grant to James Glen, July 22, 1754, *DRIA* 2:15.

41. #870 Treaty Held with Catawbas and Cherokees, February–March 1756, Cherokee response made by Culloughculla (as in Kullakulla), Little Carpenter, Loudoun Papers, Box 19, Huntington Library, 33. The Overhill leaders specifically expressed "hope my Brother will bring a quantity of Guns and a good Smith with him that he may Assist us in mending our Broken guns." Hereafter cited as Cherokee-Catawba Congress, Loudoun Papers, Huntington Library.

42. In this metaphor the king was "our common father" under whom Cherokees and the colonies were coequal. Perhaps Attakullakulla put it most clearly in 1756 at a conference with Virginia and the Catawbas. He had traveled to London in 1730, he noted, and had "seen the Great King, [who] acknowledged the Cherokees his Children as well as the English, and desir'd that we might continue Brethren forever." "Governor Glen to the Head Men of the Upper Cherokees," in *DRIA* 1:519; 2:75–78; Hatley, *Dividing Paths*, 96–97, 76. The language is reminiscent of Pulsipher's observations in *Subjects unto the Same King*. See also Boulware, *Deconstructing the Cherokee Nation*, 105–6.

43. Cherokee-Catawba Congress, Loudoun Papers, Huntington Library, 34.

44. Ibid. Merely one example: In 1754 a joint venture between Richard Pearis and Nathaniel Gist to stabilize trade with Cherokees (and Catawbas) had fallen apart because of "a quarrel between the two traders." See editor's note 9 in Adam Stephen to George Washington, November 7, 1755, *PGW* 2:161.

45. Old Hop, Little Carpenter, Great Warriour, Willanawaugh, and Standing Turkey to Robert Dinwiddie, near Tellico, August 23, 1757, in Loudoun Papers, Box 95, #4294, Huntington Library.

46. Cherokee-Catawba Congress, Loudoun Papers, Huntington Library, 33. Attakullakulla continued that "when they are secure we will immediately send a great Number of Warriors to be employed by your Governor where he shall think proper."

47. Lewis also seemed not to have understood the complexities of Cherokee political structures. As a peace chief, Old Hopp could not have authorized troop movements. Ray, "Cherokees and Franco-British Confrontation"; and Boulware, *Deconstructing the Cherokee Nation*.

48. Andrew Lewis to Arthur Dobbs, September 30, 1756, Loudoun Americana Collection, Box 43, #2783, Huntington Library.

49. Ibid.

50. Ibid. Attakullakulla was even more direct, warning at the Cherokee-Catawba Congress "that if no steps are taken for our Security, the French will extinguish the friendly Fire between us." Cherokee-Catawba Congress, Loudoun Papers, Huntington Library, 33. A year later, in a fascinating symbolic gesture, Old Hopp also took a wampum belt to Loudoun officer Paul Demere and reminded him "that when the Late Governour was at Saluday he had presented him with such a belt." He gave it to Demere "as a token of Friendship, [but] desired to Acquaint you with it." Old Hopp's Letter to William Lyttelton, August 23, 1757, enclosed in Paul Demere to Lyttelton, August 31, 1757; Paul Demere to William Lyttelton, August 31, 1757; John Stuart to William Lyttelton, July 11, 1757; all in Lyttelton Papers, Box 5, WCL.

51. Ochterlong to Loudoun, April 19, 1757, Loudoun Papers, Box 74, #3396, Huntington Library.

52. Kerlérec to ministre de la marine, December 15, 1756, Lyttelton Papers, Box 4, WCL. The proposal was substantive enough that Kerlérec contacted Vaudreuil, now governor of New France, for guidance. He wondered "whether the interests of his northern region could be reconciled with an alliance that it is very desirable that we contract for this region." Kerlérec to de Machault d'Arnouville, September 15, 1754, *MPA* 5:144. For British paranoia as context, see George Washington to Robert Dinwiddie, October 17, 1755, *PGW* 2:120–21.

53. Article 3 in William Henry Lyttelton to South Carolina Assembly, April 5, 1757, regarding intercepted letters seized by Capt. Thomson of HM's Sloop *Jamaica* from the French merchant ship *Revanche*. Enclosing Kerlérec to France, ministre de la marine, December 13, 1756, and enclosure, France and Cherokees, Articles and Preliminary Conditions of Peace, November 23, 1756, Lyttelton Papers, Box 4, WCL (hereafter cited as Franco-Cherokee Treaty, Lyttelton Papers, WCL). The chain stretching as far as Chota comes from Boulware, *Deconstructing the Cherokee Nation*, 75. Kanagatoga's presence at New Orleans comes from Reynolds, *Cherokee Struggle to Maintain Identity*, 72.

54. Franco-Cherokee Treaty, Lyttelton Papers, WCL; Boulware, *Deconstructing the Cherokee Nation*, 81.

55. Franco-Cherokee Treaty, Lyttelton Papers, WCL.

56. "Indian Intelligence of Raymond Demere," December 13, 1756, Loudoun Americana, Box 54, #2341, Huntington Library. Similarly, at the 1756 Virginia congress dominated by Catawbas and Cherokees, "only one band [of Cherokee negotiators] came from the Overhills." The rest were from the Lower towns. Oliphant, *Peace and War on the Anglo-Cherokee Frontier*, 38. See also Corkran, *Cherokee Frontier*.

57. Ludovick Grant to James Glen, April 29, 1755, *DRIA* 2:51.

58. "Indian Proceedings" at Fort Johnson, November 23, 1756, in Sullivan, *Papers of Sir William Johnson*, 9:561 (hereafter cited as *SWJP*, followed by volume number).

59. "An Indian Council, 21 July 1758," in *SWJP* 9:949.

60. Specifically, they explained an encounter they had had with Shawnees and Catawbas in Virginia. The Shawnees inquired "of what Nation we were, and as

we told them of Keowee, they pass'd us." "A Talk from Tiftoe, the Wolf, of Keowee to his Excellency the governor of South Carolina," March 5, 1759, Lyttelton Papers, Box 10, WCL. Variations for Tistoe's name also draw from Hatley, *Dividing Paths*, 92.

61. Franco-Cherokee Treaty, Lyttelton Papers, WCL; Kerlérec to ministre de la marine, December 15, 1756, Lyttelton Papers, Box 4, WCL; Boulware, *Deconstructing the Cherokee Nation*, 81.

62. Ibid. Within a year Carolina Indian trader White Outerbridge warned Lyttelton that several Cherokees from the town of "Chatoggi [Chatuga] had at two Sev'ral times kill'd Eight Chickesaws & besides had us'd 'em (the Chickesaw) Frequently Very Ill." Chickasaws apparently had not yet responded "but were very Uneasy at their Usage." Outerbridge to Lyttelton, March 8, 1757, Lyttelton Papers, Box 4, WCL.

63. It is crucial to note that there was no unanimity within the Overhill towns in terms of support for the French, which fits broader diplomatic patterns of rejecting exclusive military and economic alliances. Tellingly, Ostenaco warned Demere that his list of enemies was growing and that he might even be killed imminently. The language of the letter on the surface indicates he was referring to the French, but it could have been an allusion to other realities. See also Old Caesar of the Town of Chatuga; and evidence of Nancy Butler, both Loudoun Americana, Box 55, Huntington Library.

64. Franco-Cherokee Treaty, Lyttelton Papers, WCL.

65. Old Caesar continued that he did "not know what their Design may be but he imagines that they are to bring a Body of Troops to Join those that are to Come from the Southward and perhaps to bring Great Guns War to the Stores &c." "The information of Old Caesar of the Town of Chatuga," December 21, 1756, Loudoun Americana, Box 55, #2375, Huntington Library.

66. Reynolds, *Cherokee Struggle to Maintain Identity*, 72. Specifically, Demere warned that "the Mankiller of Tellico came here [Fort Loudoun] on purpose to see our situation and to carry of one or more of our Scalps if he possibly cou'd. she [Nancy Butler] says that the Mankiller was sent here by the Capt of the Albamas Fort to observe the Exact situation of our Fort & the Number of our Troops and to assure the French officers that there was white People here he was to carry him some Scalps, on the Rect of which the French officer promised to send a Number of Indians &c sufficient to Cut of all the White People in the Cherokee Nation. She says that the Head Men of several Different Nations of Indians together with the Creeks were at the French Fort affsd with the Mankiller of Tellico and his gang and they with the French Entered into a Strong Aliance together and agreed to assist the French in their Designs against the English now in the Cherokees Nation." Echoing Andrew Lewis, Butler claimed that Mankiller "said that [the British] had great Dependence on the Little Carpenter but we shou'd find him of very Little use to us." She also noted a lack of unanimity in Overhill country, along with a sense of what the British meant to them: "This Conversation passed between the Mankiller

and his Brother Kinoteta who made answer go on as you have begun, I am determined to stand by the English and when there fort is attacked I will be there for they belong to me." "Information given to Capt. Demere by an Indian Wench called Nancy Butler," December 20, 1756, Loudoun Americana, Box 55, #2374, Huntington Library.

67. Franco-Cherokee Treaty, Lyttelton Papers, WCL.

68. According to Kerlérec's spies, Shawnees and Cherokees already once had gone to Quebec to "negotiate the peace with M. de Vaudreuil" in 1756. Kerlérec to de Machault d'Arnouville, April 1, 1756, *MPA* 5:169.

69. Rumor had it that the French started out well. In December 1756 Cornelius Docharty heard from a "Tellico Runner who had just returned from the Allabamer's Fort" that in February "Lantignac with Sixty Frenchmen and a Number of Indians was to come to the Cold Springs on the other side of the Coosewatee River and that there is Runners sent throughout the whole Nation to invite the Indians of every Town to repair to the Cold Springs aforesaid to receive a Talk from the French and partake of about Sixty Horse Loads of Presents, which Horses are sent for from Tellico, And from the Cold springs the French are to proceed to Highwassey Old Town and Erect a Fort there." "Indian Information from Cornelius Doharty. As Reported to Capt. Raymond Demere. 2 December 1756," Loudoun Americana, Box 53, Huntington Library. Old Caesar of Chatuga reinforced the rumor, relaying that he had heard from Mankiller of Tellico "that the French are to send Sixty pack horses Loaded with Ammunition and presents, he Expects that there will be a great Number of French Troops come with them." Ibid.

70. Kerlérec to Ministre de la Marine, December 15, 1756, Lyttelton Papers, Box 4, WCL.

71. Kerlérec to D'Arnouville, April 1, 1756, *MPA* 5:169.

72. A major reason for the failure of the Articles of Friendship, perhaps, was the fact that the French never were able to provide the promised goods. In 1758 Kerlérec complained that "very far from having received what has been requested for it, we have hardly even enough in the shipment that you have made us to satisfy the nations with which we have always been in alliance." Kerlérec to Berryer, October 25, 1758, in *MPA* 5:196. He nevertheless continued to express hope that the Overhills soon "will be in a position to obtain from the French the merchandise that is necessary for it."

73. For more on this point see Ray, "Cherokees and Franco-British Confrontation."

74. McDonnell, for example, warns that scholars should be cautious not to "lose sight of how much Native American" agendas drove trans-Appalachian experiences. *Masters of Empire*, 161. See also Morrissey, *Empire by Collaboration*.

75. That Native agendas overlapped with British and French interests in the Seven Years' War was not coincidental, observes McDonnell, but they also were secondary concerns. *Masters of Empire*, ch. 4. Jane Merritt makes similar arguments about Lenapes and Shawnees in Pennsylvania. See *At the Crossroads*. Some text in

this paragraph draws from Ray, "Rethinking Indigenous Power in Trans-Appalachia," 81–84.

76. Copy of a Letter from the Twightwees to Lieu^t Govr Dinwiddie, June y^e 21st 1752, CO_5_1327, AMDC.

77. Preston, *Braddock's Defeat*, 117–18.

78. *GCDFA*, 245; Preston, *Braddock's Defeat*, 117–18.

79. As a Shawnee man living along the Muskingum River put it, "I am a Shavanah, and Head of a Town, [but] we are distributed by different names." Warren, *Worlds the Shawnees Made*, 219. Shawnee divisions included the Thawekilas, Kispokothas, Pekowithas, Mekoches, and Chalagawthas. Ibid., 22. See also Lakomäki, *Gathering Together*; and Calloway, *Shawnees and the War for America*. "The Greatest Travelers in America" comes from Warren and Noe, "Greatest Travelers in America," in Ethridge and Shuck-Hall, *Mapping the Mississippian Shatter Zone*, 163–87. See also Spero, "Stout, Bold, Cunning" (PhD diss., University of Pennsylvania, 2010).

Scholars have chronicled the consequence of such divisions in other contexts, as well as their impact upon European imperial warfare. Historian Jane Merritt, for example, has noted that internal Shawnee divisions in Pennsylvania reveals both how Native issues shaped their own actions and those of the British and French. See *At the Crossroads*. See also Silver, *Our Savage Neighbors*.

80. Warren, *Worlds the Shawnees Made*, 216. See also Dowd, *A Spirited Resistance*, chs. 1 and 2.

81. For more on Nucheconner, see Lakomäki, *Gathering Together*; Lakomäki, Kylli, and Ylimaunu, "Drinking Colonialism"; and Warren, *Worlds the Shawnees Made*.

82. Journal from the Ohio to the Twightwees and back in June 1752, June 21–August 4, 1752, CO_5_1327_Part2_022, AMDC.

83. Ibid.

84. James Glen to Edward Fenwick, June 1, 1756, Lyttelton Papers, Box 1, WCL. See also Gregory Evans Dowd, "'Insidious Friends': Gift Giving and the Cherokee-British Alliance in the Seven Years' War," in Cayton and Teute, *Contact Points*, 121; and Steele, "Shawnee Origins of Their Seven Years' War."

85. Spiritual renewal could also explain this connection. See Dowd, *Spirited Resistance*, ch. 1. As regards Shawnees specifically, see Warren, *Worlds the Shawnees Made*; and Merritt, *At the Crossroads*.

86. Kerlérec to de Machault d'Arnouville, April 1, 1756, *MPA* 5:169. Pennsylvania governor Robert Morris believed that the French were behind Shawnee-Cherokee interaction, even as he received intelligence that "they would have their own people Believe, this is Scheme to Recover their Lands, & to Reduce both the English & French to narrower Bounds." Morris to Shirley, December 3, 1755, *SWJP* 2:369.

87. "The Examination of Monsr Belestre a French Ensign," June 20, 1757, *Documents Relative to the Colonial History of the State of New-York*, 7:282.

88. "Intelligence brought by Rosa, or Silver Heels, a Seneca Indian also Peter, an Oneida Indian," February 18, 1757, Loudoun Americana, Box 64, #2853, Huntington Library.

89. Preston, *Braddock's Defeat*, 301.

90. Warren, *Worlds the Shawnees Made*, 218. Warren also points out that in 1754 Kerlérec described how "Cherokees and Shawnees had joined Chickasaws in a series of attacks on French traders on the Mississippi River." See also Hinderaker, *Elusive Empires*. Further insight into the Shawnee-Overhill connection in this period emerges from Creek country. According to Diron d'Artaguette, as early as the 1730s Shawnees operated on behalf of the Overhills by brokering peace efforts between them and Upper Creek towns. Diron d'Artaguette to Maurepas, October 24, 1737, *MPA* 4:146–47.

91. Grant to Lyttelton, July 22, 1754, *DRIA* 2:18.

92. Ibid.

93. Cherokee-Catawba Congress, Loudoun Papers, Huntington Library, 32–33.

94. Demere to Lyttelton, October 13, 1756, *DRIA* 2:218.

95. Demere to Lyttelton, May 18, 1757, *DRIA* 2:376.

96. *GCDFA*, 11.

97. Bull to Lyttelton, June 25, 1758, *DRIA* 2:474. Bull thought the western confrontations would work to the British advantage, not understanding how Native agendas were actually driving the situation.

98. Raymond Demere to Lyttelton, July 30, 1757, *DRIA* 2:395.

99. Paul Demere to Lyttelton, March 7, 1758, *DRIA* 2:440.

100. Demere to Lyttelton, March 2, 1758, Lyttelton Papers, WCL; Demere to Lyttelton, March 7, 1758, *DRIA* 2:439–40.

101. Demere to Lyttelton, March 7, 1758, *DRIA* 2:440.

102. Paul Demere to Lyttelton, Lyttelton Papers, Box 8, WCL.

103. Ibid.

104. Ibid. In May 1758 Gen. John Forbes naively informed William Pitt that he had succeeded in sending Cherokee "scouting parties to the Amount of four hundred of them (all equipt for War) who are gone upon the Ohio, above and below Fort Duquesne, in order to annoy the Enemy, get Intelligence, and bring away some Prisoners if possible." He actually was playing right into their hands—a brilliant example of the overlap of Native and European agendas. Forbes to William Pitt, May 1, 1758, in Forbes, *Writings of General John Forbes*, 77–78.

105. Rooted in decades of tension, Creek-Cherokee encounters were once again escalating in the 1750s. In 1753, for example, South Carolina was rocked by violence of notable consequence. The broad contours of the event were not in dispute: after having concluded a meeting in Charles Town with Governor Glen, a group of Cherokees from the Lower town of Estatoe were attacked by Mvskokes from Osochi town. As it happened, another delegation of Creeks led by a minor mico from Little Okfuskee—the Acorn Whistler—had been in Charles Town at the same moment. In meetings prior to the attack Acorn Whistler had seemed to lead all Mvskokes in symbolic ceremonies of friendship with the Cherokee delegates. He was likely aware of the Osochi attack before it happened, however, and in its aftermath

quickly fled the scene. Outraged, the governor eventually demanded he face justice. Glen initially blamed Lower Creeks, but within a few months he focused his ire on Acorn Whistler. He was not alone, historian Joshua Piker reminds us. By September four different storytellers had turned Acorn Whistler into a scapegoat for reasons transcending the April attack. Acorn Whistler had to die for reasons ranging from the evolving nature of the British Empire to emerging Creek nationhood, and from the protection of Indian models of local political life to the ambiguities of colonial assertions of power. See Piker, *Four Deaths of Acorn Whistler*.

In the years following the two polities would struggle over boundaries to hunting grounds on the margins of the Tennessee corridor. An era of increasingly blurred territorial lines made regional diplomacy even more uncertain. For Cherokee-Creek confrontations over hunting grounds, see Boulware, "It seems like Coming into Our Houses," in Ray, *Before the Volunteer State*, 65–82. Creek historiography for this period is outstanding. For merely a few important perspectives, see Hahn, *Invention of the Creek Nation*; Piker, *Okfuskee*; Juricek, *Colonial Georgia and the Creeks*; Sweet, *Negotiating for Georgia*; and Braund, *Deerskin and Duffels*.

106. For more on British North American success between 1758 and 1761, see Anderson, *Crucible of War*; Preston, *Braddock's Defeat*; Ward, *Breaking the Backcountry*; Hinderaker, *Elusive Empires*; or Silver, *Our Savage Neighbors*. For a global view see Baugh, *Global Seven Years War*.

107. Memoir of Silhouette, 1759, IHSHP vol. 27, 250–51; Kerlérec to Berryer, December 21, 1760, *MPA* 5:263; Kerlérec to Berryer, June 12, 1760, *MPA* 5:252–53.

108. Kerlérec to Berryer, August 4, 1760, *MPA* 5:260.

109. "Plan of Operations on the Mississippi, Ohio, & Ca.," Forbes, *Writings of General John Forbes*, 35. French soldiers in Illinois suggested the British would construct forts "at the junction of the Ohio and Wabash, or at that of the Ohio with the Mississippi."

CHAPTER 5

1. The most comprehensive accounts of the Anglo-Cherokee conflict include Tortora, *Carolina in Crisis*; Boulware, *Deconstructing the Cherokee Nation*; Kelton, *Cherokee Medicine*; Hatley, *Dividing Paths*; Williams, *The Cherokee Struggle to Maintain Identity*; and Corkran, *The Cherokee Frontier*. See also Oliphant, *Peace and War on the Anglo-Cherokee Frontier*. For a primary source account, see Timberlake, *Memoirs*.

2. For more on the mythology of this moment in western expansion, see Kevin Barksdale and Kristofer Ray, "Searching for John Sevier," in Ray, *Before the Volunteer State*; Griffin, *American Leviathan*; and Nooe, *Aggression and Sufferings*.

3. Unknown author, Campbell Family Papers, Rare Books, Manuscripts, and Special Collections, William R. Perkins Library, Duke University. Text draws from Ray, *Middle Tennessee, 1775–1825*, ch. 1.

4. Stuart to John Pownall, August 24, 1765, Shelburne Papers, vol. 60, WCL. For more on "reciprocal hatred and jealousy" see Silver, *Our Savage Neighbors*; and Nooe, *Aggression and Sufferings*.

5. For more on Cherokee nationalism see Boulware, "The Effect of the Seven Years' War on the Cherokee Nation"; and Hatley, *Dividing Paths*. On spiritual renewal movements and their impact on Cherokee country, see Dowd, *Spirited Resistance*.

6. Adair, *History of the American Indians*, 268.

7. In addition to the historiography already mentioned, see *South Carolina Encyclopedia* online, s.v. "Cherokee War, 1759–1761," by Alexander Moore, accessed December 12, 2022, https://www.scencyclopedia.org/sce/entries/cherokee-war-1759–1761/; North Carolina Department of Natural Resources, s.v. "Cherokee Clash with British along the Frontier, June 27, 2016, https://www.ncdcr.gov/blog/2015/06/27/cherokee-clash-with-british-along-frontier-1760; and *NCPedia*, s.v. "Cherokee Indians," by William L. Anderson and Ruth Wetmore, revised December 2021, https://www.ncpedia.org/cherokee/overview.

8. Kelton, *Cherokee Medicine*. On the possible 1696 outbreak, see Kelton, "Shattered and Infected: Epidemics and the Origins of the Yamasee War, 1696–1715" in Ethridge and Shuck-Hall, *Mapping the Mississippian Shatter Zone*, 312–32; and Kelton, *Epidemics and Enslavement*.

9. For more on the South Carolina outbreak, see Kresbach, "The Great Charlestown Smallpox Epidemic of 1760." For more on smallpox in the Revolutionary era, see Fenn, *Pox Americana*.

10. Kelton, *Cherokee Medicine*, 124–25. As a generalization, Grant's tactics anticipated those the British Army subsequently would use to deal with Pontiac's Rebellion. For more on this point, see Dowd, *War under Heaven*.

11. Calloway, *American Revolution in Indian Country*, 182. See also Peter Wood, "The Changing Population of the Colonial South: An Overview by Race and Region, 1685–1790," in Wood, Waselkov, and Hatley, *Powhatan's Mantle*, 65; and Thornton, *The Cherokees*, ch. 2.

12. For more on this period in terms of Euro-American migration, see Klein, *Unification of a Slave State*. See also Piecuch, *Three Peoples, One King*; Cumfer, *Separate Peoples, One Land*; and Ray, *Before the Volunteer State*.

13. The 1761 expeditionary force certainly came nowhere near completing British general Sir Jeffrey Amherst's mandate that they should not "return until [they] have compelled [Cherokees] to a peace." Kelton, *Cherokee Medicine*, 131–32.

14. On destructiveness in the Lower and Middle towns, see Boulware, *Deconstructing the Cherokee Nation*; Hatley, *Dividing Paths*; Oliphant, *Peace and War on the Anglo-Cherokee Frontier*; and Reynolds, *Cherokee Struggle to Maintain Identity*.

15. Adair, *History of the American Indians*, 269. Anecdotally, the 1760 Cherokee siege of Fort Loudoun illustrates Adair's perception. In August that year an Overhill force laid siege to the British fort on the Little Tennessee River. They offered the garrison

safe passage to Fort Prince George but attacked as it vacated, killing commander Paul Demere and twenty-three others. They also took captives. Events such as this one led Adair to believe that the war needed to serve as "a lasting caution to our colonies." In the future the army would need to "go well prepared, with plenty of fit stores, and men, against any Indian nation." After defeating their opponents, he insisted, the British would need to "treat with them" rather than engage in wanton destruction. The latter policy, he believed, rarely resulted in resounding victory. Ibid., 268.

16. Kelton, *Cherokee Medicine*, 124. Lyttelton also informed British commander in chief Jeffrey Amherst that South Carolina was "infested" by Cherokees and elaborated that Cherokee success no doubt stemmed "on account of the declivity of their stupendous mountains, under which their paths frequently run." Lyttelton to Amherst, February 2, 1760, Lyttelton Letterbook, WCL.

17. Furstenberg, "Significance of the Trans-Appalachian Frontier," 648.

18. "Check to Southern Indians" comes from Capt. Harry Gordon's 1766 observation that "on the North Western side of *Ohio*, about 11 miles below the *Cherokee* River, on a high bank, are the remains of *Fort Massac*, built by the *French*, and intended as a check to the Southern Indians. It was destroyed by them in the year 1763. This is a high, healthy, and delightful situation. A great variety of Game;— *Buffaloe, Bear, Deer*, &c. as well as *Ducks, Geese, Swans, Turkies, Pheasants, Partridges*, &c. abounds in every part of this country." *Journal of Captain Harry Gordon's journey from Pittsburg down the Ohio and the Mississippi to New Orleans, Mobile, and Pensacola, 1766*, p. 6, John Carter Brown Library.

19. "Journal of Captain Harry Gordon, 1766," in Mereness, *Travels in the American Colonies*, 470.

20. "The Aubry Manuscript," in Beckwith, *Collections of the Illinois State Historical Library*, 1:165–70.

21. Kerlérec to Berryer, October 25, 1758, *MPA* 5:195–96.

22. Old Hopp ominously warned Lyttelton that "if we should get hurt by the French and [the] fort settled by them I shall Lay all Blame on you for Ever." Agreed Oconostota, Attakullakulla, "His Brother, [and] Several other head men" in a separate communication, they could not defend against the French because they were "mostly unarmed and destitute of ammunition." Kerlérec to De Machault d'Arnouville, April 1, 1756, *MPA* 5:170; "Aubry Manuscript," in Beckwith, *Collections of the Illinois State Historical Library*, 1:165–70; Old Hopp's Letter to William Lyttelton, August 23, 1757, enclosed in Paul Demere to Lyttelton, August 31, 1757, Lyttelton Papers, Box 5, WCL; Paul Demere to Lyttelton, August 31, 1757, ibid.; John Stuart to Lyttelton, July 11, 1757, ibid.

23. "The information of Old Caesar of the Town of Chatuga," December 21, 1756, Loudoun Americana, Box 55, #2375, Huntington Library.

24. Ibid.

25. Deposition of John Charles Vian, January 30, 1758, *DRIA* 2:442; "Intelligence brought by Rosa, or Silver Heels, a Seneca Indian also Peter, an Oneida Indian," February 18, 1757, Loudoun Americana, Box 64, #2853, Huntington Library.

26. Laws "To Contribute to Defense Against French and Indians," Documents 26 and 27, in Vaughan and Rosen, *Early American Indian Documents*, 51–52; Dobbs to Loudoun, October 30, 1756, Loudoun Americana, Box 48, #2121, Huntington Library.

27. Lyttelton Letterbooks, vol. 1, WCL.

28. Dinwiddie to Lyttelton, April 2, 1757, Lyttelton Papers, Box 4, WCL. North Carolina governor Arthur Dobbs was more expansive: the French would use Fort Toulouse with Upper Creek support to stage one prong of an invasion. Overhill Cherokees would then support a second prong from the Tennessee River, while a naval squadron from Saint Domingue would lay siege to Charles Town as a third prong. Dobbs to Lyttelton, April 10, 1757, Lyttelton Papers, Box 4, WCL.

29. "Law to Assist South Carolina against French and Indians," Document 29, in Vaughan and Rosen, *Early American Indian Documents*, 54.

30. The treaty had an impact both within and beyond Cherokee country. Internally, it highlighted interregional tensions such as the fact that the Lower towns were willing to support the British and grew frustrated that more western towns seemed to drag their feet. In reporting Cherokee attacks, for example, Outerbridge observed that "the Rest of the Cherokee Towns Were Very Angry With those of the Chatoggi for their Conduct." White Outerbridge to Lyttelton, March 8, 1757, Lyttelton Papers, Box 4, WCL.

31. Paul Demere to Lyttelton, August 28, 1759; "Talk of the Indian Woman called the Buffalo Skin," August 1, 1759, both in the Lyttelton Papers, Box 11, WCL.

32. Kerlérec to Berryer, December 21, 1760, *MPA* 5:263; Kerlérec to Berryer, June 12, 1760, *MPA* 5:252–53.

33. Kerlérec to Berryer, June 12, 1760, *MPA* 5:252–53.

34. Kerlérec to Berryer, August 4, 1760, *MPA* 5:258–59.

35. Kerlérec to Cherokees, January 6, 1760, Lyttelton Papers, Box 14, WCL.

36. Ibid. He also taunted William Lyttelton, telling the delegation that the South Carolina governor "should perish" for falsely making "people believe that the Barbarians accompany [the British] to war." On the contrary, it was the French "who are influencing the other nations to go to war. The nations that accompanied [the British] initially have turned towards the goods that I had."

37. Bull to the Board of Trade, November 18, 1760, CO 5/7: Original Correspondence, Secretary of State: 1755–79, CDFA; Bull to the Board of Trade, November 18, 1760, CO 5/377, South Carolina Original Correspondence, Board of Trade: 1760–64; Bull to Amherst, November 18, 1760, WO 34/35, Letters from the Governors of North and South Carolina to the Commanders in Chief: 1756–1763, both in CDFA.

38. Kerlérec to minstre de la marine, March 1 and June 8, 1761, AC C13A/42: General Correspondence, Louisiana: 1759–64, CDFA.

39. "Agreement between Louis de Kerlérec, Governor of Louisiana, and Okana-Stoté, Chief of the Cherokee Nation," ID #6924937, RG 59, U.S. National Archives, accessed December 12, 2022, https://catalog.archives.gov/id/6924937.

40. *GCDFA*, 51.

41. Kerlérec to the ministre de la marine, June 24, 1762, AC C13A/43: General Correspondence, Louisiana: 1762–63, CDFA.

42. *SWJP* 3:886, 905, 935.

43. Timberlake, *Memoirs*, 37.

44. *GCDFA*, 99.

45. *GCDFA*, 102.

46. Croghan tied his advice to the South Carolina conflict by bluffing that Cherokees "have no other place to go; as all Nations Else is become the Subjects of great Brittain." "Proceedings of an Indian Conference, Dec. 3–5, 1760," in *SWJP* 10:200–201.

47. "Indian Intelligence," December 10, 1761, *SWJP* 3:337.

48. *SWJP* 3:555.

49. Stuart to Thomas Gage, April 1765, Gage Papers, vol. 34, WCL.

50. Text draws from Ray, "New Directions in Early Tennessee History." See also Ray, introduction to *Before the Volunteer State*, ix–xxii; and Furstenberg, "Significance of the Trans-Appalachian Frontier," 648.

51. Thomas Boone to Amherst: "On the 13th Instant, & not before, most if not all our Remaining Prisoners among the Cherokees were delivered to the Commanding Officer of Fort Prince George; This event which I have long anxiously Wished for has been brought about merely by the Restraint of the Trade from this Province; had the Contiguous Ones taken the same Effectual Steps it might have been accomplished long ago." In the same letter he enclosed a report from New Orleans that supplies had been sent to Fort Toulouse. "Paragraph of a Letter to Governor Boone, referred to in his to Sir Jeffrey Amherst, 25th June 1762," CO 5/62 036.

52. Fullagar, *Savage Visit*. See also Fullagar, *Warrior, Voyager, and Artist*; Vaughan, *Transatlantic Encounters*; and Tortora, *Carolina in Crisis*.

53. *GCDFA*, 110.

54. Taylor, *The American Colonies*, 439. In 1763 western pacification costs were projected to be somewhere in the neighborhood of £225,000 a year. The perception of wasteful spending fit broader patterns of concern relative to British North America. For more on this point, as well as the debates coming out of the Exchequer at this moment, see Ray, "Indigenous Roots of the American Revolution." See also Sosin, *Whitehall and the Wilderness*.

55. Thomas Morris, "Journal of Trip to the Wabash, August 26–September 17, 1764," Gage Papers, vol. 138, WCL. For more on this point see Ray, "Our Concerns with Indians are now greatly extended," in Furstenberg and Hubert, *Entangling the Quebec Act*, 304–34. Two excellent recent studies exploring the freneticism of the moment are Sleeper-Smith, *Indigenous Prosperity and American Conquest*; and Lee, *Masters of the Middle Waters*.

56. Gavin Cochrane to Thomas Gage, October 10, 1764, Gage Papers, vol. 25, WCL. In several cases French traders would remain in place at the request of

Spanish leaders, who "acquired" Louisiana and inherited its posts in the aftermath of the Seven Years' War. See Usner, *Indians and Settlers in a Frontier Exchange Economy*; DuVal, *Native Ground*; and Kolb, "Borderlands in Transition."

57. Specifically, Gage to John Stuart June 19, 1764, Gage Papers, vol. 20, WCL.

58. On May 27, 1764, Gage reported to Henry Gladwin that "Major Loftus was fired upon, going up the Mississippi, about Seventy five leagues from New Orleans; he lost about Six Men, and as many wounded. He is returned to pensacola. The French used to purchase the navigation of that River by presents to the Indians; and without the Navigation is uninterrupted, it's of no use, as we can't at all times be in a condition to force our way up, and down. We must try it again. I wish your Savages may not have got supplied from the Illinois, on the Mouth of the Ohio, I don't believe that any of them have been down at New Orleans. If they do recommence hostilities, they must have procured assistance from thence. I wonder they are not all returned to you from their hunt, It looks as if they were hatching some Mischief perhaps Joining the Ilinois Indians to prevent Loftus getting up, of which they have had motive before this time long, but cou'd not so soon hear of his Return, I thought you had made peace with the Powteatamies in the Fall, as well as with the rest." Gage to Gladwyn, May 27, 1764, Gage Papers, vol. 19, WCL. See also Gage to Henry Gladwyn, March 28, 1764, vol. 16; Henry Bouquet to Thomas Gage, May 27, 1764, vol. 19; and Gage to John Stuart, June 19, 1764, vol. 20, all ibid.

59. Gage to John Stuart, June 19, 1764, Gage Papers, vol. 20, WCL.

60. Ibid. Fortunately for Gage, negotiations at Detroit combined with an Ohio invasion by British forces temporarily to calm tensions related to Pontiac's Rebellion in 1765.

61. Gage to Johnson, May 4, 1764, Gage Papers, vol. 18, WCL; William Johnson to Thomas Gage, vol. 14, ibid. Two weeks later Johnson insisted that although his intelligence network could not confirm that Overhills had offered sanctuary to Shawnees, given "that as many of the latter, are in some measure connected with them, they might probably afford them a retreat on their requisition." William Johnson to Thomas Gage, May 17, 1764, vol. 18, ibid.

62. Gage to John Campbell, April 20, 1765, Gage Papers, vol. 34, WCL. For more on Odawa strategies in this period see McDonnell, *Masters of Empire*; and Witgen, *An Infinity of Nations*.

63. For his part, Gavin Cochrane feared that "Cherokees cannot be brought to employ their time at present, in cutting off the Supplies sent our enemies." The reason was rooted in a time-honored Native misdirection: "They plead its being the hunting season & the great debts they have contracted with the Indian traders." Cochrane to Thomas Gage, October 10, 1764, Gage Papers, vol. 25, WCL.

64. Boulware, *Deconstructing the Cherokee Nation*, ch. 7; Hatley, *Dividing Paths*, 158–59. See also Oliphant, *Peace and War on the Anglo-Cherokee Frontier*; and Tortora, *Carolina in Crisis*. In many ways Cherokee mobility from a central region resembles the pattern described by Jon Parmenter regarding the Haudenosaunee in *Edge of the Woods*. See also Rodning, *Center Places and Cherokee Towns*.

65. *GCDFA*, 36. Haudenosaunee scouts reinforced this intelligence, noting that an unnamed party had traveled near the Forks of the Ohio on their way "to fight the Cherokees last spring." See "Indian Intelligence," September 28, 1762, *SWJP* 10:535.

66. Griswold, *Pictorial History of Fort Wayne, Indiana*, 58–59.

67. Gladwin to Gage, June 7, 1764, Gage Papers, vol. 19, WCL; and Griswold, *Pictorial History of Fort Wayne*, 58–59. Miamis put out feelers directly to the British for supplies, too, a fact corroborated by Oconostota in reports he provided to the South Carolina Council Chamber; see *GCDFA*, 110, 310.

68. Lagautrais to Farmar, n.d. [early 1765] from Illinois, enclosed in Farmar to Gage, April 13, 1765, Gage Papers, vol. 34, WCL.

69. Pittman to Farmar, July 10, 1764, enclosed in Robert Farmar to Gage, March 24, 1765, Gage Papers, vol. 32, WCL.

70. Fraser Report, Gage Papers, vol. 137, 7–8, WCL.

71. Dowd, *War under Heaven*, 226. On Mascoutens and Kickapoos, see *GCDFA*, 52.

72. Apparently, a Cherokee prisoner was taken to Illinois at roughly the same time. *GCDFA*, 176.

73. *GCDFA*, 118.

74. Proceedings at a congress at Fort Prince George in the Cherokee Country, May 8, 1766, Great Britain Indian Department Collection, Box 1, WCL.

75. Ibid.

76. Ibid.

77. North Carolina governor Arthur Dobbs, for example, noted that the Haudenosaunee claimed everything "from the falls on the Ohio to the Mississippi on the South side of the Ohio our allies the Cherokees claim a Right and dispute it much higher of the South side with the six Nations." In the Cherokee "right" he felt North Carolina (and the British) "have a claim to these." Arthur Dobbs to the Board of Trade, December 26, 1755, *CSRNC*, 5:464.

78. Overlapping claims to extended hunting grounds were a problem for Cherokees on several fronts. For more on this point see Boulware, "It seems like coming into our Houses," in Ray, *Before the Volunteer State*, 65–82.

79. "Journal of the Superintendent's Proceedings of Congress held at Hard Labour, South Carolina. 1768 Sept 28–Oct 17," Gage Papers, vol. 137, 4, WCL. See also Boulware, *Deconstructing the Cherokee Nation*, 143–44; and Hinderaker, *Elusive Empires*.

80. For more on the Fort Stanwix negotiations, see Campbell, *Speculators in Empire*.

81. For more on Shawnee efforts in Cherokee country, see, for example, Dowd, *Spirited Resistance*; Warren, *Worlds the Shawnees Made*; and John Bowes, "Shawnee Geography and the Tennessee Corridor in the Seventeenth and Eighteenth Centuries," in Ray, *Before the Volunteer State*, 83–108. See also Hinderaker, *Elusive Empires*.

82. Speech of Oconostota, "Journal of the Superintendent's Proceedings of Congress held at Hard Labour, South Carolina," Gage Papers, vol. 137, 8. As early as 1766 Kittagusta had asked John Stuart to inform Onondaga "that the Cherokees send to ask for a Peace from their Town House in Chote where Peace has been made

before, Belts of Whampum & Pipes exchanged & Tobacco smoked." "Proceedings at a Congress at Fort Prince George in the Cherokee Country, May 8, 1766," Great Britain Indian Department Collection, Box 1, WCL.

83. Johnson to Croghan, March 16, 1768, quoted in Campbell, *Speculators in Empire*, 238n59.

84. Speech of John Stuart, "Proceedings of a Congress of the principal Chiefs and Warriors of the Cherokee Nation with John Stuart held at Congarees, South Carolina, 1770 April 3," Gage Papers, vol. 137, 3, WCL.

85. Speech of Oconostota, "Journal of the Superintendent's Proceedings of Congress held at Hard Labour, South Carolina," Gage Papers, vol. 137, WCL.

86. This statement, although about 1768, was part of a 1770 speech. Speech of John Stuart, "Proceedings of a Congress of the principal Chiefs and Warriors of the Cherokee Nation with John Stuart held at Congarees, South Carolina, 1770 April 3," Gage Papers, vol. 137, 3, WCL.

87. Ibid., 10.

88. Ibid., 16.

89. Wilkins speech to the Indians at Post Vincent, Wabash, & Ohio Rivers, Great Britain Indian Department Collection, Box 1, WCL.

90. Ibid.

91. That conviction was one part of a broader rethinking of North American policy on the part of the empire. Charles Garth would have suggested that such a position was a bit hasty, however. South Carolina's factor in London in 1762, Garth intuited that Anglo-American triumphalism was rooted in the false assumption that the British had acquired *actual* jurisdiction. The west remained Native-controlled, he understood, which suggested that the real issue was whether British North Americans should go there at all. He informed the South Carolina Assembly that "where there is no Jurisdiction, there can be no law, and where there is no Law, Villanies, Violences, Injuries, disputes & differences of all sorts for ever subsist." No colonial advantage could develop in such an environment, he suggested, in which case "it is highly proper for the Interposition of the Government, to determine a Boundary Line in some way or other." Even an "unequitable determination," he believed, seemed "better than to continue" with the ongoing system of corruption. Century-old imperial imaginations notwithstanding, without greater stability every regulation the South Carolina assembly passed "to Establish a Trade with the Indians upon a proper footing, will fail of the End wish'd for." Charles Garth to the South Carolina Legislature, August 14, 1762, Charles Garth Letterbooks, WCL.

Garth may not fully have understood it, but he put his finger on a central problem for the British Empire following the Seven Years' War: inter-Indigenous complexities in trans-Appalachia, combined with unrestricted encroachment by eastern colonials, obliterated the extension of meaningful imperial jurisdiction. That encroachment, moreover, was rooted in utterly selfish motivations, suggested Sir William Johnson. The colonies were undermining the empire, he believed, because they focused so heavily upon individual gain when "the General Interests of the Whole, & the Security of Peace on the Frontiers is what alone should be pursued." Johnson to Gage, April 23, 1768, Gage Papers, vol. 76, WCL. Colonial corruption and diplomatic cacophony were fixable problems, of course, but they would require significant investment both in terms of Indigenous diplomacy and of reforming colonial political structures unfit to accommodate evolving imperial western policies. Officials like Thomas Gage, Sir William Johnson, John Stuart, and their support networks particularly understood the situation. Between 1763 and 1775 they supported policies that would increase revenue to defray North American expenses. They called for an end to colonial corruption, something they feared undermined Indigenous diplomacy and made a mockery of the rule of law. Ultimately, they concluded that centralizing Indigenous affairs offered the best means by which to stabilize the continent. See Ray, "Indigenous Roots of the American Revolution."

92. The proclamation further attempted to stabilize commerce by requiring that trade licenses would have to come from royal governors. The Royal Proclamation-October 7, 1763, Avalon Project, accessed December 12, 2022, http://avalon.law.yale.edu/18th_century/proc1763.asp. For more on the proclamation see Calloway, *Scratch of a Pen*.

93. *OED* online, s.v. "Congress, n.," accessed December 20, 2022, https://www.oed.com/view/Entry/39158?isAdvanced=false&result=1&rskey=6gipyh&.

94. Emmerich de Vattel, *The Law of Nations*, book 2, ch. 7, 310. See also John Winthrop, "Reasons to be Considered for justifying the Undertakers of the intended Plantation in New England and for Encouraging Such Whose Hearts God Shall Move to Join Them in It (1629)," *Massachusetts Historical Society Proceedings* 8 (1864–65), 420–25; and Locke, *Two Treatises of Government*.

95. "Copy Kings Instruction to the Govr No. 109 respecting Indian lands, ca. 1760–1775," British Public Records, c. 1600–1782 [manuscript], Southern Historical Collection #517, Unit 2, University of North Carolina at Chapel Hill.

96. Ibid.

97. Ibid.

98. Iroquois-Cherokee Congress, Gage Papers, vol. 75, 18, WCL.

99. Ibid., 19.

100. Ibid.

101. "Journal of the Superintendent's Proceedings of Congress held at Hard Labour, South Carolina," Gage Papers, vol. 137, WCL.

102. Ibid., 9.

103. Speech of John Stuart, "Proceedings of a Congress of the principal Chiefs and Warriors of the Cherokee Nation with John Stuart held at Congarees, South Carolina, 1770 April 3," Gage Papers, vol. 137, 6.

104. Ibid., 6–7. Henry Stuart reinforced the point to Cherokee leadership in 1776, suggesting that "they themselves were to blame for making private Bargains for their Lands contrary to al the Talks that they had received from [John Stuart] and Mr Cameron." Henry Stuart to John Stuart, August 25, 1776, *CSRNC* 10:764.

105. Speech of Oconostota, "Proceedings of a Congress of the principal Chiefs and Warriors of the Cherokee Nation with John Stuart held at Congarees, South Carolina, 3 April 1770," Gage Papers, vol. 137, 9–10, WCL. Specifically, he expressed his "desire [that] my Father may get this matter settled for us, and the Line marked agreeable to Treaty."

106. Ibid.

107. Henry Stuart to John Stuart, August 25, 1776, *CSRNC* 10:768.

108. Gage to John Stuart, June 21, 1772, Gage Papers, vol. 112, WCL.

109. On Cherokees in Lord Dunmore's War, see Dowd, *Spirited Resistance*, 45.

110. Gage to Johnson, February 5, 1775, Gage Papers, vol. 125, WCL.

111. On Dunmore's War, see Holton, *Forced Founders*; and David, *Dunmore's New World*. For more on Henderson and the Transylvania Company, see Aron, *How the West Was Lost*; Kars, *Breaking Loose Together*; and Natalie Inman, "Military Families: Kinship in the American Revolution," in Ray, *Before the Volunteer State*.

112. "Talk by Old Tassel," in Lowrie and St. Clair, *American State Papers*, 1:42.

113. Gage to James Grant, September 29, 1764, Gage Papers, vol. 25, WCL.

114. Dowd, *Spirited Resistance*, ch. 2. See also Boulware, *Deconstructing the Cherokee Nation*; Hatley, *Dividing Paths*; and Reynolds, *Struggle to Maintain Cherokee Identity*.

115. Sleeper-Smith, *Indigenous Prosperity and American Conquest*, 224. For examples of ongoing conflict, see John Stuart to Gage, February 8, 1771, *SWJP* 8:1131–32; Gage to William Johnson, May 20, 1770, *SWJP* 12:821–22.

116. Furstenberg, "Significance of the Trans-Appalachian Frontier."

117. "New Creature, the American" draws from Crevecoeur, *Letters from an American Farmer*, Letter 3—What Is an American? 66–105.

Epilogue

1. "Family squabble" is a paraphrase of Colin Calloway's interpretation in *The American Revolution in Indian Country*. Agrees Gregory Smithers: "Most Indigenous Southerners . . . saw the Revolutionary War between the British and the American colonists as a foreign war." *Native Southerners*, 120. See also Schmidt, *Native Americans in the American Revolution*. Cameron insisted the defense of Cherokees "& their Land is one of the greatest Causes of it." His allusion points to an issue mostly overlooked by traditional explorations of what caused the Revolution. By the 1770s the combination of eastern land encroachment and inter-Indigenous complexities in trans-Appalachia had come to represent clear threats to the British Empire in North America. The officials who most closely dealt with the region increasingly concluded that removing colonists from the equation offered a crucial means by which to deal with those threats. To do so required the consolidation of Native affairs at the imperial level, which, as previously noted, was a conviction that had evolved at least over a twenty-year period. South Carolinian Jonathan Belcher succinctly

articulated the position in 1757. The only way to overcome local "jealousies, piques, and animosities," he said, was "to have an Union of the Colonies established by Act of Parliament in such a manner as that all Military Matters be concerted and enacted by one Body, binding the Whole." Belcher to Loudoun, February 21, 1757, #2883, Loudoun Papers, Box 64, Huntington Library. Agreed John Stuart in 1765: "The Laws in the American Provinces are not strong enough to operate with necessary Vigour, amongst People living so remote and who require to have the Hand of Justice perpetually stretched over them." He more directly addressed western concerns with John Pownall, explaining that "the Trade to the Cherokee Country is in the same State of Confusion, or worse than in the other Nations." The reason, he said, was because southern governors would not force colonists to abide by established regulations for western trade and land acquisition. As a consequence, ordinary people would not "pay the least attention to any Orders, or Instructions from the Superintendant, his Deputies or any other Person under him." His source for this opinion was the Mvskoke mico the Mortar, whom Stuart said had informed him "that I talk with Two Tongues, for whilst I was making Things straight in one Part of the World, our People were killing the Red Men, & stealing their Lands in another, & that he could put no Confidence in People, who act in such a Manner." John Stuart to John Pownall, August 24, 1765, Shelburne Papers, vol. 60, WCL.

By 1774 the conclusion was obvious: centralizing Indigenous affairs offered the best means by which to stabilize the continent. Only centralized authority could advance unified Indigenous diplomatic initiatives, stop corrupt speculation and trade practices, and solidify jurisdiction in trans-Appalachia. Ultimately Parliament agreed with this assessment, and in the 1774 Quebec Act imposed boundaries intended "to correct the defective state of the hinterland." Jack Sosin, *Whitehall and Wilderness*, 242. Colonials (generally) and speculators and their surveyor corps (specifically) disagreed, however, seeing trans-Appalachia as an untapped resource and imperial restraints as threats to local autonomy. They rejected giving the empire control over Indigenous affairs and used the rhetoric of British constitutional liberty to reframe corrupt behavior into something it emphatically was not. For more on the issue of centralizing Native affairs as an important but overlooked means by which to think about the coming of the American Revolution, see Ray, *Indigenous Roots of the American Revolution*; and Ray, "Our Concerns with Indians are now greatly extended," in Furstenberg and Hubert, *Entangling the Quebec Act*.

2. See, for example, Hinderaker, *Elusive Empires*; Furstenberg, "Significance of the Trans-Appalachian Frontier"; and Silver, *Our Savage Neighbors*.

3. Population figures draw from Ray, *Middle Tennessee*, 14. Another way to think about land speculation in the Cumberland district (the region surrounding modern Nashville): between 1790 and 1795 nineteen justices of the peace in Davidson County claimed an average of 7,170 acres. Four of them held in excess of 20,000 acres each. Ray, *Middle Tennessee*, 16.

4. Bloody Fellow to William Blount, September 10, 1792, *American Historical Magazine* 2 (January 1897): 70–71, quoted in Ray, *Middle Tennessee*, 24.

5. Ray, *Middle Tennessee*, 26.

6. Because Revolutionary speculators surveyed an immense volume of acreage, the stations they established led Cherokees to believe "what was told some years ago by the Kings people i.e. if our elder brothers here overcome them, they would at last take all our hunting grounds and bring us to nothing." "Journal of Daniel Smith, September 25, 1779," *Tennessee Historical Magazine* 1 (March 1915): 51.

7. Calloway, *American Revolution in Indian Country*, 48. Boulware points out, for example, that unlike during the Anglo-Cherokee War, Whigs "successfully targeted every mountain region." *Deconstructing the Cherokee Nation*, 8. "Catastrophic" comes from Richard Gildrie, "Tennessee in the American Revolution: A Reconsideration," in Ray, *Before the Volunteer State*, 119. In 1780, he observes, Arthur Campbell burned "upwards of one thousand Houses, and not less than fifty thousand bushels of corn" in the Overhill towns. A year later John Sevier, in the first of many such actions over his lifetime, burned fifteen Middle towns. Calloway, *American Revolution in Indian Country*, 50. For more on Sevier, see Barksdale, *Lost State of Franklin*; Ray, *Middle Tennessee*; and Barksdale and Ray, "Searching for John Sevier: Myth, Memory, and the History of Tennessee History," in Ray, *Before the Volunteer State*, 201–16.

8. By 1777 thousands of Anglo-Americans had settled in or near Cherokee territory. It meant that the Overhill towns (in particular) found themselves drawn into violent clashes between Patriots and Loyalists. In one particularly notable incident, in November 1775 two thousand Loyalists laid siege to nineteen hundred Patriots at Ninety-Six, South Carolina (ten miles east of modern Greenwood), over munitions allegedly sent to the Cherokees. After two days of skirmishing the two sides agreed to a peace treaty, which the Whigs very quickly broke—causing Loyalists to flee to Cherokee country. Gildrie, "Tennessee in the American Revolution," in Ray, *Before the Volunteer State*, 117.

9. Importantly, the site of the negotiation was a location the Aniyunwiya long had deemed sacred. And although they "kept formal possession of that sacred space," they did so only "by sufferance" of the Euro-Americans. Gildrie, "Tennessee in the American Revolution," in Ray, *Before the Volunteer State*, 120. From a purely legal perspective, such an arrangement anticipated the seisin versus "rights of occupancy" debates adjudicated in 1809 by the U.S. Supreme Court in *Fletcher v. Peck*. For more on that decision and its impact on Native property rights, see Ray, "The indians of every denomination were free, and independent of us," 149–51; and Watson, "The Doctrine of Discovery and the Elusive Definition of Indian Title," 1002–4. For more on *Fletcher v. Peck* generally, see Magrath, *Yazoo*; Hobson, *Great Yazoo Lands Sale*; Banner, *How the Indians Lost Their Land*; and Watson, *Buying America from the Indians*.

10. On spiritual renewal and identity formation, see Dowd, *A Spirited Resistance*; and Dowd, *War under Heaven*. The White settlement resulting from the Transylvania Purchase had an environmental as well as an "economic" consequence: the settlers fundamentally altered the landscape, threatening to devastate available game by allowing free-ranging livestock to reduce cane breaks and grasses used by

Indigenous animals for shelter. In so doing, they made the region more of a foreign landscape for the Native polities that had used it for centuries. Ray, *Middle Tennessee*, 4–5. It is also worth noting that such alteration violated central elements of Cherokee lifeways, which emphasize that because land was created first, and "men came after the animals and plants" in the order of creation, humans owe reciprocal obligations to their nonhuman kin. Mooney, *Myths of the Cherokee*, 240. For more on the nonhuman personhood and reciprocal obligations, see DeSanti, "Teaching Native American Religions and Philosophies in the Classroom," in Ray and DeSanti, *Understanding and Teaching Native American History*, 198–213. For more on European and Euro-American alteration of landscapes as a concept, see Cronon, *Changes in the Land*.

11. John Stuart to Lord George Germain, August 23, 1776, in Davies, *Documents of the American Revolution*, 12:189. Gregory Smithers observes that memory of the Anglo-Cherokee War also factored into Cherokee decision making. *Native Southerners*, 121.

12. Historians Greg O'Brien and Cynthia Cumfer give insight into the age split by revealing how younger Choctaws and Cherokees (respectively) developed power through gift giving and access to European goods rather than through bloodlines. See O'Brien, *Choctaws in a Revolutionary Age*; Cumfer, *Separate Peoples, One Land*. Similarly, Charles Weeks and Wendy St. Jean have shown how the decentralized political structure of the Chickasaws led to a division into pro-Spanish and pro-American factions by the 1780s. Weeks, "Of Rattlesnakes, Wolves, and Tigers," 493–95; and St. Jean, "How the Chickasaws Saved the Cumberland Settlements," 2–19. St. Jean writes that the pro-American faction helped ensure the survival of the White Cumberland settlements at a moment in the 1790s when they faced significant violence from Creeks and Cherokees. In addition to splits between older and younger Cherokees, tensions also developed between war and peace chiefs. Smithers, *Native Southerners*, 121.

13. On the Chickamauga split, see, for example, Henry Stuart to John Stuart, August 25, 1776, *CSRNC* 10:763–85. Colin Calloway notes that Patriot "armies marching through Cherokee country in pursuit of Chickamauga raiders did not always distinguish between Cherokee friends and Cherokee foes, thereby swelling [Chickamauga] ranks with new recruits." *American Revolution in Indian Country*, 50. See also Piecuch, *Three Peoples, One King*, 110; Ray, *Middle Tennessee*; Barksdale, *Lost State of Franklin*; and Ray, *Before the Volunteer State*. It is worth noting that Chickamauga towns included Whites and runaway slaves, meaning they were never homogeneous Cherokee populations. For more on Chickamaugas, see Mize, "To Conclude on a General Union"; Calloway, *American Revolution in Indian Country*; Cumfer, *Separate Peoples, One Land*; Finger, *Tennessee Frontiers*; Ray, "Leadership, Loyalty, and Sovereignty"; and Pate, "The Chickamauga." See also Smithers, *Cherokee Diaspora*.

14. It is a crucial reminder of Michael McDonnell's notation that distant European outposts in North America "were only one among many sites of meeting, encounter,

and community" for Indigenous polities—not a reliable claim of jurisdictional control. *Masters of Empire*, 14. For the 1630s and 1640s, see chapter 1 of this work.

15. Gildrie, "Tennessee in the American Revolution," in Ray, *Before the Volunteer State*, 122.

16. DuVal, *Native Ground*, ch. 6.

17. Henry Stuart to John Stuart, August 25, 1776, *CSRNC* 10:774.

18. *GCDFA*, 409. To help with the matter, Cherokees agreed to send "a strong party" to the confluence of the Tennessee and Ohio to help Loyalists "pass by in security." Gildrie, "Tennessee in the American Revolution," in Ray, *Before the Volunteer State*, 122. See also Nester, *Frontier War for American Independence*; and Starr, *Tories, Dons, and Rebels*, 78–121.

19. *GCDFA*, 409. For his part, Hamilton put his faith in the "Accounts of a considerable number of Southern Indians being assembled on the Cherokee River who are designed to come this way." Dowd, *Spirited Resistance*, 57.

20. Dowd, *Spirited Resistance*, 58.

21. Ibid.

22. Sleeper-Smith, *Indigenous Prosperity and American Conquest*, 224–25.

23. *GCDFA*, 529. These negotiations would inform the evolution of the Shawnee leader Tenskwatawa's Prophetstown movement in the early nineteenth century. For more on that point, see Jortner, *Gods of Prophetstown*.

24. Talk by Old Tassel, in Lowrie and St. Clair, *American State Papers, Class II, Indian Affairs*, 1:42.

25. For the small but growing number of Euro-American invaders in the Tennessee corridor, Cherokee and (and other Native southern) responses seemed to be the random attacks, as the Declaration of Independence stated, "of the merciless Indian savages, whose known rule of warfare, is an undistinguished destruction of all ages, sexes, and conditions." They might be losing their land in questionable fashion, went the evolving narrative of frontier life, but Indigenous reactions to White migration were disproportionate to the injustices perpetrated upon them. Americans were enduring "massacres" and had little choice but to respond with expeditions to protect hearth and home. Never mind that these forays commonly brought along surveyors to mark the land for future sale. Euro-American violence had a curious way of being both virtuous and entrepreneurial, it would seem—and thus served as an excellent foundation for American myth and memory. National Archives, America's Founding Documents, accessed December 20, 2022, https://www.archives.gov/founding-docs/declaration-transcript. See also, Vattel, *Law of Nations*; Peter Silver, *Our Savage Neighbors*; Nooe, *Aggression and Sufferings*; and Barksdale and Ray, "Searching for John Sevier," in Ray, *Before the Volunteer State*, 201–16.

26. *Cherokee Phoenix*, February 11, 1829, WCU Digital Collections, accessed December 12, 2022, https://www.wcu.edu/library/DigitalCollections/Cherokee Phoenix/Vo11/no48/from-the-georgian-page-2-column-1a.html.

27. For that matter, Article VI, Clause 2, of the U.S. Constitution requires that "all Treaties made, or which shall be made, under the Authority of the United States,

shall be the supreme Law of the Land." If Americans took the Constitution seriously, they would have needed carefully to consider any action that could have violated agreed terms in the Treaty of DeWitt's Corner. America's Founding Documents, accessed December 20, 2022, https://www.archives.gov/founding-docs/constitution-transcript.

28. For more systematic discussion of this phenomenon in other regions, see DeLay, *War of a Thousand Deserts*; and Hämäläinen, *Comanche Empire*. See also Waterman and Noel, "Not Confined to the Village Clearings," 44, 47.

29. Gildrie, "Tennessee in the American Revolution," in Ray, *Before the Volunteer State*, 122.

30. Robertson, "Correspondence of Gen. James Robertson," 79. See also Liette, *Memorial concerning the Illinois Country*, Ayer MS 3237, 178–81, Newberry Library.

31. Ramsay, *Annals of Tennessee*, 514.

32. Brown, *Old Frontiers*, 217–19.

33. "Washington's Memoranda on Indian Affairs, 1789," in Abbot, *Papers of George Washington*, Presidential Series, 4:481.

34. Carter, *Territorial Papers*, 4:72–73.

35. White to James Monroe, August 9, 1792, in Preston, *Papers of James Monroe*, 2:556.

36. Carter, *Territorial Papers*, 4:365; James Seagrove to William Blount, February 10, 1794, *American Historical Magazine* 3 (July 1898), 284–85, quoted in Ray, *Middle Tennessee*, 23.

37. McGillivray to O'Neil, *East Tennessee Historical Society's Publications*, vol. 9:114.

38. Furstenberg, "Significance of the Trans-Appalachian Frontier," 648.

39. Ibid., 650.

Bibliography

ARCHIVAL SOURCES

Huntington Library, Los Angeles
    James Abercromby Papers
    Loudoun Papers; Loudoun Americana
    Williams, Edward. *Virgo Triumphant, or, Virginia in general, but the south part thereof in particular* (London, 1650).
John Carter Brown Library, Brown University, Providence,
    Journal of Captain Harry Gordon's journey from Pittsburgh down the Ohio and the Mississippi to New Orleans, Mobile, and Pensacola, 1766
    Bossu, Jean Bernard. *Travels Through that Part of North America Formerly Called Louisiana. By Mr. Bossu, Captain of the French Marines. Translated from the French by John Reinhold Forster, F.A.S.* London: Printed for T. Davies in Russel Street, Covent Garden, 1771.
Newberry Library, Chicago
    Edward Ayer American Indian and Indigenous Studies Collection
    French in America Collection
Southern Historical Collection, University of North Carolina at Chapel Hill
    British Public Records, c. 1600–1782 [manuscript]
    Desmond Clarke Papers, 1726–1954, Series 1
    Preston Davie Collection, 1560–1903, Series 1, Manuscripts, 1560–1903, and undated
    William R. Davie Papers
    Arthur Dobbs Papers, 1726–1765, and undated
    Thomas Griffiths Journal
    King's instruction to the governor no. 109—respecting Indian lands, c. 1760–75
    Lenoir Family Papers
Western Carolina University, Cullowhee, NC
    Cherokee Documents in Foreign Archives, 1632–1909 (microfilm)

Cherokee Phoenix, 1828–34, https://www.wcu.edu/library
/DigitalCollections/CherokeePhoenix/
William Clements Library, University of Michigan
   Jeffery Amherst Papers
   George Clinton Papers
   Thomas Gage Collection
   Charles Garth Letterbooks
   Great Britain Indian Department Collection
   William Henry Lyttleton Papers
   Native American History Papers
   Rogers-Roche Collection
   Lord Shelburne Papers
William R. Perkins Library, Duke University
   Campbell Family Papers

Online Databases

Adam Matthew Digital Collection, Colonial America, CO 5 Series from the National Archives, Kew, UK. http://www.colonialamerica.amdigital.co.uk.
   Account of Christian Pryber's proceedings (Report, 1743/4/22), CO_5_655_Part2_009.
   Answer of the Six Nations to George Clark, June 16, 1742, CO_5_1094_Part2_034.
   Chickesaws Indian talk (Report, 1736/07/13), CO_5_654_Part1_029.
   Copy of a Letter from the Twightwees to Lieu^t Govr Dinwiddie, June y^e 21st 1752, CO_5_1327.
   Craven to Andrew Purcevall (Correspondence, 2 Dec. 1689–13 May 1691), CO_5_288_039.
   Documents relating to the building of a French fort on Indian land in breach of the [Treaty] of [Utrecht] (Correspondence; Report, 1726/07/05–1727/01/11), CO_5_1085_Part2_021.
   John Savry Declaration (Correspondence, September 18, 1728), CO_5_1337_Part1_040.
   Journal from the Ohio to the Twightwees and back in June 1752 (Report, 1752/6/21–1752/8/4), CO_5_1327_Part2_022.
   Letter from Mr. [John] [Stewart] of Carolina to the Lord Dartmouth (Correspondence, [1712]/6/8), CO_5_9_017.
   Letters concerning the interception of French letters, revealing their contravention of the [Treaty] of [Utrecht] by assisting the American Indians in the war against the British (Correspondence, 1725/03/31–1725/05/13), CO_5/752_Part1_026.

Mr. Bull to the Duke of Newcastle (Correspondence, 1739/10/5), CO_5_388_Part1_069.

Orders and Letters of the lords proprietors of Carolina relating to building churches, accusations against officials, and the outbreak of the Yamasee War (Correspondence, [1715]/3/25–1716/3/3), CO_5_390_014.

Petition of James Maxwell and Cornelius Docherty (Correspondence, 1744/06/27), CO_5_37_011.

Petition of the South Carolina Assembly to the Board of Trade (Correspondence, 1744/06/27), CO_5_37_011.

Proprietors to Seth Sothell, James Colleton, Thomas Smith, Joseph Blake, and Bernard Skinking (Correspondence), CO_5_288_039.

William Bull to the Lords Commissioners (Correspondence, March 20, 1741), CO_5_368_01.

William Bull to the Lords of Trade (Correspondence, 1740/03/20), CO_5_368_010.

William Bull to the Lords of Trade (Correspondence, 1742/06/15), CO_5_368_024.

American Antiquarian Society. Historical Periodical Series.

"Charles Town in America, July 17." *Gentleman's Magazine* 25 (October 1755). https://americanantiquarian.org/american-historical-periodicals.

American Antiquarian Society and Readex Corporation. Early American Imprints, Series I, Evans, 1693–1800.

"By the Hon. Francis Fauquier, Esq. His Majesty's lieutenant-governour, and commander in chief of the said colony and dominion: a proclamation, May 17, 1765." #41593. https://www.americanantiquarian.org/early-american-imprints-series-i-evans-1639–1800.

America's Historical Newspapers, New York Public Library

American Weekly Mercury (Philadelphia), June 20–27, 1745. https://www.nypl.org/research/collections/articles-databases/americas-historical-newspapers.

Avalon Project, Yale Law School

Charter of Carolina, March 24, 1663. https://avalon.law.yale.edu/17th_century/nc01.asp.

The First Charter of Virginia, April 10, 1606. http://avalon.law.yale.edu/17th_century/va01.asp.

Sir Robert Heath's Patent 5 Charles 1st; October 30, 1629. http://avalon.law.yale.edu/17th_century/heath.asp.

Creighton University

The Jesuit Relations and Allied Documents. Edited by Reuben Gold Thwaites. http://moses.creighton.edu/kripke/jesuitrelations/.

Documenting the American South, University of North Carolina

Colonial and State Records of North Carolina. https://docsouth.unc.edu/csr/.

Hariot, Thomas. "A Briefe and True Report of the Newfoundland of Virginia." https://docsouth.unc.edu/nc/hariot/hariot.html.

Hening's Statutes. http://vagenweb.org.

Internet Archive

"Letter from a Gentleman in Charles Town to the Carolina Agents in London." *Year Book—1894, City of Charleston, South Carolina.* http://archive.org/details/yearbookcityofchoounse_6.

Chicken, George. "Journal of the March of the Carolinians into the Cherokee Mountains, in the Yemassee Indian War, 1715–1716." *Year Book—1894, City of Charleston, South Carolina.* January 11, 1715/16. http://archive.org/details/yearbookcityofchoounse_6.

Lexis-Nexis

Robin, et al. v. Hardaway, et al. (VA Sup Ct 1772)

Hudgins v. Wrights (VA Sup Ct 1806)

National Humanities Center

Requerimiento, 1510. https://nationalhumanitiescenter.org/pds/amerbegin/contact/text7/requirement.pdf.

Proquest, Early English Books Online

"The four Kings speech to her Majesty." London, April 20, 1710. Tract Supplement/C8:2[121]. http://eebo.chadwyck.com/search/full_rec?SOURCE=pgimages.cfg&ACTION=ByID&ID=V187685.

Sabin Americana, Gale, Cengage Learning

Ash, Thomas. "Carolina; Or A Description of the Present State of that Country, and the Natural Excellencies Thereof." London, 1682. 26 pp.

Coxe, Daniel. "A Description of the English Province of Carolina, By the Spaniards called Florida, and by the French La Louisiane." In B. F. [Benjamin Franklin] French, *Historical Collections of Louisiana: Embracing many rare and valuable documents relating to the natural, civil and political history of that state.* Vol. 2. New York, 1846–51. 309 pp.

Defoe, Daniel. *A general history of trade, and especially consider'd as it respects the British commerce, as well at home, as to all parts of the world* . . . London, 1713. 48 pp.

Franklin, Benjamin. *The Works of Benjamin Franklin: Containing several political and historical tracts not included in any former edition, and many letters official* . . . Vol. 10. Boston, [between 1848 and 1850]. 561 pp.

Gentleman of America. "Some Considerations on the Consequences of the French Settling Colonies on the Mississippi: With Respect to the Trade and Safety of the English," London, 1720. 61 pp.

Knox, William. *The justice and policy of the late act of Parliament for making more effectual provision for the government of the province of Quebec asserted* . . . London, 1774. 89 pp.

Lederer, John. "The discoveries of John Lederer, in three several marches from Virginia, to the west of Carolina, and other parts of the continent." London, 1672. 34 pp.
Seventeenth- and Eighteenth-Century Burney Newspapers Collection, Gale
"Business." *Echo or Edinburgh Weekly Journal*, October 21, 1730. Link.gale.com/apps/doc/Z2000312481/BBCN?u=unihull&sid=bookmark-BBCN&xid=b9a153ec.
"Business." *Public Advertiser,* March 17, 1764. Link.gale.com/apps/doc/Z2001095908/BBCN?u–unihull&sid=bookmark-BBCN&xid=877cb765.
"News." *Daily Gazetteer*, Aug.20, 1745. Link.gale.com/apps/doc/Z2000239264/BBCN?u=unihull&sid=bookmark-BBCN&xid=3f222a17.
"News." *Daily Journal*, December 28, 1734. Link.gale.com/apps/doc/Z2000257976/BBCN?u=unihull&sid=bookmark-BBCN&xid=faabda3d.
"News." *Daily Journal*, July 16, 1736. Link.gale.com/apps/doc/Z2000261622/BBCN?u=unihull&sid=bookmarkBBCN&xid=f934182f.
"News." *London Chronicle*, March 4, 1760—March 6, 1760. Link.gale.com/apps/doc/Z2001670874/BBCN?u=unihull&sid=bookmarkBBCN&xid=fbd30ef1.
"News." *London Evening Post*, March 4, 1755—March 6, 1755. Link.gale.com/apps/doc/Z2000658291/BBCN?u=unihull&sid=bookmark-BBCN&xid=52ddda48.
"News." *London Evening Post*, September 16, 1755–September 18, 1755. Link.gale.com/apps/doc/Z2000658852/BBCN?u=unihull&sid=bookmark-BBCN&xid=476f994b.
"News." *London Post with Intelligence Foreign and Domestick*, January 26, 1700—January 29, 1700. Link.gale.com/apps/doc/Z2001389584/BBCN?u=unihull&sid=bookmark-BBCN&xid=74fa898a.
"News." *Public Advertiser*, August 30, 1753. Link.gale.com/apps/doc/Z2001066025/BBCN?u=unihull&sid=bookmark-BBCN&xid=dd82d195.
"News." *Public Advertiser*, November 26, 1759. Link.gale.com/apps/doc/Z2001077627/BBCN?u=unihull&sid=bookmark-BBCN&xid=77c13089.

Published Primary Sources

Abbot, W. W., et al., eds. *The Papers of George Washington*. Colonial Series, Vols. 1–4. Charlottesville: University of Virginia Press, 1983–93.
Adair, James. *The History of the American Indians, Particularly Those Nations adjoining to the Mississippi, East and West Florida, Georgia, South and North Carolina, and Virginia*. London: E & C. Dilly, 1775. Reprint, edited by Kathryn Holland Braund, Tuscaloosa: University of Alabama Press, 2005.
Beckwith, H. W., ed. *Collections of the Illinois State Historical Library*. Vol. 1. Springfield: Trustees of the Illinois State Historical Library, 1903.

Blackstone, William. *Commentaries on the Laws of England*. 4 vols. 1765–69. Reprint, Chicago: University of Chicago Press, 1979.
Bland, Richard. "The Colonel Dismounted: Or the Rector Vindicated (Williamsburg, 1764)." In *Pamphlets of the American Revolution*. Vol. 1: *1750–1765*. Edited by Bernard Bailyn. Cambridge, MA: Harvard University Press, 1965.
Cain, Robert J., ed. *The Colonial Records of North Carolina (Second Series)*. Vol. 8: *Records of the Executive Council, 1735–1754*. Raleigh: North Carolina Office of Archives and History, 1988.
———, ed. *The Colonial Records of North Carolina (Second Series)*. Vol. 10: *The Church of England in North Carolina: Documents, 1699–1741*. Raleigh: North Carolina Office of Archives and History, 1988.
Carter, Clarence Edwin, ed. *The Territorial Papers of the United States*. Vol. 4: *The Territory South of the River Ohio, 1790–1796*. Washington, DC: Government Printing Office, 1936.
Díaz del Castillo, Bernal. *The Conquest of New Spain*. c. 1632. Translated by J. M. Cohen. New York: Penguin Press, 1963.
Chalmers, George, Esq., ed. *A Collection of Treaties between Great Britain and Other Powers*. Vol. 1. London: John Stockdale, 1790.
Clark, William, ed. *State Records of North Carolina*. Vol. 17: *1781–1785*. Wilmington, NC: Broadfoot Publishing, 1994.
Clayton, Lawrence, ed. *The De Soto Chronicles: The Expedition of Hernando De Soto to North America in 1539–1543*. 2 vols. Tuscaloosa: University of Alabama Press, 1993.
Cooper, Anthony Ashley, Earl of Shaftsbury. *The Shaftsbury Papers*. Charleston: Home House Press for the South Carolina Historical Society, 2010.
Corbitt, D. C., and Roberta Corbitt, eds. "Papers from the Spanish Archives Relating to Tennessee and the Old Southwest, 1783–1800: II, 1786." *East Tennessee Historical Society Publications*, vol. 10 (1938).
"The Correspondence of Gen. James Robertson." *American Historical Magazine* 1, no. 1 (January 1896): 71–91.
Crévecoeur, J. Hector St. John de. *Letters from an American Farmer and Sketches of Eighteenth-Century America*. c. 1782. Reprint, New York: Penguin Classics, 1981.
Davies, K. G., ed. *Documents of the American Revolution, 1770–1783*. 21 vols. Shannon, Ireland: Irish University Press, 1972–81.
Dumont de Montigny, Jean-Francois-Benjamin. *The Memoir of Lieutenant Dumont, 1715–1747: A Sojourner in the French Atlantic*. Edited by Gordon M. Sayre and Carla Zecher. Chapel Hill: University of North Carolina Press, 2012.
Du Pratz, Simon le Page. *The History of Louisiana, or of the Western Parts of Virginia and Carolina*. 1774. Reprint, Dodo Press, 2008.
East Tennessee Historical Society. *East Tennessee Historical Society's Publications*. Vol. 9. Knoxville, TN: ETHS, 1937.
Forbes, John. *The Writings of General John Forbes Relating to his Service in North America*. Edited by Alfred Procter James. Menasha, WI: Collegiate Press, 1938.

Galloway, Patricia Kay, Dunbar Rowland, and A. G. Sanders, eds. *Mississippi Provincial Archives*. 5 vols. Baton Rouge: Louisiana State University Press, 1984.

Grotius, Hugo. *On the Law of War and Peace: In Three Books*. 1625. Edited by William Whewell, 1853. Reprint, Lexington, KY: Forgotten Books, 2010.

Hakluyt, Richard (the Younger). *The Principal Navigations, Voyages, Traffiques and Discoveries of the English Nation*. c. 1589–1600. Vol. 1. Reprint, Elibron Classics, 2005.

Harriot, Thomas. *A Briefe and True Report of the New Found Land of Virginia*. 1591. Reprint of the Theodor de Bry edition, Charlottesville: University of Virginia Press, 2007.

Historical Collections of the Michigan Pioneer and Historical Society. Vol. 34. Lansing, MI: Wynkoop Hallenbeck Crawford, State Printers, 1905.

"Historical Relation of Facts Delivered by Ludovick Grant, Indian Trader, to His Excellency the Governor of South Carolina." *South Carolina Historical and Genealogical Magazine* 10, no. 1 (January 1909).

Hudson, Charles, and Paul Hoffman, eds. *The Juan Pardo Expeditions: Exploration of the Carolinas and Tennessee, 1566–1568*. Tuscaloosa: University of Alabama Press, 2005.

Hutchins, Thomas. *A Topographical Description of Virginia, Pennsylvania, Maryland, and North Carolina*. Boston: John Norman, 1787.

Jacobs, William, ed. *The Appalachian Indian Frontier: The Edmond Atkin Report and Plan of 1755*. Lincoln: University of Nebraska Press, 1954.

Kinietz, W. Vernon, ed. *The Indians of the Western Great Lakes*. Ann Arbor: University of Michigan Press, 1965.

Labaree, Leonard et al., eds. *The Papers of Benjamin Franklin* Vol. 5. New Haven: Yale University Press, 1959.

Lambing, A. A., ed. "Céleron's Journal." *Ohio Archeological and Historical Quarterly* 29, no. 4 (October 1920): 335–423.

Lee, Henry, and Robert E. Lee. *The Revolutionary War Memoirs of General Henry Lee*. 1812. Edited by Charles Royster. New York: DeCapo Press, 1998.

Locke, John. *Two Treatises of Government*. Edited by Peter Laslett. Cambridge: Cambridge University Press, 1960.

Longe, Alexander. "A Small Postscript on the Ways and Manners of the Indians Called Cherokees." Edited by David Corkran. *Southern Indian Studies* 21 (October 1969).

Lowrie, Walter, and Arthur St. Clair, eds. *American State Papers. Class II: Indian Affairs*. Vol. 1. Washington, DC: Government Printing Office, 1932.

Mancall, Peter, ed. *Envisioning America: English Plans for the Colonization of North America*. 2nd ed. New York: Bedford/St Martins, 2016.

McDowell, William L., ed. *Colonial Records of South Carolina: Documents Related to Indian Affairs*. 2 vols. Columbia: South Carolina Archives Department, 1958.

———, ed. *Journals of the Commissioners of the Indian Trade, September 20, 1710–August 29, 1718*. Columbia: South Carolina Archives Department, 1955.

"Mémoire pour M. du Vergier, Directeur Ordonnateur de la Colonie de la Louisiane, concernant les différents opérations qu'il est chargé de faire pour perfectionner les établissements de la ditte Colonie." In Jacob Piatt Dunn, ed, *The Mission to the Ouabache*. Indianapolis: Bowen-Merrill, 1902.

Mereness, Newton, ed. *Travels in the American Colonies*. New York: Macmillan, 1916.

Mooney, James. *Myths of the Cherokee*. Reprint of the 1890 edition. New York: Dover, 1996.

———. *The Swimmer Manuscript: Cherokee Sacred Formulas and Medicinal Prescriptions*. Washington, DC: Government Printing Office, 1932.

Nairne, Thomas. *Nairne's Muskhogean Journals: The 1708 Expedition to the Mississippi River*. Edited by Alexander Moore. Jackson: University Press of Mississippi, 1988.

O'Callaghan, E. B., ed. *Documents Relative to the Colonial History of the State of New-York; Procured in Holland, England, and France*. Vol. 7. Albany: Weed, Parsons and Co., 1856.

Pagden, Anthony, and Jeremy Lawrance, eds. *Vitoria: Political Writings*. Cambridge: Cambridge University Press, 1991.

Pease, Theodore, ed. *Anglo-French Boundary Disputes in the West, 1749–1763*. Springfield: Illinois State Historical Library, 1936.

———, ed. *Collections of the Illinois State Historical Library French Series*. Vol 1: *The French Foundations, 1680–1693*. Springfield: Illinois State Historical Library, 1934.

———, ed. *Collections of the Illinois State Historical Library French Series*. Vol. 3: *Illinois on the Eve of the Seven Years' War, 1747–1755:* Springfield: Illinois State Historical Library, 1940.

Pope, Peter. *Virginia's God Be Thanked: Or, A Sermon of Thanksgiving for the Happie Successe of the Affayres in Virginia This Late Yeare*. London: Printed by I. D. for W. Sheffard and J. Bellamie, 1622.

Preston, Daniel, et al., eds. *The Papers of James Monroe: Selected Correspondence and Papers*. Vol. 2: *1776–1794*. Santa Barbara, CA: Greenwood Press, 2006.

Pufendorf, Samuel von. *The Whole Duty of Man, According to the Law of Nature*. 1691. Translated by Andrew Tooke. Edited by Ian Hunter and David Saunders. Reprint, Indianapolis, IN: Liberty Fund, 2003.

Quinn, David Beers, ed., *The Roanoke Voyages, 1584–1590*. Vol. 1. New York: Dover, 1991.

Quinn, David Beers, and Alison O. Quinn, eds. *New American World*. 5 vols. New York: Macmillan, 1979.

Robertson, James. "The Correspondence of Gen. James Robertson." *American Historical Magazine* 1, no. 1 (January 1896).

Ross, John. *The Papers of Chief John Ross*. 2 vols. Edited by Gary Moulton. Norman: University of Oklahoma Press, 1985.

Sauvole [M de]. *The Journal of Sauvole: Historical Journal of the Establishment of the French in Louisiana by M. de Sauvole*. Edited by Jay Higginbotham. Mobile: Colonial Books, 1969.

Shelley, Alexander, ed. *Narratives of Early Carolina, 1650–1708*. New York: Charles Scribner's Sons, 1911.

Simmons, R. C., and P. D. G. Thomas, eds. *Proceedings and Debates of the British Parliaments Respecting North America, 1754–1783*. Vol. 1: *1754–1764*. Millwood, NY: Kraus International Publications, 1982.

Smith, Daniel. "The Journal of Daniel Smith, September 25, 1779." *Tennessee Historical Magazine* 1 (March 1915).

Sullivan, James, et al., eds. *The Papers of Sir William Johnson*. 14 vols. Albany: University of the State of New York, 1921–65.

Traunter, Richard. *The Travels of Richard Traunter: Two Journeys Through the Native Southeast in 1698 and 1699*. Edited and introduced by Sandra L. Dahlberg. Charlottesville: University of Virginia Press, 2022.

Timberlake, Henry. *The Memoirs of Lt. Henry Timberlake: The Story of a Soldier, Adventurer, and Emissary to the Cherokees, 1756–1765*. Edited by Duane King. Cherokee, NC: Museum of the Cherokee Indian Press, 2007.

Tucker, Sara Jones, and Wayne C. Temple. *Atlas and Supplement Indian Villages of the Illinois Country*. Springfield: Illinois State Museum, 1975.

Turner, Frederick Jackson "The Significance of the Frontier in American History." *Annual Report of the American Historical Association for the Year 1893*. Washington, DC: American Historical Association, 1894.

Vassar, Rena, ed. "Some Short Remarkes on the Indian Trade in the Charikees and in Management thereof since the Year 1717." *Ethnohistory* 8, no. 4 (Autumn 1961).

Vattel, Emmerich de. *The Law of Nations*. 1758. Edited by Bela Kapossy and Richard Whatmore. Reprint, Indianapolis, IN: Liberty Fund, 2008.

Vaughan, Alden, and Deborah Rosen, eds. *Early American Indian Documents*. Vol. 3: *Pennsylvania Treaties, 1756–1775*. Bethesda, MD: University Publications of America, 1998.

Weeks, Charles A. "Of Rattlesnakes, Wolves, and Tigers: A Harangue at the Chickasaw Bluffs, 1796." *William and Mary Quarterly* 67, no. 3 (July 2010): 487–518.

Williams, George W. "Letters from the Clergy of the Anglican Church in South Carolina, c. 1696–1775." http://spinner.cofc.edu/~speccoll/pdf/SPGSeriesABC.pdf?referrer=webcluster&.

Williams, Samuel Cole, ed. *Early Travels in the Tennessee Country, 1540–1800*. Knoxville: Watauga Press, 1928.

———, ed. "An Account of the Presbyterian Mission to the Cherokees, 1757–1759." *Tennessee Historical Magazine*, Series 2, vol. 1, no. 2 (January 1931): 125–38.

Winthrop, John. "Reasons to be Considered for Justifying the Settlement of New England." In *Proceedings of the Massachusetts Historical Society*, vol. 8: 420–25. Boston: Massachusetts Historical Society,

Woodward, Henry. "A Faithfull Relation of my Westoe Voyage, 1674." In *Narratives of Early Carolina, 1650–1708*. Edited by Alexander Shelley. New York: Charles Scribner's Sons, 1911.

Wright Haile, Edward, ed. *Jamestown Narratives: Eyewitness Accounts of the Virginia Colony: The First Decade, 1607–1617.* Champlain, VA: Roundhouse Press, 1998.

Yonge, Francis. *A Narrative of the Proceedings of the People of South-Carolina, in the Year 1719 and of the true causes and motives that induced them to renounce their obedience to the Lords proprietors, and to put themselves under the immediate government of the crown.* London, 1726.

Secondary Sources

Abernethy, Thomas Perkins. *From Frontier to Plantation in Tennessee: A Study in Frontier Democracy.* Chapel Hill: University of North Carolina Press, 1932.

Ablavsky, Gregory. "Making Indians White: The Judicial Abolition of Native Slavery in Revolutionary Virginia and Its Racial Legacy." *University of Pennsylvania Law Review* 159 U. Pa. L. Rev. 1457 (April 2011): 1458–1531.

Alden, John. *The South in the Revolution: 1763–1789.* Baton Rouge: Louisiana State University Press, 1957.

Anderson, Chad. "Rediscovering Native North America: Settlements, Maps, and Empires in the Eastern Woodlands." *Early American Studies* 14, no. 3 (Summer 2016): 478–505.

Anderson, Fred. *Crucible of War: The Seven Years' War and the Fate of Empire in British North America, 1754–1766.* New York: Vintage, 2001.

Anderson, M. S. *The War of the Austrian Succession, 1740–1748.* New York: Routledge, 2016.

Anderson, William L., and James A. Lewis, eds. *A Guide to Cherokee Documents in Foreign Archives.* Metuchen, NJ: Scarecrow Press, 1983.

Aron, Stephen. *American Confluence: The Missouri Frontier from Borderland to Border State.* Bloomington: Indiana University Press, 2009.

———. *How the West Was Lost: The Transformation of Kentucky from Daniel Boone to Henry Clay.* Baltimore: Johns Hopkins University Press, 1996.

Banner, Stuart. *How the Indians Lost Their Land: Law and Power on the Frontier.* Cambridge, MA: Harvard University Press, 2005.

Barker, Eirlys. "Pryce Hughes, Colony Planner, of Charles Town and Wales." *South Carolina Historical Magazine* 95, no. 4 (October 1994): 308–9.

Barksdale, Kevin T. *The Lost State of Franklin: America's First Secession.* Lexington: University Press of Kentucky, 2008.

Basso, Keith. *Wisdom Sits in Places: Landscape and Language among the Western Apache.* Albuquerque: University of New Mexico Press, 1996.

Bauer, Brooke. *Becoming Catawba: Catawba Indian Women and Nation Building, 1540–1840.* Tuscaloosa: University of Alabama Press, 2022.

Baugh, Daniel. *The Global Seven Years' War, 1754–1763.* New York: Routledge, 2014.

Beck, Robin. *Chiefdoms, Collapse, and Coalescence in the Early American South.* Cambridge: Cambridge University Press, 2013.

Beeman, Richard. *The Varieties of Political Experience in Eighteenth-Century America*. Philadelphia: University of Pennsylvania Press, 2004.

Beeman, Richard, Stephen Botein, and Edward Carter, eds. *Beyond Confederation: Origins of the Constitution and American National Identity*. Chapel Hill: University of North Carolina Press, 1987.

Berlin, Ira. *Many Thousands Gone: The First Two Centuries of Slavery in North America*. Cambridge, MA: Harvard University Press, 1998.

Boles, John B. *The Great Revival: Beginnings of the Bible Belt*. Lexington: University Press of Kentucky, 1996.

Bossy, Denise. "Godin & Co.: Charleston Merchants and the Indian Trade, 1674–1715." *South Carolina Historical Magazine* 114, no. 2 (April 2013): 96–131.

Bossy, Denise, and Alan Gallay, eds. *The Yamasee Indians: From Florida to South Carolina*. Lincoln: University of Nebraska Press, 2018.

Boulware, Tyler. *Deconstructing the Cherokee Nation: Town, Region, and Nation among Eighteenth-Century Cherokees*. Gainesville: University Press of Florida, 2011.

———. "The Effect of the Seven Years' War on the Cherokee Nation." *Early American Studies* 5, no. 2 (Fall 2007): 395–426.

Bowne, Eric. *The Westo Indians: Slave Traders of the Early Colonial South*. Tuscaloosa: University of Alabama Press, 2005.

Bowne, Eric, and Crystal Bowne. "Natives, Women, Debtors, and Slaves: Christian Priber's American Utopia," *Native South* 11 (2018): 56–80.

Braudel, Fernand. *La Méditerranée et le Monde Méditerranéen a L'Epoque de Phillippe II*. London: William Collins Sons & Co., 1972.

Brandao, Jose Antonio. *"Your fyre shall burn no more": Iroquois Policy toward New France and Its Native Allies to 1701*. Lincoln: University of Nebraska Press, 2000.

Braund, Kathryn. *Deerskins and Duffels: The Creek Indian Trade with Anglo-America, 1685–1815*. Lincoln: University of Nebraska Press, 1993.

Brown, John P. *Old Frontiers: The Story of the Cherokee Indians from the Earliest Times to the Date of their Removal to the West, 1838*. Kingsport, TN: Southern Publishers, 1938.

Brown, Malcolm B. "'Is It Not Our Land?': An Ethnohistory of the Susquehanna-Ohio Indian Alliance, 1701–1754." PhD diss., University of Pennsylvania, 1996, Philadelphia.

Browning, Reed. *The War of the Austrian Succession*. New York: St. Martin's Press, 1993.

Caldwell, Norman W. "Fort Massac during the French and Indian War." *Journal of the Illinois State Historical Society* 43, no. 2 (Summer 1950): 100–119.

Calloway, Colin. *The American Revolution in Indian Country: Crisis and Diversity in Native American Communities*. Cambridge: Cambridge University Press, 1995.

———. *The Indian World of George Washington: The First President, the First Americans, and the Birth of the Nation*. Oxford: Oxford University Press, 2018.

———. *Pen and Ink Witchcraft: Treaties and Treaty Making in American Indian History*. Oxford: Oxford University Press, 2013.

———. *The Scratch of a Pen: 1763 and the Transformation of North America*. Oxford: Oxford University Press, 2006.

———. *The Shawnees and the War for America*. London: Viking Press, 2007.
Campbell, William J. *Speculators in Empire: Iroquoia and the 1768 Treaty of Fort Stanwix*. Norman: University of Oklahoma Press, 2012.
Cameron, Catherine, Paul Kelton, and Alan Swedlund, eds. *Beyond Germs: Native Depopulation in North America*. Tucson: University of Arizona Press, 2015.
Canny, Nicholas, and Anthony Pagden, eds. *Colonial Identity in the Atlantic World, 1500–1800*. Princeton, NJ: Princeton University Press, 1987.
Carroll, Beau Duke. "Talking Stone: Cherokee Syllabary Inscriptions in Dark Zone Caves." Master's thesis, University of Tennessee, Knoxville, 2017.
Carroll, Beau Duke, Alan Cressler, Tom Belt, Julie Reed, and Jan Simek. "Talking Stones: Cherokee Syllabary in Manitou Cave, Alabama." *Antiquity* 93, no. 368 (2019): 519–37.
Carson, James Taylor. *Searching for the Bright Path: The Mississippi Choctaws from Prehistory to Removal*. Lincoln: University of Nebraska Press, 1999.
Cashin, Edward. *Guardians of the Valley: Chickasaws in Colonial South Carolina and Georgia*. Columbia: University of South Carolina Press, 2009.
———. *The King's Ranger: Thomas Brown and the American Revolution in the South*. New York: Fordham University Press, 1999.
Cayton, Andrew, and Fredrika Teute, eds. *Contact Points: American Frontiers from the Mohawk Valley to the Mississippi, 1750–1830*. Chapel Hill: University of North Carolina Press, 1998.
Chambers, Ian. "Space, the Final Frontier? Spatial Understandings in the Eighteenth-Century American Southeast." PhD diss., University of California at Riverside, 2006.
Chmielewski, Laura M. *The Spice of Popery: Converging Christianities on an Early American Frontier*. Notre Dame, IN: University of Notre Dame Press, 2012.
Coclanis, Peter. *The Shadow of a Dream: Economic Life and Death in the South Carolina Low Country, 1670–1920*. Oxford: Oxford University Press, 1991.
Cogliano, Francis, ed. *A Companion to Thomas Jefferson*. Malden, MA: Blackwell, 2012.
Colley, Linda. *Britons: Forging the Nation, 1707–1837*. New Haven, CT: Yale University Press, 1992.
Cook, Robert A., and L. Faragher. "The Incorporation of Mississippian Traditions into Fort Ancient Societies: A Preliminary View of the Shift to Shell-Tempered Pottery Use in the Middle Ohio Valley." *Southeastern Archeology* 27 (2008): 222–37.
Cook, Robert A., and T. Douglas Price. "Maize, Mounds, and the Movement of People: Isotope Analysis of a Mississippian/Fort Ancient Region." *Journal of Archaeological Science* 61 (2015).
Corcoran, Paul. "John Locke on Native Right, Colonial Possession, and the Concept of *Vacuum Domicilium*." *European Legacy* 23, no. 3 (2018): 225–50.
Corkran, David. *The Cherokee Frontier: Conflict and Survival, 1740–1762*. Norman: University of Oklahoma Press, 1962.
Crane, Verner. "A Lost Utopia of the First American Frontier." *Sewanee Review* 27, no. 1 (January 1919): 48–61.

———. *The Southern Frontier, 1670–1732*. Ann Arbor: University of Michigan Press, 1929.

———. "The Tennessee River as the Road to Carolina: The Beginnings of Exploration and Trade." *Mississippi Valley Historical Review* 3, no. 1 (June 1916): 3–18.

Cronon, William. *Changes in the Land: Indians, Colonists, and the Ecology of New England*. New York: Hill and Wang, 1983.

Crosby, Alfred. *The Columbian Exchange: Biological and Cultural Consequences of 1492*. 30th anniversary ed. Westport, CT: Praeger, 2003.

Cumfer, Cynthia. *Separate Peoples, One Land: The Minds of Cherokees, Blacks, and Whites on the Tennessee Frontier*. Chapel Hill: University of North Carolina Press, 2007.

David, James Corbett. *Dunmore's New World: The Extraordinary Life of a Royal Governor in Revolutionary America*. Charlottesville: University of Virginia Press, 2013.

DeLay, Brian. *War of a Thousand Deserts: Indian Raids and the U.S.-Mexican War*. New Haven, CT: Yale University Press, 2008.

Demallie, Raymond J., and Alfonso Ortiz, eds. *North American Indian Anthropology: Essays on Society and Culture*. Norman: University of Oklahoma Press, 1994.

Dennis, Matthew. *Cultivating a Landscape of Peace: Iroquois-European Encounters in Seventeenth-Century America*. Ithaca, NY: Cornell University Press, 1993.

DeSanti, Brady, and Kristofer Ray, eds. *Understanding and Teaching Native American History*. Madison: University of Wisconsin Press, 2022.

Dickson, John. "The Judicial History of the Cherokee Nation from 1721–1835." PhD diss., University of Oklahoma, Norman, 1964.

Dowd, Gregory Evans. *Groundless: Rumors, Legends, and Hoaxes on the Early American Frontier*. Baltimore: Johns Hopkins University Press, 2016.

———. "The Panic of 1751: The Significance of Rumors on the Cherokee–South Carolina Frontier." *William and Mary Quarterly* 53, no. 3 (July 1996): 527–60.

———. *A Spirited Resistance: The North American Indian Struggle for Unity, 1745–1815*. Baltimore: Johns Hopkins University Press, 1992.

———. *War under Heaven: Pontiac, the Indian Nations, and the British Empire*. Baltimore: Johns Hopkins University Press, 2002.

Dubcovsky, Alejandra. "'All of Us Will Have to Pay for These Activities': Colonial and Native Narratives of the 1704 Attack on Ayubale." *Native South* 10 (2017): 1–18.

———. *Informed Power: Communication in the Early American South*. Cambridge, MA: Harvard University Press, 2016.

Dunn, Jacob Piatt. *The Mission to the Ouabache*. Indianapolis: Bowen-Merrill, 1902.

———. "Names of the Ohio River." *Indiana Quarterly Magazine of History* 8, no. 4 (December 1912): 166–70.

DuVal, Kathleen. *Independence Lost: Lives on the Edge of the American Revolution*. New York: Random House, 2015.

———. *The Native Ground: Indians and Colonists in the Heart of the Continent*. Philadelphia: University of Pennsylvania Press, 2006.

Eccles, William J. *France in America*. New York: Harper and Row, 1972.
Edelson, S. Max. *The New Map of Empire: How Britain Imagined America before Independence*. Cambridge, MA: Harvard University Press, 2017.
———. *Plantation Enterprise in Colonial South Carolina*. Cambridge, MA: Harvard University Press, 2011.
Edmunds, R. David. *The Potawatomis: Keepers of the Fire*. Norman: University of Oklahoma Press, 1978.
Edwards, Tai S., and Paul Kelton. "Germs, Genocides, and America's Indigenous Peoples." *Journal of American History* 2 (June 2020): 52–76.
Ekberg, Carl. *Francois Vallé and His World: Upper Louisiana before Lewis and Clark*. Columbia: University of Missouri Press, 2002.
———. *French Roots in the Illinois Country: The Mississippi River in Colonial Times*. Urbana: University of Illinois Press, 2000.
———. *Stealing Indian Women: Native Slavery in the Illinois Country*. Urbana: University of Illinois Press, 2007.
Elliott, J. H. *Empires of the Atlantic World: Britain and Spain in America, 1492–1830*. New Haven, CT: Yale University Press, 2006.
Ellis, Elizabeth. "The Natchez War Revisited: Violence, Multinational Settlements, and Indigenous Diplomacy in the Lower Mississippi Valley." *William and Mary Quarterly* 77, no. 3 (July 2020): 441–72.
Engelbert, Robert, and Guillaume Teasdale, eds. *French and Indians in the Heart of North America, 1630–1815*. Lansing: Michigan State University Press, 2013.
Eslinger, Ellen. *Citizens of Zion: The Social Origins of Camp Meeting Revivalism*. Knoxville: Univ. of Tennessee Press, 1999.
Ethridge, Robbie. *From Chicaza to Chickasaw: The European Invasion and the Transformation of the Mississippian World, 1540–1715*. Chapel Hill: University of North Carolina Press, 2011.
Ethridge, Robbie, and Charles Hudson, eds., *The Transformation of the Southeastern Indians, 1540–1760*. Jackson: University of Mississippi Press, 2002.
Ethridge, Robbie, and Sheri M. Shuck-Hall, eds. *Mapping the Mississippian Shatter Zone: The Colonial Indian Slave Trade and Regional Instability in the American South*. Lincoln: University of Nebraska Press, 2009.
Faragher, John Mack, ed. *Rereading Frederick Jackson Turner*. New Haven, CT: Yale University Press, 1998.
Fenn, Elizabeth. *Encounters at the Heart of the World: A History of the Mandan People*. New York: Hill and Wang, 2014.
———. *Pox Americana: The Great Smallpox Epidemic of 1775–1782*. New York: Hill & Wang, 2001.
Finger, John R. *The Eastern Band of Cherokees, 1819–1900*. Knoxville: University of Tennessee Press, 1984.
———. *Tennessee Frontiers: Three Regions in Transition*. Bloomington, IN: Indiana University Press, 2003.

Fisher, Linford. "'Dangerous Designes': The 1676 Barbados Act to Prohibit New England Slave Importation." *William and Mary Quarterly* 71, no. 1 (January 2014): 99–124.

———. "Why shall we have peace to be made slaves? Indian Surrenderers during and after King Phillip's War." *Ethnohistory* 64, no. 1 (2017): 91–114.

Fitts, Mary. *Fit for War: Sustenance and Order in the Mid-Eighteenth-Century Catawba Nation*. Gainesville: University Press of Florida, 2017.

Fixico, Donald. *The American Indian Mind in a Linear World: American Indian Studies and Traditional Knowledge*. New York: Routledge, 2003.

———. *Call for Change: The Medicine Way of American Indian History, Ethos, and Reality*. Lincoln, NE: University of Nebraska Press, 2013.

Fogelson, Raymond. "The Ballgame Cycle: An Ethnographer's View." *Ethnomusicology* 15, no. 3 (September 1971): 327–38.

Frank, Andrew. *Creeks and Southerners: Biculturalism on the Early American Frontier*. Lincoln: University of Nebraska Press, 2005.

Frank, Andrew, and A. Glenn Crothers, eds. *Borderland Narratives: Negotiation and Accommodation in North America's Contested Spaces, 1500–1850*. Gainesville: University Press of Florida, 2017.

Fried, Morton H. *The Notion of Tribe*. Menlo Park, CA: Cummings Publishing, 1975.

Fullagar, Kate. *The Savage Visit: New World People and Popular Imperial Culture in Britain, 1710–1795*. Berkeley, CA: University of California Press, 2012.

———. *The Warrior, the Voyager, and the Artist: Three Lives in an of Empire*. New Haven, CT: Yale University Press, 2019.

Fullagar, Kate, and Michael McDonnell, eds. *Facing Empire: Indigenous Experiences in a Revolutionary Age*. Baltimore: Johns Hopkins University Press, 2018.

Furstenberg, François. "The Significance of the Trans-Appalachian Frontier in Atlantic History." *American Historical Review* 113, no. 3 (June 2008): 647–77.

Furstenberg, François, and Ollivier Hubert, eds. *Entangling the Quebec Act of 1774: Transnational Contexts, Meanings, and Legacies in North America and the British Empire*. Montreal: McGill-Queens University Press, 2020.

Gallay, Alan. *Indian Slavery in Colonial America*. Lincoln: University of Nebraska Press, 2009.

———. *The Indian Slave Trade: The Rise of the English Empire in the American South, 1670–1717*. New Haven, CT: Yale University Press, 2002.

Gallivan, Martin. *The Powhatan Landscape: An Archaeological History of the Algonquian Chesapeake*. Gainesville: University Press of Florida, 2016.

Galloway, Patricia. *Choctaw Genesis, 1500–1700*. Lincoln: University of Nebraska Press, 1995.

Gould, Eliga, and Peter Onuf, eds. *Empire and Nation: The American Revolution in the Atlantic World*. Baltimore: Johns Hopkins University Press, 2005.

Gragson, Ted, and Paul Bolstad. "A Local Analysis of Early Eighteenth-Century Cherokee Settlement." *Social Science History* 31, no. 3 (Fall 2007): 435–68.

Greene, Jack P. "Colonial History and National History: Reflections on a Continuing Problem." *William and Mary Quarterly*, Third Series, vol. 64, no. 2 (April 2007): 235–50.

———. *The Constitutional Origins of the American Revolution*. New York: Cambridge University Press, 2010.

———. *Exclusionary Empire: English Liberty Overseas, 1600–1900*. Cambridge: Cambridge University Press, 2010.

———. *Negotiated Authorities: Essays in Colonial Political and Constitutional History*. Charlottesville: University of Virginia Press, 1994.

———. *Pursuits of Happiness: The Social Development of Early Modern British Colonies and the Formation of American Culture*. Chapel Hill: University of North Carolina Press, 1988.

———. *The Quest for Power: The Lower Houses of Assembly in the Southern Royal Colonies, 1689–1776*. New York: Norton, 1972.

Greer, Allan. *Property and Dispossession: Natives, Empires, and Lands in Early Modern North America*. Cambridge: Cambridge University Press, 2018.

Griffin, Patrick. *American Leviathan: Empire, Nation, and Revolutionary Frontier*. New York: Hill and Wang, 2008.

Griswold, B. J. *The Pictorial History of Fort Wayne, Indiana; A Review of Two Centuries of Occupation of the Region about the Head of the Maumee River*. Chicago: Robert O. Law Co., 1917.

Hahn, Stephen. *The Invention of the Creek Nation, 1670–1763*. Lincoln: University of Nebraska Press, 2004.

———. *The Life and Times of Mary Musgrove*. Gainesville: University Press of Florida, 2012.

Hämäläinen, Pekka. *The Comanche Empire*. New Haven, CT: Yale University Press, 2008.

———. *Lakota America: A New History of Indigenous Power*. New Haven, CT: Yale University Press, 2019.

Hamer, Phillip. "Anglo-French Rivalry in the Cherokee Country, 1754–1757." *North Carolina Historical Review* 2 (1925): 303–22.

Hall, Joseph M., Jr. *Zamumo's Gifts: Indian European Exchange in the Colonial Southeast*. Philadelphia: University of Pennsylvania Press, 2009.

Hancock, David. *Citizens of the World: London Merchants and the Integration of the British Atlantic Community, 1735–1785*. Cambridge: Cambridge University Press, 1997.

Harrison, Lowell H. *George Rogers Clark and the War in the West*. Lexington: University Press of Kentucky, 1976.

Hatley, Tom. *The Dividing Paths: Cherokees and South Carolinians through the Revolutionary Era*. New York: Oxford University Press, 1995.

Havard, Gilles. *The Great Peace of Montreal of 1701: French-Native Diplomacy in the Seventeenth Century*. Translated by Phyllis Aronoff and Howard Scott. Montreal: McGill-Queen's University Press, 2001.

Haywood, John. *The Civil and Political History of the State of Tennessee from the Earliest Settlement up to the Year 1796.* 1823. Reprint, Knoxville: Tenase Company, 1969.
Heath, Charles L. "Catawba Militarism: Ethnohistorical and Archeological Overviews." *North Carolina Archeology* 53 (2004): 80–121.
Hendrickson, David. *Peace Pact: The Lost World of the American Founding.* Lawrence: University Press of Kansas, 2003.
Hinderaker, Eric. *Elusive Empires: Constructing Colonialism in the Ohio Valley, 1670–1800.* Cambridge: Cambridge University Press, 1997.
Hobson, Charles F. *The Great Yazoo Lands Sale: The Case of Fletcher v. Peck.* Lawrence: University Press of Kansas, 2016.
Hoffer, Peter. *Cry Liberty: The Great Stono River Slave Rebellion of 1739.* Oxford: Oxford University Press, 2010.
Hofstra, Warren. *The Planting of New Virginia: Settlement and Landscape in the Shenandoah Valley.* Baltimore: Johns Hopkins University Press, 2004.
Holton, Woody. *Forced Founders: Indians, Debtors, Slaves, and the Making of the American Revolution in Virginia.* Chapel Hill: University of North Carolina Press, 1999.
Horn, James. *A Kingdom Strange: The Brief and Tragic History of the Lost Colony of Roanoke.* New York: Basic Books, 2010.
———. *A Land as God Made It: Jamestown and the Birth of America.* New York: Basic Books, 2005.
Hoxie, Frederick E. "Retrieving the Red Continent: Settler Colonialism and the History of American Indians in the US." *Ethnic and Racial Studies* 31 (2008): 1153–67.
Hudson, Charles. *Knights of Spain, Warriors of the Sun: Hernando de Soto and the South's Ancient Chiefdoms.* Athens: University of Georgia Press, 1998.
———. *The Southeastern Indians.* Knoxville: University of Tennessee Press, 1976.
Hudson, Charles, and Carmen Chaves Tesser, eds. *The Forgotten Centuries: Indians and Europeans in the American South, 1521–1704.* Athens: University of Georgia Press, 1994.
Inman, Natalie. *Brothers and Friends: Kinship in Early America.* Athens: University of Georgia Press, 2017.
———. "Networks in Negotiation: The Role of Family and Kinship in Intercultural Diplomacy on the Trans-Appalachian Frontier, 1680–1840." PhD diss., Vanderbilt University, Nashville, 2010.
Jackson, Jason Baird, ed. *Yuchi Indian Histories before the Removal Era.* Lincoln: University of Nebraska Press, 2012.
Jennings, Francis. *The Ambiguous Iroquois Empire: The Covenant Chain Confederation of Indian Tribes with English Colonies.* New York: Norton, 1984.
———. *The Invasion of America: Indians, Colonialism, and the Cant of Conquest.* 1975. Reprint, Chapel Hill: University of North Carolina Press, 2010.
Jordan, Kurt. *Seneca Restoration, 1715–1754: An Iroquois Local Political Economy.* Gainesville: University Press of Florida, 2011.

Jortner, Adam. *The Gods of Prophetstown: The Battle of Tippecanoe and the Holy War for the American Frontier*. New York: Oxford University Press, 2011.

Juricek, John T. *Colonial Georgia and the Creeks: Anglo-Indian Diplomacy on the Southern Frontier, 1733–1763*. Gainesville: University Press of Florida, 2010.

Kars, Marjoleine. *Breaking Loose Together: The Regulator Rebellion in Pre-Revolutionary North Carolina*. Chapel Hill: University of North Carolina Press, 2002.

Kawashima, Yasuhide. *Igniting King Philip's War: The John Sassamon Murder Trial*. Lawrence: University Press of Kansas, 2001.

Kelso, William. *Jamestown: The Buried Truth*. Charlottesville: University of Virginia Press, 2006.

Kelton, Paul. "The British and Indian War: Cherokee Power and the Fate of Empire in North America." *William and Mary Quarterly*, Third Series, 69, no. 4 (October 2012): 763–92.

———. *Cherokee Medicine, Colonial Germs: An Indigenous Nation's Fight against Smallpox, 1518–1824*. Norman: University of Oklahoma Press, 2015.

———. *Epidemics and Enslavement: Biological Catastrophe in the Native Southeast, 1492–1715*. Lincoln: University of Nebraska Press, 2009.

Kidd, Thomas. *The Protestant Interest: New England after Puritanism*. New Haven, CT: Yale University Press, 2004.

King, Duane, ed. *The Cherokee Nation: A Troubled History*. Knoxville: University of Tennessee Press, 1979.

Klein, Rachel. *Unification of a Slave State: The Rise of the Planter Class in the South Carolina Backcountry, 1760–1808*. Chapel Hill: University of North Carolina Press, 1990.

Kolb, Frances. "Borderlands in Transition: Acadian Immigration and British Merchant Networks in Louisiana, 1765–1790." PhD diss., Vanderbilt University, Nashville, 2010.

Kresbach, Suzanne. "The Great Charlestown Smallpox Epidemic of 1760." *South Carolina Historical Magazine* 97 (January 1996): 30–37.

Kupperman, Karen Ordahl. *Indians and English: Facing Off in Early America*. Ithaca, NY: Cornell University Press, 2000.

———. *The Jamestown Project*. Cambridge, MA: Harvard University Press, 2007.

———. *Pocahontas and the English Boys: Caught Between Cultures in Early Virginia*. New York: New York University Press, 2019.

Lakomäki, Sami. *Gathering Together: The Shawnee People through Diaspora and Nationhood, 1600–1870*. New Haven, CT: Yale University Press, 2014.

Lakomäki, Sami, Ritva Kylli, and Timo Ylimaunu. "Drinking Colonialism: Alcohol, Indigenous Status, and Native Space on Shawnee and Sámi Homelands, 1600–1850." *Native American and Indigenous Studies* 4, no. 1 (Spring 2017): 1–29.

La Vere, David. *The Tuscarora War: Indians, Settlers, and the Fight for the Carolina Colonies*. Chapel Hill: University of North Carolina Press, 2013.

Lee, Jacob. *Masters of the Middle Waters: Indian Nations and Colonial Ambitions along the Mississippi*. Cambridge, MA: Harvard University Pres, 2018.

Lee, Wayne. *Crowds and Soldiers in Revolutionary North Carolina: The Culture of Violence in Riot and War.* Gainesville: University Press of Florida, 2001.

Lefler, Hugh T., ed. "A Description of 'Carolana' by a 'Well-Willer,' 1649." *North Carolina Historical Review* 32, no. 1 (January 1955): 102–5.

LeMaster, Michelle. *Brothers Born of One Mother: British-Native American Relations in the Colonial Southeast.* Charlottesville: University of Virginia Press, 2012.

Lengel, Edward G. *General George Washington: A Military Life.* New York: Random House, 2005.

Lepore, Jill. *The Name of War: King Philip's War and the Origins of American Identity.* New York: Vintage, 1998.

Lewis, James E. *The American Union and the Problem of Neighborhood: The United States and the Collapse of the Spanish Empire, 1783–1829.* Chapel Hill: University of North Carolina Press, 1998.

Lockyer, Roger. *Habsburg and Bourbon Europe, 1470–1720.* London: Longman Group, 1974.

Lowery, Malinda Maynor. "On the Antebellum Fringe: Lumbee Indians, Slavery, and Removal." *Native South* 10 (2017): 40–59.

Lozier, Jean-Francois. *Flesh Reborn: The Saint Lawrence Valley Mission Settlements through the Seventeenth Century.* Montreal: McGill-Queens University Press, 2018.

Magrath, C. Peter. *Yazoo: Law and Politics in the New Republic: The Case of Fletcher v. Peck.* New York: Norton, 1966.

Mancke, Elizabeth, and Carole Shammas, eds. *The Creation of the British Atlantic World.* Baltimore, MD: Johns Hopkins University Press, 2005.

Mandell, Daniel. *King Phillip's War: Colonial Expansion, Native Resistance, and the End of Indian Sovereignty.* Baltimore: Johns Hopkins University Press, 2010.

Marcoux, Jon. *Pox, Empire, Shackles, and Hides: The Townsend Site, 1670–1715.* Tuscaloosa: University of Alabama Press, 2010.

Marshall, P. J., ed. *The Oxford History of the British Empire.* Vol. 2: *The Eighteenth Century.* Oxford: Oxford University Press, 1992.

McConville, Brendan. *The King's Three Faces: The Rise and Fall of Royal America, 1688–1776.* Chapel Hill: University of North Carolina Press, 2007.

McDermott, John Francis. *Frenchmen and French Ways in the Mississippi Valley.* Urbana: University of Illinois Press, 1969.

McDonnell, Michael. *Masters of Empire: Great Lakes Indians and the Making of America.* New York: Hill and Wang, 2015.

Mcilvenna, Noeleen. *A Very Mutinous People: The Struggle for North Carolina, 1660–1713.* Chapel Hill: University of North Carolina Press, 2009.

McMichael, Andrew. *Atlantic Loyalties: Americans in Spanish West Florida, 1785–1810.* Athens: University of Georgia Press, 2008.

McShea, Bronwen. *Apostles of Empire: The Jesuits and New France.* Lincoln: University of Nebraska Press, 2019.

Mellon, Knox, Jr. "Christian Priber's Cherokee 'Kingdom of Paradise.'" *Georgia Historical Quarterly*. 57, no. 3 (Fall 1973): 319–31.
Merrell, James H. *The Indians' New World: Catawbas and Their Neighbors from European Contact through the Era of Removal*. New York: Norton, 1989.
———. *Into the American Woods: Negotiators on the Pennsylvania Frontier*. New York: Norton, 1999.
Merritt, Jane. *At the Crossroads: Indians and Empires on a Mid-Atlantic Frontier, 1700–1763*. Chapel Hill: University of North Carolina Press, 2003.
Milne, George Edward. *Natchez Country: Indians, Colonists, and the Landscapes of Race in French Louisiana*. Athens: University of Georgia Press, 2015.
Mize, Jamie. "'To Conclude on a General Union': Masculinity, the Chickamauga, and Pan-Indian Alliances in the Revolutionary Era." *Ethnohistory* 68, no. 3 (2021): 429–48.
Mooney, James. "The Cherokee River Cult." *Journal of American Folklore* 13, no. 48 (January–March 1900): 1–10.
Moore, David, Robin Beck, and Christopher Rodning. "Joara and Fort San Juan: Culture Contact at the Edge of the World." *Antiquity* 78 (March 2004). https://antiquity.ac.uk/projgall/Moore/.
Morgan, M. J. *Land of Big Rivers: French and Indian Illinois, 1699–1778*. Carbondale: Southern Illinois University Press, 2010.
Morrisey, Robert. *Empire by Collaboration: Indians, Colonists, and Governments in Colonial Illinois Country*. Philadelphia: University of Pennsylvania Press, 2015.
Musselwhite, Paul. *Urban Dreams, Rural Commonwealth: The Rise of Plantation Society in the Chesapeake*. Chicago: University of Chicago Press, 2019.
Musselwhite, Paul, Peter Mancall, and James Horn, eds. *Virginia 1619: Slavery and Freedom in the Making of English America*. Chapel Hill: University of North Carolina Press, 2019.
Negrin, Hayley. "Possessing Native Women and Children: Slavery, Gender and English Colonialism in the Early American South 1670–1772." PhD diss., New York University, 2018.
Nester, William R. *The Frontier War for American Independence*. Mechanicsburg, PA: Stackpole Books, 2004.
Newell, Margaret Ellen. *Brethren by Nature: New England Indians, Colonists, and the Origins of American Slavery*. Ithaca, NY: Cornell University Press, 2015.
Newman, Simon. *Parades and the Politics of the Street: Festive Culture in the Early American Republic*. Philadelphia: University of Pennsylvania Press, 1997.
Nichols, John L. "Alexander Cameron, British Agent Among the Cherokee, 1764–1781." *South Carolina Historical Magazine* 97, no. 2 (April 1996): 94–114.
Nooe, Evan. *Aggression and Sufferings: Settler Violence, Native Resistance, and the Coalescence of the Old South*. Tuscaloosa: University of Alabama Press, 2023.
Oatis, Steven. *A Colonial Complex: South Carolina's Frontiers in the Era of the Yamassee War, 1680–1730*. Lincoln: University of Nebraska Press, 2004.

Oberg, Michael. *Dominion and Civility: English Imperialism and Native America, 1585–1685*. Ithaca, NY: Cornell University Press, 1999.

———. *The Head in Edward Nugent's Hand: Roanoke's Forgotten Indians*. Philadelphia: University of Pennsylvania Press, 2008.

O'Brien, Greg. *Choctaws in a Revolutionary Age, 1750–1830*. Lincoln: University of Nebraska Press, 2005.

Oliphant, John. *Peace and War on the Anglo-Cherokee Frontier, 1756–1763*. Baton Rouge: Louisiana State University Press, 2002.

Olwell, Robert. *Masters, Slaves, and Subjects: The Culture of Power in the South Carolina Low Country, 1740–1790*. Ithaca, NY: Cornell University Press, 1998.

Onuf, Peter, and Eliga Gould, eds. *Empire and Nation: The American Revolution in the Atlantic World*. Baltimore: Johns Hopkins University Press, 2005.

O'Shaughnessy, Andrew Jackson. *An Empire Divided: The American Revolution and the British Caribbean*. Philadelphia: University of Pennsylvania Press, 2000.

Pagden, Anthony. *European Encounters with the New World*. New Haven, CT: Yale University Press, 1993.

———. *Lords of All the World: Ideologies of Empire in Spain, Britain, and France, c. 1500–c. 1800*. New Haven, CT: Yale University Press, 1995.

Parmenter, Jon. *The Edge of the Woods: Iroquoia, 1534–1701*. East Lansing: Michigan State University Press, 2010.

Pasley, Jeffrey, Andrew Robertson, and David Waldstreicher, eds. *Beyond the Founders: New Approaches to the Political History of the Early American Republic*. Chapel Hill: University of North Carolina Press, 2004.

Pate, James. "The Chickamauga: A Forgotten Segment of Indian Resistance on the Southern Frontier." PhD diss., Mississippi State University, Jackson, 1969.

Perkins, Elizabeth. *Border Life: Experience and Memory in the Revolutionary Ohio Valley*. Chapel Hill: Univ. of North Carolina Press, 1998.

Perdue, Theda. *Cherokee Women: Gender and Culture Change, 1700–1835*. Lincoln: University of Nebraska Press, 1998.

Perley, Bernard. *Defying Maliseet Language Death: Emergent Vitalities of Language, Culture, and Identity in Eastern Canada*. Lincoln: University of Nebraska Press, 2012.

Phillips, Paul. "Vincennes in Its Relation to French Colonial Policy." *Indiana Magazine of History* 17, no. 4 (December 1921): 311–37.

Piecuch, Jim. *Three Peoples, One King: Loyalists, Indians, and Slaves in the Revolutionary South, 1775–1782*. Columbia: University of South Carolina Press, 2013.

Piker, Joshua. *The Four Deaths of Acorn Whistler: Telling Stories in Colonial America*. Cambridge, MA: Harvard University Press, 2013.

———. *Okfuskee: A Creek Indian Town in Colonial America*. Cambridge, MA: Harvard University Press, 2004.

Powell, William S. "Carolana and the Incomparable Roanoke: Explorations and Attempted Settlements, 1620–1663." *North Carolina Historical Review* 51, no. 1 (January 1974): 1–21.

———. "John Pory." *Dictionary of North Carolina Biography.* https://ncpedia.org/biography/pory-john.

———. *John Pory, 1572–1636: The Life and Letters of a Man of Many Parts.* Chapel Hill: University of North Carolina Press, 1977.

"Pownall, John (1720–95), of Wykeham, Lincs." *History of Parliament Online.* http://www.historyofparliamentonline.org/volume/1754-1790/member/pownall-john-1720-95.

Preston, David. *Braddock's Defeat: The Battle of the Monongahela and the Road to Revolution.* Oxford: Oxford University Press, 2015.

———. *The Texture of Contact: European and Indian Settler Communities on the Frontiers of Iroquoia, 1667–1783.* Lincoln: University of Nebraska Press, 2009.

Pritchard, James. *In Search of Empire: The French in the Americas, 1670–1730.* New York: Cambridge University Press. 2004.

Pulsipher, Jenny Hale. *Subjects Unto the Same King: Indians, English, and the Contest for Authority in Colonial New England.* Philadelphia: University of Pennsylvania Press, 2005.

Ramsay, J. G. M. *Annals of Tennessee to the End of the Eighteenth Century.* 1853. Reprint, Knoxville: East Tennessee Historical Society, 1967.

Ramsey, William. *The Yamasee War: A Study of Culture, Economy, and Conflict in the Colonial South.* Lincoln: University of Nebraska Press, 2008.

Ray, Kristofer, ed. *Before the Volunteer State: New Thoughts on Early Tennessee History, 1670–1800.* Knoxville: University of Tennessee Press, 2015.

———. "Cherokees and Franco-British Confrontation in the Tennessee Corridor, 1730–1760." *Native South* 7 (2014): 33–67.

———. "Constructing a Discourse of Indigenous Slavery, Freedom, and Sovereignty in Anglo-Virginia, 1600–1750." *Native South* 19 (2017): 19–39.

———. "'The Indians of every denomination were born free and independent of us': White Southern Explorations of Indigenous Slavery, Freedom, and Society, 1772–1830." *American Nineteenth Century History* 17, no. 2 (2016): 139–59.

———. "The Indigenous Roots of the American Revolution." In *The Oxford Research Encyclopedia of American History.* Edited by Jon Butler and Angela Hudson. Oxford: Oxford University Press, 2020. http://oxfordre.com/americanhistory.

———. "Interpreting *Native* Trans-Appalachia, 1670–1770: Or, How I Stopped Worrying and Learned to Read Fanni Mingo's Map." *XVII–XVIII Century Review* (Winter 2022).

———. "Leadership, Loyalty, and Sovereignty in the Revolutionary American Southwest: The State of Franklin as Case Study." *North Carolina Historical Review* 92, no. 2 (April 2015): 123–44.

———. *Middle Tennessee, 1775–1825: Progress and Popular Democracy on the Southwestern Frontier.* Knoxville: University of Tennessee Press, 2007.

———. "New Directions in Early Tennessee History, 1540–1815." *Tennessee Historical Quarterly* 68, no. 3 (Fall 2010): 204–23.

Reed, Julie. *Serving the Nation: Cherokee Sovereignty and Social Welfare, 1800–1907.* Norman: University of Oklahoma Press, 2016.

Reed, Marcelina. *Seven Clans of the Cherokee Society.* Cherokee, NC: Cherokee Publications, 1993.

Reeves, Carolyn Keller, ed. *The Choctaw before Removal.* Oxford: University Press of Mississippi, 1985.

Reid, John Phillip. *A Law of Blood: The Primitive Law of the Cherokee Nation.* New York: New York University Press, 1970.

Reséndez, Andrés. *The Other Slavery: The Uncovered Story of Indian Enslavement in America.* Boston: Houghton Mifflin, 2016.

Reynolds, William. *The Cherokee Struggle to Maintain Identity in the Seventeenth and Eighteenth Centuries.* Jefferson, NC: McFarland, 2015.

Richter, Daniel. *Ordeal of the Longhouse: The Peoples of the Iroquois League in the Era of European Colonization.* Chapel Hill: University of North Carolina Press, 1992.

Richter, Daniel, and James H. Merrell, eds. *Beyond the Covenant Chain: The Iroquois and Their Neighbors in Indian North America, 1600–1800.* University Park, PA: Pennsylvania State University Press, 2003.

Rindfleisch, Bryan. *George Galphin's Intimate Empire: The Creek Indians, Family, and Colonialism in Early America.* Tuscaloosa: University of Alabama Press, 2019.

Rine, Holly. "Mohawk Reinvention of the Fort Orange and Albany Courthouses, 1652–1677." *Journal of Early American History* 2 (2012): 3–31.

Rodning, Christopher B. *Center Places and Cherokee Towns: Archeological Perspectives on Native American Architecture and Landscape in the Southern Appalachians.* Tuscaloosa: University of Alabama Press, 2015.

Roper, L. H. *Conceiving Carolina: Proprietors, Planters, and Plots, 1662–1728.* New York: Palgrave Macmillan, 2004.

Ross, Rupert. *Returning to the Teachings: Exploring Aboriginal Justice.* Saskatoon: University of Saskatchewan Press, 1996.

Rountree, Helen Hornbeck. *Manteo's World: Native American Life in Carolina's Sound Country before and after the Lost Colony.* Chapel Hill: University of North Carolina Press, 2021.

———. *Pocahontas, Powhatan, Opechancanough: Three Lives Changes by Jamestown.* Charlottesville: University of Virginia Press, 2005.

Rushforth, Brett. *Bonds of Alliance: Indigenous and Atlantic Slaveries in New France.* Chapel Hill: University of North Carolina Press, 2014.

Sachs, Honor. "'Freedom by a Judgment': The Legal History of an Afro-Indian Family." *Law and History Review* 30, no. 1 (February 2012): 173–203.

———. *Home Rule: Households, Manhood, and National Expansion on the Eighteenth-Century Kentucky Frontier.* New Haven, CT: Yale University Press, 2015.

Saunt, Claudio. *A New Order of Things: Property, Power, and the Transformation of the Creek Indians, 1733–1816.* Cambridge: Cambridge University Press, 1999.

———. *Unworthy Republic: The Dispossession of Native Americans and the Road to Indian Territory.* New York: Norton, 2020.

———. *West of the Revolution: An Uncommon History of 1776*. New York: Norton, 2014.

Saxine, Ian. *Properties of Empire: Indians, Colonists, and Land Speculators on the New England Frontier*. New York: New York University Press, 2019.

Schmidt, Ethan. *Native Americans in the American Revolution: How the War Divided, Devastated, and Transformed the Early American Indian World*. New York: Praeger, 2014.

Shannon, Timothy. *Indians and Colonists at the Crossroads of Empire: The Albany Congress of 1754*. Ithaca, NY: Cornell University Press, 2000.

———. *Iroquois Diplomacy on the Early American Frontier*. New York: Penguin, 2009.

Shefveland, Kristalyn. *Anglo-Native Virginia: Trade, Conversion, and Indian Slavery in the Old Dominion, 1646–1722*. Athens: University of Georgia Press, 2016.

Sheidley, Nathaniel. "Unruly Men: Indians, Settlers, and the Ethos of Frontier Patriarchy in the Upper Tennessee Watershed, 1763–1815." Ph.D. diss., Princeton University, Princeton, NJ, 1999.

Silver, Peter. *Our Savage Neighbors: How Indian War Transformed Early America*. New York: Norton, 2008.

Simpson, Leanne. "Looking After Gdoo-naaganinaa: Precolonial Nishnaabeg Diplomatic and Treaty Relationships." *Wicazo Sa Review* 23, no.2 (Fall 2008): 29–42.

Skinner, Claiborne. *The Upper Country: French Enterprise in the Colonial Great Lakes*. Baltimore: Johns Hopkins University Press, 2008.

Slater, P. A., K. M. Hedman, and T. E. Emerson. "Immigrants at the Mississippian Polity of Cahokia: Strontium Isotope Evidence for Population Movement." *Journal of Archaeological Science* 44 (2014): 117–27.

Sleeper-Smith, Susan. *Indigenous Prosperity and American Conquest: Indian Women of the Ohio River Valley, 1690–1792*. Chapel Hill: University of North Carolina Press, 2018.

Smith, Theresa S. *The Island of the Anishnaabeg: Thunderers and Water Monsters in the Traditional Ojibwe Life-World*. Lincoln: University of Nebraska Press, 1995.

Smithers, Gregory. *The Cherokee Diaspora: An Indigenous History of Migration, Resettlement, and Identity*. New Haven, CT: Yale University Press, 2015.

———. *Native Southerners: Indigenous History from Origins to Removal*. Norman: University of Oklahoma Press, 2019.

———. "'Our Hands and Hearts Are Joined Together': Friendship, Colonialism, and the Cherokee People in Early America." *Journal of Social History* 50, no. 4 (2017): 609–29.

Smyth, Noel Edward. "Uncovering an Unknown Diaspora: The Natchez of Louisiana in the Caribbean." PhD diss., University of California at Santa Cruz, 2016.

Snyder, Christina. *Slavery in Indian Country: The Changing Face of Captivity in Early America*. Cambridge, MA: Harvard University Press, 2010.

Sosin, Jack M. "Louisbourg and the Peace of Aix-la-Chapelle, 1748." *William and Mary Quarterly* 14, no. 4 (October 1957): 516–35.

———. *Whitehall and the Wilderness: The Middle West in British Colonial Policy, 1760–1775*. Lincoln: University of Nebraska Press, 1961.
Speck, W. A. *The Birth of Britain: A New Nation 1700–1710*. Oxford: Blackwell, 1994.
Spero, Laura Keenan. "Stout, Bold, Cunning, and the Greatest Travelers in America: The Colonial Shawnee Diaspora." PhD diss., University of Pennsylvania, Philadelphia, 2010.
St. Jean, Wendy. "How the Chickasaws Saved the Cumberland Settlements in the 1790s." *Tennessee Historical Quarterly* 68, no. 1 (Spring 2009): 2–19.
Starr, J. Barton. *Tories, Dons, and Rebels: The American Revolution in British West Florida*. Gainesville: University Press of Florida, 1976.
Steele, Ian K. "Shawnee Origins of Their Seven Years' War." *Ethnohistory* 53, no. 4 (Fall 2006): 657–87.
Stern, Jessica Yirush. *The Lives in Objects: Native Americans, British Colonists, and Cultures of Labor and Exchange in the Southeast*. Chapel Hill: University of North Carolina Press, 2017.
Stern, Philip, and Carl Wennerlind, eds. *Mercantilism Reimagined: Political Economy in Early Modern Britain and Its Empire*. Oxford: Oxford University Press, 2013.
Stewart, James A., and Charles R. Cobb. "Fort Congaree: A Cosmopolitan Outpost on the Rim of Empire." *Native South* 11 (2018): 29–55.
Stremlau, Rose. *Sustaining the Cherokee Family: Kinship and the Allotment of an Indigenous Nation*. Chapel Hill: University of North Carolina Press, 2011.
Sweet, Julie. *Negotiating for Georgia: British-Creek Relations in the Trustee Era, 1733–1752*. Athens: University of Georgia Press, 2005.
Tankersley, Kenneth B. "Bison Exploitation by Late Fort Ancient Peoples in the Central Ohio River Valley." *North American Archaeologist* 7, no. 4 (April 1987): 289–303.
Taylor, Alan. *American Colonies: The Settling of North America*. New York: Penguin, 2001.
Teasdale, Guillaume. *The Fruits of Perseverance: The French Presence in the Detroit River Region, 1701–1815*. Montreal: McGill-Queen's University Press, 2019.
Thomas, Daniel. *Fort Toulouse: The French Outpost at the Alabamas on the Coosa*. Tuscaloosa: University of Alabama Press, 1989.
Thompson, Andrew C. *Britain, Hanover, and the Protestant Interest, 1688–1756*. Woodbridge, Suffolk: Boydell Press, 2006.
Thompson, Antonio, and Christos Frentzos, eds. *The Routledge Handbook of American Military and Diplomatic History: The Colonial Period to 1877*. New York: Routledge Press, 2015.
Thornton, Russel. *The Cherokees: A Population History*. Lincoln: University of Nebraska Press, 1990.
Tillson, Albert J. "The Militia and Popular Political Culture in the Upper Valley of Virginia, 1740–1775." *Virginia Magazine of History and Biography* 94, no. 3 (July 1986): 285–306.

Tortora, Daniel. *Carolina in Crisis: Cherokees, Colonists, and Slaves in the American Southeast, 1756–1763*. Chapel Hill: University of North Carolina Press, 2015.
Townsend, Camilla. *Fifth Sun: A New History of the Aztecs*. Oxford: Oxford University Press, 2019.
———. *Pocahontas and the Powhatan Dilemma*. New York: Hill and Wang, 2004.
Usner, Daniel. *Indians, Settlers, and Slaves in a Frontier Exchange Economy: The Lower Mississippi Valley before 1783*. Chapel Hill: University of North Carolina Press, 1992.
Vaughan, Alden. *Transatlantic Encounters: American Indians in Britain, 1500–1776*. New York: Cambridge University Press, 2006.
Waldstreicher, David. *In the Midst of Perpetual Fetes: The Making of American Nationalism, 1776–1820*. Chapel Hill: University of North Carolina Press, 1997.
Walthall, John A., and Thomas E. Emerson, eds. *Calumet and Fleur-De-Lys: Archeology of Indian and French Contact in the Midcontinent*. Washington, DC: Smithsonian Institution Press, 1992.
Ward, Matthew. *Breaking the Backcountry: The Seven Years' War in Virginia and Pennsylvania, 1754–1765*. Pittsburgh, PA: University of Pittsburgh Press, 2003.
Warren, Stephen. *The Worlds the Shawnees Made: Migration and Violence in Early America*. Chapel Hill: University of North Carolina Press, 2014.
Waselkov, Gregory. "Seventeenth-Century Trade in the Colonial Southeast." *Southeastern Archeology* 8, no. 2 (Winter 1989): 118–19.
Waterman, Kees-Jan, and Jan Noel. "Not Confined to the Village Clearings: Indian Women in the Fur Trade in Colonial New York, 1695–1732." *New York History* 94, no. 1–2 (Winter/Spring 2013): 40–58.
Watson, Blake. *Buying America from the Indians: Johnson v. McIntosh and the History of Native Land Rights*. Norman: University of Oklahoma Press, 2012.
———. "The Doctrine of Discovery and the Elusive Definition of Indian Title." *Lewis & Clark Law Review* 15, no. 4 (2011): 995–1024.
Weaver, Jace. *The Red Atlantic: American Indigenes and the Making of the Modern World, 1000–1927*. Chapel Hill: University of North Carolina Press, 2014.
Weeks, Charles. "Of Rattlesnakes, Wolves, and Tigers: A Harangue at the Chickasaw Bluffs, 1796." *William and Mary Quarterly* 67, no. 3 (July 2010): 487–518.
Weeks, Rex, and Ken Tankersley. "Talking Leaves and Rocks that Teach: The Archeological Discovery of Sequoyah's Oldest Written Record." *Antiquity* 85, no. 329 (2011): 978–93.
White, Richard. *The Middle Ground: Indians, Empires, and Republics in the Great Lakes Region, 1650–1815*. New York: Cambridge University Press, 1991.
White, Sophie. *Voices of the Enslaved: Love, Labor, and Longing in French Louisiana*. Chapel Hill: University of North Carolina Press, 2019.
———. *Wild Frenchmen and Frenchified Indians: Material Culture and Race in Colonial Louisiana*. Philadelphia: University of Pennsylvania Press, 2012.

White, Sophie, and Trevor Burnard, eds. *Hearing Enslaved Voices: African and Indian Slave Testimony in British and French America, 1700–1848*. New York: Routledge, 2020.
Williams, Robert A., Jr. *The American Indian in Western Legal Thought: The Discourses of Conquest*. Oxford: Oxford University Press, 1990.
Witgen, Michael. *An Infinity of Nations: How the Native New World Shaped Early America*. Philadelphia: University of Pennsylvania Press, 2013.
Wood, Bradford. *This Remote Part of the World: Regional Formation in Lower Cape Fear, North Carolina, 1725–1775*. Columbia: University of South Carolina Press, 2004.
Wood, Peter. *Black Majority: Negroes in Colonial South Carolina from 1670 through the Stono Rebellion*. New York: Norton, 1974.
Wood, Peter, Gregory Waselkov, and M. Thomas Hatley, eds. *Powhatan's Mantle: Indians in the Colonial Southeast*. Lincoln: University of Nebraska Press, 1989.
Yirush, Craig. *Settlers, Liberty, and Empire: The Roots of Early American Political Theory, 1675–1775*. New York: Cambridge University Press, 2011.
Zogry, Michael J. *Anetso, the Cherokee Ball Game: At the Center of Ceremony and Identity*. Chapel Hill: University of North Carolina Press, 2010.

Index

Abekas, 111
Abenakis, 28
Acorn Whistler, 191n62, 200n32, 207n105
Adair, James, 9, 76, 105–6, 110, 160n9, 170n58, 193n87, 194n92, 209n15
Alabama, 8, 19, 77–78, 107
Albamy Fort, 110. *See also* Fort Toulouse (Albama Fort, Alibamoux Fort)
Albany Congress, 200n34
Algonkins, 28
Alibamos (Alibamoux), 95, 111, 131, 142, 146–47, 151, 153
American Bottom, 1
"American confluence" region, 13, 29, 132, 164n40, 171n70
American Revolution, 4, 16, 128–34, 162n24, 217n1, 218n6; as "family squabble," 128, 216n1; Patriots and, 129, 131, 218n8; Loyalists and, 129, 131, 218n8, 220n18
Amherst, Jeffrey, 111, 113, 208n13, 208n16
ammunition, 24, 81, 84, 90, 108, 116, 169n44, 176n23, 178n58, 180n71, 199n27, 204n69, 209n22; bullets, 90, 94, 137, 153; flint(s), 94, 116, 137, 146, 153; knives, 13, 116, 117, 137, 176n23; powder, 46, 90, 94, 98, 117, 137, 153, 183n100, 189n44, 190n51, 193n87, 195n106; tomahawks, 116; war clubs, 93–94, 151–53
Anetso (Ball Game), 42, 177n30
Anglo-Cherokee encounters, 49, 60, 73, 79; Chain of Friendship, 15, 36–57, 61; frontier, 162n26, 198n23, 198n25, 199n28, 202n56, 207n1, 208n14, 212n64; interaction, 7; relationship, 7, 15, 16, 48, 52, 84–85, 115

Anglo-Cherokee Articles of Friendship (1730), 7, 38, 50, 52, 54, 55, 57, 61, 74–75, 86, 87, 99, 135–40, 181n84, 197n13; "brightening" of chain, 55, 71, 136
Anglo-Cherokee Chain of Friendship (1730). *See* Anglo-Cherokee Articles of Friendship (1730)
Anglo-Cherokee Treaty (1730). *See* Anglo-Cherokee Articles of Friendship (1730)
Anglo-Cherokee War or conflict, 16, 95, 104–14, 126, 207n1, 218n7, 219n11. *See also* Cherokees
animals and game, 164n42, 209n18; deer, 11, 209n18. *See also* skins and furs for trade
Anishnaabegs, 4, 13, 29, 57, 63, 96, 113, 159n2, 165n45, 188n22, 196n110. *See also* Odawas; Ojibwes (Chippewas); Potawatomis
Aniyunwiya. *See* Cherokees
Apalachees, 40
Appalachian Mountains, 4, 17, 122
Appy, John, 189n34, 190n46, 195n108
Arkansas River, 4, 171n70
Arthur, Gabriel, 19
Articles and Preliminary Conditions of Peace. *See* Franco-Cherokee Treaty of Friendship (1756)
Articles of Friendship (1730). *See* Anglo-Cherokee Articles of Friendship (1730)
Ash, Thomas, 26
Atkin, Edmond, 53, 83, 84, 90, 92, 93, 98
Atlantic world, 20, 27, 36, 58, 60, 68, 106, 114
Attakullakulla (Oukanekah, Little Carpenter), 15, 61, 77–79, 86, 89–92,

251

Attakullakulla (*continued*)
   98–100, 108, 118–19, 199n27, 204n66;
   delegations, 49, 86, 89, 181n79, 197n9,
   201n42; intelligence provided, 81, 84, 91;
   interpretation of Anglo-Cherokee
   Articles of Friendship, 54–55;
   relationship and interactions with
   French, 78–79, 92–95, 202n50, 209n22
Aubry, Charles Phillipe, 107, 209n22
Augusta, 84, 123, 125, 170n58
Aztec Empire, 164n45

Ball Game. *See* Anetso
Barlowe, Arthur, 23
Bauxar, Joseph, 43
Baye de Puans, 30
Belcher, Jonathan, 217n1
Bellefeuille, 31, 44
Berkeley, William, 23
Berryer, Nicolas René, Comte de La
   Ferrière, 197, 204n72, 207nn33–34,
   207nn107–8, 209n21, 210n32
Big Pigeon River, 19
Billouart, Louis, Chevalier de Kerlérec, ix,
   68, 80, 81, 92, 93, 94, 95, 98, 102, 106–7,
   109, 110, 111, 112, 114, 141, 142, 145, 146,
   148, 149, 150, 151, 153, 154, 155, 202n52,
   204n68, 204n72, 206n90
bison, 29, 30, 171n71
Bladen, Martin, 6, 48, 50, 161n14, 179n62,
   181n72, 184n109
Blainville, Pierre Joseph Céleron de, 80
Blair, Rev. John, 179n65
Blake, Joseph, 30, 174n103, 192n77
Bland, Richard, 53
Bloody Fellow, 129
Board of Indian Commissioners (South
   Carolina), 40–45, 132, 176nn21–22,
   177n43, 180n71
Board of Trade, 6, 26, 46–48, 49, 51, 52,
   54, 68, 81, 84, 87, 88, 90, 103–4, 138, 139,
   140, 161n15, 179n62, 183n100, 185n120,
   185n122, 185n1, 186n6, 200n32; on
   Anglo-Cherokee Treaty, 135–40; on
   delegations to London, 48–49, 181n72;
   on fortifications, 47, 87–90, 183n102
Boische, Charles de la, Marquis de
   Beauharnois, 63, 80
Bolstad, Paul, 11
Bonnefoy, Antoine, 63, 66–67, 188n21,
   189n41, 189n44
Boone, Daniel, 103
Boone, Thomas, 115

Bossu, Jean-Bernard, 164n42, 176n26,
   195n106
Boulware, Tyler, 12, 54
Bourbon Dynasty, 33, 46, 173n98
Braddock, Edward, 196n2, 201n31
Braudel, Fernand, 174n2
Britain. *See* British Empire
British Empire, 6, 7, 9, 35, 36–37, 46, 47, 51,
   52, 54, 57, 58, 86, 88, 103, 115, 119, 122,
   126, 162n24, 175n5, 180n66, 185n1,
   193n80, 198n27, 200n32, 207n105, 214n91,
   216n1; legacy of, 186n3; negotiations
   with Cherokees generally, 49–50; trade
   goods, 37, 52, 164n44; treaties, 46, 58,
   179n60; wars, 66, 162
British North America. *See* British Empire
Broughton, Thomas, 52–53, 184n104
Brudanell, James, 50, 161n14
Bull, William (South Carolina governor),
   59–60, 68, 72, 74, 76, 117, 185n122,
   186n11, 190n53, 191n54, 192n65, 206n97
Bull, William, II (South Carolina
   governor), 113
Bunning, Robert, 49
burdeners, 40, 44, 177n45, 180n71
Butler, Nancy. *See* Oninaa

Caesar, 40, 42, 44, 79, 108, 176n23, 177n29,
   203n63, 203n65, 204n69, 209n23
Cahokias, 27, 29, 34, 44, 120
Cameron, Alexander, 119, 125, 128,
   216n104, 216n1
Campbell, John, 103, 212n62
Canada, 8, 10, 12, 33, 65–66, 84, 87, 108, 146,
   153, 179n60, 187n15, 188n24, 190, 192
Canelle, 63, 188n27, 188n29
Canoste (Cherokee town), 99
Carlos II, King of Spain, 33. *See also*
   Habsburg Dynasty
Carolana, 22, 23, 24, 26, 168n37, 173n97,
   185n122
Carolina/Carolinians, 1, 6, 13, 26, 32, 34,
   36–41, 45, 51–55, 57, 71–72, 75, 79, 84, 88,
   103, 105, 168n44, 173n99, 175n9, 176n18,
   180n66, 186n10, 192n77. *See also* North
   Carolina; South Carolina
Carson, James Taylor, 164n45
Caskaskias. *See* Kaskaskias
Catawbas, 18, 69, 72, 76–78, 91, 92, 97, 99,
   131, 169n44, 186n6, 189n34, 201n42,
   201n44, 202n56, 203n60; interactions with
   Cherokees, 63–64, 72, 76–78, 90–92, 97,
   99–100, 192n65, 201n41, 202n50;

INDEX 253

interactions with Europeans, 90–92, 131, 169n44, 178n58, 183n95, 183n100, 191n59, 197n16; interactions with Haudenosaunees, 63–64, 69–70, 72, 76–78, 194n93
Catholic Church/Catholics, 25, 34, 46, 161n16. *See also* Protestant interest
Chain of Friendship (1730). *See* Anglo-Cherokee Articles of Friendship (1730)
Champlain, Samuel de, 28
Charles I, King of England, 22
Charles II, King of England, 26
Charles Town, 14, 26, 52, 60, 68–73, 84, 174n103; attacks on, 34, 38, 41–42, 109, 210n28; commodities and trade in, 11, 27, 30, 33, 40, 169n44; interactions with Cherokees, 71–73, 78, 81, 86, 102, 186n6, 206n105. *See also* South Carolina
Charlevoix, Pierre de, 32, 45, 172n90, 178n51, 190n49
Chartier, Peter, 77
Chattahoochee River, 19
Chatuga (Cherokee town), 94, 108, 203n62, 204n69
Cheawee. *See* Keowee (Cherokee town)
Cherikees. *See* Cherokees
Cherokee-Catawba Congress (1756), 99, 201n41, 201n43, 201n46, 202n50, 206n93
Cherokee Phoenix, 132
Cherokee River. *See* Tennessee River (Cherokee River, Riviere des Cherakis, Long Man)
Cherokees (Tsalagis): and Anglo-Cherokee War, 16, 95, 104–15, 126, 207n1, 218n7, 219n11; and British Empire, 49–54, 57, 68–69, 75–79, 83–85, 101–2; Carolina, relationship with, 8, 34–48, 57, 59–60, 71–73, 86–91; clans, 9, 162n26; commercial and trade relationships, 12–14, 19, 36, 41–42, 52–53, 132–33; Creek confrontations with, 18, 39–40, 101, 206n105; dialects and languages, 9, 55; fortifications and, 9, 32, 60, 62, 65, 79, 80, 81, 83–87, 89, 95; France and French colonies, relationship with, 14, 42–43, 47, 63–68, 73–74, 92–95, 106–14; and Georgia, 55; Haudenosaunee confrontations and relations with, 69–72, 119–21, 124; interregional relations, 54–55; migration, 17–19, 104; mines and mining, 73–75; and other Native polities, 39–42, 62–65, 69–71, 96–101, 108, 129–30; Overhill-Miami confrontations and relations, 100–101; religion, spirituality,

and culture, 9–11, 17–18, 47, 55; settlement and territory, 4, 5, 18–19, 62; and slavery, 14, 37, 43–45, 75–77; smallpox and aftermath, 105–6; Spain and Spanish colonies, relationship with, 40–41; and Tennessee Corridor, 60–61, 71, 128–29; towns, 43, 66, 67, 73, 86, 92–93, 94, 99, 106, 108, 109–10, 118, 131, 177n28, 178n53, 197n12, 198n27, 202n53, 206n105; Virginia, relationship with, 6, 7, 27, 38, 47–48, 51–53, 55, 72, 91–92, 99–100, 124–26. *See also* Overhill Cherokee region; Valley Cherokee region
Chestowee (Yuchi town), 38, 41–43, 45, 70, 75, 77, 166n14, 166nn28–29, 166n35, 181n79, 194n91
Chickamaugas, 127, 130–32, 219n13
Chickasaws, 1, 11, 12, 13, 30–31, 34, 53, 62, 64, 65, 67, 68, 81, 84, 94, 96, 102, 130, 131, 151, 159n3, 173n102, 178n46, 186n6, 190n54, 203n62, 206n90, 219n12. *See also* Fanni Mingo (Squirrel King)
Chicken, George, 44, 48, 49, 51, 176n18, 176n23, 178n48, 181n73, 183n94
Chincanacina (Dragging Canoe), 130
Chiscas, 18
Choctaws, 30, 34, 53, 64, 97, 111, 130, 131, 154, 171n65, 173n100, 186n6, 188n24, 219n12
Chota (Cherokee town), 66, 67, 73, 86, 92–93, 99, 109–10, 118, 131, 178n53, 197n12, 198n27, 202n53. *See also* Overhill Cherokee region
Chowan River, 21
Clea, Benjamin, 43
Clinton, George, 67, 89, 159n2, 190n50, 200n33
Clogoillah, 135
Cochrane, Gavin, 116, 212n56, 212n63
Cofitachequi Chiefdom, 23, 166n10
Colannah, 135
Colbert River, 30. *See also* Mississippi River
Comanchería, 165n45
commodities, 8, 11, 13–14, 19, 22, 26–27, 30, 36, 62, 66–67, 78, 110, 190n51, 199n27; corn, 42, 48, 50, 61, 73, 108, 129, 136, 137, 195n106, 218n7; flour, 8, 61, 87, 164n42, 187n12, 187n13; rice, 74, 186n4
Commons, British House of, 83
Congress of Hard Labour, 57, 124, 125
Conjuror, The (Charite Hagey), 40–42, 44, 79, 176n22, 183n93

Connecorte. *See* Kanagatoga
Conowes, 44
conquistadores, 25, 164n45
Cooper, Anthony-Ashley, Third Earl of Shaftesbury, 73
Coosa Chiefdom, 18
Coosa River, 8, 19, 41
Countie of Albemarle, 26
coureur de bois, 26
Courtonne, Jerome, 81, 84, 196n113
Couture, Jean, 26, 170n58, 192n77
Covenant Chain, 7, 69, 78, 96, 120, 160n13, 174n103, 182n88
Cowetas, 39, 176n23. *See also* Creeks; Mvskokes
Coxe, Daniel, 33, 173n97
Creeks, 34, 39, 41, 47, 53, 56, 64, 65, 66, 67, 69, 83, 84, 97, 98, 101, 109, 130, 132, 133, 166n7, 175n12, 176n17, 180n65, 186n6, 187n11, 189n41, 190n54, 191n62, 197n16, 200n32, 203n66, 206n90, 206n105, 210n28, 219n12. *See also* Mvskokes
Croghan, George, 98, 114, 117–18, 120, 211n46, 214n83
Cumberland River, 4, 27, 32, 67, 128, 132–33, 190
Cuming, Alexander, 49, 135, 181n79, 182n87
Cunneshote (Standing Turkey), 198n27, 199n27

Daniel, Robert, 178n58
D'Arnouville, Jean Baptiste de Machault, 92, 95, 189n36, 196n114, 202n52, 204n68, 204n71, 205n86, 209n22
deerskin map, 1, 159n1
De la Galissonière, Roland-Michele Barrin, 65, 80
Delaware River (valley), 69–70
Delawares. *See* Lenapes
DeLay, Brian, 164n45
Demere, Paul, 100, 178n53, 202n50, 202nn99–102, 209n15, 210n31
Demere, Raymond, 100–101, 108, 202n56, 203n63, 203n66, 204n69, 206nn94–95, 206n98
D'Iberville, Pierre Le Moyne, 30–31
Dinwiddie, Robert (Virginia governor), 83, 88, 90, 91, 96–97, 109, 197n7, 198n25, 200nn30–31, 210n28
Dobbs, Arthur (North Carolina governor), 109, 161n15, 185n120, 186n6, 210n28, 213n77

Docherty, Cornelius [Doherty, Dougherty], 15, 61, 73–74, 76, 89
Dominique, Paul, 50
Douglas, James, 43
DuVal, Kathleen, 24, 130

Edenic boosterism, 20, 22, 24, 26, 97, 128
Ekberg, Carl, 45
embargo(es), 88, 101, 199n28
English Declaration of Right (1689), 7
Espionage, 43
Estatoe (Cherokee town), 106, 206n105
Ethridge, Robbie, 27–28. *See also* Mississippian Shatter Zone
Étienne François, Duc de Choiseul, 8, 62, 111, 187n12
Euphase (Cherokee town), 43, 177n28
Exchequer, 59, 115, 186n4, 211n54

Fancourt, John, 44, 177n46
Fanimingo. *See* Fanni Mingo
Fanni Mingo (Squirrel King), 1, 2, 159n3, 169n44; map of, 2
Farmar, Robert, 118, 213nn68–69
Fauquier, Francis, 199n28
Five and Six Nations of Iroquois. *See* Haudenosaunees
Fixico, Donald, 14, 165n46, 165n2
Fletcher v. Peck (1809), 218n9
Flint (Overhill man), 42, 44
Forbes, John, 102, 206n104, 207n109
Forks of the Ohio River, 80, 83, 98, 196n2, 196n3, 213n65
Fort Ancient (people), 4, 171nn70–71
Fort Arkansas, 60, 107
Fort Chartres, 56, 60, 81, 108
Fort Congaree, 41, 79, 121, 177n27, 214n84, 215n103, 216n105
Fort Cuskuskia (Caskaskia), 45, 108
Fort Duquesne, 80, 95, 98, 101, 111, 199n27, 206n104
Fort Johnson, 202n58
Fort Loudoun, 202n50
Fort Massac, 81, 84, 95, 101, 106–8, 110, 114, 116, 172n88, 190n49, 196n111, 209n18
Fort Necessity, 78, 96. *See also* Seven Years' War
Fort Ouiatenon, 60, 159n6. *See also* Ouiatanons
Fort Pitt, 101, 118
Fort Prince George, 13, 78, 87, 105, 110, 119, 209n15, 211n51, 213n74, 214n82
Fortress Louisbourg, 66, 189n45

INDEX 255

Fort Stanwix, 57, 119, 120, 123, 213n80
Fort Tombecbe, 60
Fort Toulouse (Albamas Fort, Alibamoux Fort), 8, 41, 43, 58, 60, 68, 77, 91, 95, 110, 143, 146, 153, 176n26, 187n11, 190n54, 203n66, 210n28; negotiations at, 37, 56, 65, 92, 189n41; trade at, 47, 56, 94, 190n51, 211n51
Fort Vincennes, 32, 56, 121, 130–32, 172n83, 172n88, 172n91, 178n52, 190n49
Four Iroquois Kings, 181n84
Fox, Joseph, 76–77
France, 8, 34, 41, 45, 46, 52, 62, 65, 66, 85, 87, 161n16, 162n22, 164n42, 179n60, 190n45, 195n106
Franco-Cherokee Treaty of Friendship (1756), 9, 16, 61, 77, 81, 85, 92–95, 106, 109, 114, 141–56, 202n53
Franco-Overhill Treaty (1756). *See* Franco-Cherokee Treaty of Friendship (1756)
Fraser, Alexander, 118
French Broad River, 18–19
French North Americans, 8, 104, 162n22
Furstenberg, François, 133

Gage, Thomas, 114, 116, 117, 118, 125, 126, 211n49, 212n58, 212nn60–61, 212n63, 215n91
Galissonière, Roland-Michel Barrin de la, 65, 80
Gallay, Alan, 28
Gălûñ'lătĭ, 17
Garth, Charles, 214n91
"Gentleman of America," 47, 179n63
Gentleman's Magazine (London), 5
George II, King of England, 49, 50, 55, 57, 58, 66, 77, 79, 135, 139
George III, King of England, 123
Georgia/Georgians, 6, 72, 76, 103, 114, 123, 133, 186n6, 199n27; relationship and interaction with Cherokees, 13, 57, 66, 84, 88, 183n102, 198n21, 199n27; Spanish attack, 76, 192n66; statute requiring nonresidents to obtain trade license (1736), 52; tensions with Virginia and South Carolina, 7, 38, 51–53, 55–57, 73, 88
Gist, Nathaniel, 201n44
Gladwyn, Henry, 117, 212n58
Glen, James (South Carolina governor), 5, 57, 59, 67, 70–72, 77, 78, 81, 83, 84, 86–91, 96, 97, 117, 159n2, 180n65, 186n6, 192nn70–72, 197n9, 197nn13–14, 197n16, 200n32, 200nn34–35, 206n105

Gordon, Harry, 107, 209nn18–19
Gower, Richard, 42
Gragson, Ted, 11
Grant, James, 126
Grant, Ludovick, 49, 54, 70, 78, 84, 87, 88, 99, 181n79, 194n88, 194n98, 195n103, 197n10
Great Buzzard, 17
Great Lakes, 1, 4, 28, 29, 36, 63, 108, 188n22
Great Warrior of Tellico. *See* Oconostota
Green Corn Ceremony, 42
Guale missions in La Florida, 20
Guales, 34. *See also* Guale missions in La Florida
Gulf Coast, 173n100, 180n66
guns, 13, 19, 29, 45, 51, 77, 81, 108, 116, 136, 137, 169n44, 178n58, 195n106, 199n27, 200n35, 201n41, 203n65

Habsburg dynasty, 33. *See also* Carlos II, King of Spain
Hagey, Charite (The Conjuror), 40–42, 44, 79, 176n22, 183n93
Hahn, Steven, 39
Halifax, Lord, 200n31
Hard Labor, South Carolina, 57, 119, 120, 123–25
Harriot, Thomas, 21–24
Hastings, Theophilus, 40–41, 44, 56, 180n71
Hatton, William, 39, 43, 51, 182n93, 183n94
Haudenosaunees (Five Nations, Six Nations, Iroquois), 6, 12, 48, 76, 83, 131, 159n6, 160n11, 160n13, 164n45, 191n59; British interactions with, 46, 56, 78, 124, 174n103, 181n84; Cherokee interactions with, 56, 63–64, 68–72, 93, 96, 119–21, 189n41, 191n61, 194n93, 213n65; French interactions with, 46; territorial expansion, incursions, cessions, 4, 29, 57, 120, 161n15, 185n120, 186n10, 213n77. *See also* Cayugas; Mohawks; Oneidas; Onondagas; Senecas; Tuscaroras; Walking Purchase (1737)
Heath, Robert, 22
Henderson, Richard, 126, 129, 132
Henri IV, King of France, 28
Hicks, Charles (Cherokee), 19, 167n21
Hiwassee (Cherokee town), 99
Hiwassee River, 19, 43
Holston River, 19, 103, 129
Hootlebayau (Warrior of Tugaloo), 40
horses, 45, 204n69; in battle, 23, 108; as commodity, 13, 51, 132, 183n95; loss or taking of, 13, 129, 133

Howard, Henry Frederick, Lord Maltravers, 22
Hudson, Charles, 11–12, 17
Hughes, Price (Pryce), 33
Hurons. *See* Wendats

Illinois/Illinois country, 1, 4, 12, 32, 45, 121. See also *pays des Illinois*
Illinois (polities), 13, 14, 30, 43, 47, 98, 99, 111, 118, 171n71, 175n4, 212n58
Indian Commissioners. *See* Board of Indian Commissioners (South Carolina)

Jamestown, 21, 22, 28, 185n122
Jenkins, Robert, 59, 60, 66
Jesuits, 13, 165n45. *See also* Catholic Church/Catholics
Joara, 18, 23
Johnson, Robert, 52, 87, 185n1
Johnson, William, 93, 98, 109, 111, 114, 116, 117, 119–21, 124, 212n61, 215n91

Kanagatoga (Connecorte, Old Hopp), 78, 89, 90, 92–94, 100, 101, 107, 195n103, 199n27, 201n47, 202n50, 209n22
Kanawha River, 19, 57, 119, 120, 126
Kaniatarowanenneh valley, 28. *See also* St. Lawrence River
Kaskaskia (town), 30, 131
Kaskaskias, 9, 29, 34, 44–45, 100, 120, 131, 159n2
Kaswentha, 12
Kelton, Paul, 18
Keowee (Cherokee town), 13, 78, 79, 87, 93, 99, 106, 197n13, 203n60
Kerlérec, Louis Bullouart, Chevalier de, 68, 80, 81, 92–95, 98, 102, 106, 107, 109–12, 114, 141, 142, 145–51, 153–55, 202n52, 204n68, 204n72, 206n90
Kickapoos, 4, 34, 62, 116, 118, 120, 131
King George's War, 66, 77, 79
Kinoteta, 204n66
kinship, 9, 29
Kittagusta (Prince of Chota), 118–20, 214n82

La Belle Rivière. *See* Ohio River
"La Demoiselle," 195n110
Lady of Cofitachequi, 23
Lagautrais, 118
Lake Erie, 18, 80, 115, 171n70
Lane, Ralph, 21, 23
Lantagnac, Antoine, 68, 110, 111
La Salle, Robert de, 30

Lederer, John, 26, 167n26
Legge, William, Lord Dartmouth, 34, 180n66
LeMoyne, Jean Baptiste, Sieur de Bienville, 32, 45
Lenapes, 4, 69, 98, 116, 120, 121, 126, 131, 205n75
Lewis, Andrew, 91, 203n66
Liette, Pierre de, 13
lifeways, Native, 7, 27, 72, 219n10
Little Carpenter. *See* Attakullakulla
Little Okfuskee (Mvskoke town), 65, 207n105
Little River, 19
Little Telequa (Cherokee town), 99
Little Tennessee River. *See* Tennessee River
Lochaber, South Carolina, 123
Locke, John, 26, 122
Loftus, Arthur, 117, 118, 212n58
London, 52, 59; Cherokee delegations visit, 7, 23, 37, 48, 49, 54, 73, 78, 115, 193n84, 201n42, 214n91; merchants, 21; newspapers and magazines published in, 5, 22, 33, 77, 181n84
Longe, Alexander, 41–43, 75
Long Man. *See* Tennessee River
"long-Savanna People." *See* Shawnees
Lord Dunmore's War, 126
Lords of Trade, 55, 60, 74
Louisbourg, 66
Louis XIV, King of France, 33. *See also* Bourbon Dynasty
Louisiana (French), 12, 14, 16, 34, 43, 45, 60, 65, 66, 68, 69, 79–81, 84, 87, 101, 102, 104, 106, 108, 113, 117, 164n42, 172n82, 185n1, 188n24, 189n41, 195n106, 212n56; and Cherokee alliance, 9, 69, 77–79, 92; concerns about Carolina-Cherokee alliance, 8–9, 54, 60–64, 66; role in Anglo-Cherokee War, 109–11. *See also* Fort Massac; New France
Lower Cherokees, 19, 51, 69, 70, 169n44; towns, 13, 38, 40–42, 56, 66, 78, 79, 87, 94, 97, 105, 168, 174n103, 186n6, 202n56, 210n30
Lower Chickasaws, 1
Lower World, 11
Lyttelton, William, 90, 106, 107, 109, 113, 117, 199nn27–28, 203n62, 209n16, 209n22

Malatchi, 191n62
Mankiller. *See* Oconostota
Manteo, 23

Marcoux, Jon, 19
Marquette, Jacques, 13
Maryland, 83
Mascoutens, 4, 9, 34, 62, 113, 118, 120, 159n6
Mauchault D'Arnouville, Jean Baptiste de, 92, 95
Maurepas, Comte de, 64, 187n15, 188n24, 195n106
Mawmees. *See* Twightwees
Maxwell, James, 15, 61, 73, 74, 76, 89
McDonnell, Michael, 25
McGillivray, Alexander, 133
Medicine Way, 14–15, 165n46
mercenaries, 31
Meschacebe. *See* Mississippi River
Miamis. *See* Twightwees
Michilimackinac, 29, 188n22
Middle towns (Cherokee), 4, 18, 49, 103, 105, 106, 218n7
mines and minerals, 21, 23, 25, 26, 73–79, 174n103; copper, 21, 22, 27; gold, 21, 26, 27, 170n58; iron, 21; lead, 13; silver, 21, 26, 27, 170n58
ministre de la marine, 92, 107, 110, 188n24, 195n106
Mississippian Shatter Zone, 27–28. *See also* Ethridge, Robbie
Mississippian world, 17, 23, 27–29, 165n4, 171n65
Mississippi River, 30, 33, 34, 57, 100, 102, 109, 118, 159n3, 173n97, 192n77, 194n92, 212n58; and Cherokee territory, 5; fortifications, 58, 65, 102, 107, 189n37, 207n109; as Haudenosaunee territory boundary, 161n15, 185n120, 213n77; role in trade and commerce, 8, 31, 33, 87, 190n49, 206n90
Mississippi valley, 1, 29, 30, 32, 36, 50, 165n4
Mobile (French settlement), 34, 60, 65, 77, 94, 180n66
Mohawks, 96, 116, 131, 160n13
Montagnais, 28, 165
Montgomery, Alabama, 8
Montreal, 31, 68, 94, 95, 101, 111, 142, 150, 180n66
Mooney, James, 11, 19
Moore, James, 32, 34, 174n103
Moore, Maurice, 38, 39, 40, 42
Morris, Thomas, 115–18
Morrisey, Robert, 61
Mortar, The, 69, 217n1
Moytoy of Tellico, 49, 50, 55, 75, 76, 135, 136, 139, 184n114

munitions, 46, 90, 94, 98, 117, 137, 153, 183n100, 189n44, 190n51, 193n87, 195n106
Mvskokes, 8, 18, 34, 56, 97, 109, 111, 176n23, 184n114, 191n62, 206n105; interactions with British, 34, 39, 55, 173n100, 180n66, 217n1; interactions and relations with Cherokees, 39, 51, 68–70, 166n7, 175n14; interactions and relations with French, 77, 97, 109; territory, 8, 18. *See also* Creeks; *names of specific towns*

Nadouessians, 30
Nairne, Thomas, 36, 37, 47, 175n4
Nantarialy (Cherokee town), 99
Natchez Rebellion. *See* Natchez War
Natchez War, 64, 68, 166n14, 171n65, 188n30
Natchitoches, 187n16
native ground concept, 15, 24, 25, 28, 168n44
Needham, James, 19
Nequassee (Cherokee town), 49
Newcastle, Duke of, 6, 7, 46, 71, 179n62
New France, 54, 62, 63, 65, 68, 80, 94, 101, 104, 107, 155, 172n82, 192n77, 202n52
New Orleans, 58, 60, 68, 102, 111, 117, 185n1, 202n53, 211n51, 212n58; commerce and trade, 8, 61, 87, 94, 164n42, 193n87; as place of negotiation for Franco-Overhill Treaty, 92–95, 114, 149–56
New River system, 19
New York, 4, 56, 67, 71, 78, 89, 119, 123, 174n103, 182n88
Nicolas René Berryer, Comte de La Ferrière. *See ministre de la marine*
Nikossen, 135
Noewee, 99
Nolichucky River, 19, 166n13
North Carolina, 18, 21, 26, 69, 103, 109, 123, 126, 129, 133, 161n15, 170n53, 179n65, 185n120, 186n6, 210n28, 213n77
Notawaugees, 45
Nova Scotia, 83, 180n66
Nucheconner, 98. *See also* Shawnees

Oakchoi (Mvskoke town), 109
Ochterlong, David, 92
Oconostota (Great Warrior of Tellico, Mankiller of Tellico, Okana-Stoté), 92, 100, 101, 111, 120, 121, 124–25, 201n45, 203n66, 204n69, 209n22, 213n67
Ocunnee Mountain (South Carolina), 133
Odawas, 9, 29, 31, 77, 79, 114–16, 131, 188n22, 212n62. *See also* Anishnaabegs

Oglethorpe, James, 64, 75
Ohio River (La Belle Rivière), 1, 8, 19, 31, 33, 57, 61, 80, 83, 96, 97, 101, 102, 106, 115, 117, 121, 126, 128, 131, 174n103, 197n7
Ojibwes (Chippewas), 131, 163n28. *See also* Anishnaabegs
Okfuskee (Mvskoke town), 65
Okana-Stoté. *See* Oconostota
Old Hopp. *See* Kanagatoga
Old Tassel, 126, 132
Oneidas, 206n88
O'Neil, Arturo, 133
Oninaa (Nancy Butler), 94, 203n63, 203n66
Onondagas, 48, 69, 93, 96, 120, 213n82
Osages, 13, 130–31
Ostenaco (Jud's Friend), 92, 94, 101, 203n63
Ouabache, 31, 64. *See also* Wabash (Ouabasch) River/valley/system
Oucounacou, 135
Ouiatanons, 31, 64, 65, 100, 116, 117, 118, 120
Oukanekah. *See* Attakullakulla
Outalassi, 132
Outerbridge, White, 203n62, 210n30
Out towns (Cherokee), 4
Overhill Cherokee region, 1, 3, 4, 5, 7, 8, 9, 12–16, 18, 20, 30, 34, 37, 38, 40–45, 47, 48, 49, 51, 52, 54–57, 59–70, 72, 73, 75–79, 81, 84–88, 90, 92–111, 113, 114, 115, 117–21, 125, 127, 131, 134, 160n8, 169n44, 178n23, 177n28, 189n41, 191n54, 193n87, 196n110, 197n14, 198n27, 200n35, 201n41, 202n56, 203n63, 204n72, 206n90, 209n15, 210n28, 212n61, 218nn7–8. *See also* Cherokees

Pacific Ocean, 21, 25, 26, 167n26
Panis, 13
Pardo, Juan, 23, 26, 166n10, 166n13
Parliament (British), 48, 59, 80, 126, 167n30, 173n97, 217n1
Parmenter, Jon, 12
Partridge (Cherokee man), 42–44
pays d'en haut, 29
pays des Illinois, 1, 8–10, 13, 16, 29, 30, 34, 36, 37, 45, 57, 60, 62, 65, 69, 80, 85, 107, 115, 116, 118, 119
Pearis, Richard, 201n44
Pearls, 20, 22
Pelham-Holles, Thomas, 46, 179n62
Pennsylvania, 4, 56, 69, 80, 83, 131, 191n59, 205n75, 205n79, 206n86
Peorias, 9, 13, 29, 34, 159n2
Perier, Étienne, 8, 62, 187n12

Philip (grandson of Louis XIV), 33. *See also* Bourbon Dynasty
Piankeshaws, 4, 9, 65, 131, 159n2, 172n84
Pickawillany, 80, 96, 195n110. *See also* Twightwees
Pinckney, Charles, 84
Pisgah-Quallah, 165n4
Pittman, Philip, 118
Plains of Abraham, 101. *See also* Seven Years' War
Point aux Cedrés, 115
Pontiac, 115, 116
Pontiac's Rebellion. *See* Pontiac's War
Pontiac's War, 106, 115, 116
Porto Bello (Panama), 59, 186n3
Pory, John, 21–24, 167n30, 168n31
Potawatomis, 9, 114, 116, 131. *See also* Anishnaabegs
Powhatan Chiefdom, 22, 23, 28, 165n45
Pownall, John, 104, 217n1
Priber, Christian, 15, 61, 75–77, 89, 193n84, 193n85, 193n87, 194n88, 194n92, 194n98
proprietors (Carolina), 26, 32, 38, 167n26, 174n103, 175n9, 185n122
Props of the Longhouse, 69–70, 191n60
Protestant interest, 7, 25, 34, 47, 59, 161n16

Quanasee (Cherokee town), 40, 44
Quawpaws, 4, 30, 34, 171n70
Quebec, 28, 98, 101, 142, 150, 194n92, 204n68
Quebec Act of 1774, 217n1
Quebec City, 101
Queen Anne, 33, 34, 53, 176n24
Queen Anne's War, 20, 34, 36, 37, 58, 66, 76, 180n65

raids and raiding, 31, 37, 63, 118, 173n99, 191n59, 191n61, 195n110, 197n12, 219n13; on Chestowee, 42–43, 70, 77, 166n14, 177n29; on British settlements or posts, 65, 67; slave raiding, 30, 34, 37, 43–45, 168n44, 173n102
Rale, Sebastian, 46
Ramsey, William, 43
Raudot, Antoine Denis, 13
Red Clay State Park, Tennessee, 166n7
Requerimiento, 36
Revanche (French merchant ship), 202n53
rice, 74, 186n4
Richardson, William, 198n27
Rigaud Vaudreuil, Pierre François de, 62, 80
Riggs, Brett, 43
Rivière des Cherakis. *See* Tennessee River

INDEX 259

Roanoke, 20–23, 185n122
Robinson, Thomas, 83, 89, 197n13, 198n25
Rodning, Christopher, 12
Rosa (Silver Heels), 98
Roubaud, Pierre, 114
Royal Navy, 59, 101, 180n66, 189n45
"Rule Britannia," 186n3

Salmon, Edmé Gatien, 188n24
Saluda agreement. *See* Saluda treaty
Saluda congress. *See* Saluda treaty
Saluda Creek, 86, 89
Saluda treaty, 85, 89, 90, 91, 92, 97, 99, 200n35, 202n50
Sauvole, 31, 172n82
Savanas. *See* Shawnees
Savannah, Georgia, 72, 84
Savannah River, 4, 19, 31, 86, 168n44
Savannahs. *See* Shawnees
Savry, John, 39, 41, 47, 175n4, 176n15, 176n24
Scalelasken Ketagusta, 135
Scayagusta Oukah, 135
Seagrove, James, 129
Senecas, 4, 44, 45, 46, 70, 71, 98, 131, 159n2, 191n62
1730 accords. *See* Anglo-Cherokee Articles of Friendship (1730)
1730 agreement. *See* Anglo-Cherokee Articles of Friendship (1730)
1730 treaty. *See* Anglo-Cherokee Articles of Friendship (1730)
1756 treaty. *See* Franco-Cherokee Treaty of Friendship (1756)
Seven Years' War, 9, 15, 16, 26, 84, 96, 98, 99, 101, 103, 109, 115, 195n110, 205n75, 212n56, 214n91. *See also* Fort Necessity
Shawanese. *See* Shawnees
Shawnees (long-Savannas, Savanas, Savannahs, Shawanese), 4, 18, 57, 69, 90, 91, 120, 121, 126, 131, 159n2, 168n44, 171n70, 195n103, 196n110, 199n27, 203n60, 204n68, 205n75, 205n79, 220n23; Cherokee relationship with, 40, 64–68, 70, 77–79, 81, 85, 97–99, 116–18, 131, 188n24, 189n34, 205n86, 206n90, 212n61; Haudenosaunee relationship with, 93
Shirley, William, 66, 189n45
Silhouette, 101
Simpson, Leanne, 55
Six Nations. *See* Haudenosaunees
Skiagunsta, 78, 79

skins and furs for trade, 28, 29, 31, 39, 41, 44, 51, 164n42, 182n88; beaver, 44, 178n58; deer, 1, 20, 27, 28, 30, 40, 44, 190n51
Slave Catcher of Chota, 109, 178n53
slavery/enslaved people, 14, 28, 30, 31, 34, 39, 44, 45, 75, 77, 137, 140, 170n60, 171n62, 177n41, 178n46, 178n53, 187n13; branding or marking, 46; Indians as slaves, 20, 27, 30, 44, 45, 53, 151, 167n23, 177n29, 177n45, 177n56, 178n54; patrols, 75, 182n91; raids and raiding, 30, 37, 38, 43, 44, 168n44, 173n102, 191n63; rebellion, 75, 84; runaways, 219n13; traders, 46
smallpox, 103, 105, 171n62
Smith, John, 23
Society for the Propagation of the Gospel in Foreign Parts, 47
Soto, Hernando de, 23, 27
Soton, 31, 44. *See also* Bellefeuille
South Carolina, 1, 7, 13, 19, 27, 36, 38, 39, 47, 50–53, 56, 58–60, 62, 66, 74, 75, 79, 81, 84, 86–92, 108, 109, 115, 119, 121, 123, 127, 129, 132, 133, 135, 159nn2–3, 161n17, 174n103, 175n12, 177n27, 186n6, 199n27, 206n105, 209n16, 211n46, 218n8; assembly, 52, 53, 68, 71, 73, 87, 183n102, 185n1, 194n92, 197n13, 200n32, 214n91; governor of, 5, 30, 50, 57, 67, 68, 83, 87, 106, 107, 113, 115, 159n2, 178n58, 180n65, 192n77, 198n25, 210n36; Indian Trade Commission, 36, 56
Spain, 33, 41, 46, 52, 164n45, 168n44, 173n95, 174n2, 185n1; colonizing, colonies, and explorations, 7, 12, 13, 16, 18, 20, 21, 25, 38, 41, 59, 73, 76, 161n17, 186n6, 192n66, 212n56, 219n12; encounters with Indians, 16, 34, 41, 58, 128, 131, 133; goods and trading, 13, 19, 174n103, 199n27; Requerimiento, 36; War of the Spanish Succession, 33, 46. *See also* War of Jenkins' Ear
"Spaniard of Movela," 41
Spanish Missions Indians, 34
Spelman, Henry, 165n45
Spirito Sancto (Mississippi River), 33
Spotswood, Alexander, 6, 48, 51, 180n70, 183n94
Squirrel King. *See* Fanni Mingo
Standing Turkey. *See* Cunneshote
St. Augustine, 58
St. Denis, Louis Juchereau de, 62

St. Denys, Charles Juchereau de, 32, 190n49
Stewart, John, 34, 173n100, 176n24, 180n66
St. Genevieve, 45
St. Joseph's River, 116
St. Lawrence River, 28, 69, 101, 114, 185n1
Stono Rebellion, 75
St. Simon's Island, Georgia, 76
Stuart, Henry, 125, 215n104, 219n13
Stuart, John, 90, 103, 108, 114, 117–21, 124, 125, 129, 131, 214n82, 214n86, 215n91, 216n104, 217n1
surveyors and speculators, 122, 130, 217n1, 217n3, 218n6, 220n25
Swannano, North Carolina, 133

Talbot, William, 26
Tallapoosa River, 8, 41
Tascaluza Chiefdom, 164n45
Tellico (Cherokee town), 40, 44, 49, 55, 63, 66, 75, 76, 91, 92, 99, 203n66, 204n69
Tennessee (state), 18, 19, 128, 131, 133, 166n7
Tennessee Corridor, 1, 2, 4–6, 8, 9, 12, 14–16, 44, 48, 57, 58–82, 105, 128, 130, 131, 207n105, 220n25; British activity within, 33, 59, 88, 94; Cherokee activity within, 4, 6, 9, 14, 20, 42, 60–61, 101, 106, 127; French activity within, 32, 67, 84, 106, 111
Tennessee-Ohio-Wabash system. *See* Tennessee Corridor
Tennessee River (Cherokee River, Riviere des Cherakis, Long Man), 5, 18, 19, 32, 42, 57, 62, 63, 118–20, 131, 132, 142–44, 163n28, 190n49, 190n54, 210n28, 220n19; fortifications, 8, 62, 67, 81, 99, 196n111, 200n35, 209n15, 209n18; and French, 31, 48, 107, 108; relationship to, use of, and importance to Cherokees, 11, 14, 32, 37, 45, 60, 84, 100; and trade, 30, 31, 33, 36, 44, 87, 94
Tennessee River valley, 1, 2, 5, 129
Tethtove, 135
Thomson (captain of HM's Sloop *Jamaica*), 202n53
Tiftoe (Tistoe, Wolf of Keowee), 93, 203n60
Timberlake, Henry, 111, 199n27
tobacco, 21, 22, 26, 163n36, 169n45, 214n82
Tomatly (Cherokee town), 99
Tonti, Henri, 30
Trail of Tears, 166n7
Transylvania Company, 126, 129
Transylvania Purchase, 126, 132, 218n10

Traunter, Richard, 26, 73
Treaty of Aix-la-Chappelle (1748), 79, 190n45
Treaty of DeWitt's Corner (1777), 129, 132, 221n27
Treaty of Friendship (1756). *See* Franco-Cherokee Treaty of Friendship (1756)
Treaty of Utrecht (1713), 41, 46, 50, 58, 61, 161, 179n60, 179n62
Treaty of Whitehall. *See* Anglo-Cherokee Articles of Friendship (1730)
Trent, William, 97, 98
Tryon, William (North Carolina governor), 123
Tsalagis. *See* Cherokees
Tuckaleechee Cove, 19
Tugaloo, 38–40, 44, 45, 51, 70, 121, 175n14, 176n23
Tugelo, Georgia, 133
Tuscaroras, 35, 37, 38, 69, 70, 75, 92, 191n63; and war, 38, 70, 75, 175n9
Twightwees (Miamis, Mawmees), 4, 30, 34, 80, 96, 99, 100, 101, 108, 113, 115, 116, 118, 120, 131, 159n2, 190n49, 195n110, 197n7, 213n67

Uchizes. *See* Yuchis
unlicensed traders, 48, 181n75

vacuum domicilium, 20, 167n24
Valley Cherokee region, 4, 8, 18, 19, 34, 37, 40, 42, 43, 44, 45, 70, 73, 79, 176n23, 177n29
Varnod, Francis, 47
Vattel, Emmer de, 122
Vaudreuil, Pierre François de Rigaud, 62–67, 80, 98, 107, 142, 143, 146, 147, 150, 151, 155, 187n15, 187n17, 189n34, 190n47, 195n106, 202n52, 204n68
Vaughan, Alden, 50
Vergier, Messeur de, 31
Vernon, Edward, 59, 186
Versailles, 60, 65, 66, 80, 95, 109
Vian, John Charles, 108
Vincennes, Sieur de, 31, 32, 121, 130–32, 172n84, 190n49
"virgin soil" thesis, 171n62
Virginia/Virginians, 21–23, 83, 88, 94, 108, 131, 150, 169n45, 174n103, 182n93, 183n95, 183nn97–98, 200n31, 203n60; Cherokee relationship and interaction with, 6, 47–48, 66, 72, 79, 88, 99, 124–26,

129, 199n28, 201n42, 202n56; and French encroachment, 47, 83, 109; and South Carolina and Georgia, 7, 27, 38, 51–53, 55–57, 73, 199n27; trade, 19, 51, 85, 90–92, 101, 183n100. *See also* Fort Necessity
Virginia Charter (1606), 21
Virginia Company, 21
Virginia congress (1756), 202n56
Volday, William, 21
Voyageurs, 13, 32, 44

Wabanakis, 46
Wabash (Ouabasch) River/valley/system, 97; Indians and polities, 107, 118, 130–32; river, 1, 19, 44, 60–67, 84, 87, 99, 100, 102, 116, 121, 132, 159n6, 173n97, 187n16, 187n17, 190n47, 207n109; valley, 1, 4, 8, 9, 13, 31, 32, 34, 37, 45, 56, 64, 99, 100, 121, 172n84, 187n15, 190n49
Wakatomica (Shawnee town), 77, 78
Walking Purchase (1737), 69
Walpole, Robert, 179n62
wampum, 12, 72, 73, 77, 93, 96, 109, 110, 138, 195n103, 202n50
Wanchese, 23
war hawks, in British Parliamentary, 59
War of Jenkins' Ear, 60, 66
War of the Austrian Succession, 60, 71
War of the Spanish Succession, 33, 46
Washington, George, 83, 98, 129, 133
Watauga River, 19
Waties, William, 46
Wattis, Captain, 191n63

Weas, 100, 116, 117, 120. *See also* Ouiatanons; Twightwees
"well-willer," 22–24, 26, 168n35
Wendake (Huronia), 29
Wendats (Wyandots, Hurons), 4, 28, 29, 63, 65, 68, 114, 131, 165n45, 188n24
West, Thomas, Second Baron De La Warr, 21
Westminster, 49, 87
West Virginia, 57
White, James, 133
Whitehall, 73
Wiggan, Eleazar, 41–43, 181n79
Wilkins, John, 121
Willanawaugh, 201n45
William III, King of England, 26
Williams, Edward, 22–24, 26, 169n44
Williamsburg, Virginia, 51, 72, 73, 92, 199n28
Wilmington, North Carolina, 26
Windsor Castle, 49
Wingina (Roanoke Weroan), 23
Wolf (Mvskoke *mico*), 65, 93
Wood, Abraham, 168n44
Wood, Peter, 28
Woodward, Henry, 73, 168n44, 169n44
Wyandots. *See* Wendats

Yamasees, 35, 37, 38–40, 175n9, 177n46
Yamasee War, 32, 39, 45, 51, 56, 74, 79, 81, 161n17, 175n9, 182n93
Yonge, Francis, 38, 161n17
Yuchis, 19, 40, 41, 42, 43, 44, 70, 75, 77, 131, 166n14

www.ingramcontent.com/pod-product-compliance
Lightning Source LLC
Chambersburg PA
CBHW021342230426
43666CB00006B/375